101 913 139 X

D1343359

~~KEY TEXT~~

REFERENCE

Understanding Youth Offending

Risk factor research, policy and practice

Stephen Case and Kevin Haines

WILLAN
PUBLISHING

Published by

Willan Publishing
Culmcott House
Mill Street, Uffculme
Cullompton, Devon
EX15 3AT, UK
Tel: +44(0)1884 840337
Fax: +44(0)1884 840251
e-mail: info@willanpublishing.co.uk
Website: www.willanpublishing.co.uk

Published simultaneously in the USA and Canada by

Willan Publishing
c/o ISBS, 920 NE 58th Ave, Suite 300,
Portland, Oregon 97213-3786, USA
Tel: +001(0)503 287 3093
Fax: +001(0)503 280 8832
e-mail: info@isbs.com
Website: www.isbs.com

First published 2009

ISBN 978-1-84392-341-1 paperback
      978-1-84392-342-8 hardback

British Library Cataloguing-in-Publication Data

A catalogue record for this book is available from the British Library

FSC
Mixed Sources
Product group from well-managed
forests and other controlled sources

Cert no. SGS-COC-2482
www.fsc.org
© 1996 Forest Stewardship Council

Project managed by Deer Park Productions, Tavistock, Devon
Typeset by TW Typesetting, Plymouth, Devon
Printed and bound by T J International Ltd, Trecerus Industrial Estate, Padstow, Cornwall

Contents

Acknowledgements

We are grateful for the comments and constructive feedback on our ideas that we have received from a number of colleagues. The final arguments set out in this book remain, of course, the responsibility of the authors.

List of acronyms

APIS	Assessment, Planning Interventions and Supervision
CtC	Communities that Care
DEAT	Development Ecological Action Theory
DYS	Denver Youth Study
ESRC	Economic and Social Research Council
ICAP	Integrated Cognitive Antisocial Potential theory
ISP	Individual Support Plan
ISRD	International Self-Reported Delinquency
KEEP	Key Element of Effective Practice
MLES	Montreal Longitudinal and Experimental Study
OCJS	Offending, Crime and Justice Survey
PADS	Peterborough Adolescent Development Study
RFR	risk factor research
RFPP	risk factor prevention paradigm
RYDS	Rochester Youth Development Study
SCoPIC	Social Contexts of Pathways in Crime
SPooCS	Sheffield Pathways out of Crime Study
SSDP	Seattle Social Development Project
YIP	Youth Inclusion Panel
YIPs	Youth Inclusion Programmes
YISP	Youth Inclusion and Support Panel
YISPMIS	Youth Inclusion and Support Panel Managment Information System
YJB	Youth Justice Board
YJS	Youth Justice System
YLS	Youth Lifestyles Survey
YOT	Youth Offending Team

Introduction

Risk factor research

For some people, risk factor research represents the most important and significant breakthrough in understanding and explaining juvenile delinquency. Unencumbered by complex, implicit or dubious social theories and free of political bias, risk factor research represents the appliance of science to understand social problems. Through the use of pure scientific method, the individual and social factors prevalent in the lives of young people that predict future delinquency are uncovered and the causes and predictors of delinquency are laid bare.

As if this were not achievement enough, risk factor research (RFR) also paves the way for preventing future juvenile delinquency. The list of risk factors for future offending produced by RFR, provides academics, policy makers and practitioners with a ready set of targets for intervention. If the factors in the lives of young people that have been shown to predict and cause future offending can be changed or mitigated then delinquency can be averted or prevented. This potential of RFR to identify the causes and predictors of delinquency and, simultaneously, to offer a 'cure', has proven to be irresistible. This 'irresistability' has been bolstered by the fact that both the science and the practicality of application of its main findings in concrete, pre-determinable interventions is inherently logical, relatively simple and easily understood – it all makes sense.

Such is the power and influence of RFR that it has come to dominate much juvenile criminology across the (Western) world. More so, RFR is increasingly dominating juvenile justice policy and practice in many countries, notably England and Wales. However, to what extent is this dominance justified? How far is RFR the pure, value free appliance of science and how much has it been influenced by particular theories? Are the findings of RFR so unequivocal? Has RFR really laid bare the causes of delinquency? Are the implications of RFR for policy and practice as clear as has been claimed? Is the link between cause and treatment so conclusive that systems of juvenile justice can be confidently built on this foundation? These questions are central to this book. Thus, the overall intention here is to expose the corpus of RFR to critical exposition and appraisal by charting its historical development and by subjecting RFR to a sustained, judicious and balanced evaluation.

The influence of risk factors

We live in a 'risk society' characterised by rapid and far-reaching social changes, increasing globalisation and socio-economic uncertainty (see, for example, Beck 1992). The rhetoric of risk is universal and fundamentally negative. Thus 'risk' itself has been overwhelmingly presented by politicians, the media and academia as a potential threat or harm to be managed or mitigated, as opposed to a positive sensation where risk might be pursued for excitement or gratification (see Katz 1988). The perception of risk amongst the general public is particularly acute in relation to young people and the risk of harm they ostensibly pose to themselves and others (Case 2006; Goldson 2003). Indeed, the 'respectable fears' (Pearson 1983) of the adults of each successive generation have been visited on the young such that populist portrayals of 'risk' and 'young people' have demonstrated striking similarities throughout the twentieth century, with both elements viewed as uncertain, unpredictable, uncontrollable and unwelcome.

Largely in response to the concerns of New Right governments in Western countries regarding increased youth offending, the failures of deterrence, the prohibitive cost of youth custody and the need for public protection (Kemshall 2007), there has been an explosion in the popularity of research that seeks to identify factors in childhood that 'predict' or increase the 'risk' of offending by individuals in their teenage years and over their life course. This research has typically employed longitudinal designs to identify the distinguishing characteristics (what are now known as 'risk factors') of groups of young people usually in the pre-teen years and then to track their offending trajectories (sometimes called 'pathways') into and out of crime (Burnett 2007) throughout adolescence and sometimes into adulthood. More recently, cross-sectional RFR has risen to prominence as a method of accessing larger samples and producing more up-to-date risk factor findings for ready application by policy makers and practitioners in the youth justice field.

As two of the leading life course researchers in the US have noted:

> the risk-factor and prediction paradigms have taken hold of criminology, especially for those interested in crime prevention and crime control policies. (Laub and Sampson 2003: 289)

The academic field of criminology, sometimes under considerable political pressure or inducement, has conducted research to identify the risk-

related characteristics of young people that allegedly ren
iour more predictable and consequently more controllal
able. Followers of criminology at the present time canno
of the notion of risk and the growing body of research in
youth offending, all of which has been readily tran
industrial complex of punishment and control into the c
mantra of 'prevention prevention prevention' and slogans such as
'nipping crime in the bud' (see, for example, Garland 2002).

RFR has become increasingly popular in the industrialised Western world as a means of exploring the origins and development of youth offending and for informing 'interventions designed to prevent the development of criminal potential' (Farrington 2000: 3). This body of research has had particular appeal to politicians, policy makers and some practitioners due to its advocacy of 'scientific' methods of generating and applying evidence of risk. Much RFR has been grounded in positivism – the view that social scientists are able to generate objective, value free knowledge by using 'empirical' methods (direct observation, measurement and experimentation) to quantify different elements of observable human behaviour into factors/variables. The purported major 'scientific' strength of positivist methodology is that statistical manipulation of these factors can be employed to identify *causal relationships* between them. Positivist RFR has, therefore, identified what have been viewed as constant and predictable causal relationships between a range of risk factors and offending behaviour. Thus, a major attraction of positivist RFR to, for example, policy makers, has been its apparent utility in producing data that is replicable, generalisable, defensible and ostensibly value free. Positivist RFR has been championed for its ability to provide clear, unambiguous findings which can underpin controlled interventions to target risk factors and reduce youth offending – all in a demonstrable and defensible 'what works' and 'evidence-based practice' context.

According to Mason and Prior (2008), the generation of a knowledge base of research evidence relating to risk factors has been central to the policy and practice of the Youth Justice System of England and Wales because these factors offer valuable indicators of suitable targets for preventative interventions and the ready identification of 'effective' programmes for 'treating' young people who offend (see also Prior and Paris 2005). The identification of a group of replicable risk factors which have a demonstrable statistical relationship with and impact on offending has allowed the government and the Youth Justice Board to promote a very particular risk centred 'evidence-based' approach to youth justice, both in the realms of prevention and intervention. Thus, RFR has provided government with: (1) a rationale for distancing youth justice policy and practice away from previously held beliefs about the causes and subsequent treatments of juvenile delinquency; (2) a 'third way' alternative to traditional pre-occupations with welfare or justice; and (3) a chanism for building a youth justice system capable of managing the youth 'problem' (France 2008: 3). However, the government's belief in positivist RFR is more akin to a blind faith in what may be called the 'psychosis of positivists' – the conviction that valid representations of the real world can be attained through artefactual quantification and subsequent statistical manipulation, to the denial of the existence of much wider influences on behaviour that are not measured.

The exponential prioritisation of risk-centred, *evidence-based practice* within the Youth Justice System of England and Wales not only reflects a response to the uncertainties of the risk society and the increasingly pervasive and invasive audit-based mentality of modern public sector managerialism, but also concerns within government and the Youth Justice Board about 'undue' youth justice practitioner discretion, perceptions of poor practice and a perceived ineffectiveness in the system in controlling young people and crime. For youth justice staff, these developments have been most keenly experienced in terms of the top-down imposition of evidence-based risk management. There is a statutory obligation on youth justice staff to obtain evidence of the risk that young people may reoffend (using quantitative risk assessment tools) and to match 'what works' interventions to this evidence of risk. Arguments for the evidence-based management of risk through increasingly prescribed practices are persuasive – the process, it is argued, can provide standardised (and thus consistent and predictable) methodologies for dealing with the perceived accelerating local, national and globalised risk presented by young people. As Stephenson *et al.* maintain, evidence-based risk management offers an:

> ostensibly neat and coherent approach to the messy and ill-defined complexities of practice ... (that) promises a consistent risk management methodology resting on a platform of knowledge ... a cautious and defensive response to the challenges of modern society. (Stephenson *et al.* 2007: 3–4)

The risk with risk

In an era of modernisation, managerialism, audit culture and quality assurance in the public sector, RFR, it seems, has facilitated defensible, accountable and transparent youth justice and youth crime prevention policy and practice predicated on a robust empirical evidence base (see Brown 2005; Bateman and Pitts 2005). RFR has provided researchers, politicians, policy makers and practitioners with an expedient method of controlling and managing risk in an age where uncertainty and anxiety hold sway. Where little in life is certain, RFR provides a touchstone. However, RFR has been accused of perpetuating 'governmentality' – the political mindset that prioritises the efficient governance, control, monitoring and management of, in this case, offending populations, over other concerns such as welfare, justice or rehabilitation (Muncie 2004; Armstrong 2004). This governmentality has been allegedly compounded by the over-control and prescription of the practice of youth justice staff at the expense of practitioner expertise and discretion (Pitts 2003a). It has been alleged that the UK government has exploited the epidemiological nature and medicalised language of RFR to portray offending as a symptom of individual pathology (see Stephenson *et al.* 2007) and not a problem of social policy. Quantitative, positivist approaches to RFR have underpinned government policies that have committed to managing the youth offending 'risk' (Armstrong 2004) to the extent that the quantitative interpretation of risk factors has evolved from an explanation of the multivariate analyses of longitudinal data to become 'fact' in the social world (Haw 2007: 77) at the expense of alternative (e.g. qualitative or non-psychosocial) explanations. There is a stand-off with regards to RFR between politicians and academic supporters of the government's commitment to RFR as an effective, practical approach and critics who characterise RFR as sterile, self- and policy-referencing research, or what House (2007: 15) calls 'status quo thinking'.

Thinking about and researching risk

It should already be clear that RFR and risk factor researchers have made some bold claims about understanding and predicting juvenile delinquency. It should also be clear that some people (notably, particularly in England and Wales, in government and the Youth Justice Board) have bought into and possibly over-estimated these claims: their veracity, validity and practical utility. Others, meanwhile, have raised voices of concern or opposition to RFR and its uses.

This book will show how the ability of RFR to uncover replicable and generalisable predictors and causes of youth offending is not as strong as many have claimed. Nor is the link between the findings and claims of RFR and effective interventions as clear cut as some would assert. Indeed, scratch the surface of RFR and one finds that it is not one consistent enterprise that has logically and inexorably contributed to a coherent and growing understanding of juvenile delinquency. Instead, RFR is a collection of differing and sometimes competing paradigms. Rather than being scientific, value free and essentially positivist, RFR has been based on a number of distinct theoretical platforms and researcher biases, which have led to the use of different methodologies and produced sometimes contrasting conclusions and interpretations. Surprisingly, perhaps, these nuances, the fallibilities of RFR and its uses remain under-explored and poorly understood.

The central aims of this book, therefore, are: to expose RFR to a comprehensive critical exposition and evaluation; to draw out the different theoretical underpinnings and biases of RFR researchers; to make clear the implications of these theoretical and personal biases for the types of research conducted and the conclusions reached; to critically evaluate the research methodologies used in RFR; to assess the validity and veracity of the knowledge produced; and to re-evaluate the extent to which RFR provides a solid, evidenced basis on which youth justice policy and practice can be built.

RFR has become an international academic enterprise, at least in the so-called modern industrialised countries and this book reflects that internationality in the research that is described and discussed within it. Relationships to policy and practice, however, are drawn out more domestically with primary reference to England and Wales, partly because this is the jurisdiction we know best and partly because the UK government and the Youth Justice Board for England and Wales have gone further than any other country in structuring the Youth Justice System around risk, risk assessment and risk-based interventions. Of course, there is an inherent logic to the policy and practice implications of RFR findings and conclusions. The link is simple – once you have identified the factors that are statistically shown to be causal or predictive of youth offending behaviour it then becomes a straightforward matter of targeting and changing those factors, confident in the belief that future offending will be mitigated or averted. However, there is a leap of faith required to reach a belief that if these factors are targeted and changed then the outcome (offending) can also be changed. The inherent logic of risk factors and their commonsense linkages to youth justice policy and practice form the basis on which the critical analysis in this book is based.

Chapter synopses

In the opening chapter, the methodological premises of RFR are set out and evaluated in terms of the purported benefits espoused by proponents of 'factorised' and 'aggregated' explanations of risk (what is generally known as artefact RFR). These processes of RFR are then set against the alleged disadvantages highlighted by critical opponents. Particular attention is paid to the positivist, scientific, developmental, simplistic, definitive and universalised nature of the RFR conclusions that have been utilised to inform policy makers and risk-focused preventative interventions, including the determinism of the paradigm and its reductionist and psychosocial biases. The chapter draws out six key themes that underpin the evaluation of RFR throughout the book and discusses these in the form of unresolved methodological paradoxes for RFR:

- the *simplistic over-simplification* of the methodologies, analyses, findings and conclusions of RFR;

- the *definitive indefinity* with which researchers have disseminated simplistic, policy-friendly conclusions based on the ill-defined and poorly understood central concepts of 'risk factor', 'offending' and the nature of the relationship between the two;

- the restricted conception of *risk-dependent protective factors* entirely defined in relation to risk, largely through the use of over-simplified dichotomisation techniques;

- the *replicable incomparability* of the globalised, generalised conclusions from RFR which have been founded on the application of aggregated results to the level of individual explanation and the assumption that replicability necessarily implies comparability in the risk-factor–offending relationship across different samples of young people;

- the *unconstructive constructivism* of the emerging constructivist strand of RFR, which has simultaneously evolved understandings of risk and moved RFR away from simplistic, practical findings with clear policy utility;

- the *heterogeneous homogeneity* of the RFR movement, wherein replication and ostensible cohesion belies a paradigm of disparate research strands and perspectives.

Chapter 2 focuses on the origins and development of RFR. The theoretical development of RFR is traced chronologically from the seminal studies of Sheldon and Eleanor Glueck, which introduced a risk focus to criminological research with young people, onto the Cambridge-Somerville Youth Study of the Gluecks' colleague, Richard Cabot, which introduced the notion of risk-focused developmental crime prevention. From there, discussion moves to the hugely-influential Cambridge Study in Delinquent Development, founded by Donald West and taken forward by David Farrington, which established developmentalism as the cornerstone of RFR and youth justice policy and practice responses to young people. There follows an explication of the Criminals Coming of Age study (Bottoms and McClintock 1973), which explored the influence of immediate situation and context on the likelihood of reoffending in adulthood. The Social Development Model of David Hawkins and colleagues is then discussed as a strand of RFR in its own right; one which introduced a focus on the influence of risk and protective factors on prosocial as well as antisocial processes. The re-evaluation of the Gluecks' research by Robert Sampson and John Laub is then addressed, as this research helped to develop a life course approach to risk-focused developmental criminology and introduced the notion that risk factors could be dynamic as well as stable. What follows is a discussion of the ecological approach to RFR that was formulated as an examination of the interaction between individual and environmental risk factors. Following an exposition of the constructivist pathways approach to RFR that has been embodied in the Pathways Into and Out of Crime partnership (Jean Hine, Derek Armstrong, Alan France, Hazel Kemshall and others) and the Teesside Studies (Colin Webster, Robert McDonald and Donald Simpson), the theoretical review concludes with a discussion of the recent integrated models of RFR put forward by Farrington (the Integrated Cognitive Antisocial Potential theory) and Wikström (the Developmental Ecological Action Theory). The chapter ends with a discussion of the different strands of RFR that have evolved over the past 80 years. Hitherto, RFR has assumed a homogeneous and rather simplistic character. Challenging these notions, this chapter draws out the important differences between the strands of RFR, whilst also showing (with the notable exception of the constructivist pathways strand) how RFR has remained faithful to an implicit deterministic and developmental understanding of the predictive influence of psychosocial measures of risk on youth offending.

In Chapter 3, the theoretical bases, methodologies and empirical claims of longitudinal RFR are evaluated, with particular focus on the (in)ability of longitudinal designs to identify causal and predictive risk factors and to measure within-individual changes in exposure to risk and offending behaviour. The chapter exposes the most important longitudinal RFR studies in England and Wales to critical scrutiny with regards to their aims and objectives, designs, methods, findings and conclusions. Particular attention is paid to evaluating the hugely influential Cambridge Study in Delinquent Development, along with other notable studies that have been inspired by it, including the Home Office Offending Crime and Justice Survey and the SCoPIC partnership founded in ecological RFR. Finally, there is an evaluation of the main empirical bases of constructivist RFR: the Pathways Into and Out of Crime partnership and the Teesside Studies. Chapter 3 concludes that longitudinal RFR studies in England and Wales have evolved RFR through methodologies involving the prospective measurement of risk collected from multiple data sources. However, confident robust conclusions regarding the predictive validity of risk factors have relied on imputation of the nature of the risk-factor–offending relationship largely based on oversimplification of their temporal relationship.

Chapter 4, 'Cross-sectional risk factor research in England and Wales – Achievements, limitations and potential', places the aims, methods, analyses, findings and conclusions of several notable cross-sectional studies under the microscope: the Home Office Youth Lifestyles Survey, the Communities that Care Youth at Risk survey, the On Track Youth Lifestyles Survey and the Youth Justice Board Risk and Protective Factors and Role of Risk and Protective Factor studies. There is a critical evaluation of the ability of cross-sectional RFR to generate up-to-date indicators of risk in large, representative samples (often used as guides to policy and practice), weighed against the methodological limitations of a design with an inability to examine causality and prediction (within cross-sectional RFR studies as they have been designed to date) and an inability to contribute to explanations of the relationship between risk and offending. The chapter concludes by setting out a series of common weaknesses within cross-sectional RFR in England and Wales, notably: lack of definitiveness regarding temporal issues (due to an inability or unwillingness to examine the temporal ordering of risk and offending), the uncritical importation of developmental risk factors into an incompatible research design, psychosocial reductionism, the homogenisation and aggregation of risk and offending and an overriding policy focus that has prioritised immediate, practical findings (e.g. the identification of risk factors in current life) over long-term aetiological and explanatory goals.

In Chapter 5, the global movement of RFR is explored (having been introduced in Chapter 2) through a theoretical and methodological evaluation of the pursuit of globally-applicable, 'universal' risk factors. The chapter begins with scrutiny of two major reviews of RFR: Understanding and Preventing Youth Crime (Farrington 1996) and Antisocial Behaviour by Young People (Rutter et al. 1998). From there, a series of large and influential international RFR studies are critically reviewed: the Europe-based International Self-Reported Delinquency survey (led by Josine Junger-Tas), the USA-based Causes and Correlates studies (led by Terrence Thornberry), the New Zealand-based Dunedin Study Sex Differences in Antisocial Behaviour project (led by Terri Moffitt), the Montreal Longitudinal and Experimental Study (led by Richard Tremblay), the Seattle Social Development Project (led by David Hawkins) and the Edinburgh Study of Youth Transitions and Crime (led by David Smith). The chapter concludes with a discussion of how the pursuit of universal risk factors has exacerbated the extant methodological weaknesses of RFR (artefactualism, developmental determinism, psychosocial bias, homogenisation, aggregation, imputation of a predictive risk factor-offending, prioritising replication above validation) by perpetrating and perpetuating these weaknesses on a much larger scale than ever before. These pervasive weaknesses raise serious questions about the validity of the search for globally-applicable risk factors.

Chapter 6, 'Risk assessment in the Youth Justice System: Application without understanding?', outlines and evaluates the way in which the findings from RFR have been applied to work with young offenders and young people considered to be at risk of offending in England and Wales. The political origins of risk-focused policy and practice with young people in England and Wales are outlined, leading into a critical discussion of how actuarial justice and the applied arm of RFR, the risk factor prevention paradigm, have been animated by risk assessment. What follows is a detailed critique of the theoretical and methodological basis of risk assessment in the YJS in the form of the *Asset* and *Onset* instruments and their extrapolation within the *Scaled Approach* to risk-focused youth justice intervention. Risk assessment in the Youth Justice System is criticised for maintaining ambiguous (even contradictory) foci and objectives, the uncritical transposition of RFR findings into risk assessment tools, the 'technicised' prescription of youth justice practice and the drawing of confident and definitive conclusions of predictive utility and intervention effectiveness on the basis of imputation from a sparse evidence base and perpetuation of an uncritical, narrow understanding of risk prescribed by the Youth Justice Board for England and Wales. It is concluded that the UK government has privileged pseudoscientific, psychosocial, reductionist methods of risk assessment that have relied on crude, broadly-phrased statistical measures of risk and offending and that prioritise the repeatability of established methods and findings over the validation of risk measures themselves. It is argued that this is a self-perpetuating process that has allowed the Youth Justice Board to prescribe the nature and outcomes of youth justice practice on the non-evidenced basis of a narrow, self-replicating 'evidence base' and the mis-appliance of RFR.

The final chapter, 'Revisiting risk factor research, policy and practice', draws together the common critical themes of the previous chapters and evaluates them in relation to the methodologies, analyses and conclusions of RFR. Discussion focuses on:

- the widespread reductionism and over-generalisation manifested in and perpetuated by positivist methods, the factorisation of risk, the aggregation of risk measures, the homogenisation of categories of offending and groups of young people, psychosocial bias;

- the utility of between-groups analysis for identifying causes and predictors of offending by individual young people, the imputation of causality and predictive validity on the basis of the temporal precedence of the measurement of risk;

- the extent to which many of the conclusions from RFR (particularly in its artefact form) have been developmental, deterministic, over-simplified, over-generalised, partial and poorly-understood. The notion of young people as 'crash test dummies' on an irrevocable course to offending is reintroduced, as are previous criticisms of the inappropriate and invalid transference of methods, analyses and conclusions between studies, groups of young people, countries and RFR designs.

The constructivist RFR alternative is then re-explored in terms of its emphasis on currency (active risk in daily life), construction (young people's differential meanings and experiences of risk) and context (how and where risk is experienced). Constructivist RFR is then taken to task for a failure to acknowledge inherent similarities with artefact RFR, particularly in relation to developmentalism, determinism, lack of control, psychosocial bias, predictive risk factors, homogenisation and aggregation.

The book concludes with a section tracing the authors' journey through the process of evaluating RFR. The authors offer a personal reflection on the exploration and evaluation of RFR that has underpinned the arguments in the book, concluding by questioning the capability of RFR to identify valid, meaningful measures of risk and to explain the relationship risk and offending.

Chapter I

Examining the unresolved methodological paradoxes of risk factor research

A large body of research investigating the risk factors associated with youth offending has been developed by criminologists working predominantly in Western Europe, North America and Australasia. The majority of this risk factor research has been positivist in nature and empirically led – typically viewing risks as quantitative, quantifiable, objective, value-fee and scientific 'facts' with a consistent, predictable and possibly causal relationship with offending. To this end, risk factor research (RFR) has mainly utilised quantitative methodologies such as structured observation, standardised surveys, psychometric testing, secondary data analysis, random/representative sampling and the statistical control and analysis of variables to reach its ultimate conclusions. These methods have enabled measurement of the prevalence of certain characteristics, circumstances, experiences, behaviours, attitudes, perceptions etc in the lives of young people. This measurement of 'risk' has been facilitated by a process of quantification or 'factorisation' – attributing a numerical or ordinal value to real world observations to produce 'variables' that are amenable to statistical testing. Subsequent statistical analysis has then been conducted on these 'independent variables' to ascertain their relationship with the 'dependent variable' – offending. Those independent variables (or factors) which are statistically shown to be predictive or causal of the dependent variable (offending) are labelled as 'risk factors'. In much RFR these risk factors have been identified at an early stage in a child's life (at age ten years or less) and shown to be statistically *predictive* of offending, usually in the mid-teenage years.

The scientific, empirical, technical and standardised nature of the dominant methodologies of RFR has led to the identification, replication and generalisation of risk factors across different populations of young people, in various countries at different times. Thus, it is claimed, RFR has produced an expanding and robust evidence-base of the psychosocial characteristics of young people which predispose them to offending. In many countries, particularly England and Wales, this research-based knowledge has been transferred into youth justice policy – underpinned by the assumption that if risk factors can be identified then interventions targeted on changing them for the better will reduce the likelihood of offending. Moreover, interventions predicated on this model are often labelled 'what works' in reducing youth offending and are offered as prescriptions for 'effective practice'. Taken together, the identification of risk factors through RFR and their targeting in youth justice policy and practice constitute a 'risk factor prevention paradigm'. Ostensibly, this paradigm has offered a simplistic, comprehensible and 'evidence-based' approach to controlling and managing youth crime and young offenders. Thus, one of the major proponents of RFR, David Farrington, has asserted:

> A key advantage of the risk factor prevention paradigm is that it links explanation and prevention, fundamental and applied research, and scholars and practitioners. Importantly, the paradigm is easy to understand and to communicate, and it is readily accepted by policy makers, practitioners, and the general public. Both risk factors and interventions are based on empirical research rather than theories. (Farrington 2000: 7)

However, in reality, the RFR that has underpinned the risk factor prevention paradigm (RFPP) has not been as scientific, value-free, definitive or unequivocal as has often been claimed or depicted. This terrain has, in fact, been quite heavily contested, as has been reflected in the emergence of two very distinct camps and perspectives concerning the generation and application of knowledge through RFR. The first camp is an increasingly large number of researchers across the globe who have pursued quantitative RFR as a valid and productive way of understanding and explaining juvenile delinquency, buttressed by supporters and believers in political and policy-making offices (including many of those responsible for deciding how research funding is spent); the second camp is a smaller, disparate group of academics who have sought to evolve, reorientate, challenge, criticise and oppose the RFR movement and the manner and extent to which this research has been used to inform and develop youth justice policy and practice.

These two camps have proffered disparate views of both the methodological robustness and the practical and policy utility of RFR. Proponents have championed RFR methodology as both *scientific* (e.g. empirically-based, variable focused and statistically robust) and *clinical* (e.g. enabling the objective identification of risk as a set of factors that are purportedly predictive or causal of offending and that are amenable to treatment or change). These same proponents have accentuated the empirical basis and sustained validation, replicability and universality of risk factors as robust, conclusive research-based evidence of the utility of RFR for shaping policy and practice, protecting the public and reducing offending and/or re-offending by young people exposed to identified risks. Many opponents, on the other hand, have questioned the methodological, ethical and political bases of RFR and have doubted the validity of the conclusions drawn. Critics have asserted, for example, that the 'factorisation' of risk equates to a reductionism that oversimplifies the context and operation of risk, individualises responsibility for subsequent offending and individualises responses to risk; arguing that such pervasive individualisation stigmatises and harms young people rather than helps them (O'Mahony 2008; White 2008). What has emerged has been a polarisation of opinion and a lack of direct engagement between the two camps. RFR has continued to spread and replicate itself, largely without reference to the valid (or otherwise) arguments of the critics. The cries of the critics have, for the most part, gone unheard by risk factor researchers, politicians and policy makers.

Our position does not fit neatly into either camp. We have carried out and published RFR (e.g. Case and Haines 2004, 2007, 2008; Haines and Case 2005), but simultaneously have taken a critical approach to the methodology and conclusions drawn of much pre-existing RFR (e.g. Haines and Case 2008; Case 2006, 2007; Case et al. 2005). In many ways, this book represents the process through which we have developed our own research and the conclusions we have reached about RFR and the uses to which it has been put in the development of youth justice policy and practice.

RFR has potential benefits, not least in affording a practical, real-world methodology for testing theoretical premises, identifying promising targets for intervention and applying knowledge of risk factors to the development of interventions. However, these strengths have been variously overstated and misrepresented by proponents of RFR, too often crudely understood by politicians and policy makers (and others) and frequently clumsily implemented in policies and programmes. On the other hand, critics have tended to proffer generalised critiques of RFR and its uses; criticisms that have often been based on an anti-positivist philosophy, moral or ethical objections and questions concerning the politics of crime control. Much of this critical work provides an important socialising counterbalance to the 'psychosis of positivists': the over-riding belief that the complexities of the human social world are reducible to a series of measurable factors which can be shown to exist in statistical relationships to the denial of alternative ways of knowing or understanding. However, rarely have the critics engaged with the substance and actuality of RFR. RFR has, therefore, until now, largely escaped the detailed critical analysis and exposé this book aims to provide.

The RFR movement has emerged from a body of longitudinal studies in the industrialised Western world (discussed in more detail in Chapter 2) that claim to have identified a range of 'factors' in childhood that predict an increased statistical likelihood of offending in adolescence. The prediction of adolescent offending from childhood factors has promulgated a very specific (yet almost exclusively implicit) within-individual, *developmental* understanding of exposure to early-life risk factors as the explanation of adolescent offending and/or antisocial behaviour. This developmental RFR has identified risk factors primarily within domains that have been labelled 'psychological' (e.g. relating to cognition, emotion, temperament) and 'social', the latter of which has typically been predicated on a restricted definition of the social as relating to the family, school, neighbourhood, peer group and lifestyle, rather than broader socio-*structural* factors such as gender, class, poverty, societal access routes to opportunities (France and Homel 2006) and the criminalising tendency of interactions with official agencies (McAra and McVie 2005; Armstrong 2004). As a result, a select group of psychological and social (otherwise known as 'psychosocial') risk factors for offending have been widely replicated across different groups of young people (e.g. different age groups, genders) across time, place and culture. This sustained and far-reaching replicability has been seen as a major strength of RFR and has been drawn on to impute a robustness and validity to the research findings.

The apparent predictive validity of a widely-replicated, globally-applicable set of psychosocial risk factors generated through RFR has been enormously attractive to politicians, policy makers and practitioners. For many such people, a developmental understanding of the risk-factor–offending relationship has provided clear, evidence-based targets for preventative and ameliorative (early) interventions that have the potential to 'nip crime in the bud'. Thus, RFR has directed the limited time, resources and finances of policy makers and practitioners towards the most promising targets for intervention and afforded a convenient, commonsense and defensible response to a significant public and political concern.

However, critical criminologists have taken issue with the governmentality and interventionism arising from RFR (see, for example, Armstrong 2004; Pitts 2003a). These same critics have also expressed serious concerns over the methodological robustness and validity of the RFR paradigm; concerns that we intend to evaluate, extrapolate and add to throughout this text. In particular, it has been suggested (see, for example, Haines and Case 2008; O'Mahony 2008; Case 2007; Kemshall 2003; Pitts 2003a) that RFR has:

- relied inordinately on measuring and analysing risk as a broadly-phrased, quantitative factor that is aggregated across groups, thus encouraging a focus on the replication of statistical differences between-groups rather than within-individual changes;

- become dominated by deterministic and probabilistic developmental understandings of predictive, childhood risk factors at the expense of alternative and more holistic and complex explanations;

- lacked coherence and a clear, well-developed understanding of its central concepts, namely the definition of risk factors and the nature of their relationship with offending;

- produced findings that have been applied uncritically and over-simplistically by policy makers more interested in broad headlines than addressing the details and limitations of the research.

Exploring the unresolved methodological paradoxes of RFR

Thinking critically about RFR brings to light a number of inherent methodological issues that can be perceived as paradoxes that beset RFR. These paradoxes are by no means easy or even possible to resolve and (to a greater or lesser degree) reflect the current state of ability and knowledge in the field. Nevertheless, it is essential to illuminate these paradoxes and evaluate their impact on the reliability, validity and practical utility of the conclusions drawn from RFR. These methodological paradoxes are mutually exclusive but they also reinforce each other. They are reflected to a greater or lesser extent across the entire field of RFR as well as manifest variously in individual studies.

- *Simplistic over-simplification* – RFR has relied on the factorisation of risk in order to produce clear, comprehensible and practical findings. However, the greater the extent of factorisation, the greater the simplification of the lived real-life experiences of young people and the less accurate and representative of real life the data becomes. Moreover, factorisation has been combined with the aggregation of risk and the homogenisation of categories of offending and young people. These methodological and analytical processes have combined to radically over-simplify the lived real-life experiences of young people. Consequently, the data becomes less accurate and less representative of real life. In efforts to try to explain more, RFR is actually able to explain less.

- *Definitive indefinity* – researchers have confidently disseminated simplistic, clear-cut, evidence-based conclusions which have, in reality, been predicated on indefinite, unspecific and inconsistent definitions and understandings of key concepts. In particular, there has been ambiguity and lack of consensus over how to understand 'risk factors', 'offending' and the nature and temporal order of the risk-factor–offending relationship (e.g. deterministic or probabilistic, causal or predictive). Thus the attribute of 'indefinity' (i.e. a lack of definitiveness) in key concepts is what has enabled and promoted definitive conclusions.

- *Risk-dependent protective factors* – there has been a lack of consensus about the definition and understanding of so-called 'protective factors'. The various definitions proffered have, however, explored the concept of protection almost exclusively as a 'factor' and in relation to risk (factors) and the prevention of negative outcomes, rather than as powerful elements exerting independent, autonomous and potentially-positive influences. Thus, attempts to explain non-offending, reductions in reoffending or positive outcomes have been limited in scope by notions of risk.

- *Replicable incomparability* – the development of an impressive range of 'universal', globally applicable risk factors has relied on studies collecting and analysing aggregated data. Aggregation has, however, rendered research findings largely unrepresentative of any particular individual differences or contextual differences relating to, *inter alia*, locality, nation, culture. Thus, the apparent replicability in the risk factors identified has not necessarily implied *comparability* in the nature or function of these risk factors across different samples.

- *Unconstructive constructivism* – a constructivist strand of RFR has challenged dominant quantitative, developmental understandings of risk and begun to address the aforementioned methodological paradoxes by exploring young people's ability to construct, negotiate and resist exposure to risk in their interactions with their environment. Constructivism, however, has been simultaneously wedded to dominant developmental definitions of risk factors (at least in part) and intent on exploring qualitative, nuanced, individualised and context-specific understandings of risk and its relationship to offending. Thus, the more constructivism has attempted to challenge and problematise factorised RFR, the less it has actually been able to offer genuine and practical alternatives, findings and conclusions.

- *Heterogeneous homogeneity* – RFR has been characterised and presented as if it were a homogeneous, coherent, progressive and reinforcing field of research. Yet, in reality, there have been significant theoretical and methodological differences between separate RFR strands and studies. Thus, heterogeneity has been presented as homogeneity in underpinning the grand claims of RFR.

17

The paradox of simplistic over-simplification

The apparent scientific robustness, clarity and consistency of findings and the inherent simplistic logic in translating these research findings into policy and practice has been at the heart of the appeal of RFR for many researchers, politicians, policy makers and others of a non-technical background. There has been little reflection by risk factor researchers on the potentially-deleterious effects of the methodological shortcuts that have found their way into RFR. These shortcuts include, but are not limited to, the factorisation of risk, the limitations of aggregate analyses for understanding and explaining individual behaviour and the psycho-social and developmental biases manifested in the purportedly coherent, cohesive and atheoretical risk factor paradigm.

Artefact risk factor research and risk factorology

The focus of much RFR has been on the transformation of 'risk' into objectively-knowable, measurable, quantitative risk 'factors' or 'artefacts' that are amenable to probabilistic calculation (France 2008; Horlick-Jones 1998). This factorisation process, which France (2005) dubbed 'risk factorology', is fundamental and necessary to RFR. Factorisation has been achieved, for example, through gathering quantitative data (e.g. official records, psychometric test scores) or using quantitative response and rating scales to convert individual, personal or social information (such as association with peers, quality of family relationships) into quantitative measures (e.g. high–low, frequent–never, 1–5 etc). Thus questions such as 'How good do you think your relationship with your parents is?' (please circle the number that applies. 1 = poor, 5 = good) readily turn the quality of family relationships into a number. The resultant quantitative factors – no matter how crudely they represent or measure real life – have been plugged into statistical analyses (as independent variables). The relationships between these independent variables with quantitative measures of offending (taken from official records and/or self-report inventories) have been produced. Those factors which are shown to correlate with offending are thus presented in the form of risk factors for offending. The positivist conception, measurement and analysis of risk variables has been characterised by Kemshall (2003) as the *artefact model* of RFR.

Factorisation of risk and the risk-factor–offending relationship

The process of factorisation in RFR has been enabled by the collection of quantitative data from surveys, behavioural ratings scales, psychometric tests and official records, plus the quantification of essentially qualitative risk data obtained from interviews and observations. Some form of factorisation is central to much social research, however, factorisation has become a particular problem within RFR. The factorisation of risk data through the use of, *inter alia*, quantitative scales, psychometric testing and qualitative data analysis has typically involved allocating risk information to broad risk 'categories' that are subjectively defined by the researcher, such as 'inadequate parental supervision', 'academic underachievement' and 'criminogenic neighbourhood'. Consequently, factorisation has encouraged the oversimplification of potentially-complex, multi-faceted and subjective risk processes into crude, abstract, broadly-phrased factorised variables that may be unrepresentative of the phenomena being measured and may lack meaning to the individuals to which they are attributed. For example, what constitutes 'academic underachievement' to one individual may not to others (at least to the same degree), even if they obtain similar grades at school. Similarly, young people may have disparate perceptions and ratings of levels of 'parental supervision', even if these young people are siblings within the same family. The effects of reliability and validity of the ambiguous categories of risk and the relative nature of responses to them is compounded by the potential for young people's perceptions to change over short periods of time. Regardless of this dynamism, quantitative ratings of risk are typically viewed by researchers as stable and representative of young people's perceptions over long periods of time (e.g. 12 months).

Therefore, the factorisation of risk has been a blunt tool used to carve out risk factors and 'at risk' populations of young people to enter into statistical analyses. Moreover, the factorisation of risk measurement and analyses have produced statistical artefacts (i.e. risk factors) whose relationship with offending can only be explored and understood in generalised, statistical, abstract terms and solely in relation to the (typically psychosocial) factors originally programmed into the analyses. This technical, mechanical and narrow methodological approach not only limits the search for risk factors to a pre-determined list – failing to quality check this list or generate possible new risk factors – but it also restricts understanding of risk. Conclusions regarding the nature of the relationship between risk factors and offending, particularly the much-neglected and poorly-theorised explanations of risk processes, have been largely underpinned by imputation and uncritical comparisons with previous RFR. Many of the conclusions from RFR have been born of the false confidence generated by the positivist, 'scientific' basis of the artefact paradigm and have rested on risk factors that some consider to be little more than 'vague, inadequate proxies for putative causal processes' (O'Mahony 2008).

Ignoring the meaning and construction of risk

Notwithstanding the vagaries of the process of factorisation itself – whether individual and social information can be and has been factorised in a meaningful and useful manner, there are additional questions concerning what is captured and what is left out in this process. The artefact model's reductionist simplification of complex, in-depth individual and social information to quantitative factors has overlooked and washed away the original subjectivity within the young people's responses. What has been lost in the factorisation process is any *meaning* that an individual assigned to particular risks and the possibility that young people can, to some extent, take an active role in shaping or constructing their exposure to and responses to risk – as the *constructivist* approach to risk emphasises (Kemshall 2003). This is important because the active human agent may be a crucial determinant in the outcome of any risk-factor–offending (or non-offending) outcome. The lack of attention to the active human agent, particularly in developmental RFR, gives rise to the notion of the 'crash test dummy' – the proposition that young people are inexorably conditioned by early life factors to become offenders in adolescence.

There are important questions about measurement and about what is being measured in artefact approaches to RFR. The use of quantitative response scales in RFR has privileged standardisation and quantification over qualitative exploration of the individual value and meanings that young people attribute to questions about different risk factors and how they respond to them. For example, a young person reporting high levels of family problems may interpret 'high levels' and 'family problems' as entirely different concepts than another young person offering the 'same' response, particularly when individuals' understandings of risk, social contexts and age, gender, cultural and historical differences are taken into account (Case 2006). In artefact RFR, therefore, it is difficult to be certain about exactly what is being measured – particularly when, as is common, complex social dynamics (such as family or peer relationships) are 'assessed' in a limited number of questions.

Furthermore, artefact RFR presents risk as a series of static and stable variables and tends to negate the notion of risk as complex and dynamic *processes* which are subject to construction, reconstruction and flux. Pitts (2003a) has criticised the artefact approach for transforming a dynamic, interactive set of risk processes into static relationships and for treating diverse phenomena (e.g. unemployment, attitudes) as if they were equivalent variables that could be assigned reliable numerical values capable of statistical manipulation and understanding. More recently, proponents of RFR have begun to acknowledge and address these limitations and the concern that 'the focuses of attention should be on the *processes* or mechanisms, rather than on variables' (Rutter 1987: 320). Wikström (2006b; Farrington 2005) and Farrington (2007) in particular have formulated multi-faceted explanatory theories of risk factor influence that have prioritised examinations of what exactly puts the risk into risk factors (Wikström and Butterworth 2006), although these 'social context' theories have been artefactual and have also been accused of reductionism and psychosocial bias (see Chapter 2 for a full discussion of these theories and their attendant criticisms).

The artefact approach to RFR has, therefore, not only overlooked the possibility that young people can actively construct, interpret and negotiate their responses to risk factors, but it has made two other notable assumptions:

- that the response to (or effect of) risk factors is either known or predictable, thereby discounting the possibility of different responses or effects;

- that the response or effect of risk factors is uniform, thereby discounting the possibility of different (possibly non-factorised) responses/effects at different times (e.g. during specific developmental periods, at times of transition) or in different social contexts (e.g. home, school, leisure time).

The crude factorisation of risk, prevalent within artefact RFR, has, therefore, simplistically over-simplified the concept of risk and its function. RFR is trapped. In order to enable the prediction of delinquency, it has been necessary to construct a definitive list of measurable variables, but to produce this list, these variables have inevitably been imprecisely-defined and crudely measured. Oversimplification and imprecision have thus inevitably engendered misrepresentations of the reality of young people's lives. The paradox is, therefore, that the more simplistic the research has been and the greater its ability to produce definitive results and conclusions, the more distant these research outcomes have been from the complexities of the social phenomenon they are trying to explain.

An additional, related, matter concerns the extent to which risk has been constructed by researchers themselves. Researchers have exercised subjectivity when interpreting risk through the initial choices they have made regarding the key risk factors to target in their research, through the response scales used in their research, through the process of factorisation and by their chosen methods of analysis. For example, Armstrong (2004) has argued that the use of concepts such as 'good and bad parenting' and 'community disorganisation' is a subjective process. Similarly, defining levels of risk as 'low' or 'high' involves a degree of imputation (see France and Crow 2005). In this way, as Armstrong (2004) has argued, social scientists socially-construct risk through the categories they use to describe it. Lupton has asserted a similar view:

A risk is never fully objective or knowable outside of belief systems and moral positions: what we measure, identify and manage as risks are always constituted via pre-existing knowledge and discourses. (Lupton 1999: 29)

Here, both Armstrong and Lupton dispute the claims of neutrality, objectivity and scientific method within RFR. They argue instead that the individualised, psychosocial nature of the commonly-employed risk factors has reflected the theoretical preferences of the researchers who have driven the RFR agenda (see also Susser 1998) – contra the positivist view of risk as a set of objective, scientific and 'value-free' measures (see, for example, Hansen and Plewis 2004). Consequently, the definition, collection and analysis of quantitative statistical risk factor data in standardised forms has provided a scientific gloss to a paradigm ripe with theoretical, methodological and personal biases that have a strong tendency to oversimplify, misrepresent and depoliticise a complex, theory-driven and politically-motivated field of research (see, for example, Pitts 2003a).

Psychosocial reductionism

There is another sense in which RFR (particularly artefact RFR) has tended towards simplistic over-simplification – the artificial restriction of the range of factors explored. The origins of RFR lie in social science (primarily psychology) that has tended to emphasise individualistic approaches to the understanding of human behaviour to the relative neglect of sociological perspectives. Thus these theoretical preferences and biases have been reflected in an implicit biopsychosocial reductionism in the RFR literature that has privileged individualised risks at the expense of socio-political, structural and constructivist understandings (see France 2008). Measuring risk as 'the psychogenic antecedents of criminal behaviour' (Armstrong 2004: 103) in the domains of family, school, peers, neighbourhood, lifestyle and psychological/emotional has neglected the potential (possibly independent and direct) influence of socio-structural and socio-political factors (see France and Homel 2006), social exclusion and the impact of locally-specific policy formations (Cuneen and White 2006). Therefore, the dominance of the psychosocial focus has restricted the breadth and depth of RFR by' electing to ignore (or, at least, much under-emphasise) sociological processes, influences and explanations of human behaviour. This psychosocial reductionism has produced, at best, a *partial* (in the dual sense of limited and biased) understanding and explanation of youth offending.

For some, the broad psychosocial reductionism and the attestation that RFR is scientific, robust, atheoretical and evidence-led coalesces with the government agenda. Thus, psychosocial reductionism has been encouraged by governmental demands for simplistic and practical targets for policy that are, at the same time, morally neutral, politically attractive and evidence-led. Central to this argument is the way in which psychosocial risk factors have tended to situate offending within individual pathologies that have encouraged a 'morality of blame' (Armstrong 2004) and have produced conclusions that are ripe for short-term, cheap, quick fix responses from a government seen to be 'doing something' about youth crime. In this way, risk becomes a symptom of the individual and attention is drawn away from structural, social inequalities for which government itself has some responsibility (see White 2008). As O'Mahony asserts in his forceful critique of RFR:

> inherent deterministic and reductionist bias gives virtually no consideration to key issues like justice, equality, human agency, moral development, human rights and restrictions on the state's power over the individual. (O'Mahony 2008)

The homogenisation of 'offending'

In much the same way that the measurement of risk has been oversimplified, so too measures of 'offending' have been over-simplified within RFR. Much RFR has measured offending as a broad and ostensibly homogenous category, such as:

- *Lifetime* – young people self-report whether they have *ever* committed any offence on a given offending inventory.

- *Active* – young people self-report that they are offending in their current lives and/or that they have offended over a given period (usually 12 months).

- *General* – young people report having committed any offence on an inventory, regardless of the type or seriousness of the offence. General offending can be lifetime or active unless specified.

- *Serious* – young people report that they have committed any offence on an offending inventory that has been classified as 'serious', such as offences of violence, sexual offences, drugs offences, burglaries/robberies and vehicle theft.

However, there are inherent weaknesses with these generic and insensitive categorisations of offending. For example, the measure of lifetime offending is far from a guarantee that young people are *current* offenders, so identified 'risk' factors for lifetime offending may be linked to a behaviour that is no longer relevant or active. Similarly, young people admitting to any offence on an inventory of active/current offending can also be classified as 'lifetime' and 'general' offenders. However, the risk factors associated with this behaviour offer little of explanatory value, not least because the aggregated measures of, for example, general offending, against which risk factors are measured may be constituted by vastly different forms of offending, so the dependent variable in this case is highly insensitive. The same can be said of aggregated measures of 'serious' offending, typically comprised of admissions of any one of a number of (potentially disparate) serious offences on a generic inventory.

There has been relatively little exploration of the relationships between risk factors and more specific forms of offending (e.g. specific property, violent and sexual offences) or for different features of the criminal career (e.g. offending frequency, duration, seriousness, escalation, persistence, specialisation). RFR has been equally silent on issues of temporality – the 'lag' between risk exposure and offending outcome. As a result, studies of the risk-factor–offending relationship have been overly superficial, generalised and insensitive – over-relying on measuring the statistical link between over-simplified conceptions of risk and over-simplified categories of offending. There has, thus, been a lack of clarity in much RFR as to precisely what risk factors are predictive of.

This situation has been exacerbated by the internationalisation of RFR (evaluated in detail in Chapter 5), which has:

- been founded on the uncritical acceptance of universalised categories of 'crime', 'offending' and 'antisocial behaviour';

- ignored fundamental historical, socio-cultural, legal, political and contextual differences and ambiguities within and between the definitions of offending and antisocial behaviour that risk factors have been linked to;

- neglected to explore risk factors relative to the perceived seriousness of these broad categories of behaviour and their component behaviours (e.g. specific types of offence).

The lack of precision in the definition of offending as the dependent variable in the risk-factor–offending relationship is an important and serious matter. Much is made in RFR of the high degree of replicability of risk factors for offending across different studies conducted over time and in different contexts and countries. Yet when the dependent variable has such malleable qualities and has been so variably and loosely defined and differently measured, the basic validity of the statistical relationship between independent and dependent variables must be questioned. Where measures of offending differ between studies, the issue becomes one of whether the 'replication' of risk factors for offending is an indication of the robustness of multiple research findings or some crude statistical artefact.

The simplistic-oversimplification of risk

By design RFR conceives of risk as a static, quantifiable variable, measured at a single point in time. However, the nature of the risk-factor–offending relationship is likely to be more dynamic and subject to construction/reconstruction by the young person than artefact approaches have ever begun to comprehend or address. Artefact approaches have tended to ignore the notion of risk as a process or, indeed, even a set of interacting processes. This has led artefact RFR to overlook, *inter alia*, the perhaps less quantifiable, more subtle, more processual and more long-term potential influences on offending such as structural and political processes and the young person's interactions with significant others, the community and the state.

Artefact RFR has demonstrated, but not acknowledged, notable reductionist tendencies, evidenced through factorisation, partial understandings of the risk-factor–offending relationship, lack of recognition of agency and an unwillingness to explore young people's ability to construct risk. Armstrong (2004: 111) has accused artefact RFR of being founded on a quasi-experimental pseudoscience that has privileged 'naïve scientific-realist assumptions about the identification of relationships between "risk" and offending through the use of probabilistic statistics' that have reduced complex experiences to 'objective' naturalistic categories. These 'shaky scientific credentials' (O'Mahony 2008) have produced methods and content that have been castigated for promoting a deterministic and narrow view of the developmental influence of a limited body of childhood, psychosocial risk factors on young people's future behaviour (Brown 2005). Accordingly, young people have been portrayed as the passive recipients and 'victims' of exposure to risk factors – as crash test dummies. Such simplistic-oversimplification has been attractive to politicians and policy makers seeking practical solutions to social problems, more effective targeting of interventions and the efficient deployment of resources (see Kemshall 2008). However, the already discussed theoretical biases and methodological inadequacies of much RFR bring into question any claims to progress detailed and realistic understandings of risk or the relationship between risk factors and offending.

The paradox of definitive indefinity

RFR has been characterised by the definitiveness with which results, interpretations and conclusions have been presented – notably in relation to the predictive and causal nature of risk factors for offending. For example, advocates of developmental RFR have claimed that:

> *Causal risk factors* are risk factors that can change and, when changed, cause a change in risk for the outcome. (Murray *et al.* in press)

> Causal risk factors are the 'gold' of risk estimation. They can be used both to identify those at high of the outcome and to provide the bases for interventions to prevent the outcome. (Kraemer *et al.* 2005: 32–3)

> risk mechanisms ... are directly associated with causation. (Rutter *et al.* 1998: 18)

> systemic reviews of longitudinal research and the use of meta-analytic statistical techniques have been used to produce much shorter lists of major risk factors that appear to be implicated in causation. (YJB 2005a: 6)

However, detailed scrutiny of studies shows that the confident conclusions of RFR have been based on concepts and methodologies which have remained malleable, unspecific and indefinite in design and interpretation. Indeed, there remains much uncertainty and ambiguity concerning the aims of RFR, the definition and nature of risk (and protective) factors and the relationship between risk and offending. There has been, in fact, as much difference and disagreement within RFR on these key concepts as there has been between RFR and its critics. Therefore, just how scientific is it for research based on such poorly-defined and partially-understood concepts and methodologies to have confidently reached such a definitive set of conclusions? The level of indefinity regarding exactly what has been measured, what can be understood and what can be claimed must be assessed against the definitiveness of the conclusions reached. Not surprisingly, the simplistic, definitive and replicated understanding of risk factors as predictors of offending (and for easy targeting by crime prevention programmes or interventions) has been criticised as an inherently flawed, over-estimation of what can be concluded from the available research (France 2008; Case 2007) – a definitiveness achieved out of indefinity.

Indefinite definitions of risk: What is a risk factor?

The concept of a criminogenic 'risk factor' has been defined fairly simplistically as relating to factors statistically 'associated with an increasing likelihood of the commencement, frequency and duration of offending' (Stephenson *et al.* 2007: 9). However, in practice, the over-simplicity and inadequacy of this definition has been exposed by the inconsistency with which the concept of a 'risk factor' has been defined and explored across RFR. It has proven extremely difficult, if not impossible, to provide a universally-agreed *operational* definition of risk factors for offending (e.g. to specify what they are and how they work) or to reach consensus on how they should be measured and interpreted (see France and Crow 2005; Hill *et al.* 2004). Instead, a host of diverse and competing alternative definitions and understandings of the nature and functions of risk factors have been put forward and used by proponents of RFR (see Pitts 2003a). The effects of risk factors on offending have, for example, been variously characterised as:

- *Causal* – factors that determine or cause different forms of offending at different stages of the criminal career. Such factors may be developmental or proximal or a mixture (Rutter *et al.* 1998; Farrington 2007). According to Murray *et al.* (in press), causal risk factors can only be identified if the researcher is able to (experimentally) control for the extraneous influences on the internal validity of the risk factors measured, specifically: *selection effects* (differences between those exposed to a risk factor and those who are not), *history* (events concurrent to the risk factor that may influence the outcome), *maturation* (naturally occurring changes), *attrition* (sample members dropping out) and *regression to the mean* (natural fluctuations in risk levels).

- *Predictive* – criminogenic factors that increase the statistical probability of offending at a later stage (Kazdin *et al.* 1997).

- *Linear* – factors that operate on a continuum or scale. For example, risk of conviction could be higher for males in large families, but constant for lower levels of family size (Farrington and Hawkins 1991).

- *Catchall* – sufficiently broad concepts that apply to all young people at some point (R. Smith 2006), depending on how they are defined by the researcher/practitioner. In this way, risk factors can provide universalised explanations of offending, yet consequently may lack discriminatory power and practical utility.

- *Multiplicative, cumulative or additive* – the more risk factors a young person is exposed to, the more likely they are to offend, regardless of which specific factors are present (e.g. Farrington 2007; YJB 2005a, 2005b). However, Kraemer *et al.* (2001: 848) have stated that 'accumulating risk factors and either counting or scoring them does little to increase the understanding of etiologic processes'.

- *Interactive* – different combinations of risk factors may exert different effects when experienced together by the same young person, so the specific constellation of risks may be more important than the total number of factors. Cashmore (2001) has argued that the complex relationship between risk factors could be both multiplicative and interactive and that the effects of these factors are dependent on the context in which risk factors are experienced and the timing of exposure to them.

- *Overlapping* – factors that are correlated with each other and both related to the outcome, but with neither having 'temporal precedence' in the causal chain (Kraemer *et al.* 2001). The combined effect of factors increases the probability of offending, so exposure to multiple risk factors outweighs the 'additive' effect of the sum of those factors' independent effects (Agnew 2005; Durlak 1998).

- *Correlational* – risk factors as correlates of offending, both coterminous symptoms of some other unknown cause. According to Pitts (2001), it has been extremely difficult to distinguish the 'causal primacy' of risk factors, namely whether they are antecedents of offending behaviour or symptoms/effects. Indeed, some risk factors may not be 'causes' at all, but merely correlates of offending, whereas others could be both correlates *and* causes depending on, for instance, social context, situational influences and age (Farrington 2007). For example, chronic drug use could be a cause of offending distinguished by differences between-individuals as well as a cause within the same individual (e.g. offending more whilst under the influence of drugs).

- *Multi-stage* – a risk factor (e.g. neighbourhood disadvantage, lack of educational qualifications) could increase the likelihood of another risk factor (e.g. unemployment or low socio-economic status), which in turn could lead to offending (Farrington 1996). Similarly, problem behaviours could also serve as risk factors for one another (e.g. the apparently reciprocal relationship between substance use and disaffection or between truancy and educational failure). Risk factors may also form part of a larger multi-component risk factor, but, in isolation, may not effect offending at all (see 'Proxy risk factors' below). According to Kraemer *et al.* (2001), there is a need for the further investigation of individual risk factors as components of larger risk domains in order to enhance understanding of the causal processes of youth offending.

- *Proxy* – factors correlated with risk factors for offending but which are not risk factors in their own right. However, these factors may show up in statistical tests as risk factors because of their correlation to 'real' risk factors. To date, however, there has been little analysis to statistically-distinguish proxy risk or 'risk indicators' (Rutter *et al.* 1998) from 'causal' risk factors or 'risk mechanisms' (Rutter *et al.* 1998), so the danger of identifying faux risk factors remains a real yet unknown possibility. This resonates with the statistical phenomenon of 'multicol-linearity', where two or more 'predictor variables' in a regression model are so closely correlated with one another that they may be, in effect, representing the same thing (see Field 2005). For example, if truancy and disaffection from school were both identified as risk factors for offending, but were also highly correlated with each other, truancy might, in fact, be an integral component of and/or proxy measure for the risk factor 'disaffection from school'.

- *Challenging* – exposure to certain risk factors may inoculate young people against exposure to and/or the effects of further risk factors. For example, if a young person has experienced a stressful life event, they may be more resilient to future stressful life events (Ungar 2004).

- *Reciprocal* – risk factors and offending exist in a reciprocal, mutually-reinforcing relationship where each can influence, perpetuate and exacerbate the other (in line with Thornberry's interactional theory). For example, association with delinquent peers may precipitate offending, which in turn may increase the likelihood of and exacerbate the effects of future associations with delinquent peers.

- *Symptomatic* – 'risk factors' emerge as the outcomes of offending. Factors statistically associated or correlated with offending may not, in fact, precede or cause it, but may be products of the processes (individual, family, social, structural) that accompany offending. Therefore, these factors are not actually 'risk' factors at all, but symptoms of offending. Alternatively, certain factors may be both correlated with offending and symptomatic of it. Farrington (2007: 605) concedes that 'it is difficult to decide if any given risk factor is an indicator (symptom) or a possible cause of offending . . . some factors may be both indicative and causal'.

Defining risk factors for offending and understanding their effects has been far from straightforward and even proponents of the risk factor approach remain discordant in their views. This situation matters because when researchers talk about risk factors they may actually be talking about different things, but they may be read (by other researchers or consumers) or assumed to be talking about the same thing. Moreover, risk-factor–offending relationships based on one understanding may not mean the same thing as risk-factor–offending relationships based on another. Obfuscation rather than clarity has been the result and it is a weakness of the RFR literature that there has been little discussion or analysis, for example, of the possibility that risk factors may exhibit all, some or none of these characteristics at different times or in different contexts, between or within individuals.

Indefinite relationships between risk factors and offending: Determinism or probabilism?

Reflecting the disparate definitions and understandings of risk factors in RFR, there has been a lack of clarity concerning the precise nature of the relationship between risk factors and offending. This lack of clarity inevitably questions the validity of conclusions that risk factors are either causal or predictive of offending. Both proponents and opponents of RFR (e.g. Farrington 2007; Pitts 2003a) have noted that statistical analyses have thus far been unable to conclusively evidence whether or not:

- the risk-factor–offending relationship is indeed causal/predictive, in what direction this causality/prediction flows (e.g. it is possible that offending behaviour could cause risk factors such as poor relationships with parents or truancy from school to emerge);

- risk factors and offending function within a relationship of reciprocal causal/predictive influence (see, for example, Thornberry's Interactional Theory);

- the true nature and complexity of the relationship between risk factors and offending lies outside the scope of simplistic understandings;

- risk factors may simply be statistical artefacts with no dynamic, actual relationship with offending whatsoever other than at the statistical level.

Artefact RFR, particularly in its developmental form (which is discussed fully in the next chapter) has promoted a simplistic, deterministic, passive model of behaviour (see Armstrong 2004). Children and young people have been portrayed as victims of predictive risk factors; as conditioned by the exigencies experienced early in life to become offenders in their teenage years; as 'crash test dummies' hurtling towards a series of negative outcomes later in life. Herein there has been no conception that a young person may, for example, grow out of crime or that they may be able to actively construct, manage, redefine, negotiate or resist risk (see Hine 2005) over the life-course, or indeed of the propositions of any other criminological theory. Thus, these so-called predictive risk factors, identified and measured in childhood, have been assumed to remain active influences on and, indeed, determinants of young people's behaviour in their later years, irrespective of the influence of life circumstances and events that have occurred in the intervening period or the direct and current circumstances and events which characterise a young person's life in the here and now.

Recent commentaries on RFR (see, for example, Wikström 2008; Moffitt 2005) have argued, however, albeit perhaps with the benefit of hindsight, that most RFR has focused on identifying predictive risk factors that increase the statistical *probability* of later offending, rather than identifying the causal risk factors *determining* offending (i.e. the model is probabilistic rather than deterministic). This is an important distinction. If RFR claims to be deterministic in its findings and conclusions then these findings and conclusions are simply not sustained by the methodology or the analysis employed – if for no other reason than RFR has not demonstrated that intervening circumstances and events have no effect. If, on the other hand, RFR is merely probabilistic then the potential impact of circumstances and events in the intervening years between the identification of risk factors and the outcome offending is not negated. Rather, early life factors may retain some explanatory credibility and practical utility (e.g. as potential targets for risk-focused intervention at an 'early' age when these factors are still live). However, such RFR is not able to demonstrate the validity or credibility of these early life factors as potential targets for risk-focused intervention in the teenage years because the impact of the intervening years is neither measured nor known. Regrettably, RFR is rarely, if ever, so clear on such important caveats when discussing methodology (and its potential and limitations) or when presenting its results and discussing their import. All too often, probabilism has deteriorated into determinism or the distinction has been rendered irrelevant in arguments that whether deterministic or probabilistic, the identification of risk factors at the pre-offending stage allows for crucial *risk-focused* early intervention and has the potential to prevent negative outcomes for the young person and society (see Blyth *et al.* 2007). Such arguments contain so much imprecision as to render them almost useless and potentially dangerous. Even risk factor researchers who have been careful to technically define the probabilistic limits of their research have tended towards determinism in their conclusions concerning the practical utility of their findings. There has been a persistent incongruity between the tentative, guarded statements concerning the probabilistic influence of risk factors on future offending and the deterministic confidence with which RFR findings have been presented, championed and applied in risk-focused, preventative and curative interventions (e.g. by the Youth Justice Board of England and Wales – see Chapter 6). This determinism is exemplified by Graham and Bowling, who concluded a major government research project, the first Youth Lifestyles Survey (see Chapter 4), with the decisive conclusion that:

> Criminality prevention . . . can be achieved by developing a range of policies which impact on the (risk) factors which predispose young people towards committing offences. (Graham and Bowling 1995: 83)

Is RFR probabilistic or deterministic? In practice there is no simple or single answer to this question. Much will depend on the theoretical influences of risk factor researchers, their assumptions and the methodologies they employ. Much also depends on the accuracy of the language they use to describe their research and findings. In respect of all of these matters, RFR has been characterised more by imprecision and ambiguity than technical scientific rigour. By itself this is a serious criticism of RFR but, to make matters worse, it has permitted (and, indeed, at times seemingly actively encouraged) government and policy makers to imbue determinism and certainty into what is all too often little more than speculation.

Causal or predictive risk factors?

> The claim that past behaviour is the best *predictor* of future behaviour does not mean that past behaviour *causes* future behaviour. (Wikström 2008: 133)

In the natural sciences, particularly within laboratory experiments, researchers manipulate elements of the environment or behaviour (independent variables) in order to measure the effect on another aspect of the environment or behaviour (the dependent variable), whilst controlling for the influence of extraneous variables (factors that have not been or cannot be manipulated but which may have an influence on the dependent variable). The systematic manipulation of independent variables and the control of potentially extraneous variables has allowed scientific researchers to identify 'cause and effect' relationships between independent and dependent variables. The artefact approach to RFR has been based on a similar methodology applied to real-world (rather than laboratory-based) behaviour. Factors have been measured in terms of, *inter alia*, their presence, frequency, intensity and (less often) duration in the lives of young people. Statistical analyses have been employed to identify those factors most strongly associated with offending. These factors have been labelled 'risk factors' for offending. In this way, risk factors have been treated as if they were independent variables, with offending behaviour as the dependent variable. Thus, in RFR, causality in the relationship between independent and dependent variables is typically demonstrated statistically, rather than experimentally.

Following their extensive review of RFR related to youth antisocial behaviour across the Western world, Rutter *et al.* (1998: 378) identified five distinct types of risk factor that could, in their view, be seen as explicitly causal:

- factors responsible for individual differences in liability to offend (e.g. early-onset hyperactivity);

- factors translating liabilities into acts (e.g. peer group influences)

- factors causing changes in differences in overall levels of crime (e.g. cultural change, availability of guns);

- factors leading to situational variations in delinquency (e.g. environmental and architectural differences in the local area);

- factors responsible for the persistence of behaviour over time in an individual's life (e.g. an unsupportive marriage to a deviant spouse).

However, there is a subtle, yet substantive difference between concluding that risk factors are *causal* (i.e. they determine offending – Rutter *et al.* 1998) and that they are *predictive* (i.e. they increase the probability of offending – Farrington 2002). This difference harkens back to the determinism-probability issue discussed above (i.e. causal implies determinism, whereas predictive suggests probability), although both imply more than the identification of risk factors as statistical *correlates* with offending. However, as Farrington (2000: 8) has noted, 'a problem of the risk factor paradigm is to determine which risk factors are causes and which are merely markers or correlated with causes'. As noted by the symptomatic definition of risk given above, there has been a pervasive lack of clarity within RFR as to whether factors correlated with offending actually represent causes (and therefore risk factors for offending) or whether they are symptoms of offending or cannot be considered to be risk factors in any sense. This has led to a confusion between whether risk factors are firstly measured and then portrayed as either causal or predictive, when, in fact, these concepts are neither synonymous nor equivalent (Wikström 2008).

A particular limitation of RFR has been the lack of detailed understanding of risk factor influence on any level; descriptive, exploratory or explanatory, other than statistical. Many risk factors have been factorised, aggregated and generalised in order to impute causality, but without exploration of 'a plausible mechanism (process) linking the suggested cause and effect' (Wikström 2005: 237). In other words, RFR has tended to rely on demonstrating causality through statistical relationships and has not been concerned to explain how risk is related to offending, or what processes link the two. Without identifying such mechanisms/processes, RFR remains restricted to understanding causation as indicated by regular associations. In this view, risk factors can only be confidently identified as correlates with offending, albeit regular correlates that facilitate consistent predictions (Wikström 2008). Conversely, by identifying the mechanisms/ processes by which certain factors produced offending, RFR could progress understandings of risk factors to causal and explanatory levels. In practice, however, the artefact approach has offered a superficial conception of risk factors as either causal or predictive of offending, but without the ability to explain or demonstrate either. The focus of concern has been on the quantity of inputs (risk factors) and the quantity of outputs (offending), rather than the quality of either of these measures or, more importantly, the pursuit of any informed understanding of what is happening between inputs and outputs to link the two. As Porteus has argued:

> The problem of causation tends to be sidestepped in risk-factor research, resulting in a kind of 'black box' explanation ... whereby causal links are assumed rather than specified. (Porteous 2007: 271–2)

Within RFR there has been an inadequate understanding of the relationship between risk factors and offending and inadequate to non-existent explanations of the processes and mechanisms through which risk factors allegedly translate into offending behaviour (see Wikström 2008; see also Pawson and Tilley 1998). Farrington (2000: 7) has acknowledged that it is 'important to establish processes or developmental pathways that intervene between risk factors and outcomes'. However, Kemshall cautions that to gain this understanding requires the recognition that pathways into offending are multi-causal, social processes and that 'pre-determined pathways' have not always turned out to be that 'determined' (Kemshall 2008: 27).

Despite the best efforts of researchers employing complex and cutting edge statistical modelling and analysis techniques, there remains a large degree of imprecision in much artefact-based RFR (see also Kraemer *et al.* 2001). As a result, RFR continues to present an over-simplified, reductionist and even misleading picture of the relationship between risk factors and offending behaviour. There has been a fundamental incompatibility between the pseudoscientific methods of artefact RFR and the conclusions of causality and predictive validity that have often been drawn. Researchers have measured the social behaviour of human beings in real-world settings, but the measurement of social behaviour simply disallows the adequate control and manipulation of risk factors in the systematic manner of an experiment in order to impute or explain causality or predictive validity. Devoid of the ability to control and manipulate putative causes and observe their effects, RFR is empirically and theoretically constrained to the post-hoc statistical analysis of superficial, non-random correlations (see Wikström 2008); what Bunge (2006: 119) calls the 'mindless search for data and statistical correlations among them'. Indeed, the predominantly survey-based (rather than experimental) methodologies of RFR (with their accompanying correlational, regression-based analyses) mean that issues of causality or prediction remain clouded. In practice, therefore, the complexities of measuring social behaviour in real-world contexts and subjecting these measures to systematic and scientifically predictable forms of physical manipulation and control represent very real limitations to the possibilities of RFR. It is very difficult, if not impossible, for RFR to counter the influence on offending behaviour of all potential (extraneous) variables/factors and researchers have not attempted to do so. Instead, researchers have attempted to 'control' for the influence of independent variables (risk factors) and the dependent variable (offending) through statistical modelling and analysis – thus substituting experimental control with statistical control as if the latter equated to 'scientific control . . . (to) take the place of hunches and guesswork' (Glueck and Glueck 1934: 297).

However, there is a pressing need for RFR to develop more informed understandings of the differences between the putative 'causal' risk factors that can explain offending and risk factors that are merely correlates and can facilitate the prediction of offending (Wikström 2008). In reaching conclusions about causality or prediction, RFR may have stepped beyond the limitations of statistical control and inappropriately drawn inferences from experimental methods. Ultimately, the methodologies of RFR may be unable to resolve or to answer questions concerning causality or prediction and, in fact, the established list of risk factors for offending may not actually be either causal or predictive. This is not the fault of RFR, *per se*, but an attribute of methodology, but the implications of these limitations for the claims made by RFR are very serious.

Indefinitive temporality

Conclusions that risk factors can exert a causal or predictive influence on offending have highlighted the under-explored issue of *temporality*. Causality and prediction both imply a time lapse between the measurement of risk factors at point A and the measurement of offending at some latter time B. Accordingly, factors have been ascribed a temporal precedence over offending and have been heralded as 'risk' factors for post-dated, 'consequent' offending behaviour. Notwithstanding problems relating to the researcher's ability to fully control for extraneous variables in order to attribute change in offending to changes in the independent variable (risk factor), issues of temporality themselves require specific attention.

Researchers conducting longitudinal RFR have lauded its ability to track changes over time and thus to explore issues of temporality relating to the occurrence and timing of risk factors and offending. In particular, developmental risk factor researchers have concentrated on identifying risk factors in childhood that appear to pre-date official and self-reported measures of offending later in life – usually during adolescence. The analysis and interpretation of longitudinal data by developmentalists has imbued risk factors with a predictive influence and thus a temporal precedence over offending. However, much longitudinal RFR (as will be discussed in Chapter 3) has contained crude, insensitive temporal measures and has instead relied on commonsense imputation to assign temporal precedence to risk factors over offending.

When measuring exposure to risk and the incidence of offending over a set period of time (e.g. 12 months) or even an ambiguous measure of 'current life' (whatever period of time this category is intended to cover), both longitudinal and cross-sectional RFR have tended to view the measurement period as homogenous, paying limited attention to the precise timings of exposure to risk factors and offending behaviour within it. Factors that may have been experienced in September, for example, have been statistically linked to offending that may have occurred previously in, say, March – in the same year. It is possible, therefore, and often not demonstrated otherwise, that the offending preceded the risk. It is also possible that so-called 'risk' factors and offending behaviour occurred concurrently and are equally devoid of causal relations. Consequently, (risk) factors have been assumed to be correlates with and even predictive of offending behaviour (the latter conclusion implying that they have temporal precedence over offending), when there has been little to no sensitivity as to exactly when factors and offending have occurred in relation to one another (e.g. the onset of risk is almost never measured).

Therefore, it is moot as to whether these factors actually represent a 'risk' of offending at all.

Furthermore, there has been little exploration of potential explanatory mechanisms/processes that could indicate the causal influence of risk factors at a given point in time, beyond a merely predictive utility in statistical terms. Even if it could be established that the onset of a risk factor pre-dated the onset of offending behaviour, further investigation would be needed to establish the existence and nature of any relationship between the two, as this relationship could be solely temporal and statistical, rather than actual. For example, it could be that the risk factor does not influence the onset or recurrence of offending at that point in time (even though it predates it), but may do so when the young person is further exposed to the risk factor at a subsequent point. In this way, even if the onset of offending behaviour has pre-dated the onset of the risk factor, the risk factor could still be predictive of future offending at another stage. However, without more detailed investigation to pursue explanations of how risk and offending interact, these conclusions are beyond the capability of factorised methodologies and statistical analyses.

Statistical association and time-ordering are necessary, but not sufficient, to established causation. As Wikström (2008) has argued, explanatory mechanisms and causation may operate over a very short time period (e.g. milliseconds), so potentially even cross-sectional RFR can be capable of establishing causality – although, to date, research has failed to penetrate to this detail of measurement and analysis. Typically, cross-sectional RFR has employed a single data collection episode, often measuring risk factors and offending contemporaneously, across a generic and homogenised measurement period (e.g. 12 months), which offers no capability of tracing the development of the risk-factor–offending relationship over a prolonged period (see Chapter 4 for a fuller discussion of these issues).

The insufficient attention paid to temporal issues has further oversimplified understandings of the risk-factor–offending relationship by neglecting to explore the impact of *duration* of exposure to risk factors (e.g. chronic versus acute, prolonged versus one-off) on the extent and nature of both offending and other risk factors. Neither has the contemporaneous measurement of factorised risk and offending been able to (or been inclined to) explore the *intensity* of exposure to risk within individuals, preferring to investigate less sensitive measures of aggregated risk and relative (rather than absolute) differences between groups (see O'Mahony 2008). For example, a risk factor predating offending may not be experienced for long enough or in sufficient intensity to induce offending at that point, but repeated, prolonged and/or intense exposure may lead to offending at another point in time. Furthermore, RFR has struggled to address the issue of the *weight/strength* of influence of different risk factors (Kemshall 2008). The neglect of these issues has exacerbated the difficulty that risk factor researchers have had in linking specific risk factors and groups of these factors to predictable trajectories/pathways of offending.

The indefinity of RFR

There has been an alarming disparity between the degree of confidence placed in RFR findings by academics, policy makers and practitioners and the general lack of understanding of what risk factors are and how they work. Definitive conclusions regarding the predictive and causal influence of risk factors have been founded on a degree of abstraction, imputation and extrapolation that has not been sufficiently addressed by researchers or acknowledged by policy makers. Although (over)simplification has been helpful in directing practice (see Stephenson *et al.* 2007), there has been an implicit reductionism in factorising risk and privileging of psychosocial risk factors. When this reductionism is considered in combination with aggregation, assumption of control over variables, lack of consensus regarding how to define risk factors and different under-standings of the nature and temporal order of their relationship with offending, the definitive conclusions from RFR become laced with an indefinity regarding exactly what is happening, to who, when, how and why. The espoused validity and legitimacy of artefact RFR has been undermined by the technicisation, quantification and reduction of com-plex human social behaviour to ostensibly measurable and controllable variables. However, it is highly unlikely that the true extent and nature of risk in the real world are amenable to probabilistic calculation and comprehensive and definitive understanding; nor can researchers be definitive regarding the breadth, depth and complexity of risk at all times in all places.

Some commentators point to the standardisation of methods and the 'appliance of science' (Porteous 2007) as methodological strengths that encourage essentially valid and replicable findings. Inconsistencies in defining the precise aims of RFR and the inability to fully explain how risk factors operate are not necessarily flaws in the paradigm if they prompt further study to produce more complex and comprehensive explanatory models. However, critics have suggested that the investigation of an ill-defined and poorly-understood body of psychosocial risk factors, with little recourse to individual, socio-cultural or historical differences be-tween and within samples (France 2008) offers little more than a methodological self-fulfilling prophecy that replicates limited and pre-scribed understandings of risk (Case 2007). This once again raises the issue of how definitively researchers should promulgate their conclusions on the basis of poorly defined concepts and potentially over-simplified and indefinite methods and analyses.

To compound the over-simplification and indefinity surrounding the nature of risk factors, offending and the relationship between them, the aims of RFR have remained ambivalent in the literature and have been rarely discussed, poorly-operationalised and often left implicit. For example, RFR has variously aimed to:

- identify risk factors in general populations;
- predict offending by individuals (often using aggregation from group-level results);
- identify pre-teen factors that explain teenage offending in general;
- develop predictive tests for use in clinical or professional assessments of individuals who can be targeted by early (childhood) intervention;
- provide assessments of teenagers that lead to risk-focused interventions with this age group;
- predict *re*offending amongst known offenders.

Therefore, the simple conclusion that risk factors have a statistical relationship with offending (and reoffending) and that these risk factors are equivalent in nature, frequency, intensity, duration and impact is rendered highly problematic if the key variables (risk factors, offending) and the aims of the research cannot be operationalised in a consensual, reliable or clear manner across the breadth of RFR. Consequently, the explanatory power and predictive utility of outcomes of RFR remain indefinite and partial in the absence of:

- a clearer understanding of the precise aims of RFR;
- consistent understandings and agreement of the precise definitions of the risk factors and offending behaviour (or other target variable) being measured;
- acknowledgement of the extent and nature of the researchers' lack of control over the measurement of risk factors;
- more precise understandings of the nature of the risk-factor–offending relationship.

The paradox of the risk-dependent protective factor

A sister project has evolved within RFR that has focused on the other side of the risk factor coin – the so-called 'protective factor' (see West 1982). Protective factors have been simply defined as 'any influence that ameliorates or reduces risk' (Hackett 2005). Accordingly, the concept of protection has been generally understood in terms of 'factors' that either decrease the statistical likelihood of future offending (amongst non-offenders, current offenders or both) or increase a young person's resilience to the effects of exposure to risk factors (see, for example, Schoon 2006).

Set in context, protective factors have been relatively neglected in relation to the exploration of risk (see France and Homel 2006). More so, protective factors have been commonly understood in a narrow, reductionist manner as the simple quantitative dichotomy of a risk factor (e.g. high academic achievement as protective, low academic achievement as risk). Indeed, certainly in early RFR, the most common conception of the relationship between risk factors and protective factors has been that they represent two sides of the same coin; a *dichotomous variable*. In the hugely influential Cambridge Study in Delinquent Development, the study which popularised the concept of a protective factor in RFR (see West 1982), the researchers simply dichotomised variables into risk/protective factors to increase the ease with which results could be communicated to policy makers and practitioners, to simplify the production of risk 'scores' to identify young people with problems and to study the interactions between different factors (see Farrington 2005). Dichotomisation of this kind has standardised the way factors have been measured in order to compare their ability to predict outcomes. Loeber and Farrington (2000) have argued that the benefits of dichotomising risk/protective factors outweigh the disadvantages for the purposes of analysing and interpreting risk through standardised, simplified and readily-understandable output. However, others counter that dichotomisation of the complex phenomena of risk lacks statistical sensitivity and further simplifies the factorisation process by treating all cases above and below a set threshold as bi-polar equivalents, thus aggregating or 'rounding up' their breadth, depth, scope and potential influence or explanatory power (Kemshall 2008; Haines and Case 2008; Case 2007).

The study of protective factors has received further impetus from a growing body of prospective longitudinal surveys and studies of resilience that have highlighted how young people exposed to multiple risk factors can lead non-problematic and successful lives (see for example, Schoon 2006). However, the vast array of studies focused on risk factors, resilience, desistence, and positive youth development have yet to establish a consensual definition of a 'protective factor'. This situation is partly born out of a lack of specific research. However, it is also the product of the inability of existing research to offer an unequivocal explanation of the relationship between protective factors and problem/positive behaviours and the failure to establish the nature of the protective factor–risk factor relationship.

The concept of a 'protective factor' has not been employed consistently across RFR (see Farrington 2000). Rather than existing as the simple dichotomies discussed above, some researchers have mooted that protective factors (when conceived of as variables with explanatory utility) could be:

- *Linear, catchall, multiplicative/cumulative/additive or interactive* – see the equivalent definitions of risk factors in the section 'Indefinite definitions of risk'.

- *Standalone* – a factor with no dichotomous risk effects. Farrington (2000) offers 'high income' as an example of a standalone protective factor, which could decrease the likelihood of offending, whereas low income may not increase this likelihood. In this case, high income is a protective factor but low income is not a risk factor.

- *Compensatory* – individual or environmental characteristics that increase *resilience* to risk by mitigating negative behaviours or promoting positives outcomes amongst at risk groups. Protective factors can also be compensatory in promoting adaptation and coping following exposure to stressful life events or other biopsychosocial risk factors (Ungar 2004). However, as Ungar goes on to assert: 'researchers have largely avoided the thorny issue of definitional ambiguity in the resilience construct' (2004: 347).

- *Moderators or mediators* – factors that modify or mediate the effects of particular risk factors on offending (Pollard *et al.* 1999). A moderating protective factor must occur after the risk factor it mediates (so the risk factor has 'temporal precedence') and prior to non-offending (Kraemer *et al.* 2001). However, explorations of the relationship between risk factors and protective factors as their mediators or moderators has been largely evaluated in cross-sectional studies, which are unable to investigate temporal patterns and relationships between co-terminously collected variables (Kraemer *et al.* 2001).

- *Causally-reciprocal* – one or more risk factors may cause certain protective factors to emerge and vice versa (Thornberry 1987). For example, peer pressure as a risk may induce a young person to develop protective, resistance strategies to counteract risk. Conversely, attempts to provide the protective measure of 'effective parenting' may actually produce maladaptive behaviour in the young person. In this causally-reciprocal model, risk and protection are not dichotomous, the risk factor and the protective factor may comprise independent behaviours that are causally related to each other in certain circumstances, yet not necessarily related to offending or non-offending.

Thus far, a precise, consensual definition of the protective factor has been beyond RFR. There has been a lack of attention paid to investigating the nature and influence of protective factors, which has resulted in definitional ambiguities and partial, under-developed understandings of the risk/protective factor relationship. In addition, little is understood regarding the relative weight of influence of different protective factors, the interactions between different protective factors and the possibility that protection operates as a dynamic process (see Kemshall 2008; Hackett 2005).

Promoting positive behaviour?

The consistent focus on risk and deficit has distracted risk factors researchers from examining the potential of protective factors to promote positive outcomes. A possible explanation for the limited focus on preventing the negative may be found in the psycho-criminological background of key investigators whose thinking has been bounded by efforts to explain offending (a *negative* behaviour) and a lack of concern with explaining positive pro-social development. Herein lies a striking limitation to the perspective and ambition of RFR – the pigeon holing of protective factors as existing entirely in relation to risk-based, criminological foci. Thus, protective factors have been conceived and analysed in terms of their potential to mitigate or obviate risk factors and thus to reduce or remove the likelihood of offending. The risk-dependent protective factor is neither conceived nor analysed in terms of its utility in promoting positive behaviour – it is inherently limited to the avoidance of negative outcomes.

Whilst there is, indeed, some merit in being able to show which factors protect against the negative effects of risk and, more importantly, understanding the dynamic of the risk/protective factor relationship, this is only a very partial element of the story. By only attempting to explain why young people do *not* offend, a whole explanatory edifice concerning the promotion of positive behaviours has been missed. A more holistic, dynamic and potentially profitable standpoint for RFR (in practical, political and methodological terms) would be to explore protective factors as mechanisms/processes (rather than discrete variables) that encourage positive behaviours or outcomes. This potential has not been entirely ignored, as evidenced by more recent reconceptions of protective factors as *promotive* factors (see Prelow *et al.* 2007; McCarthy *et al.* 2004; Catalano *et al.* 2004). Ashcroft *et al.* (2004), for instance, stated that protective factors can be associated with prosocial relationships and healthy bonding in the key domains of young people's life (family, education, peers, community). So, even if protective factors are seen as dichotomous to risk factors, they can also be seen as *promoting positive outcomes* rather than simply reducing negative outcomes such as offending. These arguments remain, however, relatively under-developed.

Furthermore, in practice, even the nascent focus on 'promotive' factors for positive behaviours has been theoretically-underpinned by the assumption of a commonality (even a common aetiology) of factors for both negative and positive behaviours. This commonality has been grounded in the somewhat uncritical importation of established lists of risk factors into concepts of protection and promotion limited to the psychosocial domains (e.g. Catalano *et al.* 2004). Protective or promotional factor research (if there is such a thing) has retained risk, deficit and problem behaviour as its normative touchstone. Consequently, research addressing protective factors has been beset by many of the limitations of RFR, notably: developmental determinism, psychosocial reductionism and individualisation, within a field redolent with concepts that are imprecise, poorly-defined and contested.

Therefore, much research into protective factors to date has, perhaps unwittingly, colluded with the agenda of developmental criminology by lackadaisically accepting that the established body of psychosocial, individualised and community-based risk factors offers an exhaustive and apolitical list of influences on youth behaviours and outcomes. The self-perpetuating framing of protective factors solely in terms of established and replicated risk factors speaks of a general malaise within (artefact) RFR. There appears to be a self-created comfort zone wherein a rudimentary understanding of a hugely-complex area has been deemed sufficient, thus precluding further investigation or a more holistic critique of the working concept of the protective factor. In particular, the risk-dependent protective factor exemplifies a pervasive over-simplification and fixedness within much RFR, whereby behaviour has been dichotomised as either one thing or the other (e.g. risk or protection, offending or non-offending, prosocial or antisocial) with little recognition of the spatial, temporal and personal complexities of young people's lives (see France 2008).

RFR, therefore, has remained just that: *risk factor* research, with the merest nod in the direction of exploring and explaining protection or the promotion of positive behaviour. Crucial, inextricably-linked, questions concerning the nature of the risk/protective factor relationship (e.g. the nature of the temporal precedence, interactions and causal relationships between the two) and the independent effect of preventative or promotional factors have been under-explored and remain poorly understood.

The paradox of replicable incomparability

The emergence, growth and hegemony of artefact-based RFR has encouraged researchers to explore the possibility of identifying *universal* risk factors that can be generalised to the broadest possible level (e.g. across different countries, different times and different groups of young people). The intention has been to find universal risk factors that can contribute to a 'universalised explanatory edifice' (D. Smith 2006) for youth offending. This 'mission' has been buttressed and fed by the seemingly impressive extent of replicability of risk factor findings across different groups of young people in different countries and cultures over different historical periods (see Chapter 4 for a more detailed evaluation of the global replicability of risk factors).

Indeed, according to Farrington, 'the most important risk factors are replicable over time and place' (2003: 5). In order to legitimate this claim, Farrington has cited the commonality of childhood risk factors between the Cambridge Study in Delinquent Development (which began in England in the early 1960s) and the Pittsburgh Youth Study (which began in the USA in the late 1980s). A comparison of the two studies showed a significant overlap in risk factors for offending (e.g. hyperactivity, impulsivity, low school achievement, poor parental supervision, large family size, low family income), despite considerable social, cultural and temporal differences (Farrington and Loeber 1999). There have been further replications of the Cambridge Study risk factors across international surveys in, *inter alia*, the USA (Thornberry and Krohn 2003), Canada (Tremblay *et al.* 2003), Sweden (Farrington *et al.* 1994), Finland (Pulkkinen 1988), Europe in general (Junger-Tas *et al.* 2003) and other Western industrialised countries (see Rutter *et al.* 1998).

In fact, RFR has presented a veneer of homogeneity and consensus, substantiated by the ostensible replicability and global-applicability of RFR findings and the definitive understandings of the risk-factor–offending relationship that they have allegedly facilitated. In practice, however, RFR is distinguished more by heterogeneity than homogeneity in aims and methods. As O'Mahony has argued:

> Risk, indeed, has become a sort of superconductor term attracting and organising numerous distinct but interrelated ideological, methodological and academic discourses. (O'Mahony 2008)

The heterogeneity of RFR has been evidenced in disparate research aims and differences in the definition, measurement and understanding of risk and offending. Unfortunately, the pursuit of a veneer of homogeneity has led researchers to eschew a detailed analysis of individual, localised, cultural and historical differences in the definition of offending, the choice of target variable (e.g. offending, antisocial behaviour, delinquency) and the extent, nature, distribution, influence and construction of risk factors. The replicability of risk factors between studies has been promulgated by an androcentric, ethnocentric and temporally-bound artefact movement that has engendered a 'spurious universalism' (R. Smith 2006) within RFR. Such replication does not necessarily imply comparability in the nature of the risk-factor–offending relationship across studies, nor are the aggregated findings necessarily representative of any individual within a specific sample.

The aggregation of risk

The majority of RFR has explored aggregated differences between-groups (typically broad dichotomies such as offenders–non-offenders and at risk–no risk) as a means of identifying risk factors for offending. The subsequent degeneralisation or 'rounding down' of these group differences to the individual level has uncritically assumed that identified risk factors are equally applicable to all young people in a given sample. For example, an individual young person in a group measured to be 'high risk' of future offending would be assumed to share the group's risk profile/status and their need for responsive, risk-focused interventions, regardless of his/her personal exposure (or lack of exposure) to risk factors. Consequently, aggregation has precluded detailed investigations of within individual change that would more adequately address issues of causality (see Farrington 2007), not to mention considerations of contextual – or cultural-specificity in exposure to and construction of, risk.

The aggregated, between groups focus has been born out of practical and financial necessities to analyse large groups of young people and to produce generalisable and universalised findings that can inform policy and practice. However, the emphasis on group exposure to risk has led to the inadvisable homogenisation of large and often disparate samples of young people that may vary widely in relation to, *inter alia*, age, gender, ethnicity, locality, culture and background. These methodological shortcuts have been inherently insensitive to within individual change and have washed away potential individual differences in exposure to risk factors and their effects. Statistical analysis has only been able to identify *what* risk factors predict offending at the group level – the analysis has not established *how* these factors may relate to offending or how these risk factors are experienced by individual members of the samples in question. In this way, aggregation and between groups analysis has further over-simplified processes of identifying risk factors for offending. The result is an even more crude identification of risk factors and a more abstract conception of the risk-factor–offending relationship.

This problem, of course, relates to individual studies. Efforts to establish universal risk factors for offending magnify the error by compounding, *inter alia*, measurement laxity across studies. Thus, a poorly measured factor in study A is combined with the same poorly measured factor in study B to reach a more definitive conclusion of the influence of this factor to much wider and potentially diverse populations of young people.

The paradox of unconstructive constructivism

Constructivist RFR (Kemshall 2003) has sought to move away from static quantitative models and methodologies and, instead, to conduct qualitative studies with dynamic and agentic foci to better understand the construction and operation of risk in the real lives of young people. Constructivist RFR emerged, at least in part, in response to the developmental determinism of the artefact model. However, the degree to which constructivist explanations of risk and offending have truly broken free from positivist, developmental understandings of risk and offending is moot (see Chapter 7 for a fuller discussion of this issue).

Webster (2007) has spoken of a 'qualitative consensus' within RFR in the UK that has pitted itself against deterministic approaches and which has emphasised instead: choice, contingency and contextual-correctness over statistical-correctness. In particular, constructivist RFR has challenged the artefact model claim of a supposed tight causal fit between risk factors and offending (see Macdonald 2007) and the view of young people as behaving in a 'mechanistic and dehumanised fashion abstracted from day-to-day lives and contexts' (Lawy 2002: 408). Accordingly, constructivist RFR has offered a less simplistic, more qualitative, interpretive, appreciative and ethnographic perspective to assert that risk and risk factors are experienced, constructed, resisted and negotiated by young people in specific social contexts through interactions with significant others and their environment. Constructivist RFR has also recognised and explored the broader, risk-based impact of social context, relations of power, opportunity/constraint and institutional factors on youth offending (see France and Homel 2006; Macdonald and Marsh 2005).

Constructivist researchers have employed narrative, interpretivist methodologies for a number of cogent methodological reasons:

- to explore the influence of risk as a dynamic and complex process operating at social, contextual, political levels, rather than as a static predictive 'factor' resting solely within the individual young person;

- to explore how young people understand and make meaning of risk as a reality in their lives;

- to give a voice to marginalised groups, particularly young people;

- to examine more closely how race, gender and class affect personal definitions of risk, to challenge the adult-centric perspective of risk;

- to account for neglected local discourses;

- to investigate the interaction between developmental pathways and societal access routes to opportunities.
        (see France and Homel 2006, 2007; see also Ungar 2004).

Kemshall et al. (2006, 2007) have identified three forms of constructivism, each with a differing view of the relationship between agency and structure:

- *Weak constructivism* – focuses on the immediate situational context in which risk decisions are made by examining the interaction between a young person's propensity to respond to situational temptations and the social mechanisms that influence that young person's routines and decision-making processes. Consequently, weak constructivism has prioritised agency and the individual, whilst containing a limited notion of the 'social' – viewing risk as an objective hazard that is mediated through socio-cultural processes.

- *Moderate constructivism* – sees pathways into and out of offending as negotiated processes dependent on continuing interactions between agency (individual choice and decision-making) and structure (e.g. power relations and cultural processes within a society). This interaction can determine the contexts and opportunity routes within which decisions whether to offend are made.

- *Strong constructivism* – emphasises the pivotal role of social structure and cultural understandings of risk rather than the individual's risk decisions. Strong constructivism challenges the traditional academic understanding of risk and the policy-related language that surrounds the concept as inextricably linked to processes of individualisation and responsibilisation, whereby social risks (e.g. unemployment) are transformed into individual faults (e.g. lack of skill or effort). Strong constructivism, therefore, views risk as a historical, social and political product.

(Kemshall *et al.* 2007: 356–7; see also Lupton 1999)

Constructivist RFR studies have evolved the methodologies and foci of RFR by examining young people's narratives and biographies and by exploring influences beyond traditional psychosocial domains of risk. Studies employing a constructivist perspective have attempted to expand RFR by countering the factorisation and psychosocial reductionism that has perpetuated over-simplified, deterministic, developmental understandings of risk and conceptions of young people as passive 'crash test dummies' when exposed to early-life risk. However, there has been an accompanying focus on how agency (individual choice, decision-making) can be bounded by *socio-structural factors* (e.g. social class, gender, race, social exclusion – see Furlong and Cartmel 2006), *culture/habitus* (the knowledge, values, rules and resources drawn on to inform life choices – Bourdieu 1977) and *social power relations* (which influence access to social capital, social networks and opportunities – Boeck 2006).

The constructivist perspective of risk is not necessarily new, owing an intellectual debt to theories of social constructionism (see Berger and Luckmann 1966) and interactionism (see Mead 1934), but constructivist understandings of risk *factors* for offending do, at least, attempt to provide something new. The application of constructivist discourses within RFR has promoted qualitative, interpretive and ethnographic methodologies and understandings of how young people and risk factors function within relationships of reciprocal influence. Constructivists have not necessarily claimed that the psychosocial risk factors first identified in artefact approach to RFR do not exert an influence on youth offending, but rather that the nature of their influence should be explored in ways that can augment or replace traditional deterministic, developmental, over-simplified, indefinite and universalised understandings. For example, constructivist studies of resilience have concluded that the relationship between risk and protective factors is 'nonsystemic, nonhierarhcial ... chaotic, complex, relative and contextual' (Ungar 2004: 341).

Constructive constructivism?

Constructivists have held few (explicit) pretensions to be able to control the variables they have measured and not measured. They have, for the most part, shied away from pursuing causal and predictive risk factors, acknowledging that their qualitative, interpretive methodologies and analyses have been incompatible with this aim and that their priorities have been to gain an understanding of risk from the young person's perspective. However, constructivist understandings of risk have offered something different for RFR. Through constructivist RFR, there has been a more concerted effort to understand 'what is going on' in terms of the dynamic and negotiated nature of risk factors and their relationship with offending. In particular, constructivists have pursued understandings of the processes (pathways) linking risk factors and offending (as well as desistance from offending) and have thus attempted to *explain* the relationship between risk and offending rather than to simply identify and replicate lists of risk factors statistically linked to offending. The focus on pathways *out of* crime (i.e. processes of desistence from offending and resilience to risk) has encouraged more investigation of the extent and nature of protective factors and the processes by which they influence risk factors and offending; a notable advancement from the risk-dependent protective factor perpetuated by artefact RFR. Constructivist RFR has also introduced more detailed investigations of the much neglected roles of (bounded) agency and structure, moving understandings of risk away from the psychosocial bias and dubious 'value free' positivist concepts of artefact RFR by incorporating notions of subjectivity, power and socio-political influence. For example, moderate constructivists have argued that socio-structural context can place external constraints on agency and on young people's opportunities to both resist risk and to succeed in life (see France and Homel 2006). There has been, therefore, a move away from developmental and deterministic understandings towards a view of risk as constructed in the present day through interactions between subjective/agency factors and social/environmental factors (see also LeBel *et al.* 2008). Indeed, Kemshall *et al.* (2006) suggest that constructivism's attention to socio-structural factors, social processes and social context can progress RFR 'beyond traditional risk factors'.

Unconstructive constructivism?

There remains, however, a paradox deep in the heart of constructivist RFR. Constructivism has not broken free from the developmentally-established list of predictive risk factors for offending (but added to it) and placed an understanding of the influence of risk factors in a context which is immediate, dynamic and inherently anathema to prediction. Unconstructive constructivism, therefore, relates to the extent to which constructivism remains largely wedded to traditional lists of risk factors, but renders generalisable understandings and explanations of risk factor influence beyond reach.

The extent to which constructivist RFR has retained traditional artefactual risks as factors to be investigated represents a limitation to the extent to which this approach truly breaks free from previous RFR (as opposed to attempts to debunk it). This constitutes a missed opportunity to redefine what risks are actually risks or even redefine the notion of risk itself. Apart from the intention to challenge established RFR, why, for example, has constructivist RFR taken traditional risk factors as a starting point instead of starting afresh by asking young people themselves to set the risk agenda? Such an approach is not so radical, as it would be entirely concordant with much child-focused, child-centred research taking place today (e.g. Hill *et al.* 2004).

Constructivist RFR has prioritised alternative theorising about risk factor influence (the nature of the risk-factor–offending relationship), but this theorising has been (and has been recognised as) highly individually-, temporally- and contextually-specific. There has also been a tendency for theorising to be targeted at providing alternative explanations to various established tenets of traditional RFR (e.g. individual agency as a counterpoint to developmental determinism). The constructivist approach, therefore, has been characterised by diversity of approaches and plurality in explanations and, consequently, an absence of any grand explanatory theory or framework. As a result, it is difficult to find within constructivist RFR a clear, understandable or definitive alternative model or explanation of the risk-factor–offending relationship and particularly one that could be tested and applied in direct work with young people.

Constructivist critiques have sought to evolve understandings of risk, whilst undermining the definitiveness of artefact RFR and the confidence placed in its conclusions. In doing so, however, the strand has problematised RFR to the point where the ability of RFR in any form to *ever* produce generalisable definitions of risk and explanations of risk factor influence, particularly explanations that are amenable to predictable and controlled ameliorative interventions, has been rendered highly questionable.

The paradox of heterogeneous homogeneity

The apparent similarities in the results and messages from global RFR (a homogeneity) is actually the product of different and sometimes incompatible models and methodologies (a heterogeneity). Thus, the apparent coherence and consistency in RFR is actually born out of difference. Partial, selective and even inaccurate understandings of risk factors, protective factors, offending and the relationships between them have emerged from, and are reflected in, a confused RFR literature. A disparate collection of uncoordinated strands of RFR have evolved and yet been presented in research, policy and practice as an homogenous, coherent and comprehensive method of understanding and explaining (as well as preventing and responding to) youth crime. There has been no consensus around the term 'risk factor research', yet it has been employed as a generic descriptor of the broad range of approaches found in this field of research. In practice, however, RFR can be (and needs to be) divided into and understood as comprising a range of distinctively different approaches or 'strands' which can be summarised as follows:

- *Developmental criminology* – the identification of risk factors early in life that predict the onset of later offending. Key examples of this approach include the longitudinal research of David Farrington, which has been strongly influenced by developmental psychology.

- *Life course criminology* – this perspective considers the influence of risk factors and one-off life events at different developmental stages on an individual's offending behaviour. The life course approach constitutes an extrapolation of developmental criminology because it explores the influence of risk factors and life events in adolescence and adulthood (not just childhood) and considers the potential for offending trajectories to change rather than to remain stable and dictated by childhood influences. The emphasis on risk and protective factors within life course criminology has been most notably promulgated by the work of Sampson and Laub.

- *The Social Development Model* – a stand-alone theory of how risk and protective factors influence antisocial and prosocial behaviour by young people. The model has integrated theoretical constructs from Social Learning Theory, Differential Association Theory and Social Control Theory. This model was developed by Catalano and Hawkins and forms the basis of the Communities that Care approach to community crime prevention.

- *Ecological research* – a sociological strand of RFR that seeks to identify community and neighbourhood influences on offending and to explore how they interact with individual/psychosocial risk factors to shape the behaviour of young people. The approach has been animated by the ESRC-sponsored Social Contexts of Pathways In Crime (SCoPIC) research partnership.

- *Integrated approaches* – these are somewhat pragmatic approaches to both the design and interpretation of RFR, which attempts to augment traditional (developmental, life course and ecological) conceptions of psychosocial risk and protective factors with an examination of the influence of situational contexts and rational choice/human agency on decisions to offend. Examples of this approach include Farrington's Integrated Cognitive Antisocial Potential theory and Laub and Sampson's revised age-graded theory of informal social control.

- *Constructivist/Pathways models* – an avowedly ahistorical branch of longitudinal research, which focuses on how young people make meaning of and negotiate critical moments and transitions in their daily lives which can influence their pathways into and out of offending (often called 'trajectories'). As such, the focus of this research has been current events rather than on the influence of early life risk factors. An example of this approach is the ESRC-sponsored Pathways Into and Out of Crime partnership of projects.

Rather than representing a single coherent enterprise, RFR has adopted a diversity of theory, definition, method and analysis. Homogeneity has been constructed artificially and superficially from heterogeneity to present clear, coherent, confident, certain and practical messages/conclusions. These conclusions, as the critical scrutiny developed in this book demonstrates, have served more to obfuscate than promote understanding of the causes of juvenile delinquency.

Conclusion: the unresolved methodological paradoxes of RFR

There are underlying tensions within RFR that are animated by the unresolved methodological paradoxes that drive the paradigm. There is an urgent need to reconcile practicality and policy relevance with a more reflective and realistic interpretation of what can be concluded from RFR thus far. The potential of RFR to produce clear, commonsense and understandable findings for the public, politicians, policy makers and practitioners is manifest. However, methodological over-simplification, homogenisation and over-generalisation of research findings has precipitated conclusions and recommendations founded on partial, ambiguous and potentially-invalid understandings of complex concepts.

The forthcoming chapters will evaluate the degree to which the methodological paradoxes have been reflected, acknowledged, addressed or remain unresolved in longitudinal and cross-sectional RFR in England

and Wales and internationally. The central aim is to evaluate the validity and robustness of the methods, results, conclusions and applications of RFR and the implications for the development of risk-related theory, policy and practice.

Chapter 2

The origins and development of risk factor research

Risk factor research has been promoted as an empirically-grounded, atheoretical and value-free method of investigating the circumstances and features of young people's lives that are predictive of later delinquency (see Farrington 2002). Proponents have characterised RFR as 'science', by which they mean to imply that the methods used and the 'evidence' it has produced have been uncontaminated by political philosophies and the ideologies of the social sciences (towards which there is a degree of antipathy on the part of, at least, some researchers and politicians). A paradigm of artefact RFR has flourished by drawing simplistic, definitive and generalised conclusions regarding the nature of risk factors, their relationship with offending and the potential for interventions to influence that relationship. However, a number of critical issues must be addressed:

- Just how valid is the claim that RFR has been 'atheoretical' and that it has produced value-free, pure information that has been unencumbered by theoretical and moral considerations?

- To what extent should politicians, policy makers, practitioners, researchers and the general public accept uncritically that evidence from RFR has been obtained and interpreted in an objective and unequivocal manner, as opposed to employing hidden theoretical and methodological agendas and expressions of narrow, privileged readings of the data?

- To what extent have the key figures in the evolution of RFR been willing or able to acknowledge the limitations and weaknesses of their own theoretical and methodological preferences on the extent, nature and validity of RFR evidence?

France (2008) has asserted that RFR has been underpinned by a series of assumptions that have guided researchers' understandings of human nature and the origins of social problems. In practice, the underpinnings of RFR have both broad and deep implications that have shaped the nature of this research and what it can and cannot tell us. The uncritical assumption that RFR has been and continues to be homogenous in theory, purpose and approach must be challenged, not least because on close inspection, there is a prima facie heterogeneity in the theoretical bases, methodology and conclusions drawn from RFR. Consequently, it is too simplistic to conceive of RFR as constituted by two generalised, discrete approaches – the artefact and the constructivist (see Kemshall *et al.* 2007). There are discernible differences between and within approaches to RFR and these can be both extreme and subtle. To properly understand and evaluate RFR, these differences must be exposed and understood. This means being clear about how these different strands emerged, what underpins them and how these underpinnings have influenced what the research does, the way in which it does it and the types of conclusions that can legitimately be drawn.

Any journey through the development of RFR must start with the Gluecks. Their work not only set the theoretical and methodological bases of much RFR that was to follow, they also laid down the fundamental list of risk factors for offending which remain hugely influential today.

Sheldon and Eleanor Glueck: the originators of risk-focused, developmental criminology

The origins of criminological RFR can be traced to the groundbreaking work of Sheldon and Eleanor Glueck at Harvard University in the US. The Gluecks' research, first published in the 1930s, was heavily influenced by two developments in unrelated academic areas. In 1915, William Healy's classic criminological study The Individual Delinquent introduced consideration of psychiatric factors and treatments into a criminological discipline traditionally dominated by a European focus on genetics and biology. Elsewhere, in the medical field, Richard Clarke Cabot was using the methodology of clinical follow-ups to assess the accuracy of cardiac illness diagnosis. The Gluecks were inspired by both studies and consulted both Healy and Cabot (with the latter helping them to obtain their initial funding) as they resolved to fill a perceived gap in the penology research literature concerning the effectiveness of penal treatment for young offenders and how it could be improved. The Gluecks noted that existing research into the effectiveness of reformatories, for example, had consisted of piecemeal investigations into various unrelated phases following incarceration and that there had been no reliable research tracing the self-reported life histories of 'prisoners' before, during and after imprisonment (Glueck and Glueck 1930).

In *500 Criminal Careers*, Glueck and Glueck (1930) investigated 510 young male adults who had been incarcerated in the Massachusetts Reformatory from 1911–1922 and released between 1926–1927. Through observation and interviews with the young men and their families, the Gluecks traced the men's life histories before sentence, during imprisonment, on parole and for five years after completing their sentence. An 80 per cent recidivism rate during the post-parole period prompted the Gluecks to posit that the reformatory had been a failure in reforming the young men. This led them to question whether there were factors in the young men's life histories (i.e. personal characteristics that they were bringing with them on arrival at the Reformatory) that predisposed them to offending and which could be better addressed by the Reformatory programmes. From their interviews, the Gluecks' identified several psychological and social (or 'psychosocial') characteristics and circumstances common in the pre-reformatory lives of the young men, mainly in the family domain. The Gluecks set about quantifying or 'factorising' these characteristics and circumstances through the use of ratings and categorisation tables. For example, different 'principle components' of family relationships were rated as 'good', 'fair' or 'poor'. This factorisation enabled a value to be placed on these characteristics which was then statistically correlated with the onset and frequency of offending and thus, as the Gluecks put it, related to 'ultimate criminal status' (Glueck and Glueck 1930: 313). Having factorised the interview data, the Gluecks formulated an innovative prediction table (although crude by today's standard of advanced statistical techniques) that cross-tabulated a range of factors with measured offending in the pre-reformatory period. According to the Gluecks' early analysis, factors that were present in early childhood and early adolescence and related to later onset of recorded offending were:

- *Family* – official record of arrest amongst family members, economic hardship, poor parental education, abnormal or unhealthy home situation, long/complete absence of parent(s), rift in home, insufficient parental oversight (supervision), intemperate (excessive use of alcohol, violent behaviour) or immoral mother, foreign or mixed parentage, child moved about during childhood or adolescence, child left parental home prior to sentence.

- *School* – educational retardation.

- *Lifestyle* – illicit heterosexual relations, gambling, alcoholism, keeping bad company, infrequent church attendance, open conflict with social authorities (school or law).

- *Personality/Intelligence* – dull or borderline intelligence, psychotic or psychopathic, neuropathic traits – extreme suggestibility, emotional instability, impulsiveness.

- *Employment* – unskilled/semi-skilled worker prior to incarceration.
(see Glueck and Glueck 1930)

The Gluecks also employed factorisation to examine the elements of offenders' pre-reformatory, reformatory, parole and post-parole histories that were correlated with post-parole recidivism. This supplemented the identification of factors in childhood and adolescence linked to offending with a measure of factors linked to *re*-offending in young adulthood. Once again, the factorisation process facilitated the use of a statistical prediction table with which to identify the factors most statistically 'predictive' of post-parole reoffending. These factors (which are mostly related to current circumstances) were:

- unconstructive pre-reformatory/post-parole work habits;

- negative family attitude post-parole;

- being incompatibly married or single;

- living in unfavourable homes and neighbourhoods post-parole;

- economic dependence;

- unconstructive use of leisure time.
(see Glueck and Glueck 1930)

The Gluecks claimed that through their longitudinal empirical research, certain factors could be identified in young men's pre-offending life, in childhood and adolescence, that disposed them to offending later in life; what they called 'the early genesis of antisocial careers' (Glueck and Glueck 1930: 142–3). They also claimed that they were able to identify factors that were 'associated with success or failure in criminal conduct during the five-year post-parole period' (1930: 313). For the Gluecks, their findings suggested that the reformatories could not be entirely blamed for their failure to reform offenders as they were essentially being asked to mitigate and cure factors that were a result of the deep-rooted failings of broader social institutions such as the family and school.

The factors identified by the Gluecks as predisposing young people to offend and to reoffend following incarceration are the earliest conception of predictive *risk factors* for offending. The work of the Gluecks clearly represents a methodological and criminological breakthrough in understanding and explaining juvenile delinquency, but their work and the conclusions they reached are not without their problems.

The Gluecks formulated a methodology for RFR that was essentially founded on developmental understandings of risk as psychosocial factors experienced in childhood and influential on later behaviour. Their view of the risk-factor–offending relationship was, however, somewhat simplistic; assuming a linear relationship between risk factors as predictors and offending as the inevitable result. The Gluecks did not consider alternative explanations of their findings, such as the possibility that risk factors could be correlates with offending or that offending could 'cause' the appearance of risk factors. Heavily influenced by developmentalism and the work of Cabot, the Gluecks believed that risk factors measured in childhood must have caused or precipitated later official offending simply because they pre-dated its measurement. However, the Gluecks crucially overlooked several potentially confounding issues in drawing such confident conclusions, *inter alia*:

- that unofficial, non-convicted offending by the young men may have pre-dated their official convictions;

- that non-convicted offending may have pre-dated the risk factors measured;

- that the temporal precedence of risk over offending in a statistical relationship does not necessarily indicate any explanatory influence in the real world.

Moreover, the Gluecks' view of risk was simplistic, culturally bound and value laden (e.g. intemperance, church attendance). Measurement was reliant, at least in part, on malleable judgements about the quality of different factors (e.g. family dynamics). These subjective processes were compounded by over-simplified factorisation (e.g. 'good, fair or poor') and simplistic correlational analysis between factors and offending.

There was also a degree of confusion in the Gluecks' research due to their dual focus on studying factors determining both offending and reoffending in the same study, without a clear demarcation of the two or adequate discussion of the implications of these findings. In *500 Criminal Careers*, the Gluecks studied early life risk factors for offending *and* the impact on reoffending of risk factors over the life-course up to five years post-parole – two very different studies which produced quite different sets of risk factors for offending. The Gluecks were clearly concerned by their findings as they returned to this issue in a ten year post-parole follow-up of the same group of males (*Later Criminal Careers* – Glueck and Glueck 1937). This later study found little difference in the pre-reformatory (early life) characteristics of recidivists and non-recidivists, offering confirmation and validation, for the Gluecks, of the predictive risk factors for reoffending. Notwithstanding the broader concerns with simplistic factorisation and basic statistical analyses, these findings suggest that either the risk factors for offending and reoffending may differ or that the developmental hypothesis is either incorrect or too simplistic – with dynamic life course events being more important in understanding and explaining delinquency than static developmental factors. The problem is, this conundrum was not and cannot now be resolved on the basis of the Gluecks' analysis.

The Gluecks followed up *500 Criminal Careers* with *One Thousand Juvenile Delinquents* (Glueck and Glueck 1934), which set out to explore the 'highly disappointing' attempts by state agencies (courts and family clinics rather than reformatories in this case) to reform juvenile delinquents and to investigate the backgrounds to juvenile delinquency; otherwise known as 'the factors conditioning crime' (Glueck and Glueck 1934: xv). In this study, the opening volume of the *Harvard Law School Survey of Crime in Boston*, the Gluecks investigated 1,000 male delinquents who had been referred to the Boston Juvenile Court and subsequently to the Judge Baker Foundation (a family guidance clinic) from 1917–1922. Following from *500 Criminal Careers*, the Gluecks emphasised the importance of identifying the traits, family background and social situations that young offenders brought with them to their first court appearance, what they called the 'early danger signals' for delinquency (Glueck and Glueck 1934: xv). The Gluecks also stressed the importance of understanding the psychosocial and environmental reasons for recidivism following exposure to the court and the clinic. Their intention was, of course, to identify risk factors that could then be targeted by ameliorative interventions to reform young offenders.

Statistical analysis of the data from interviews with the young offenders identified numerous factors evident in childhood and adolescence that increased the risk of the young men coming before the court as an official offender. There was a significant overlap between the risk factors identified here and those in *500 Criminal Careers*, notably in the domains of:

- *Family* – very large family, poor parental education, parents separated or divorced, parents unduly quarrelsome, insufficient parental oversight (supervision) and discipline, parents(s) intemperate (excessive use of alcohol, violent) or immoral, foreign or mixed parentage.

- *School* – educational retardation, leaving school early in life, truancy.

- *Lifestyle* – hanging around the streets during leisure time.

- *Personality/intelligence* – sub-normal intelligence, marked emotional and personality handicaps.

- *Employment* – unskilled /semi-skilled workers prior to incarceration.

(see Glueck and Glueck 1934)

Turning to an exploration of post-treatment behaviour and using a five year post-parole follow-up period (as in *500 Criminal Careers*), the Gluecks concluded that post-treatment recidivism 'may be due to one or more of a large number of causes, operating in varying and virtually immeasurable degrees of strength and interpenetration' (Glueck and Glueck 1934: 243). They concluded that, in searching for explanations of post-treatment behaviour, 'statistical technique will not help us here; we must rely on as fair and accurate an appraisal of the major influences involved in the process as it is possible to obtain' (Glueck and Glueck 1934: 243). Such a bold and damning conclusion is remarkable when re-evaluated in the light of a RFR movement based on positivist methodology, artefactualism and statistical predictions that has flourished on the 'strength' of the Gluecks' work.

In practice, the Gluecks came to very similar conclusions as they had for reformatories regarding the inability of the juvenile court, the family guidance clinic and community facilities to prevent recidivism. Similar to *500 Criminal Careers*, in *One Thousand Juvenile Delinquents* they concluded that socio-economic conditions represented 'wider and deeper forces . . . beyond the control of the modern clinician, judge and community worker' (Glueck and Glueck 1934: 279). Thus, despite their implications that, in terms of the onset of offending, the die was cast by early-life factors, especially 'biologic conditions' (e.g. psychopathology, poor physical health, mental deficiency), the Gluecks concluded that there were signifi-cant immediate socio-economic influences on recidivism. The respective psychosocial and structural/socio-economic determinism of the Gluecks' explanations of offending and recidivism led them to the same fatalistic conclusion – that post-offending interventions were impotent in address-ing reoffending behaviour.

More importantly, however, and a finding that strikes at the heart of developmental RFR, was the Gluecks' conclusion that none of the factors measured prior to incarceration were actually causes or the best predictors of desistance from offending post-release. In *Later Criminal Careers*, for example, the Gluecks concluded that any physical and mental changes that had 'predicted' desistance were actually correlated with a more influential factor, *maturation through aging* or the 'natural accompaniment of the "settling down" process of growth or maturation' (Glueck and Glueck 1937: 200). This is an astonishing conclusion in retrospect given the continued prominence of developmental and deterministic understand-ings of how childhood risk inevitably influences later behaviour in the work of the Gluecks and others. In particular, it appears incongruous that an industry of risk-focused intervention has flourished on the basis of the 'findings' of authors who ultimately concluded that 'the reform of criminals . . . is now bought about largely by the natural process of maturation' (Glueck and Glueck 1937: 206).

If indeed maturation has such a significant impact on desistence then is a risk-focused form of early intervention necessary at all or will young people simply grow out of crime? In other words, are young offenders in need of reform or will they simply reform themselves given time? The Gluecks intention was to provide 'scientific knowledge about the criminal and his environment – not *a priori* assumptions nor massed generalities' (Glueck and Glueck 1934: xv). This aim has proven prophetic in its emphasis on the 'scientific knowledge' provided by much subsequent RFR. However, the aim has subsequently become highly ironic due to the Gluecks' counter-evidential adherence to a developmental theory that has underpinned the theoretical 'a priori assumptions' of much subsequent RFR, methodologies grounded in 'massed generalities' and positivist conclusions on the basis of aggregated data. The Gluecks were insensitive to their methodological fallibilities and resistant to counter- or non-developmental readings of their findings which ran counter to their developmental biases – a developmental tunnel vision and dogmatic drive to confirm a priori theory that continues to shape much RFR.

Nevertheless, the die was cast. The Gluecks had opened up a new and potentially powerful explanatory paradigm and 'scientific' methodology in juvenile criminology. They had also, simultaneously, reduced debate and limited analysis to a relatively narrow interpretation of their findings, choosing to set aside potential explanations of delinquency (e.g. the influence of risk factors in current life, the effects of maturation) that did not fit comfortably with their developmental pre-conclusions that early life factors determined later offending.

The Gluecks' early research introduced a reductionist (developmental, factorised, psychosocial) and deterministic understanding of risk into criminology by identifying psychosocial risk factors in childhood and adolescence that were allegedly predictive of offending in later life. The practical implications were that these childhood factors offered potential targets for the classification and treatment of young offenders in reformatories and could be targeted through early intervention before they manifested themselves in the form of offending behaviour. The Gluecks concluded that prognostic instruments such as prediction tables should be used by 'judges and administrative agencies concerned with the scientific administration of justice' (Glueck and Glueck 1930: 313) and that these instruments 'have significant research value for both the causation and the therapy of criminality' (Glueck and Glueck 1930: 334). Curiously prophetic of an over-confidence placed in simplistic and distorted readings of RFR, whatever the motivation, Richard Cabot argued that reformatories could significantly improve their practice by offering individualised treatments based on classifications of young people in relation to preoffending factors, rather than having young people 'massed together and treated alike ... (due to a) short-sighted policy of economy' (Cabot, in Glueck and Glueck 1930: x). In short, there has been a confusion or obfuscation between the influence of early life, current life and maturational factors on offending, sometimes accompanied by assumptions being made and conclusions drawn that do not directly fit the evidence provided.

The Gluecks' early research

The *500 Criminal Careers* and *One Thousand Juvenile Delinquents* studies were clearly the genesis of criminological RFR. These studies introduced new ways of thinking about juvenile delinquency and its treatment as well as introducing some methodological innovations. In both respects, however, these studies also introduced some enduring weaknesses into the new field of RFR, notably:

- the crude factorisation of risk and the use of basic statistical analyses to reach conclusions;

- the explanation that these 'risk factors' are linked to offending and reoffending, but with a failure to address the substantive and qualitative differences between the two behaviours and their precursors;

- not exploring the possibility that risk factors experienced by young men who have 'officially' offended may differ from the risk profiles of those who have offended, but have yet to be caught or convicted – thereby conflating criminality with conviction. For example, certain risk factors, such as working class status, may increase the likelihood of the young men coming to the attention of the authorities;

- limited and insensitive exploration of *how* risk factors may precipitate offending and reoffending, the nature of their relationship with offending/reoffending, whether risk factors differ for sub-types of offending (e.g. violent versus property) and at which specific ages in childhood and adolescence these risk factors are experienced and are most influential;

- drawing definitive conclusions that fail to acknowledge or address the indefinite nature of what form of offending is being predicted, for whom, at what point in their life and how predictive risk factors actually influence the offending behaviour measured.

Unraveling Juvenile Delinquency: moving risk factor research forward

We cannot, in truth, know for sure what motivated the Gluecks. They did provide some evidence in their early studies of developmental risk factors for offending, yet, at the same time, they also produced findings that emphasised the importance of current social circumstances for behaviour that, at the very least, brought the developmental hypothesis into question. Nevertheless, by the time they had moved on to their next research, any such questions were evidently set aside in favour of an avowedly developmental and deterministic approach.

The Gluecks followed their earlier studies, this time, with a prospective longitudinal study of juvenile delinquency known as *Unraveling Juvenile Delinquency* (Glueck and Glueck 1950). Here the Gluecks were clearly motivated by the importance of developing knowledge about how to prevent and cure the 'maladaptions of youth' and to identify the exact causes of this maladjustment to inform effective responses by the courts, probation and parole systems (Glueck and Glueck 1950). *Unraveling Juvenile Delinquency*, as the name suggests, was particularly concerned with identifying factors as predictive of first time official offending (rather than reoffending) in order to facilitate early, pre-emptive intervention. As the Gluecks said:

> The selection of potential delinquents at the time of school entrance or soon thereafter would make possible the application of treatment measures that would be truly crime preventive. To wait for certain manifestations of delinquency before applying therapy is to close the barn door after the horse has been stolen. (Glueck and Glueck 1950: 257)

Thus, although their previous research had shown that different risk factors were associated with offending at different ages or stages of a young person's development and the importance of maturation for cessation of offending, the Gluecks set aside these more complex ideas and pursued a more basic and simplistic developmental hypothesis.

In *Unraveling Juvenile Delinquency*, 500 officially delinquent and 500 officially non-delinquent white males aged 10–17 years were drawn from lower-class neighbourhoods in Boston, US and were studied prospectively over a 14 year period (1949–1963). The young men in both groups were matched on age, race/ethnicity, residence in underprivileged neighbourhoods and measured intelligence. Extensive official record checks were conducted, along with interviews with the sample members, their families, teachers, neighbours, recreational leaders, employers, police and social workers. The Gluecks collected a wide range of data concerning each young person's social, psychological and biological characteristics, family life, school performance, work experiences, recreational activities, criminal career histories and experience of criminal justice interventions. Once again, the interview data was converted into a quantitative form (factorised) amenable to statistical analysis.

Through basic statistical cross-tabulations, the Gluecks identified strong associations between a range of biological, psychological and social risk factors measured in childhood and subsequent youth offending, notably:

- *Body type* – stocky, muscular mesomorphs.

- *Temperament* – restless, impulsive, extroverted, aggressive, destructive.

- *Attitude* – hostile, defiant, resentful, suspicious, stubborn, assertive, adventurous, not submissive to authority.

- *Psychological* – tending to think in concrete (rather than abstract) terms.

- *Family* – lack of parental discipline, poor supervision and low family cohesiveness.

(see Glueck and Glueck 1950)

These 'biopsychosocial' risk factors reflected, but were not entirely co-incident with, the childhood risk factors identified in *500 Criminal Careers* and *One Thousand Juvenile Delinquents* that appeared to predict the onset of offending in adolescence amongst officially-recorded offenders. However, the design of *Unraveling Juvenile Delinquency* differed from the Gluecks' earlier studies. Notably, in *Unraveling Juvenile Delinquency* the Gluecks did not confuse or conflate risk factors for offending with those for reoffending and the research made use of an innovative prospective longitudinal design that sought to identify early childhood risk factors that were predictive of later offending through drawing statistical comparisons between offenders and non-offenders (akin to the experimental distinction between control and treatment groups). Arguably, therefore, the methodology of *Unraveling Juvenile Delinquency* represented a more robust design than either *500 Criminal Careers* or *One Thousand Juvenile Delinquents*, but the differences in the results from these studies were not dealt with or explained. The Gluecks' intention was, of course, to identify early childhood risk factors for offending that could provide promising targets for ameliorative/preventative interventions at the early childhood stage – although this latter point was not fully drawn out and the Gluecks' research had little impact on policy and practice at the time.

The Gluecks' multi-factor, multi-causal developmental approach to investigating youth offending emerged from their eclectic, multi-disciplinary background. Despite their research emanating from Harvard's Law School, the Gluecks drew from criminology, psychology, sociology, social work, social ethics, law, psychiatry and education. Their research pioneered longitudinal and follow-up prediction studies using multiple data sources to identify biopsychosocial risk factors in key domains and at key stages in the lives of young people. These methodological innovations were imbued with an apparent clarity and statistical robustness founded in empiricism which certainly would have appealed to modern day policy makers.

However, the Gluecks' RFR had relatively little impact on criminological policy, practice, research or theory for over 40 years following *Unraveling Juvenile Delinquency*. At the time of its publication, the Gluecks' early work and their assertions about the factors correlated with and predictive of offending were subject to intense methodological criticisms, particularly from the eminent sociologist Edwin Sutherland. Sutherland

(1934) believed that criminology should be a sociological discipline and he firmly opposed the multi-factor, developmental approach taken in *Unraveling Juvenile Delinquency*, especially as, in his view, the preference for biological and psychological factors underplayed the influence of sociological variables such as peer group, culture and community. There were two key strands to the debate at the time:

• The Gluecks believed that their work reflected an 'anti-theory approach', arguing that abstract theory was speculative and unscientific. Clearly, Sutherland had particular problems with this, arguing that the Gluecks' work was avowedly theoretical, even if they denied it (see Sampson and Laub 1993).

• Sutherland (1934) claimed that the Gluecks made little attempt to evaluate the representativeness of their offending sample (see also Hirschi and Selvin 1967), nor were they entirely open and honest about the 'statistical manipulation' that enabled them to achieve their results. The implication here was that the Gluecks used selective analyses to identify only the narrow range of (risk) factors that fitted their developmental preconceptions of the aetiology of offending. Sutherland's critique intimated that the Gluecks had preferred a developmental, individualised, micro-level analysis to any macro analysis of neighbourhood organisation or 'broader economic and social organisation' (Sutherland 1934).

Following the publication of *Unraveling Juvenile Delinquency*, further criticisms were levelled at the perceived methodological weaknesses of the Gluecks' research. Notably, their research was criticised for using unrepresentative samples (a 50/50 split of offenders/non-offenders which was not reflected in the general population), a poor quality matching design (especially relating to age) and uncritical use of official data to distinguish offenders from non-offenders (Reiss 1951; Wilkins 1969). Further, Hirschi and Selvin (1967) took issue with the Gluecks' somewhat crude statistical approach to determining predictive influence; an approach that relied on cross-tabulations and basic correlations. They argued that as a consequence, the analyses 'fail to distinguish consistently between factors that preceded delinquency and those that may well have resulted from either delinquent acts or institutionalisation' (Hirschi and Selvin 1967: 54). Consequently, the earliest exemplar of RFR was criticised for proffering definitive conclusions regarding risk factor influence that were based on assumptions and a limited understanding of the nature of the risk-factor–offending relationship. Indeed, it seems the Gluecks' conclusions over-stepped the boundaries of the data. With their rudimentary measures of risk, inability to control for extraneous variables and their underdeveloped statistical techniques, the Gluecks could not hope to adequately understand the nature of the risk-factor–offending relationship.

The notion that the Gluecks uncovered the 'risk factors for youth offending' requires additional clarification. A neglected issue with the Gluecks' research lies in the andocentric, ethnocentric and class-biased nature of their research design. A major limitation of the findings was the extent to which the Gluecks' risk factors, identified with a narrow sample (working-class boys in an American city), could be properly extrapolated and applied to disparate groups of young people (e.g. girls, black and ethnic minorities, different age groups etc) beyond those represented in their study. No matter how well-intentioned, over-confidence and over-generalisation appear to have been imbedded within RFR from its earliest beginnings.

The developmental legacy of the Gluecks

The Gluecks' body of research is the obvious forerunner to what we know today as 'risk factor research'. The Gluecks paved the way for new understanding and explanations of juvenile delinquency, but their research also institutionalised some major weaknesses in RFR.

In the introduction to *Unraveling Juvenile Delinquency*, the Gluecks insisted that researchers should not be overawed by or overemphasise any branch of science or methodology to the neglect of others, because 'bias must weaken the validity of both method and interpretation' (Glueck and Glueck 1950: 5). However, the Gluecks under-emphasised their own theoretical inspirations and set aside findings which did not accord with their pre-suppositions. This 'psychosis of positivists', whereby researchers conducting artefact RFR argue that their approach is atheoretical, scientific and value-free, belies a deep denial about the extent to which their theoretical predilections have guided and influenced their studies. The Gluecks did caution that the factors that emerged from their prediction tables were not isolated influences, but interrelated within a 'perplexing' system of biocultural forces. However, this acknowledged complexity did not prevent them championing certain risk factors as predictive of offending and as promising targets for preventative and post-offending interventions. The Gluecks thus set the ball rolling for a RFR movement that has since privileged a staunchly developmental perspective which views young people as the passive recipients of the negative impact of childhood risk factors – helpless 'crash test dummies' careering towards pre-determined and inevitable offending outcomes. The crash test dummy model has, therefore, privileged risk factors experienced in childhood over evidence of factors emerging and exerting influence in later life.

Of course, once the Gluecks had set in stone their developmental understanding of risk factors for offending, there was only one conclusion they could come to regarding recommendations for interventions that had any possibility of changing future outcomes – to intervene 'early' to change these developmental factors for the better and thus change the predetermined offending outcome to a new predetermined non-offending outcome. Notwithstanding the counter-factual adherence to the developmental hypothesis, this conclusion is based on supposition and not on evidence. There was no available evidence base that targeting these risk factors at an early stage in the life course actually reduced or prevented future offending – the Gluecks merely concluded that this would happen based on speculative, imputed and over-simplified readings of the risk-factor–offending dynamic.

In order to effectively intervene early, it was considered necessary to identify the risk factors for offending. Here too, there are problems with the work of the Gluecks that remain reflected in much RFR. Sample populations restricted by age, geography, class and gender and a restricted set of factors within the psychosocial domain inevitably place limitations on the claims to generalisability of the research findings. The Gluecks and those who have sought to interpret and use their findings have failed to adequately situate their conclusions within a proper consideration of these limitations. This problem has been exacerbated by processes of factorisation (i.e. the extent to which researchers are able to accurately quantify risk factors). Whilst factorisation is endemic and, indeed, essential to much social scientific research, there are still questions concerning the accuracy or quality of these measurements. The factorisation employed by the Gluecks was, by any standard, fairly crude and their failure to problematise and discuss this issue undermines the definitiveness of their conclusions. Taken together, the critiques presented here cause, at the very least, serious questions to be raised about the methodology, analysis, findings and conclusions of the Gluecks. Whilst they did open up new areas of enquiry, the Gluecks' achievements have been flawed. These flaws that emerged in the foundations of RFR will be shown to echo and reverberate to the present day.

The Cambridge-Somerville Youth Study: early risk-focused, developmental crime prevention

The 30-year longitudinal *Cambridge-Somerville Youth Study* began in 1939 under the supervision of Richard Clarke Cabot, a contemporary of and inspiration to the Gluecks. Cabot's study evaluated a programme of delinquency prevention conducted in Cambridge and Somerville, MA, US. Cabot's main aim was to address the 'dispiriting findings' of the *500 Criminal Careers* study and to explore the potential for a scientific approach to delinquency prevention by focusing on the key risk factors for youth offending that could be identified early in a child's life (Cabot 1940).

Cabot studied 650 boys aged between seven and 12 years whose behaviour and personality was rated as either 'average' or 'difficult' by a selection committee of three judges, all practitioners from the youth justice field: a psychiatrist, a social worker and the Director of Casework at Massachusetts Reformatory (the site of *500 Criminal Careers*). The judges examined the findings of home visitor interviews with the boy's mother/ chief carer, which gathered (risk) information regarding the boys' 'developmental history' in relation to:

- *Habits* (e.g. eating, sleeping).

- *Recreation* (e.g. gambling, un/supervised activities).

- *Personality* (e.g. aggression, irritability, leadership).

- *Family and home conditions* (e.g. broken home, parental discipline, parental and sibling personality).

- *Neighbourhood* (e.g. presence of gangs, general conditions, criminogenic nature, recreation opportunities).

(Powers *et al.* 1951)

No information has been provided as to what underpinned the choice of factors to examine in the home visitor interviews, but it does not require a huge analytical leap to note the degree to which many of the factors resonate with the original criminogenic influences identified by the Gluecks. Upon examination of the home visitor interviews, the selection committee then made a prognosis of each boys likelihood of delinquency using a predictive scale ranging from minus five (extreme probability of delinquency) to plus five (extreme probability of non-delinquency). Ratings were accepted if it least two of the judges agreed on them.

Following the predictive ratings, half of these boys were randomly allocated (by coin toss) to a control group and the other half were randomly allocated to a treatment group. The treatment group received interventions that sought to reduce and prevent the perceived predetermined impact of childhood risk factors. In practice, Cabot simply advised counsellors to do 'whatever they thought best' to ameliorate the risk factors present (Cabot 1940; see also Powers *et al.* 1951; McCord and McCord 1959). For example, the treatment group boys variously received counselling, academic assistance, family guidance and extra curricular leisure opportunities.

The study results focused on two key areas – the predictive ability of the judges ratings and the efficacy of the treatment programme. The judges' prognostic ratings were disappointing. When a sub-sample of 200 boys were followed up 9–10 years following the initial ratings, there was a significant over-prediction of delinquency (i.e. the identification of 'false positive' boys who were predicted to offend who did not), with only 33 per cent of the treatment group and 40 per cent of the control group who were originally predicted to offend actually becoming delinquent (Powers et al. 1951). The impact of the preventative treatment programme on offending was assessed at four points. The first assessment took place while the treatment programme was in progress, consisting of psychological tests of school adjustment and a review of official court records. In 1948, three years after the preventative treatment programme ended, the boys' official court records were reviewed again. A final assessment of official court records was made in 1956 when the boys were traced into adulthood by McCord and McCord (1959).

At each of the first three stages, there was no significant difference between the offending behaviour of the treatment and control groups. Cabot concluded that any preventative benefits of the intervention given to the treatment group did not translate into decreases in offending, even when the potential risk factors of parental affection, parental discipline, neighbourhood and personality were controlled for. Following their detailed review of the study, Powers et al. (1951: xix) stated that 'none of the evaluative methods employed indicates any great degree of success for the treatment program'. A 30 year follow-up of the sample by Joan McCord went further by concluding that not only did the treatment program fail to prevent offending, but it 'had negative side effects as measured by criminal behaviour, death, disease, occupational status, and job satisfaction' (McCord 1978: 284). McCord (1978: 288) analysed the lives of 235 of the original sample (113 treatment, 122 controls) and discovered that the treatment group men, 30 years on from the programme, were more likely than the control group to: have committed a second crime, show signs of alcoholism, manifest signs of serious mental illness, die younger, hold low prestige occupations and report job dissatisfaction.

The Cambridge-Somerville Youth Study was an early (if not the earliest) example of the developmental approach to crime *prevention*. It was also the forerunner of the 'what works' approach to evaluating crime prevention programmes using a 'scientific' experimental methodology. Despite being heralded by Tremblay et al. (2003) as the best designed longitudinal-experimental study of delinquency prevention in the twentieth century, the lack of positive impact on offending and, indeed, the deleterious impact on the treatment group of the risk-focused interventions in the Cambridge-Somerville Youth Study strikingly contradicted the central developmental hypotheses of the programme. This lack of impact may be attributable to a range of possible explanations, such as:

- The childhood risk factors that were 'linked' to future offending may have been correlates, symptoms or even non-influential, statistical artefacts rather than causes or predictors of offending. Thus, targeting these factors with interventions was never going to have an impact on future offending because there was no causal relationship between them.

67

- That the treatments offered were inappropriate or simply ineffective. It is, possible, for example, that the correct risk domains were targeted, but in the wrong way. For example, McCord and McCord (1959) identified a link between exposure in childhood to the family risk factors of poor parental supervision, aggressive discipline and marital discord and offending behaviour in adulthood; providing some indication that family factors were among the most important predictors of offending. However, these factors were not directly targeted by any intervention given to the treatment group in the Cambridge-Somerville Youth Study. In addition, no attempt was made to link individually assessed risk with specific interventions. Thus, the experimental group were subjected to interventions taken from a pre-determined list that was only loosely, if at all, relevant to any individual young person.

- The risk factors targeted by the interventions in Cabot's study were essentially those identified by the Gluecks. Cabot was, therefore, not only guilty of a partial reading of the Gluecks' work (of uncritically accepting that they had indeed identified the risk factors for offending – despite their own contrary evidence), but he also assumed that these risk factors were salient to the boys in his treatment group. This was an early example of the now commonplace assumption in risk focused interventions, that the risk factors for one population or group are equally applicable to other populations or groups.

- The poorer overall set of outcomes for the treatment group, later identified by McCord, are actually testament to the validity and accuracy of the predictive factors – or the interventions in the lives of the treatment group had negative iatrogenic consequences.

- Even if these childhood risk factors had some applicability to Cabot's sample, they may have long since ceased to exert an active influence on the behaviour of the young men. Factors present in early childhood that are predictive of later delinquency may, in fact, be quite unrelated to explaining *current* adolescent behaviour, thus the interventions may have been targeting outdated factors with no currency. Conversely, Powers *et al.* (1951) suggested that perhaps the results were analysed too soon and that the treatment programme had been given an insufficient time to bear fruit.

Overall, Cabot's study provides a neat example of the flaws in RFR and exemplifies what tends to go wrong in risk-focused interventions. In particular, the uncritical transfer and application of psychosocial risk factors across studies demonstrates a series of common weaknesses within RFR, such as the assumption of the unproblematic (almost unquestionable) replicability and the taken-for-granted applicability of risk factors between groups and studies, despite the absence of an explicit, validated (rather than merely assumed) model of the risk-factor–offending relationship and weak, poorly-understood links between identified risk factors and risk-focused interventions. Furthermore, the Cambridge-Somerville Youth Study typifies the dual weaknesses of over-reliance on weak prognostic prediction techniques (e.g. the crude allocation of young people to treatment or control groups) and over-emphasis on preventing offending to the detriment of promoting positive outcomes; weaknesses that have pervaded much subsequent risk-focused crime prevention. Cabot's research also demonstrates the simplistic oversimplification of developmental, predictive understandings of risk, which rely on the assumption that risk factors first experienced in childhood (rather than emerging in adolescence or adulthood) continue to affect behaviour into adolescence and adulthood, despite substantive changes in the nature, extent, presence and salience of these risk factors as young people mature (as the Gluecks found).

Paradoxically, perhaps the most telling conclusion from Cabot's study is what it *cannot* tell us. Cabot's methodology did not, for example, allow for exploration or explanation of the nature of the relationship between risk factors and offending. Neither was the methodology flexible enough to enable alternative, non-developmental understandings of this relationship to emerge, or to facilitate explanations of why the risk-focused interventions did not reduce offending. The theoretical and methodological over-reliance on the 'black box' approach to understanding the risk-factor–offending relationship thus not only impeded any empirical attempt to explain how risk factors and offending might be related, but diminished the quality of interventions predicated on this relationship. This 'black box' approach, which measures inputs (e.g. interventions) and outputs (e.g. impact on offending) with little understanding of how or why these interventions work or do not work, imbues any conclusion with an inherent lack of specificity. Therefore, the Cambridge-Somerville Youth Study has contributed little substantive evidence that risk-focused intervention is effective or has any impact on young people other than a negative one, as 'evidenced' by ultimate conclusion of the thirty year follow-up study, which stated that 'intervention programs risk damaging the individuals they are designed to assist' (McCord 1978: 289). Nevertheless, the study's lack of positive evidence has seemingly been overlooked within a subsequent body of RFR that has enabled the risk-focused intervention approach to flourish due to a much-heralded apparently solid 'evidence-base'.

The Cambridge Study in Delinquent Development: establishing developmental criminology and risk factor research

Moving from the US to the UK, the Cambridge Study in Delinquent Development began in 1961 with the aim 'to investigate the development of juvenile delinquency in a normal population of boys ... (and why) certain groups, identifiable at an early age, are peculiarly vulnerable' (West and Farrington 1973: xiii). The founder of the Cambridge Study in Delinquent Development (commonly known as the Cambridge Study), Donald West, noted that it has its origins in *Unraveling Juvenile Delinquency* and Cambridge-Somerville studies, which both, he said, 'pointed to the strong and continuing influence of early upbringing and family circumstances in determining who became delinquent' (West 1982: 3). Thus, Donald West and David Farrington (who later became the main author of the study), acknowledged the theoretical and methodological parity of their study to that of the Gluecks, although they were keen to emphasise two key methodological differences in their work (see West and Farrington 1973, 1977):

- they would focus on *normal children* rather than on contrasts between existing delinquents and specially selected non-delinquent controls;

- they were to adopt a prospective longitudinal design that would hopefully avoid the retrospective bias inherent to the study of *known delinquents*.

Rather than starting with a sample of teenage delinquents and retrospectively tracing their history and development (i.e. a retrospective longitudinal study such as those conducted by the Gluecks), West and Farrington identified 411 working-class males born in South London in 1953–1954. The study has tracked this group (prospectively) over time from age eight years to the present day, making it the longest running longitudinal study of the impact of risk factors on delinquency. A methodology of regular interviews with the sample members, interviews with peers, psychological tests and secondary data analysis of official records has been used to measure the impact of life events and to identify risk factors for offending in key domains of the young people's lives. Over the course of the Cambridge Study, risk factors have been identified which are associated with different elements of the criminal career, particularly onset, duration, frequency, continuity, escalation and specialisation of offending. These risk factors have been located in the family, school, neighbourhood, peer and behavioural domains (West and Farrington 1977) and mostly in childhood. At a later stage in the research, the authors introduced an investigation of the *protective* factors which appeared to insulate the young person against future criminality (West 1982), albeit factors that were conceived entirely in terms of their risk factor dichotomies/counterparts.

The central claims of the Cambridge Study have revolved around the risk factors identified when the sample boys were aged 8–10 years that were statistically linked to official and self-reported offending at age 14–15 years. West has concluded that these factors were essentially 'predictive' of later offending. The strongest predictors of future offending amongst boys aged 8–10 years were identified as poor parenting, family criminality, family poverty, academic underachievement, hyperactivity/impulsivity/attention deficit and antisocial behaviour in childhood (West 1982).

The Cambridge Study has consolidated and progressed the Gluecks' multi-causal, multi-factor and factorised approach to the study of risk and the positivist developmental understanding of the risk-factor–offending relationship. Contemporaneously to their definitive conclusions, however, the authors have acknowledged (as had the Gluecks) that the risk factors they identified represented complex elements that were not fully understood and that this 'left the way open for a variety of speculative interpretations' (West and Farrington 1973: 191). Farrington himself has more recently conceded that 'little is known about the causal processes that intervene between risk factors and offending' (2003: 207), thus questioning previously taken for granted conclusions from RFR. Notwithstanding the limitations of the Cambridge Study, it has been adjudged, even by vociferous critics of RFR, to be 'among the most complete studies of the relationship between risk and offending' (Armstrong 2004: 105).

What is most definitely not in question with regards to the Cambridge Study is the predictive validity of Radzinowicz's quote in the introduction to West and Farrington's *Who Becomes Delinquent*:

> the findings recorded here will hold their own as a point of reference for discussion of juvenile delinquency and criminal behaviour for many years to come. (Radzinowicz 1973: v)

Indeed, the Cambridge Study has been hugely influential. More so than the work of the Gluecks and Cabot (which remain relatively unacknowledged), the Cambridge Study both established and popularised risk-focused developmental criminology. The Cambridge Study has become the acknowledged starting point, particularly within the UK, for much subsequent RFR and has been the touchstone of prevention policy and practice with young people in the UK across a range of policy areas, including but not limited to youth offending (see France and Homel 2006) – especially since the 1990s.

Such has been the importance and influence of the Cambridge Study that its place in the chronology and development of RFR must be marked and recognised. RFR is probably the largest single area of criminological research and it is still growing. It has become probably the most influential area of criminological research on policy and practice worldwide. Much of this influence is due to the Cambridge Study and its simple, commonsense linking of a discrete set of childhood risk factors with adolescent offending. However, it is important to question whether the developmental, deterministic arguments of West and Farrington (latterly Farrington on his own), so rooted as they are in the flawed work of the Gluecks, have been so theoretically biased and so underpinned by unresolved methodological paradoxes as to undermine the validity of their findings and their application to policy and practice. These issues are explored at length in Chapter 3.

Criminals coming of age

In 1962, discussions between researchers at Cambridge University in the UK and treatment personnel working with young offenders, brought to light the ineffectiveness of the borstal system for preventing reoffending. These discussions highlighted a pressing need to investigate this failure (similar to the objectives of the Gluecks' early research). What emerged from the discussions was the Criminals Coming of Age study, also known as the Dover Borstal Study. Under the direction of Frank McClintock and Tony Bottoms, the study set out to identify the psychosocial background factors linked to later offending and to evaluate the impact on these factors and on reoffending of a modified Borstal regime. The three main stated aims of the study were:

- to analyse and classify the information on the patterns of criminal behaviour and kinds of social background of the young men sent to the institution, with a view to ascertaining the extent of the problems requiring individualised treatment;

- to study the salient features of the institution and the process by which it was modified in an attempt to develop a more effective system for dealing with the individual problems of offenders;

- to evaluate the impact of the institutional regime upon the young offenders and its effectiveness in preventing further criminal behaviour.
(Bottoms and McClintock 1973: 3)

The project particularly warrants inclusion in this book due to its attempts to explore the extent to which 'social problems' (what can be seen as risk factors) in young adulthood are predictive of offending and whether targeting these factors through individualised treatment programmes reduce the likelihood of reoffending post-Borstal release. This offers a useful point of comparison with the Cambridge Study of Delinquent Development, which focused primarily on the influence of risk factors in the early years of a child's life. It is also interesting to note that the research took place in the 1960s at Cambridge University at the same time and in the same building from which West and Farrington were conducting the Cambridge Study.

The Criminals Coming of Age study was situated in a borstal in Dover, UK. The authors assessed the effects of a modified, individualised training regime on 306 young men aged 18–20 years referred to the institution from the first of January 1965. The basic fieldwork was conducted from 1963–1967 and the young men were followed up following their release, with data collection in the aftercare period finishing in 1969. Data was collected from official administrative documents, records completed by staff, researchers notebooks, questionnaires and interviews with inmates. The intention was to compare the treatment group to a control group (who had entered the borstal from 1959–1961 and had received the traditional, generic training regime) on three dimensions:

- personal characteristics and criminal and social background;

- the processes of training and treatment and the offender's reaction to them;

- behaviour immediately post-release.

(Bottoms and McClintock 1973: 8)

The researchers and the institution staff were particularly interested in the link between 'social and personal characteristics' (otherwise 'risk factors') and delinquency, in order that individualised training programmes could be constructed to address these features and prevent future offending. Previous studies had identified the risk factors for offending amongst young men sent to Borstal institutions (e.g. Rose 1954, Gibbens 1963) and these were the starting point in the investigation of social problems in the Dover sample. However, the research team concluded that there were no previous classifications of offenders and risk factors that were directly applicable to their study, so it was considered necessary to construct two new measures that would aid them in planning individualised training regimes: a penal problem score indices and a social problem score indices:

- *Penal problem score indices* – this measured previous convictions, criminal record (major or minor offending) and the extent of previous penal experience.

- *Social problem score indices* – this measured family structure and family conflict, marital and paternity problems, employment problems, leisure time activities, psychiatric history, drink and drug problems and sexual problems.

Young people were asked to rate the extent to which they considered the factors within each of the indices was a problem for them ('not at all' to 'major problem') – thus enabling risk to be factorised within the study.

Bottoms and McClintock acknowledged that their penal and social problem score indices were relatively crude measures of the extent and nature of young people's problems. However, the scores served as a starting point from which to conduct a more detailed investigation of how the Borstal's resources could be utilised more effectively for individualised and risk-focused training programmes. The control group had been in receipt of the traditional training regime, which consisted of training through work, recreation and education, along with the development of relationships with institution staff. For the treatment group, on the basis of their penal and social problem scores, an individualised (risk-focused) training programme was devised. Following initial diagnosis of problem areas through the problem indices, supplemented by an examination of case history files for each young person, a training plan was developed that identified appropriate ways of tackling the problems relevant to each individual. This was followed by a series of individual discussions between institution staff and the offender, along with group discussions directed by a member of staff, which sought to facilitate the implementation of a training plan and to critically evaluate how the institution's resources (e.g. in terms of employment and education) could be utilised in a more individualised way.

On the basis of post-release reconviction rates, Bottoms and McClintock discovered that there were no significant differences in the extent and nature of reoffending between the young people who participated in the modified training programme and those young people in the institution under the traditional regime. Although the treatment had a small impact, it was short-term and was fairly rapidly washed away and supplanted by the immediate social situation in which the boys found themselves after release. Bottoms and McClintock concluded, therefore, that the immediate social environment had more impact on offending behaviour than did risk factors in childhood, risk factors in adolescence or risk-focused intervention.

These results and conclusions are important (although this importance has gone largely unrecognised in subsequent RFR) in two main ways:

- Bottoms and McClintock's findings, whilst clearly compatible with the Gluecks' early conclusions regarding the influence of current risk factors on post-parole recidivism (Glueck and Glueck 1930, 1934), run counter to the developmental bias, emphasis and conclusions predominant within RFR discussed above (including that of the Gluecks). In short, Bottoms and McClintock demonstrated that current life circumstances have a much greater influence on behaviour than early-life risk factors.

- The conclusion that risk-focused intervention was largely ineffective (particularly in relation to the effects of post-parole situational and contextual influences) accords also with Cabot's findings from the Cambridge-Somerville Youth Study. Bottoms and McClintocks's findings, therefore, further questions the validity and counter-factual 'evidence base' of developmental risk-based intervention with young people.

Criminals Coming of Age was not a practical 'success' in terms of applying a risk-focused intervention to reducing reoffending. However, in theoretical and empirical terms, the study undermines the overwhelming emphasis upon risk factors in childhood for later offending and reorientates the research focus towards immediate, current life circumstances. Criminal Coming of Age offered an empirical evolution of RFR by conducting a robust controlled experiment that integrated a sensitive within-individual analysis of the retrospective and prospective influence of risk factors on offending, the effects of intervention on individuals and the influence of situational and contextual factors on behaviour. Ultimately, however, the major contribution of Criminals Coming of Age to the legacy of RFR has been the problematisation of the developmental evidence base – questioning the developmental influence of childhood risk factors on later behaviour (relative to 'current' life circumstances) and questioning the efficacy of risk-focused intervention to ameliorate risk and effect behaviour. For these reasons, Criminals Coming of Age should be best remembered by a reflective body of RFR. Unfortunately, it is likely that these very reasons actually explain why the study has been largely ignored by risk factor researchers and others seduced by the simplistic and convenient conclusions of developmental RFR.

The Social Development Model

Beginning their work in the 1980s, two social work professors at Washington University, Seattle, David Hawkins and Richard Catalano, with support from research colleagues (notably Joseph Weis), developed a multi-factor model of how risk factors operate together to influence antisocial and prosocial behaviour in young people (Hawkins and Weis 1985; Catalano and Hawkins 1996). Essentially, Hawkins and Weis (1985) set out to synthesise the key tenets of different theories of delinquent development into a coherent paradigm that, they argued, helped to understand and interpret the disparate findings from RFR.

Following a review of prevention programmes and secondary analysis of available data at the National Center for the Assessment of Delinquent Behavior and its Prevention (in Seattle, NA), Hawkins and Weis concluded that there were multiple 'correlates and causes' of antisocial behaviour and youth offending. These correlates and causes (which the authors acknowledged as equivalents to risk factors), allegedly operated within the institutional domains of family, school, peer and community and were more or less salient at different stages of a young person's

75

development. The researchers resolved to construct a dynamic, multi-faceted and developmentally-sensitive theory of how these 'etiological factors' or 'causes' emerge and interact to increase the probability of youth antisocial behaviour or reduce its likelihood. Initially, Hawkins and Weis (1985) focused on integrating Social Control Theory (Hirschi 1969) and Social Learning Theory (Akers 1985) by drawing on:

- the key units of socialisation (family and school) as the location for potential causes of antisocial behaviour/offending and prosocial behaviour/conformity (cf. Social Control Theory);

- reinforcement as the *process* by which antisocial behaviour or offending behaviour is learned or extinguished (cf. Social Learning Theory).

The Social Development Model hypothesised that four factors interacted to influence antisocial and criminal behaviour, namely:

- *perceived opportunities for involvement and interaction* with significant others in conventional activities;

- *degree of involvement and interaction*;

- *skills* of the young person to participate in these involvements and interactions;

- *perceived reinforcements for behaviour* that determine whether association with family, school or peers produces a strong bond.

(Hawkins and Weis 1985)

The Social Development Model certainly offered a more interactive and dynamic, though no less speculative, hypothesis of the influence of risk on offending than had previously been offered by artefact-based, developmentally-dominated RFR. The four elements of the model were conceived as mutually-reinforcing and interdependent, suggesting a dynamic element of change, influenced by an active, agentic young person and the possibilities of multifarious outcomes – in contrast to seeing the young person as a passive crash test dummy soaking up the deleterious, predetermined consequences of exposure to risk for inevitable future offending. For example, opportunities for involvement and interaction, it was argued, only created a bond if they were positively experienced by a young person. This positive experience was, in turn, dependent on the dynamic mix of the skills that young people brought to the involvement/interaction and the availability of consistent positive reinforcement. At the core, therefore, the Social Development Model was concerned to explain the *processes* that linked factors with outcomes and in doing so it introduced two new ideas to RFR:

- early life factors shape later behaviour, but so does what is happening during the teenage years affect teenage behaviour;

- young people are themselves active ingredients of the risk-factor–outcome relationship.

The authors asserted that the theory that underpins the Social Development Model organises the evidence regarding risk and protective factors for delinquency 'by hypothesising the theoretical mechanisms through which these factors operate to increase or decrease the likelihood of antisocial behaviour' (Catalano and Hawkins 1996: 154). However, the original Social Development Model was not necessarily the radical departure from developmental RFR that it may have seemed. Whilst Hawkins and colleagues did develop a model that was non-deterministic and more sensitive to notions of interaction, change and agency, they imported typically developmental risk factors into their new model rather than questioning the validity, appropriateness, applicability/generalisability and comprehensiveness of the factors themselves. The Social Development Model replaced a developmental definitiveness (where outcomes can be predicted) with a processual definitiveness (but where outcomes, positive or negative, cannot be predicted), whilst retaining a narrow focus on developmentally determined risk factors. Moreover, just like their developmental predecessors, the model was speculative and lacked an empirical, evidential basis.

Noting some limitations to the explanatory utility and theoretical breadth of the Social Development Model, Catalano and Hawkins set about extending and elaborating the original paradigm. In 1996, Catalano and Hawkins augmented the Social Development Model with ideas from Differential Association Theory (Sutherland and Cressey 1974) to help them to identify separate causal paths for antisocial behaviour that were related to association with delinquent peers. The updated Social Development Model also included three new variables that were considered to be 'exogenous' (external) to the original theory:

- *Constitutional and physiological traits* – cognitive ability (reading, verbal), difficult temperament, aggression, depression, hyperactivity, attention-deficit (factors that influence skills), low arousal of the nervous system (which influences the ability to perceive reinforcement).

- *Socio-structural status* – age, gender, race, socio-economic status (factors which affect available opportunities).

- *External constraints* – social reactions to behaviour that could be formal (police and other official sanction) or informal (ridicule, ostracism, disapproval) and the clarity of rules, laws, expectations for behaviour and the monitoring of behaviour (which affect the degree of perceived reinforcement for involvement in behaviour).

(see Catalano *et al.* 2005)

These exogenous variables, according to the authors, contributed to an increased likelihood of antisocial behaviour, but they could also be 'mediated by other social development model constructs' (Catalano and Hawkins 1996: 160). The revised Social Development Model further theorised that different (risk/protective) factors were more strongly associated with antisocial and prosocial behaviour at different phases of social development, namely:

- *Pre-school* (below six years of age) – family and caregivers as significant factors;

- *Elementary school* (6–11 year olds) – family, classmates and teachers as influential;

- *Middle school* (11–14 year olds) – family, peers, school personnel and school activities as important factors;

- *High school* (14–18 year olds) – family, peers, school personal, community members and community activities as the most influential factors.

(see Catalano and Hawkins 1996)

According to Catalano and Hawkins, each developmental phase is marked by major transitions in socialisation environments (e.g. in the elementary school phase, the school becomes the dominant institution over the family). At each of these stages, developmental processes involving the five Social Development Model constructs are hypothesised that influence antisocial behaviours (typically characterised as delinquency and substance use) and prosocial behaviours (typically defined in a limited manner as the absence of antisocial behaviours).

Overall, the Social Development Model is something of a Curate's egg. In its original form, the Social Development Model promised something radically different from developmental RFR, namely:

- a model of risk factor influence that was dynamic and provided for greater temporal affinity between factors and outcomes;

- a consideration of individual agency on the part of young people in constructing their responses to their life circumstances.

However, the Social Development Model retained developmental risk factors as potentially explanatory variables and replaced developmental determinism with a processual determinism that was speculative and un-evidenced – a definitive indefinity.

Recognising the limitations of this model, Hawkins and colleagues, rather than rectifying them, have actually compounded these problems. In seeking to make their model more comprehensive and in expanding the range of factors linked to outcomes, Hawkins and colleagues have deepened their adherence to what were essentially developmentally-defined risk factors. Furthermore, in seeking to sharpen their analyses of processes, Hawkins and colleagues merely introduced some rather blunt processual phases of social development. For example, the suggestion that certain factors and processes are equally representative and salient to all young people within the 'high school' phase (14–18 years old) assumes an unlikely homogeneity within that phase between, *inter alia*, 14 year olds and 18 year olds, boys and girls, young people of different ethnic groups and young people living in different localities. The end result is a model weakened by its adherence to developmentally determined risk factors and able to provide little or no predictive or causal explanatory utility.

Crime in the making: the emergence of risk-focused life course criminology

In 1972, the raw data from the Gluecks' *Unraveling Juvenile Delinquency* study was donated to Harvard University Law School. Two sociologists, Robert Sampson and John Laub, came across the data in 1985 in the basement of the Law School and, from that point, set about a meticulous and extensive process of restoring, reconstructing, validating and re-analysing it. Initially, Sampson and Laub computerised the entire data set, before subjecting the data to a series of statistical analyses that were unavailable to the Gluecks at the time of *Unraveling Juvenile Delinquency*. The recoding and re-evaluation of the Gluecks' data by Sampson and Laub attempted to address some of the original methodological limitations by:

• statistically controlling for age differences in the original data;

• statistically controlling for 'extra-legal' factors in the original matching criteria (age, race, neighbourhood socio-economic status, IQ) that may influence official responses to youth offending;

• using multivariate analyses techniques to test for the relative strengths of biological, psychological and social factors (rather than giving equal weight to all factors as did the Gluecks).

The central tenet of the Gluecks' research was that early life experiences predict future delinquency. However, the Gluecks also highlighted (but did not explore) the role of maturation as the main influence on desistance (Glueck and Glueck 1930, 1934, 1937), a conclusion that was inconsistent with their central deterministic theory. The challenge for Sampson and Laub, they felt, was to construct and test a theoretical model of individual development in childhood, adolescence *and* adulthood to expand the Gluecks' focus on early life experiences and to explore the possibility of stability and change in offending behaviour over the life course. Following an extensive process of reanalysis of the Gluecks' data, Sampson and Laub put forward their theory of age-graded informal social control and offending in the seminal text *Crime in the Making* (Sampson and Laub 1993). Their tripartite theory posited that:

- structural context (e.g. social class, ethnicity, gender, poverty, broken home, household overcrowding, parental employment) mediated by informal family and school social controls explains delinquency in childhood and adolescence;

- there is strong continuity in antisocial behaviour from childhood to adulthood in a variety of life domains;

- informal social bonds to family and employment in adulthood explain changes in criminality over the lifespan despite early childhood propensities.

(Sampson and Laub 1993: 7)

According to Sampson and Laub's theory, a young person's behaviour (prosocial or antisocial) is met with a range of formal and informal responses (e.g. offending may result in official sanction, parental discipline, approval/disapproval of peers). The nature of these responses interacts with existing risk factors to shape the individual's future behaviour. For example, official sanctions may diminish educational or vocational opportunities by incarcerating the young person and thus removing them from school or they may set the young person on a prosocial pathway by rendering a neglected education compulsory. In this way, the interaction between risk/protective factors and formal/informal responses to behaviour can form either vicious or virtuous circles. Sampson and Laub also added the notion of individual agency into their theory. Thus, risk factors and formal/informal responses to behaviour were not seen as wholly determinative of future behaviour but as providing the context which shapes the decisions an individual makes about how to behave (Sampson and Laub 1993).

Re-analyses of the Gluecks' data forced Sampson and Laub to challenge the crash test dummy determinism of the original conclusions and to posit a theory to explain both stability and change in offending over the life-course. The *age-graded theory of informal social control* set out in *Crime in the Making* introduced the idea that RFR should be conducted across the *life course*. This went beyond the early childhood focus of developmental criminology (of, for example, the Gluecks and Farrington) and broadened the scope of RFR, which had largely restricted investigations to childhood or discrete developmental stages (usually childhood and adolescence – see Catalano and Hawkins 1996).

Sampson and Laub made a particularly important contribution to RFR by identifying *life events* that could be demonstrated to interrupt the supposedly pre-determined criminal career path and which undermined the previously held belief that risk factor influence was stable over the life course. The concept of a stable path of criminal development or an offending *trajectory* had become a popular focal point of developmental and life course criminology in the early 1990s due to Farrington's criminal careers research (Farrington and Hawkins 1991) and Moffitt's studies of 'adolescence-limited' and 'life-course persistent' offenders (Moffitt 1991). However, the research of Sampson and Laub identified the possibility that offending trajectories could change in times of *transition* – significant periods in an individual's life (e.g. moving or leaving school, gaining or losing employment, getting married or separated). Thus, for Sampson and Laub, transitions and/or exposure to short-term, often abrupt, life events could promote offending or desistance from offending. Where this occurred, a substantive change in an individual's offending trajectory could result – what Sampson and Laub called a *turning point*. Re-analysis of the data from *Unraveling Juvenile Delinquency* identified employment, marriage and military service as crucial transition points that offered opportunities for the 'chain of adversity to be broken' (Rutter *et al.* 1990: 137) and which generated turning points in the life course of the young person through motivating choices/decisions to desist from offending.

Prior to Sampson and Laub's work, RFR had predominantly focused on the developmental influences of childhood risk factors and had uncritically assumed a continuity and stability of maladaptive behaviours (e.g. offending) over the life course. For many developmentalists conducting RFR, criminal propensity was established in early life and the potential impact of life events occurring in the intervening period between early childhood and adolescent offending were simply not considered. Although Sampson and Laub (1993) accepted the importance of early childhood experiences in influencing later problem behaviours, they rejected the developmental determinism and consequent simplistic over-simplification of risk factor influence prevalent in previous approaches. Sampson and Laub argued that an individual's behaviour is also shaped by the risk factors (including socio-structural factors) they are exposed to and the life events they experience throughout the life course. In this way, Sampson and Laub's life course model moved RFR forward from a narrow, artefact-based over-reliance on quantitative, developmental and deterministic understandings of the impact of early life risk factors (see France and Homel 2007) towards *constructivist* explanations of the individual's ability to actively influence their *pathways* into and out of crime – although this ability is shaped and constrained by extant risk factors and societal responses to previous behaviour. Importantly, Sampson and Laub came to these conclusions through an empirical and more sophisticated re-analysis of the Gluecks' original data set, thereby further calling into question the conclusions of the Gluecks – conclusions which not only formed the terrain of much RFR, but which remain influential today.

However, Sampson and Laub's age-graded theory of informal social control does not represent a complete break from traditional developmental criminology. Their re-analysis of the *Unraveling Juvenile Delinquency* data demonstrated that the propensity to offend is linked to psychosocial risk factors and the influence of these factors can be stable over the life course, with offending usually increasing through adolescence and slowly falling away in adulthood (in line with the Gluecks' view of maturation as the most significant influence on desistance).

In reaching their conclusions, of course, Sampson and Laub were inevitably wedded to the Gluecks' original, narrow set of simplified, factorised psychosocial risk factors. Their updated analysis and interpretation of the Gluecks' data still relied on a limited and possibly outdated set of factors that were identified in childhood using a staunchly developmental approach inspired by psychiatric and medical research. These constraints, although inevitable, do place limits on the scope and range of Sampson and Laub's conclusions. For example, there remains an unresolved tension between the determinative influence of early life risk factors and the possibilities for varied outcomes resulting from the impact and influence of dynamic social processes and the impact of immediate social circumstances (cf. Bottoms and McClintock 1973).

Intuitively, the elements of Sampson and Laub's theory elaborating the impact and importance of contemporary 'factors' and social processes seems much better able to capture the realities and dynamism of social life than the less fluid, more developmentally-deterministic, psychosocial and artefactual nature of the Gluecks' findings and conclusions. It remains unclear, however, whether life events and risk factors (early life and current) are substantively different concepts and, if so, how they differ. It also remains unclear how and to what extent early life risk factors, current risk factors and life events influence behaviour or how they combine to influence behaviour over the life-course. More sophisticated statistical analyses than that employed by Sampson and Laub would be needed to resolve these questions, but the availability and feasibility of such analyses is currently moot.

Whilst Sampson and Laub's analysis clearly calls into question notions of developmental determinism, they posited a cumulative theory consisting of vicious and virtuous circles between risk/protective factors and outcomes that was ultimately redolent with a lack of clarity about its key concepts, restricted by pre-determined lists of risk factors, beset by somewhat crude measurements and hypothetical in its explanations of the impact of risk factors, social processes and individual agency on future behaviour.

The ecological approach: the importance of socio-structural risk factors

An 'ecological' strand of RFR has emerged that has taken issue with the overriding individualised and psychosocial focus of much developmental RFR that has gone before it. Ecological RFR has built on Bronfenbrenner's 'ecology of child development', which postulated that:

> Child development takes place through processes of progressively more complex interaction between an active child and the persons, objects and symbols within its immediate environment. (Bronfenbrenner and Morris 1998: 996)

In other words, in this model, children are affected by the settings or systems they spend time in, notably the:

- *microsystem* – immediate influences in the family, school, neighbourhood, peer group;

- *mesosystem* – intermediate influences such as social institutions;

- *macrosystem* – the most removed influences, including international, regional or global changes.

(see Bronfenbrenner and Morris 1998)

Thus, while the ecological strand avers developmental determinism, it does not reject a developmental approach or the importance of childhood psychosocial risk factors, but it also seeks to address the relative neglect of neighbourhood/community-based and socio-structural risk factors and their potential influence on psychosocial risk factors and behaviour (see, for example, Wikström and Loeber 2000; see also Wikström and Loeber 1998).

In a bid to break away from what they viewed as the 'common but unfruitful' division of crime theories into individual and ecological explanations and to address concerns that RFR has neglected situational influences and individual agency, Per-Olof Wikström and Rolf Loeber have offered an ecological understanding of the interaction between risk factors measured in the individual and the social setting (see Wikström 2005). Along with noted colleagues such as Robert Sampson, Wikström and Loeber argued that within traditional developmental criminology, psychosocial risk factors have been interpreted deterministically without considering the impact of the wider structural context on the nature and extent of these risk factors (Wikström and Loeber 2000) and on the individual's perceived degree of 'social capital' (e.g. investment in, commitment to and attachment to their locality, social networks within and outside of the local community – see Boeck *et al.* 2006). Cuneen and White (2006) have argued, for example, that the so-called 'social' risk factors identified in traditional quantitative RFR, such as low socio-economic status and unemployment, should not be treated as specific individualised and causal risk factors, but rather as the *consequences* of wider socio-structural features, as contexts which shape young people's exposure to (varying levels of) 'risk' and within which young people grow up and are therefore influenced.

Wikström and Loeber (2000) have noted that previous studies of 'person-context interaction' have focused on the limited interaction between community context on the one hand and isolated individual or family characteristics on the other (e.g. family interaction – Lindstrom 1996). Concerned to deepen the ecological approach and using what they termed an 'holistic and epidemiological' analytical strategy, Wikström and Loeber set out to explore the interaction between risk factors in the individual and the community on a much broader level by identifying and exploring risk in four categories:

- *community structural characteristics* – poverty, high residential mobility, population heterogeneity, family disruption;

- *immediate social context* – aspects of the environment that affect individual decisions to offend such as temptations (e.g. attractive commodities), provocations (e.g. insults and threats), risk of punishment (formal and informal sanction);

- *individual social situation* – family, school, peers;

- *individual disposition* – impulsivity, guilt.

(see Wikström and Loeber 2000: 1114; emphasis added)

Their aim has been to proffer a more complex understanding of risk factor influence than developmental artefact models by considering:

- the interaction between individual/psychosocial risk factors and community/structural risk factors; and

- the interaction between developmental risk factors in childhood (individual social situation, individual disposition, community structural characteristics) and extant risk factors in current life (e.g. immediate social context, changes in community structural characteristics).

However, to date, the evidence base for ecological RFR has been under-developed and inconclusive. For example, following factorisation and analysis of data from the Pittsburgh Youth Study, Wikström and Loeber (2000) found that neighbourhood/community risk factors exerted little independent effect on offending and that most of their influence was mediated by individual risk factors. Other research, has found only an indirect effect of neighbourhood risk factors on offending through their influence on other risk factors such as family functioning (Sampson and Laub 1993). Sampson *et al.* (1997) concluded that neighbourhood characteristics *can* significantly predict (violent) offending, although not to the extent of individual characteristics. However, this is a claim without a strong empirical foundation.

The ecological approach has extended traditional RFR with an exploration of neighbourhood/community-based structural risk factors, which have been largely neglected by the more individualised, psychosocial foci of previous studies. However, ecological RFR has remained partly tied to developmentalism through its emphasis on how individualised childhood risk factors, personal disposition (akin to criminal potential/propensity) and the child's legacy of community structural disadvantage may be influential on, and influenced by, immediate social context. Notwithstanding this developmental element, ecological RFR has addressed previously overlooked areas in attempting to explain the influence of risk factors, particularly the interaction between childhood and present-day experiences, situational/contextual elements that may precipitate offending and a tentative consideration of the role of bounded agency (young people's ability to choose/decide to offend, as constrained by individual and neighbourhood factors) – see also Wikström's Developmental Ecological Action Theory (Wikström 2005). The tentative introduction of *agency* and *social processes* into ecological RFR arguably has addressed two of the ongoing limitations of Sampson and Laub's age-graded theory of informal social control, by adding greater depth to the range of current risk factors they had explored. However, the analytical intentions of ecological RFR have remained explicitly positivistic, exemplified by the factorisation of complex structural processes and the constant statistical comparisons between the predictive utility of neighbourhood and individual risk factors; both of which procedures have diminished the analytical and explanatory utility of this approach.

Shared Beginnings, Divergent Lives: the revised age-graded theory of social control

Sampson and Laub revisited and extended their age-graded theory of informal social control ten years after *Crime in the Making* in *Shared Beginnings, Divergent Lives* (Laub and Sampson 2003). In this follow-up research, Laub and Sampson contacted 52 men from the original delinquent group studied by the Gluecks in *Unraveling Juvenile Delinquency*

(Glueck and Glueck 1950). They conducted detailed life history interviews with the men as they approached 70 years of age, supplemented by analyses of the criminal histories and death records of all 500 men who formed part of the original sample of delinquents in the Gluecks' study. The qualitative, narrative life history approach moved RFR further away (than *Crime in the Making* already had) from its traditional emphasis on quantitative, variable-based methods and towards a focus on the life stories of the individual, in an attempt to obtain richer, more comprehensive data to illuminate why some people persisted with and others desisted from crime across the whole life course (Laub and Sampson 2003). Although this research was not focused on young people, Laub and Sampson were addressing a crucial contradiction within the developmental approach of the Gluecks and others – that childhood risk factors apparently determine offending in later life, yet young people also seem to grow out of crime.

The *Shared Beginnings, Divergent Lives* study identified four main self-reported transitions in the lives of the delinquent sample that functioned as turning points promoting desistance from offending in adulthood: marriage, joining the military, attending reform school and moving to a more prosperous neighbourhood. The interviewees reported that each of these transitions had offered them the opportunity to change the direction of their lives, to receive supervision, monitoring and social support, to bring change and structure to their routine activities and to transform their identity (Laub and Sampson 2003). Therefore, according to Laub and Sampson, desistence from an offending career was dependent on two central developments in the life of sample members: 'knifing off' from one's immediate environment and obtaining 'structured role stability' across the life domains (e.g. marriage, work, community). Knifing off enabled the desisters to transform their identities into a more positive form and to access social support. Structured role stability enabled the young men to have structure to, certainty in, and support for, their routine activities. In contrast, the sample members who remained frequent and persistent offenders or who desisted at a much later age appeared to lack these supportive structures throughout their life course, particularly relationships that provided informal social control and social support. Sample members reported that lack of support structures and lack of informal social control rendered them unable to forge attachments to significant others. In addition the men sampled believed that the general lack of structure in their lives exposed them to more criminogenic situations on a routine basis.

Laub and Sampson concluded that their original age-graded theory of informal social control (Sampson and Laub 1993) had failed to examine the *progression* (or 'pathways') of change in behaviour over the life course, particularly in relation to desistance from offending. Consequently, the authors revised their theory on the basis of an analysis of the life history narratives they collected. Using the life history data, Laub and Sampson developed an integrated theory of the life course that accounted for the respective role and impact of risk factors in adulthood (as opposed to just childhood and adolescence), individual agency and choice, situational factors, routine activities, culture and historical context. Laub and Sampson drew on constructivist understandings of risk to explore what they termed the 'inner logic of lives' (Laub and Sampson 2003: 8). By studying individuals through adulthood, by using qualitative research methods and by focusing on individual agency, situational factors and cultural and historical contexts, Laub and Sampson claimed to be 'reconsidering the risk-factor paradigm' (Laub and Sampson 2003: 289) and enabling a richer, more holistic understanding of persistence and desistance in offending careers.

In explaining their findings, Laub and Sampson eschewed theories of deterministic pre-programming that view the life course as 'an unwinding, an unfolding, or an unrolling of what is fundamentally "already there"' (Sampson and Laub 2005: 178) and they rejected the view of young people as crash test dummies on an unstoppable course/pathway towards life-long offending. Moreover, Laub and Sampson's revised theory rejected the 'structural determinism of turning points in the life course' by arguing that 'desistance is best viewed as a process realized over time, not a single event' (2003: 278). The authors therefore extrapolated their original age-graded theory of informal social control 'to include, among others, the idea of situated choice as central to an understanding of crime from childhood through old age' (2003: 293).

The revised age graded theory of social control challenged RFR by placing a hitherto-overlooked focus on the *whole* life course. The theory introduced examinations of the role of human agency and the process of desistence, both of which had, to that point, been marginalised within RFR, even within allegedly 'integrated' theories such as the Social Development Model. On the basis of their findings, Laub and Sampson (2005) came to view (young) people as active participants in constructing their own lives within a dynamic social world which has opportunities and constraints – a constructivist model of RFR to challenge and supplement traditional artefact-based understandings.

The key question is, of course, does the discovery of human agency and the potential for change through constructed and negotiated pathways into and out of offending undermine or make now redundant the deterministic developmental hypothesis? The *Shared Beginnings, Divergent Lives* study does not offer enough of substance or detail to sufficiently address this question. Crucially, due to its emphasis on desistence in adulthood, the revised theory does not explore why young people offend. There is also a tentative and limited understanding of the precise role of agency and its interaction with risk factors and risk processes in different domains of life, in different contexts and at different ages. For example, Laub and Sampson appear to suggest that changes in social and situational circumstances can prompt changes in behaviour, notably desistance from offending. However, the authors offered a limited explanatory understanding of the influential aspects of these social circumstances (e.g. contact with official agencies, increased informal social support, effects on situated choices, chance) and the processes of change that they may promote.

The pathways approach: experiencing and negotiating risk in the socio-structural context

The constructivist *pathways* approach to RFR has emphasised how young people experience, negotiate and, therefore, construct their own developmental pathways into and out of crime. The pathways model has also explored how young people's experiences and ability to negotiate risk factors can be mediated by socio-structural context (e.g. neighbourhood socio-economic status, poverty, unemployment, localised cultural influences, political influence – see France and Homel 2007). According to Elder *et al.* pathways RFR goes beyond age-specific studies of childhood and early adulthood and focuses on:

> social pathways, their developmental effects, and their relation to personal and social-historical conditions. (Elder *et al.* 2004: 7)

The notion of a 'pathway' infers a developmental life course understanding that young people's patterns of experience over time and their interactions with social institutions have a beginning, an 'interim' and an end, but not necessarily in a deterministic, 'crash test dummy' sense. In this model, therefore, young people can be seen as active agents in their own lives and active constructors and interpreters of risk factors and risk processes. However, this agency is *bounded* – their opportunities, choices and ability to negotiate and resist risk are limited, constrained or shaped by contextual and structural factors outside of their control. Thus, every young person makes decisions about how to behave (hundreds of decisions every day), but these decisions are shaped and constrained (not all options are open) by the nature of the structural, institutional and social context in which they are made.

France and Homel have described the pathways approach as:

> A life-course perspective that explores the intra-individual and inter-individual aspects of 'experience' as critical to understanding the pathways into and out of crime. (France and Homel 2007: 4)

The pathways approach understands risk and its effects as a dynamic process, subject to change and construction by young people, as opposed to a collection of static factors or variables that can be readily measured and that have effects which remain stable across the life course. Pathways RFR has been animated by two sets of studies in the UK: the Pathways Into and Out of Crime projects and the Teesside Studies.

Pathways Into and Out of Crime – a partnership of longitudinal studies sponsored by the Economic and Social Research Council (ESRC). The partnership has focused on how young people are able to negotiate and make meaning of their pathways into and out of crime and how social processes and demographic characteristics can mediate the influence and experience of risk factors (Hine 2005). Consequently, the focus has been on how risk factors in *current* lives can be constructed and negotiated (France and Homel 2007).

The Pathways Into and Out of Crime projects have each utilised qualitative methodologies (although there has also been a strong quantitative element in certain projects) to engage with hard to reach and minority groups of young people (substance users, excluded from school, behaviour problems, offenders, those with parents in prison, Black and Asian ethnic groups) – see Chapter 3 for a full discussion of the methods, results and conclusions of the different projects. The partnership has adopted a social constructivist approach to exploring risk and to developing an understanding of how young people become involved in offending. In particular, the approach has attempted to explain the complex mechanisms that link 'risk' with offending behaviour; an explanation that is beyond the capabilities of restricted artefact RFR (see France and Homel 2007). Indeed, the pathways approach in general and the Pathways Into and Out of Crime partnership in particular was developed specifically as a reaction to the traditional artefact form of RFR; taking issue with the manner in which it framed the risk 'problem' in an oversimplified, factorised, deterministic and individualised fashion (see France and Homel 2007; Webster 2007). Thus, the Pathways Into and Out of Crime partnership of studies has eschewed linear, positivistic interpretations of causality and the deterministic nature of early life experiences promulgated by artefact RFR; preferring to explore the social actor in its research – a social actor who experiences, feels, perceives and makes meaning. Pathways RFR in general has asserted the role of the individual in a reflective and reactive relationship with their social and physical environment over the developmental life course, rather than the individual as a passive and helpless recipient or 'victim' of exposure to the inevitable effects of childhood risk factors.

The Teesside Studies – an important body of three studies has emerged from Teesside University, which have taken a biographical approach to examining how young people construct and deal with risk in their daily lives (see Chapter 3 for a fuller discussion of all three studies). An integral component of the Teesside Studies, illustrative of their approach and conclusions, has been Poor Transitions:

Young Adults and Social Exclusion, a qualitative, retrospective longitudinal study of socio-structural and contextual influences on offending such as neighbourhood destabilisation and socio-economic deprivation (Webster *et al.* 2004). In *Poor Transitions*, Webster *et al.* (2004) took issue with the plethora of 'backward looking' developmental risk-focused studies that had characterised offending as strongly linked to negative experiences in early life. Following a series of retrospective biographical interviews with young people aged 16–25 years, the authors concluded that risk factors emerging in the teenage years and early adulthood were influential on behaviour, but had been neglected by 'traditional' analyses and that risk factors had been interpreted deterministically without exploration of their interrelationships with other risk factors. Webster *et al.* (2004) argued that socio-structural risk factors have been narrowly defined by a RFR movement obsessed with individualised and psychosocial risk factors. The research team concluded that the Teesside sample faced 'a myriad of risks scarcely recognised in risk and prediction studies' which inextricably linked biography, place and social structure (Webster *et al.* 2004: 15). The young people experienced transitions in their lives that were fluid, unpredictable and chaotic. Therefore, their exposure to, and ability to resist risk factors was influenced by accelerated socio-economic change which destabilised neighbourhoods and precipitated unpredictable life events.

Constructing pathways

The constructivist discourse of the Pathways Into and Out of Crime partnership and the Teesside Studies has challenged the inherent determinism, psychosocial bias and artefact focus of much RFR. The constructivist and socio-structural elements of the pathways perspective has prioritised examination of the ways in which individuals negotiate their environments and has explored the 'chaotic, complex, relative, contextual' relationships between risk factors and offending across diverse cultures, social contexts and political settings (see Ungar 2004), emphasising (although not quantifying) both individual agency and the structural limitations to individual agency. The positivist, deterministic search for globally-applicable causal and predictive risk factors has been rejected as androcentric, ethnocentric, over-generalised and unable to accommodate the plurality of meanings that young people negotiate in their constructions of self.

Pathways RFR has prioritised qualitative, narrative research methods that address much-neglected foci within RFR, particularly:

- giving a voice to young people, especially marginalised groups of young people;
- examining more closely how race, gender and class affect personal definitions of risk;

- challenging the adult-centric perspective of risk; challenging aggregated and globalised accounts of risk that neglect local discourses.

(Webster *et al.* 2006; Hine 2005; Ungar 2004)

This constructivist pathways approach to RFR has acknowledged the complexities and difficulties in young people's lives and has attempted to understand how they make meaning of risk and being 'at risk' (France and Homel 2007). Pathways RFR has intended to offer a direct challenge to quantitative, statistical 'artefact' approaches to RFR (see Kemshall *et al.* 2007) and developmental approaches that have been more age-specific in their focus on childhood, adolescence or early adulthood (see Elder *et al.* 2004). Pathways research has analysed the influence of structural, political and cultural processes and contexts on young people's *current* behaviour and *current* exposure to risk factors and how young people themselves feel that they are affected by these processes in the present (France and Homel 2007). Consequently, the results and conclusions from pathways RFR have been generally less definitive and less simplistic than those from artefact RFR. Of course, creating uncertainty and complexity presents problems to those concerned to develop policy and practice, but the challenge to the determinism of artefact RFR presented by the findings from pathways approaches must be recognised. If social life is chaotic, unpredictable, diverse and highly individualised and cannot be reduced to neat boxes of predictable understanding and explanation, then the practical claims and consequences of artefact RFR have little or no real world credibility.

De-constructing pathways

The relative utility and credibility of the nebulous 'approximations' of risk (see Webster *et al.* 2006) and its influence provided by studies within the pathways strand also remains open to debate. Pathways RFR has yet to do enough to escape the positivist pull towards over-simplification through factorisation and the aggregation of individual results into offending typologies – processes that have reduced diversity to uniform actuarial descriptions (Nagin and Tremblay 2005; Sampson and Laub 2005). Therefore, it is moot as to how far the pathways approach has evolved an understanding of risk that is sufficiently removed from the psychosocial bias and pervasive factorisation of artefact RFR (although not so much in the Teesside Studies, which have been more concerned with transitions than risk of offending *per se*). There is a sense that the espoused developmental determinism of psychosocial risk factors has been taken for granted and serves as the normative touchstone from which the pathways strand has evolved. Despite its constructivism and prioritisation of engaging, qualitative methodologies, the pathways approach has arguably privileged the exploration of adult-prescribed meanings relating to the psychosocial risk factors established in quantitative developmental research, rather than starting afresh with an inductive investigation of which risk factors young people themselves perceive as influential in their lives and pursuing explanations of how these risks may operate as dynamic and fluid processes. The developmental baggage remains. There has been an apparent drive and necessity to understand risk factors in non-traditional, non-developmental ways (e.g. in terms of their current, active influence and how they are constructed and resisted by young people). However, the methods and foci of the pathways approach remain wedded (at least in part) to a developmental, deficit-based model that places at its centre a view of young people as defined in relation to the risk in their lives – a risk that, however it is cut, can be readily factorised and statistically linked to offending. Unless and until the nascent pathways approach can develop an identity, theoretically and empirically, that is sufficiently removed from its deterministic and narrowly focused predecessors, it is could be doomed to perpetuate the biases of artefact RFR and to evolve as a more complex and interpretive 'variation on a theme'.

Integrated theories: making sense of risk factor research?

Risk factor research, as this chapter has shown, is not an homogeneous paradigm. Indeed, RFR has been deeply riven with complementary, competing and even contradictory theories and models which variously try to identify risk factors for offending and explain the link between risk factors and offending. Such are the divisions in RFR that one might begin to question its coherence and validity. Can RFR, as a body of research, actually help to understand and explain juvenile offending? In this context it is perhaps unsurprising to find key proponents of RFR thinking about new ways of understanding and making sense of the role of risk factors in the lives of young people.

According to Farrington, 'the modern trend (is) to try to achieve increased explanatory power by integrating propositions derived from several earlier theories' (Farrington 2007: 620). Two such attempts to rescue and reconcile the divisions in RFR in integrated theories of risk factor influence have been Farrington's Integrated Cognitive Antisocial Potential theory and Wikström's Developmental Ecological Action Theory.

The Integrated Cognitive Antisocial Potential theory

Artefact RFR has been criticised for focusing on empirical variables at the expense of developing underlying theoretical constructs (Farrington 2005). In response, David Farrington, has developed the Integrated Cognitive Antisocial Potential (ICAP) theory. The ICAP theory has adopted a dual focus on investigating between individual differences in *criminal potential* (a traditional concern of developmental and life course criminology) and within-individual differences in the *commission* of offences (a much neglected topic within developmental and life course criminology).

Farrington's integrated theory is a hypothetical (rather than evidence based or empirically grounded) synthesis of several theories of crime causation – strain, control, social learning, labelling and rational choice (see Farrington 2005). The ICAP theory uses the concept of *antisocial potential* as the linchpin to explain how risk factors become actualised in offending behaviour. According to Farrington (2005), antisocial potential is determined by the nature and extent of the risk factors that young people are exposed to in their everyday lives. This antisocial potential is translated into offending behaviour by cognitive processes (thinking and decision-making) that take account of the opportunities to offend and the availability of victims in different situations.

In this theory, a crucial distinction has been drawn between long-term antisocial potential that differs between individuals and short-term antisocial potential that varies within individuals:

- *Long-term antisocial potential* – actualised by impulsiveness, strain, modelling, socialisation and negative life events (e.g. divorce, separation from a partner, losing a job). Farrington has hypothesised that risk factors such as disrupted families/broken homes, inconsistent parental discipline, exposure to antisocial role models, low anxiety, impulsivity and criminogenic (high crime) schools and neighbourhoods create a long-term antisocial potential. This potential is then energised (activated) by the young person's desire for material possessions, status seeking among significant others and the pursuit of excitement and sexual satisfaction. In contrast, positive attachment, prosocial socialisation and positive life events (e.g. marriage, leaving a high crime area) can inhibit long-term antisocial potential. Farrington has, therefore, hypothesised a more complex and less deterministic, developmental theory of how childhood risk factors can impact on later offending by suggesting that they can be activated in later life by the choices that young people make.

- *Short-term antisocial potential* – dependent on motivating (risk) factors such as school failure, unemployment and low income, which are energised by boredom, anger, drunkenness, frustration and peer encouragement. Short-term antisocial potential also depends on situational factors such as suitable opportunities and victims. The actual decision to offend in a given situation has been hypothesised to be dependent on a cognitive appraisal (costs–benefits analysis) of immediate situational factors affecting the likelihood of rewards/reinforcement (material, financial, peer approval) compared to the likelihood of being caught and sanctioned (punished, subjected to family

93

and peer disapproval), the amount of effort needed to offend and the individual's perceived physical ability to commit the offence. Therefore, when explaining the commission of offences, Farrington's focus has been on the interaction between active risk factors, agency, cognition and situational factors.

Farrington has asserted that offending results from rational choices made by young people during interactions between individual characteristics (e.g. short- and long-term antisocial potential) and aspects of the environment (e.g. opportunities for crime and available victims). Thus, the ICAP theory has expanded developmental understandings of risk factors by supplementing the traditional focus on childhood risk factors with emphasis on young people's *current lives* – fusing the developmental and the current/active within the same theory. Furthermore, the ICAP theory has extended traditional deterministic RFR by incorporating consider-ations of agency and the influence of situational aspects when exploring how risk triggers offending.

Farrington has attempted to provide a dynamic theory of action to identify and explain the mechanisms that animate, 'energise' and actualise risk factors and turn them into offending behaviour. However, his hypothetical explanations sit uncomfortably within an otherwise empiri-cally-grounded body of RFR. It is far from clear, for example, what precise empirical evidence has underpinned the propositions and conclusions of ICAP theory and whether it is little more than speculation.

The ICAP theory rests on an excessive and invalidating reductionism due to its oversimplification of offending into the product of a relationship between a flawed (pathologised) individual and their dysfunctional community (see also Armstrong 2004). Thus, in order to reach this conclusion, it has been necessary to attribute definitiveness to what are actually indefinitive research findings. Paradoxically, of course, the end result is a theory with a reduced predictive utility and reduced explana-tory power, because it relies on concepts and constructs which are poorly-defined and offers little to explain the nature of the relationships between one and another concept and construct.

Perhaps most notable has been the extent to which Farrington, the champion of developmental RFR, and ICAP, are distanced from the developmentalism and determinism that has characterised his previous conclusions and influenced an entire industry of RFR (see also Sutton *et al.* 2004).

The Developmental Ecological Action Theory of Crime Involvement

Concerned that empirical research in criminology had become dominated by a 'risk factor approach' that was fixated on identifying non-random correlates with offending and devoid of theoretical guidance, Wikström set out to establish a 'scientific realist' theory of the relationship between risk and offending (see Wikström 2005 2006). Wikström has emphasised the need to address the problem of determining causality within RFR by pursuing an *explanatory* approach focused on identifying the *causal mechanisms* linking risk factors with offending (Wikström 2005, 2008). His subsequent *Developmental Ecological Action Theory* hypothesised that changes and stability in individual development, in the settings in which individuals 'participate' and in individual reactions to these settings, are to be found the *mechanisms* that link both the individual and the setting to *action* (in the form of offending in the current lives of young people). Wikström has postulated that these mechanisms can offer much-needed information about the causal processes underpinning the transformation of risk factors into offending behaviour, which is particularly useful because:

> Research on individual risk factors has largely failed to specify in any detail the causal mechanisms that link the risk factors to acts of crime and pathways in criminality. (Wikström and Sampson 2003: 119)

The empirical basis for the Developmental Ecological Action Theory (DEAT) dates back to Autumn 2000, when Wikström commenced his cross-sectional Peterborough Youth Study. The overarching aims of the Peterborough Youth Study were to expand on the understanding of risk factors within ecological RFR and to gain an enhanced understanding of adolescent involvement in crime by:

> studying the relationships between *family social position* (parents occupational social class, family structure and family ethnicity), the *adolescents' social situation* (family and social bonds), their *individual dispositions* (morality and inability to exercise self-control) and *lifestyles* (as implicated by their peers' delinquency, their own activities and alcohol and drug use) and how these factors relate to their involvement in crime as offenders (and partly as victims). (Wikström and Butterworth 2006: 6)

The study was built on a random sample of 1,957 young people (boys and girls) aged 14–15 years from all 13 state schools in Peterborough. Each young person completed a questionnaire that measured risk factors and self-reported offending, whilst 339 of the sample were also interviewed (Wikström and Butterworth 2006).

Analyses of the Peterborough Youth Study data highlighted a group of allegedly 'explanatory factors'. Wikström and Butterworth (2006) argued that young people's routines, lifestyles, dispositions (morality, self-control) and the social situations they were exposed to (parental monitoring, bonds to family and school) were significant predictors of offending behaviour. For example, a low degree of involvement and activity with the family or school, coupled with spending time with delinquent peers in high-risk environments (e.g. neighbourhoods with high rates of crime and drug use) or truanting from school, exposed young people to a higher situational risk of offending than young people who were positively/constructively engaged with family or school. Therefore, the mechanisms active in linking factors with outcomes were the *interactions* of risk factors and not just the risk factors themselves. The authors described risk factors thus:

> their role in crime causation is important but indirect (they are the causes of causes – that is, they influence the individual and environmental factors that, in turn, make individuals see certain action alternatives and make certain choices that may cause them to commit acts of crime). (Wikström and Butterworth 2006: 242)

On the basis of these findings, Wikström and Butterwortth postulated the Situational Action Theory of crime causation (the precursor to the DEAT), which states that:

> Adolescent offending is best interpreted as the consequence of perception of action alternatives and processes of choice made against the background of the interplay between the youths' individual characteristics and their behavioural contexts. (Wikström and Butterworth 2006: 241)

The Situational Action Theory offered an important analytical step forward for RFR by questioning the deterministic and explanatory sufficiency of individual risk factors as causes of later behaviour. Consequently, the Situational Action Theory sought an enhanced understanding of what makes a risk factor an 'active' predictor/cause of later or current behaviour – which was concluded to be its *interaction* with other risk factors. In other words, causality is a construct of the relationship between individual and setting (Wikström 2005). However, the model was still somewhat deterministic to the extent that specific interactions were held to be predictive/causal but, in the real world, these predictions often do not come true. It was in response to this problem that Wikström developed the DEAT (Wikström 2006a).

The Developmental Ecological Action Theory explains offending through a focus on young people's moral behaviour – why they break or conform to rules about what is right or wrong. Following from Situational Action Theory, Wikström has proposed that offending is the result of an *intersection* (interaction) between the *individual* (their current characteristics and experiences) and the *setting* (the people, objects, events and locations to which the young person is exposed and reacts). In the DEAT, the *situational mechanisms* that 'activate' the interaction between individual and setting (i.e. what turns it into offending behaviour) are twofold – the young person's *perception of alternative actions* and their *process of choice*. Wikström proposed that a young person's perception of alternative actions is affected by the setting in which they find themselves and this setting is determined (to a certain extent) by the young person's characteristics and social circumstances. Perception of alternative actions in a given situation is allegedly activated by a number of mechanisms within both the individual (moral judgement) and the setting, namely temptations (perceived opportunities to satisfy their desires unlawfully) and provocations (perceived attacks on the person, property or self-respect that precipitate a criminal response). The young person's decision to act on the perceived alternative action (their process of choice) is influenced by their own individual self-control and by deterrence (per-ceived risk of interventions and sanctions) within the setting (Wikström and Butterworth 2006).

Situational Action Theory and the DEAT have both fused an ecological approach with considerations of agency (including morality), rational-choice and socio-structural influences. Consequently, these theories have provided a more holistic and dynamic explanation of risk factor influence than have traditional developmental theories with psychosocial or deter-ministic biases. They have claimed to offer a scientific realist explanation of crime that has accounted for differing individual constructions of the same reality (thus encompassing elements of a weak constructivism) and individual responses to risk factors as artefacts, by exploring the mechan-isms of change and (unobservable) processes that have been neglected by positivist approaches (Wikström 2008).

However, in the enthusiasm to formulate an all-embracing, holistic explanation of youth offending, reductionism and imputation have replaced robust methodology and strong empirical evidence. Indeed, Wikström has acknowledged that his (supposedly dynamic and innova-tive) ecological theory has been underpinned by 'rudimentary' measures of social context, which offer only a 'rough picture' of the structural and social contexts of school and neighbourhood, but little detailed knowledge about the influential elements of each or the processes by which they influence young people's actions (Wikström and Butterworth 2006).

It is not just a matter, however, of what has been measured (and the quality of these measurements) but also of *when* things have been measured. The dynamic 'theory of action' and 'explanatory' risk factors underpinning Wikström's ideas have been generated from a cross-sectional design that has measured inputs and outputs at the same time. Any notions of causality, therefore, remain beyond such research.

Wikström is well aware of this limitation and although he argues (with justification) that cross-sectional designs are able to address issues of temporal precedence if they employ sensitive measures of temporality and causal ordering of (risk) factors and offending (Wikström, 2008), this was not achieved in the Peterborough Youth Study, which took a generalised, vague measure of offending ('in the last year') that did not enable young people to specify a precise time or time period over which they had been exposed to the so-called risk variables. Thus, it was entirely possible that offending pre-dated the risk variables or occurred at exactly the same time. Consequently, the Peterborough Youth Study resorted to assuming a spatio-temporal and therefore predictive link between risk factors (as putative causes) and offending behaviour (as the putative effect). The Peterborough Youth Study, therefore, cannot provide empirical evidence for the DEAT.

Furthermore, the DEAT remains wedded to a simplistic and artefactual understanding of risk as something that can be factorised and identified statistically as a predictor/cause of future offending. By dint of this artefactualism and the lack of any qualitative exploration or understanding of how young people actually make sense of their behaviour, Wikström and the DEAT are unable to offer an adequate description of causal processes and, for example, the absence of a simplistic link between risk factors and offending. Variance in outcomes or the failure of the model to correctly predict offending have been explained by individual morality and choice – which, of course, is not/cannot be easily measured or factorised. Ultimately, therefore, whether a young person offends or not comes down to a matter of individual choice and responsibility – which seems to be a very reductionist conclusion to a theory which claimed to offer much wider and more explanatory utility. Overall, we are left with a theory that is riddled with contradictions. The DEAT is simultaneously developmentally based and about current circumstances, is structural and individualistic, is deterministic and unpredictable – yet unable to offer anything more than speculation on the relative importance and nature of the relationship between these polarised variables.

The evolution of risk factor research

This chapter has addressed the important task of explicating and evaluating the theoretical and methodological evolution of RFR by tracing its chronological journey since the groundbreaking research of the Gluecks up to the present day. At each stage, attempts have been made to draw out the theoretical bases of the most influential empirical research studies and explanatory models and to show the threads that bind them as well as the differences and discontinuities between them.

The chronological critique of RFR has illuminated several distinctive research strands, which are set out in Table 2.1 below. The table summarises the chronological development of criminological RFR with reference to the most important studies, but the information is not meant to imply a systematic and iterative development between the strands. Indeed, despite commonalities, there have been significant divergences in approach, particularly in recent years. Moreover and to the detriment of the development of RFR and its uses, the theoretical underpinnings and inherent biases of RFR have too often remained insufficiently explored or left implicit within the literature and sometimes hidden behind a veneer of neutral, value free scientific gloss. Better and more explicit recognition of these theoretical underpinnings might have led to a greater robustness in the development of RFR – a process which has been undertaken and provided here to better evaluate RFR and its various contributions to understanding and explaining juvenile delinquency.

The explanatory models underpinning each of these strands of RFR have predominantly focused on the influence of psychosocial risk factors at the developmental stages of childhood and adolescence and have thus primarily adopted a developmental understanding of the relationship between early risk factors and later offending. Where the strands have differed most significantly has been in their views of:

- the most appropriate domains in which to look for influential risk factors;

- the extent to which the risk-factor–offending relationship is predetermined;

- the simplistic, unidirectional, linear nature of the relationship between risk factors and offending;

- the replicability and applicability of findings to young people as a generalised group.

The history and evolution of RFR has been characterised by the privileging of individualised risk factors in psychosocial domains. In recent years, new research strands have emerged which have augmented this psychosocial focus with an investigation of interactions between individualised factors and macro-level socio-structural factors (e.g. the life course and ecological strands), situational factors and rational choice (e.g. the revised life course strand, the DEAT, the ICAP theory) and the young person's ability to construct and negotiate risk (the pathways strand). However, few of these strands have challenged the origins of the 'established' body of psychosocial risk factors first illuminated by the Gluecks and consolidated by the Cambridge Study and few have challenged the validity of these factors (with pathways RFR as an exception). This suggests a taken-for-grantedness regarding the validity of these factors as essential building blocks in any comprehensive theory emerging from RFR.

The artefact-based strands of RFR in particular (e.g. developmental, ecological, social development model, integrated) have perpetuated a deterministic understanding of the stable and enduring influence of risk factors on offending, which has been founded on a simplistic (yet oversimplified) and definitive (yet indefinite) reading of the output of statistical analyses. The simplistic factorisation of risk at a given point in time and the subsequent measurement of offending within longitudinal research has apparently convinced advocates of artefact RFR of the unequivocally causal/predictive nature of risk factors – a conclusion that has even pervaded cross-sectional RFR (as Chapter 4 will discuss). There has been little or no recognition of researchers' inability to control for extraneous variables, the possibility that offending could create risk factors (rather than vice versa), that measuring risk factors in childhood and official offending in adolescence imbues their relationship with a vagueness regarding temporal precedence or that alternative, more complex explanations of offending may exist. The life course strands of Sampson and Laub were the first to address this latter point through a re-analysis and reorientation of the Gluecks' deterministic theory; by acknowledging and exploring the young person's potential to change over the life course. The pathways strand has taken this argument forward by exploring the extent and nature of young people's ability to construct their understanding of responses to risk and consequently to determine (to some degree) their own pathways into and out of crime in different social contexts. Therefore, the life course and pathways strands have reorientated the perception of young people within RFR away from the passive 'crash test dummies' of previous deterministic artefact strands and towards a consideration of active, agentic constructors and experiencers of risk.

The emergence in recent years of the ecological, pathways and integrated strands of RFR has progressed understandings of risk factors (or at least increased the complexity with which researchers have *tried* to understand these factors) into a more complex and multi-faceted arena than previously visited. The developmental research of the Gluecks, West and Farrington and Hawkins and Catalano has been considered multi-causal and eclectic in its methodology and foci, but at its heart this research has been a basic examination of the role of psychosocial risk factors in childhood in determining later offending, with no exploration of interactions with socio-structural risk factors, the mechanisms that activate risk factors, situational influences, agency or the construction of risk. However, even the more complex contemporary explanatory models have struggled to break the developmental shackles put in place by the Gluecks and the Cambridge Study. It is difficult to pinpoint an example of RFR that has not taken the developmental influence of psychosocial risk factors as its theoretical starting point and utilised the factorisation and statistical analysis of risk as its methodological basis. Even studies conducted within research strands that have eschewed deterministic understandings of risk factors in favour of their active influence in current lives (e.g. the pathways strand) have appeared to accept 'established' psychosocial risk factors as influential on offending and have (possibly invalidly) assumed that these factors, first identified in childhood, can exert an influence during adolescence and adulthood.

The predilection for assuming a unidirectional relationship between 'predictive' risk factors and consequent offending on the basis of supposedly 'scientific' statistical analyses of factorised psychosocial risk factors illustrates a cluster of methodological weaknesses and limitations that remain relatively unexplored within RFR. The individual and combined effects of each of these issues on the validity of RFR methodologies has been compounded by the definitiveness with which findings have been viewed as universally applicable to the youth population, despite having their methodological origins within studies of narrow samples of white working-class boys in industrialised Western societies. Although contemporary studies have drawn on more varied and representative samples of young people and have not sought to generalise their findings beyond that group, their methodologies have more often than not been informed by the findings from the most influential, yet undeniably androcentric, ethnocentric and class-biased RFR studies (e.g. *500 Criminal Careers*, *Unravelling Juvenile Delinquency*, the Cambridge-Somerville Youth Study, the Cambridge Study in Delinquent Development).

The chronology of RFR indicates the extent to which simplistic and definitive conclusions of risk factor influence have been promulgated on the basis of oversimplified (e.g. aggregated, factorised, psychosocial, androcentric) and imputed, even hypothesised, understandings of the risk-factor–offending relationship. The methodological weaknesses (paradoxes) of simplistic over-simplicity (including the identification of risk-dependent protective factors), definitive indefinity, replicable incomparability and unconstructive constructionism, in combination with deep-rooted theoretical biases, have simultaneously limited RFR and enabled it to replicate itself into a flourishing global research movement that has been at once homogenous in its findings and heterogeneous in its methods.

Table 2.1 The chronological evolution of risk factor research

Began	Theory	Central tenets	Key publications
1930	Multi-factor developmental	Biological and psychosocial characteristics measured in childhood and adolescence correlate with official offending in adolescence.	*500 Criminal Careers, One Thousand Juvenile Delinquents, Unravelling Juvenile Delinquency* (Glueck and Glueck 1930, 1934, 1950)
1939	Developmental crime prevention	Biological and psychosocial factors measured in childhood can be linked to official offending and can be targeted by preventative interventions.	*Cambridge-Somerville Youth Study* (Cabot 1940; Powers and Witmer 1951; McCord and McCord 1959; McCord 1978)
1961	Risk-focused developmental	Childhood risk factors, protective factors and life events in the psychosocial domains of family, school, neighbourhood and the individual, exert a developmental influence on the extent and nature of official and self-reported offending in adolescence and later life.	Cambridge Study in Delinquent Development (West and Farrington 1973; West 1982; Farrington 2007)
1963	Situational/contextual (nascent interactional theory of desistance)	An individual's immediate social environment in early adulthood exerts a stronger influence on the likelihood of reoffending than childhood risk factors or risk-focused interventions.	*Criminals Coming of Age* (Bottoms and McClintock 1973)
1985	Social Development Model	Opportunities for, and degree of, involvement and interaction, skills and perceived reinforcements for behaviour, function as broad psychosocial risk categories. These categories interact with cognitive ability, socio-structural status and external constraints to cause antisocial and prosocial behaviour at different developmental stages related to school age (pre-school, elementary, middle and high school).	Hawkins and Weis (1985); Catalano and Hawkins (1996); *Communities that Care* (Hawkins and Catalano 1992); Seattle Social Development Project (Hawkins et al. 2003)

1993	Age-graded theory of informal social control	Informal social controls in the family and school mediate the influence of structural context (structural background factors) and cause stability in offending behaviour in childhood and adolescence. In adulthood, informal social bonds can explain changes in offending over the lifespan, whilst significant transitions and critical life events can function as turning points in the trajectory (pathway, development) of offending over the life course.	*Crime in the Making* (Sampson and Laub 1993)
1997	Ecological	Psychosocial risk factors interact with socio-structural context (e.g. community characteristics, immediate situational factors) in childhood and adolescence to influence offending at different times and in different places. Consequently, risk factors related to individual characteristics and social context should be examined together rather than separately.	Wikström and Loeber (1998; 2000); Sampson *et al.* (1997)
2003	Pathways	Young people identified as at risk of offending have varying patterns of experience over time and can actively construct and negotiate their pathways into and out of crime. Social processes (protection, resilience, resistance) and socio-structural context can mediate risk factors along these pathways.	France and Homel (2007); Webster *et al.* (2006)
2003	Revised age graded theory of informal social control	Risk factors in adulthood are mediated by agency, situational factors, routine activities and cultural and historical context.	Laub and Sampson (2003)
2005	Integrated approaches: DEAT / Situational Action Theory, ICAP	Risk factors in psychosocial and structural domains interact with human agency and situational influences to affect the individual's motivations and decisions to offend. The focus is on contexts and processes surrounding risk factor influence.	Wikström and Butterworth (2006); Wikström (2005, 2008); Farrington (2005, 2007)

Chapter 3

Longitudinal risk factor research in England and Wales – achievements, limitations and potential

The risk factor research movement has been characterised by a number of distinct research strands, each with their own theoretical and methodological bases and biases, which, in turn, have influenced the nature of the research and the conclusions drawn from it. In the previous chapter, these constituent strands of (RFR) were described and their differences and limitations/implications explored. In this chapter the focus shifts to a closer inspection and critical evaluation of the methodologies, scope and conclusions of the major longitudinal risk factor studies in England and Wales.

The most influential RFR in England and Wales (indeed, across the globe) has been longitudinal in design, developmentally based, committed to the factorisation of risk and dependent on statistical analyses to demonstrate the relationship between risk factors and offending. As Crawford and Newburn have noted:

> The study of youth justice and young offenders in the UK is currently dominated by ... highly empirical, relatively technically sophisticated longitudinal studies ... of risk factors. (Crawford and Newburn 2003: 234)

At the heart of the appeal and confidence in this research has been its claims to scientific rigour and the purported ability of the research to identify causal and predictive risk factors for offending. Longitudinal research tracks the development of behaviour (e.g. offending) and experience (e.g. exposure to risk) over a long period of time. In its *retrospective* form, longitudinal research enables an individual's life history to be analysed by looking back and tracing the development of past behaviour up to the present day (e.g. the use of biographical accounts within life course and pathways RFR). In contrast, *prospective* longitudinal designs follow a sample from the present day into the future. The early studies of the Gluecks, for example, adopted a longitudinal design that was both retrospective (looking back on boys' behaviour in childhood and adolescence prior to entering the reformatory or youth court) and prospective (following boys for set periods 'post-parole') (Glueck and Glueck 1930, 1934, 1937). Most longitudinal RFR has tended to be prospective in design. In this type or research, samples of children and young people have been regularly assessed (e.g. annually), typically using interviews with the young people and significant others (e.g. parents, friends, teachers), questionnaires and analysis of official records. Regular episodes of data collection have enabled longitudinal researchers to explore how the (statistical) relationship between risk factors and offending develops over time, typically from early childhood into young adulthood or throughout the life course. Consequently, advocates of RFR have heralded several major potential benefits of longitudinal designs, particularly when compared to one-off cross-sectional RFR, most notably:

- *Causality and prediction* – the measurement of risk factors before offending has taken place has permitted researchers to identify risk factors with purportedly causal and predictive relationships with offending and, therefore, factors that can be targeted by preventative early interventions (see Thornberry and Krohn 2003).

- *Within-individual differences* – analysis of within-individual change (compared to aggregated between-group changes) can increase confidence in the validity of judgments of causality and renders control groups unnecessary because offenders and non-offenders emerge naturally over time (Farrington 2007).

- *Multiplicity of outcomes* – although they can be resource intensive and time consuming, the long-term nature of longitudinal studies enables the collection of more detailed quantitative and qualitative risk factor data from a variety of sources for a multiplicity of outcomes, including those outside of the field of criminology and criminal justice (e.g. social exclusion, school exclusion, teenage pregnancy). Thus, longitudinal research provides the opportunity for the collection of broader, deeper and more sensitive data, plus the facility for more sophisticated and comprehensive analysis (see Farrington 2003).

Research in the social sciences is rarely, however, so clear-cut and definitive. Real world research struggles to approximate the conditions found in laboratories. The relationship between theory and methodology is complex. Research is beset by problems of measurement and issues of quality and validity. Producing findings and reaching conclusions is rarely, if ever, a simple matter of 'reading off' the results of statistical tests (see Armstrong 2004; White 2008). It is important, therefore, to explore the extent to which RFR in England and Wales has been shaped, developed, enhanced, constrained and confused by longitudinal approaches. What are the potential strengths and benefits (or weaknesses and limitations) in longitudinal RFR? Have the potential benefits of longitudinal methodologies been realised by researchers? In other words, has the fanfare surrounding longitudinal RFR in England and Wales and the voracious dissemination and application of its findings, notably in the policy and practice of the Youth Justice System (see Chapter 6 for a detailed discussion of risk assessment and risk-focused crime prevention) actually been underpinned by a valid methodology for identifying and interpreting the influence of risk factors on young people and offending?

There are many important questions that need to be addressed. Firstly, has the research been able to accurately measure the full range of potential risk factors that the young person has been exposed to, whilst simultaneously controlling for the extraneous affects of unmeasured influences on offending? Secondly, have these studies been truly longitudinal in nature in terms of assessing risk across the full life course and building on previous findings at each successive research stage? Conversely, have studies tended to measure causality and predictive utility over a limited period (typically between childhood and young adulthood) and simply retested and replicated a narrow body of early childhood psychosocial risk factors at each stage in a manner more akin to a repeated cross-sectional study? Thirdly, has longitudinal RFR oversimplified and misunderstood the risk–offending relationship through a reductionist and deterministic overemphasis on viewing risk in terms of statistical *factors* that can be readily measured and by privileging developmental understandings of the stable, predictive and definitive (rather than probabilistic) influence of these risk factors identified in early childhood? The findings and conclusions from longitudinal RFR in England and Wales urgently need to be placed in context and evaluated in the light of a deeper understanding of the theoretical inspiration of the research and how it has actually been conducted, analysed and interpreted. To this end, in order to evaluate the achievements to date of longitudinal RFR in England and Wales, a number of key theoretical and methodological questions will be asked of the most high profile studies, specifically:

- What have been the theoretical bases of the main studies and have these been compatible with the research design employed?

- How have risk factors and offending been measured?

- How has data been analysed and what conclusions have been made regarding the prevalence, extent and nature of relationships between risk factors and offending by young people?

- Have these conclusions been justified/legitimised by the methodology employed, the quality of the data and the nature of the analyses?

- Have longitudinal designs offered a sensitive, flexible and valid method of evolving RFR and our understanding of the concept of a risk factor?

Any consideration of the contribution of longitudinal RFR in England and Wales to our understanding of the development of youth offending must start with the Cambridge Study in Delinquent Development. The Cambridge Study is probably the single most influential RFR of all time – certainly within the UK and possibly, also, around the world. It is the study which established and popularised RFR and its influences are to be found in the basis of much, if not all, subsequent RFR. The study has resulted in over one hundred publications and the influence of its results on youth justice policy and practice in England and Wales from the 1990s onwards is unparalleled.

The Cambridge Study in Delinquent Development

The Cambridge Study in Delinquent Development commenced in 1961 under the direction of Donald West at Cambridge University (hence the study name). He was joined in 1969 by David Farrington, who has been the sole director of the study since 1981. Since its inception, the Cambridge Study has been primarily funded by the Home Office and to a lesser degree by the Department of Health.

In *Present Conduct and Future Delinquency*, West (1969) set out the Cambridge Study's main aim 'to trace the influence of community, family and individual factors, as seen at this early age, on personality, performance and social adjustment in later years' (West 1969: 1). The 'early age' in question was 8–10 years of age, which was considered by West to offer a practical compromise once he had ruled out the 'ideal method of starting with a sample of babies' (West 1969: 5). The 'community, family and individual factors' were largely based on the factors that had been identified by the Gluecks and further tested in the Cambridge-Somerville Youth Study as the causes and correlates of youth offending by inner city males. The Cambridge Study's prospective longitudinal design was intended to enable the researchers to trace the emergence and development of offending over time, to explore the key features of the 'criminal career' (i.e. onset, duration, continuity, desistance), to assess the impact of life events on the development of offending and to investigate the extent to which offending in adolescence could be predicted by early life experiences. Within the Cambridge Study, the authors articulated a 'developmental' approach to criminology that was inspired by the (developmental) psychological backgrounds of both directors and, as a consequence, was an approach that sought to locate the causes of crime in individual characteristics that either developed or were present in early childhood.

The Cambridge Study methodology

The Cambridge Study has investigated 'a traditional White, urban, working class sample of British origin' (Farrington 2003: 139). All boys in the sample were born in 1953–1954 in an area of South London, England. The majority of the boys (97 per cent) were from six state primary schools within close proximity to the original research office. The remaining 12 boys were sampled from a local school for the 'educationally subnormal' (Farrington 2003).

Interviews were conducted in school by psychologists when the boys were aged approximately 8–9 years, 10–11 years and 14–15 years. The sample was then interviewed in the study research office by graduate students when aged 16, 18 and 21 years and in their homes at age 25, 32, 46 and 50 years. The entire sample was interviewed at seven of the nine data collection stages, with a sub-sample interviewed at ages 21 and 25 years. The early interviews explored a variety of psychological and social factors in childhood and adolescence, including domestic arrangements, relationships (with parents, siblings and peers), illnesses and injuries, leisure activities, alcohol and drug use, physical fighting and offending behaviour (West and Farrington 1973, 1977). These factors have been subsequently supplemented in the adult interviews (aged 18 years and above) by gathering information on employment histories, adult relationships and children of the sample (Farrington 1988).

A variety of additional research methods have been employed to gather information to complement the interview data, including:

- *In-school tests of individual characteristics* (when the boys were aged from 8–15 years) focused on measuring intelligence, academic attainment, personality traits and level of impulsivity.

- *Annual interviews with parents* (when the boys were aged from 8–15 years) collected information concerning family income, family size, parents' employment histories, child-rearing practices (including attitudes, discipline, parental disharmony), closeness of supervision of the child, separations from the child and child's risk-taking behaviour.

- *Teacher questionnaires* (from when the boys were aged 8–15 years) collected data about the boys' troublesome and aggressive school behaviour, restlessness and poor concentration, school achievement and truancy.

- *Peer ratings* (when the boys were in primary school) measured daring, dishonesty, 'troublesomeness' and popularity.

- *Official statistics* relating to the delinquency rates of boys' secondary schools (from the local education authority) and the offending of sample boys and their parents, siblings, partners and co-offenders (accessed from the Criminal Records Office).

(see Farrington 2003)

In their seminal text *Who Becomes Delinquent?*, West and Farrington (1973) made initial statistical comparisons between sample boys with official criminal records ('delinquents') and those without an official record ('non-delinquents'). The authors acknowledged that this was a 'crude dichotomy', albeit one that 'satisfactorily revealed the essential characteristics of the delinquent group' (West and Farrington 1973: 187). However, West and Farrington had little confidence in the validity and reliability of these characteristics because of the potential for each category to be unrepresentative and misleading, for example, due to the delinquent group containing one-off, trivial offenders and the non-delinquent group containing offenders who had escaped conviction. This ambiguity prompted the formulation of 'a more realistic index of delinquent behaviour' (West and Farrington 1973: 188) combining official criminal records and self-reported offending.

Using statistical comparisons between delinquents and non-delinquents, West and Farrington (1973) attempted to identify *explanatory risk factors* that were measured when the boys were aged 8–10 years and which could be demonstrated to statistically predict future official and self-reported offending at age 14–15 years. In order for a factor to be considered to be 'explanatory', it had to be shown in statistical analyses to precede offending (i.e. have temporal precedence) and significantly statistically predict future offending. Factors that appeared to measure the same underlying theoretical construct as offending (e.g. drug use, antisocial personality) were labelled 'non-explanatory risk factors'. Using these definitions, the range of factors measured when sample members were aged 8–10 years was reduced to a set of approximately 20 'explanatory risk factors' following statistical tests to control for multicollinearity (the statistical phenomenon of different factors measuring the same underlying variable or construct). This set of explanatory risk factors was then entered into statistical regression analyses to explore their effects as *independent predictors* of official and self-reported offending. An explanatory risk factor was considered to have an 'independent' and 'causal' effect on offending if it was still significantly linked to offending 'after controlling for the other possible explanatory variables' (Farrington 2003: 151).

Statistical comparisons between the delinquent and non-delinquent groups have been conducted from the outset of the Cambridge study, with the most recent round of analysis completed in 2006 (Farrington *et al.* 2006).

The Cambridge Study findings and conclusions

In 1973, West and Farrington highlighted five explanatory 'background factors' that were significantly associated with offending independently of all other factors measured in the Cambridge Study: low family income, large family size, parental criminality, low intelligence and poor parental behaviour (West and Farrington 1973). Noting the resemblance between these factors and those identified by the Gluecks through their social prediction table, West and Farrington (1973) concluded that the initial results from the Cambridge Study were 'undramatic and unfashionable' – supportive of previous retrospective studies of the personal and background factors underlying offending. The main conclusion of the *Who Becomes Delinquent* study was that:

> Many of the features that are apparent among older delinquents were demonstrably present by the age of ten and were significantly predictive of future delinquency. (West and Farrington 1973: 189)

However, the authors went on to dramatically qualify and temper their definitive findings and conclusions by cautioning that:

- the Cambridge Study had focused on individual characteristics and so was a 'predominantly psychological enquiry';

- the five key factors identified were 'not necessarily more closely associated with delinquency than some of the others investigated', they were simply more well-defined and more carefully-measured;

- almost every factor investigated 'proved to be associated to some extent with future delinquency';

- factors were predictive only in the sense of them demonstrating an association with delinquency rather than indicating a causal influence.
                                                   (West and Farrington 1973: 189–91)

Each of these post-hoc qualifications of the findings and conclusions raises serious issues regarding the lack of explanatory utility of the key so-called 'predictive' factors in the initial Cambridge Study analysis and, as acknowledged by the authors, 'left the way open for a variety of speculative interpretations' of the data (West and Farrington 1973: 191).

In his book *Delinquency*, West (1982) introduced an important developmental milestone into the Cambridge Study by attempting to identify factors that appeared to protect the boys against the development of offending. When the sample boys were aged around 30 years, the study first reported on these so-called *protective factors* (West 1982; see also Farrington 1988). Protective factors in the Cambridge Study were divided into two separate, yet closely associated groups – factors that appeared to protect against the *onset* of offending in the first place and factors that encouraged *desistance* from offending once it had begun. Factors protecting against the onset of offending were assessed by exploring the lives of the 25 per cent of boys who scored highly on a 'vulnerability' (to future offending) measure in childhood but who had not been convicted of an offence by the age of 32 years (Farrington 1988). Analyses identified that at age 8–10 years, being nervous, having a shy, introverted personality and being rated favourably by their mothers appeared to insulate boys against future offending and predicted an increased likelihood of living a successful and prosocial life at age 32 years. Factors promoting desistance by existing offenders (official and self-reported) were typically centred on influential life events such as moving away from London (West 1982), marriage or partnership with a prosocial, non-convicted female and spending less or no time with delinquent peers.

When the boys were aged 32 years, Farrington (1990) re-analysed the Cambridge Study data. He established that the best independent pre-dictors (measured when the boys were aged between 8–18 years) of convictions at age 32 were troublesomeness, having a convicted parent, high daring, academic underachievement, poor housing and separation from a parent (see also Farrington 2003). Farrington has since concluded that 'the best predictors of convictions tended also to be the best predictors of the worst self-reported offenders ... of 39 key risk factors measured between ages 8 and 18 years, 35 were significantly related to both official and self-reported delinquency' (Farrington 2003: 154).

Since drawing the original 'crude dichotomy' between official delin-quents and non-delinquents, Farrington has attempted to distinguish independent predictors at age 8–10 years for *persistent* young offenders (three or more convictions). The best independent predictors of persistent offenders (compared to *occasional* offenders with one or two convictions) have been identified as low family income, poor concentration, lack of parental involvement in the boy's leisure activities, low socio-economic status and having delinquent siblings (Farrington 1999). Persistent offend-ing (compared to non-offending) from the age of 21 years and beyond was significantly predicted by low verbal intelligence at age 8–10 years, lack of parental involvement in the boy's leisure activities at age 12 years, unemployment at age 16 years and heavy drinking at age 18 years (Farrington and Hawkins 1991).

In a review of the legacy of the Cambridge Study, Farrington (2003: 153) has subsequently claimed that the 'most important predictors, at age 8–10 years, of later offending (whether measured by convictions or by self-reports) could be divided into six categories of theoretical constructs':

- *Antisocial behaviour in childhood* – including troublesomeness, dishonesty, aggressiveness.

- *Hyperactivity-impulsivity-attention deficit* – including poor concentration, restlessness, high daring (risk-taking), psychomotor impulsivity.

- *Low intelligence* and *low school achievement*.

- *Family criminality* – including convicted parents, delinquent older siblings, siblings with behaviour problems.

- *Family poverty* – including low family income, large family size, poor housing.

- *Poor parenting* – including harsh and authoritarian discipline, poor supervision, parental conflict, separation from parents.

(see Farrington 2003)

Following re-interviews with the boys at age 50 years, Farrington *et al.* (2006) have identified four distinct groups within the Cambridge sample: *persisters* (convicted before and after the age of 21 years), *desisters* (convicted before the age of 21 years only), *late-onset* (first convicted at age 21 years or older) and *unconvicted* (never convicted). The independent predictors for persisters (compared to unconvicted sample members) were having a convicted parent, high daring, having a delinquent sibling, low popularity, coming from a disrupted family and large family size. The independent predictors for desisters (compare to unconvicted) were poor housing, having a convicted parent, high daring, low academic attainment in junior school, high nervousness and coming from a disrupted family. Finally, the predictors for late-onset males compared to those unconvicted were poor housing and low non-verbal IQ.

The findings presented above give a flavour of the widely-reported results from the Cambridge Study. All in all, the various incremental additions to the Cambridge Study analyses in terms of exploring protective factors, predictors of different elements of the criminal career (e.g. persistence, late-onset, desistance) and predictors of offending at different ages, have remained faithful to and have consolidated, Farrington's developmental hypothesis that risk factors identified in early childhood can predict future delinquency. However, analysis of the Cambridge data has not been entirely developmental. One notable exception was a study published in 1986 by Farrington, Gallagher, Morley, St. Ledger and West in which they examined the impact of unemployment and school leaving on offending (between the ages of 16–18 years). The authors concluded that offending was higher amongst the sample members during periods of unemployment, but slightly lower once the boys had left school, suggesting that the influence of risk factors was stronger in current life and late adolescence/early adulthood than in childhood.

Criticisms of the Cambridge Study

Not surprisingly, given its prominence within RFR, the Cambridge Study has attracted a considerable amount of critique. Indeed, the Study's main author, David Farrington, has recognised a number of limitations within the study's methodology, such as:

- failing to investigate the potentially confounding effects of repeated testing episodes on the sample members (e.g. the 'social desirability bias' of boys predicting the required answers to interview questions; the 'retrospective bias' of current responses being influenced by responses in previous data collection episodes);

- using 'inadequate' measures of biological, individual and neighbourhood factors, making it impossible to investigate the interaction between individual development and neighbourhood context;

- failing to maintain a consistent and equitable focus on protective factors, resilience, strengths and positive outcomes from the Study's outset, because far more was known at the time about the influence of risk factors on negative outcomes.

(Farrington 2003: 168–70)

It could be argued that the limitations acknowledged by Farrington have been little more than self-administered friendly fire as he has sought to head off some of his more strident critics. Indeed, Farrington has subsequently addressed many of his self-criticisms (with varying degrees of success and attention) or brushed them off. The potentially-confounding effects of repeated testing, for example, could have seriously damaged the internal validity and reliability of every single finding from the Cambridge Study, but this concern has since disappeared into the ether – as if it has been assuaged by the widespread replicability of the findings. The use of 'inadequate' measures and poor quality measurement are serious threats to the validity of the research and its conclusions, yet these issues remain largely unexplored. Likewise, the inability to measure the interaction between individual development and neighbourhood context (a central premise of subsequent life course, ecological and integrated stands of RFR) has been seemingly relegated to the background because subsequent analysis has identified the significance of individual childhood risk factors on offending. Finally, the reason why more is known about risk than protection within RFR is precisely because protective factors have not been studied in any depth and almost always in terms of risk, rather than independently – the risk dependent protective factor paradox. The Cambridge Study has not been so much atheoretical as unconcerned with reflecting on its own theoretical preferences for developmental understandings of risk factors. Accordingly, Farrington's self-criticisms have been overwhelmingly methodological rather than theoretical and focused on study administration and the definition of constructs, whilst leaving the main conclusions largely untouched.

Numerous other methodological criticisms have been levelled at the Cambridge Study. These criticisms have, in the main, been acknowledged by Farrington, but have been far more difficult to deflect as they strike at the heart of the weaknesses and biases of the Cambridge Study, particularly in relation to:

- *Urban-bias* – the original sample was taken from an inner-city area, so the findings cannot be assumed to be representative of boys from rural or mixed (urban/rural) areas – or for girls at all. Not only that, but the inner city in question was a small area of a larger city (London), so findings may only be representative of the opportunity sample of young males drawn from that specific local area at that specific time (see also Muncie 2004).

- *Class-bias* – West and Farrington focused on an entirely working-class sample, so their findings were not necessarily applicable or transferable to young people from, for example, middle-class neighbourhoods (see Armstrong 2004). The significance of this class bias in sampling is amplified when interpreting the results of the research. Research with young people from a particular stratum of society who are known to possess specific characteristics (e.g. the presence of multiple risk factors) will almost inevitably confirm the presence of many these characteristics and their statistical salience for explaining delinquency (Haines 1999). Thus, the research becomes little more than a distorted self-fulfilling prophecy,

- *Outdated* – the key risk factors in the study (with the notable exception of the unemployment study – Farrington *et al.* 1986) were identified when the boys were aged 8–10 years (in the late 1950s, early 1960s). It is important, therefore, to ask: 'How useful is data about the experience of early childhood and adolescence in the 1950s for an understanding of youth today?' (Haines 1999: 266). It is an inevitability that developmental longitudinal research rapidly loses the ability to capture the importance/impact of social change. This tendency has been exacerbated in the Cambridge Study as subsequent analyses of current behaviour have been related to the presence of risk factors prevalent in early childhood. The Cambridge Study has, consequently, tended to resemble a repeated cross-sectional survey more than a longitudinal design due to its relentless focus on replicating the same set of childhood psychosocial risk factors over the life course, rather than adopting a reflexive and adaptable methodology that has built incrementally on the findings at each successive stage in true longitudinal fashion (e.g. seeking to identify and test a new set of risk factors at each measurement episode). This has limited the study to drawing conclusions restricted to the continued predictive validity of childhood risk factors (and a very limited group of factors measured in adulthood – see Farrington 1988) rather than identifying risk factors that may have salience at different stages over the life-course.

- *Psychosocial-bias* – in terms of the data collected, there has been a distinct bias towards psychological (e.g. emotional, cognitive) and social factors (with 'social' typically taken to mean family, school and neighbourhood-based), particularly the role of family-based risk factors. This familial bias was reflected in West and Farrington's early claim that 'delinquency arises from a complex interaction between the individual home atmosphere, the personal qualities of the boy and the circumstances in which the family live' (West and Farrington 1973: 201). However, this psychosocial bias has come at the expense of exploring the broader socio-political, economic, cultural and historical context in which the behaviour of the boys has taken place during the study (see Armstrong 2004; Pitts 2003a).

- *Developmental determinism* – the Cambridge Study has privileged early life experiences and developmental milestones as explanatory factors for offending in later life (Webster *et al.* 2006). According to Pitts (2003a: 83), this 'transforms crime, a dynamic, interactive process, into a static 'effect' of developmental anomalies' and imputes a determinism, which leads to the conclusion that if one wishes to change teenage behaviour it is necessary to intervene at an earlier age. This determinism has implicitly neglected the possibility of influential risk factors emerging in adolescence and adulthood and/or being amenable to change by the young person, rejecting the potential for a young person to construct and actively respond to risk, thus writing off as hopeless and helpless any young person displaying problems at a later age. As a consequence, determinism has evolved into fatalism, thus diminishing its explanatory power and practical, ameliorative potential.

- *Androcentrism* and *ethnocentrism* – the Cambridge Study has produced findings and conclusions from research conducted exclusively with males (Armstrong 2004), which have then been applied to females in an uncritical fashion (see, for example, Farrington and Painter 2004). Such androcentrism disallows investigation of potential gender-specificity and gender differences in the salience, application, operation, influence and interpretation of risk factors. Similarly, the presentation of findings as representative of risk for all adolescent boys, despite the original sample consisting almost entirely of *white* boys (from an industrialised Western country), imbues the Cambridge Study's conclusions with an unhelpful and invalidating ethnocentrism.

These criticisms have reflected the degree to which West and Farrington adopted the content of the Gluecks' methodology, analysis, findings and conclusions in an uncritical and wholesale manner and applied these to a younger sample in another culture 30 years later, without questioning the validity or applicability of the Gluecks' original risk factors for the Cambridge sample. However, two specific methodological issues have yet to be addressed by Farrington or critics of the Cambridge Study, yet require acknowledgement and further exploration:

- *Crude measures of delinquency* – despite West and Farrington's (1973) original acknowledgement of the crude dichotomy between official delinquents and non-delinquents and their subsequent attempts to formulate a more 'realistic' measure of delinquency as the combination of official and self-reported offending, Farrington has continued to prioritise the investigation of risk factors for official delinquency (convictions) over a combined measure of delinquency. This once again raises the issues initially acknowledged by West and Farrington (1973), namely that official records do not and cannot represent the dark figure of unreported and unrecorded offending, so any statistical contrasts between official offenders and unconvicted sample members (some of whom may have offended but not have been caught or convicted) are likely to be unrepresentative and thus invalid. This criticism also applies to the subsequent analysis of different types of convicted offender (e.g. persistent, occasional, desistent, late-onset) which, although more sensitive than the crude homogenisation of delinquents and non-delinquents, remains wedded to the inherent limitations of relying on official measures of delinquency. Any claim to identify risk factors for offending is only as good (valid) as the measure of offending used.

- *Predictive invalidity* – the psychosocial background factors linked to future delinquency in the Cambridge Study have been labelled 'risk factors' and 'independent predictors' in each iteration of the study on the basis that the longitudinal design used has enabled the authors to ascribe temporal precedence to these factors (measured at age 8–10 years) over delinquency (measured at age 14–15 years and onwards). However, this ostensible temporal precedence only relates to the ages at which the factors and delinquency were measured, rather than necessarily indicating temporal precedence in the onset of, or exposure to, the factors. For example, because delinquency was not measured until the age of 14–15 years, this allows for the possibility that it had occurred before then, even if it had not yet been officially-recorded or self-reported. If this was the case, then initial episodes of delinquency in the boys' lives could have actually pre-dated the so-called predictive risk factors or delinquency and risk factors could have occurred concurrently. Even if the temporal precedence of these factors could have been established (which it was not) or could be taken for granted (which it should not), temporal precedence alone only equates to 'causation as a regular association' (Wikström 2008) and is insufficient to explain the presence or nature of any potential influence of these factors on offending other than in their role as correlates.

The Cambridge Study as RFR

When reflecting on the value of the Cambridge Study and its contribution to criminological RFR in the light of existing criticism, Farrington asserted that 'the benefits of this project in advancing knowledge have greatly outweighed its costs' (Farrington 2003: 172). This is a substantial claim and, indeed, one that must be tested. This is particularly so, because, beyond the body of existing criticism, the basis of the Cambridge Study, its findings and the presentations of its results have been contested. It is one thing, for example, to show that certain childhood risk factors are statistically predictive of offending in adolescence, it is quite another thing to claim that 'antisocial children tend to grow up into antisocial adults'. One of the major apparent strengths of the Cambridge Study has been the consistency with which childhood risk factors have been related to later offending. As such, the stability and continuity in offending behaviour found in the sample members between the ages of 18–32 years has been somewhat contradictory to Sampson and Laub's claims of change over the life course and has offered strong support for the existence of an 'antisocial potential' (see Farrington's ICAP theory) underpinned by childhood risk factors that are predictive of future self-reported and official offending (cf. Farrington 2003). On the other hand, it could be that Farrington's sample simply never changed their circumstances significantly (e.g. due to low social mobility or the impact of socio-structural factors not measured by the study), yet Sampson and Laub's sample (i.e. the Gluecks' original sample) did. Taken alone, Farrington's research cannot resolve this issue and, as such, its claims to have advanced knowledge must be questioned.

Another major claim, attesting to the validity and robustness of the Cambridge Study, is that it has been the pursuit of pure science, unencumbered by sociological theory or the biases of the researchers. This is patently untrue – at least in part. Theoretically, the study has progressed the developmental understanding of risk factors as predictive of offending first mooted by the Gluecks. More so, the study's adherence to developmentalism is based on a counterfactual (and arguably biased) reading of the Gluecks' results concerning the significance of maturation. The Cambridge study is thus avowedly theoretically informed and has been significantly shaped by this researcher bias. This, in itself, is not necessarily surprising. Only the most ardent of positivists would claim that research is anything other than a social product. But to deny the influence of theory and researcher bias and to claim a hegemony of knowledge is disingenuous and acts to prevent a full and proper evaluation of the contribution of particular studies to the wider production of social scientific knowledge – it acts to obfuscate and not to advance knowledge. If nothing else, theory informs researchers' decisions about what data is to be collected. As developmentally informed psychologists, therefore, West and Farrington quite naturally focused their data collection on psychosocial variables to the exclusion of structural or sociological variables. Any conclusions they draw, therefore, are inevitably partial and need to be understood and interpreted in this context.

Turning to methodology and to the appliance of scientific methods to the collection of data, a mixed picture emerges here too. For its time, the Cambridge Study represented a robust and innovative methodology, initially constructed by Donald West and subsequently taken on by David Farrington. The major strengths of the Cambridge Study lie in its prospective longitudinal design and its capacity to access multiple sources of information, both official and self-reported, both quantitative and qualitative. The use of multiple sources of data (interviews with children, parents, teachers, official and self-reported measures of offending, psychological testing) represented comprehensive and robust data collection processes enabling the study findings to be triangulated, thus enhancing the validity and reliability of subsequent analysis. The factorisation of this information over a significant period of time and the use of multivariate analysis has enabled the authors to simplify the complex and copious information obtained from these multiple sources and to statistically identify predictive risk factors for offending in the psychosocial domains of young people's lives (especially the family and school). The standardised methodology, which has included the collection of data from the same sources, using the same methods, the factorisation of this data and subsequent analysis using the same techniques, has facilitated the long-term, consistent replication (and ostensibly the validation) of a small group of influential developmental risk factors for offending. Such has been the accord afforded to the Cambridge Study that its methodology has been vigorously replicated and pursued by a new generation of risk factor researchers eager to produce replicable, generalisable and easily digestible understandings of risk factors for offending that can inform evidence-based policy and practice development.

The methodology of the Cambridge Study also imported and utilised some questionable techniques. To be accepted as valid and robust, the findings of RFR depend, in part, on the processes of factorisation. The central question here is the extent to which factorisation represents or distorts 'reality'. There are those critics (see O'Mahoney 2008; Armstrong 2004; Pitts 2003a) who oppose factorisation for its reductionism and the way in which dynamic processes are reduced to static statistical relationships. It is likely that such critics would never be convinced by the processes of factorisation – despite the fact that some form of measurement of social phenomena is fundamental to the social sciences. The crucial question, of course, concerns the quality or robustness of these measures. The use of multiple data sources and multiple measures in the Cambridge Study has already been mentioned and has been widely reported (e.g. Farrington 1988, 1990, 2000, 2007). However, nowhere in the vast number of publications emanating from the Cambridge Study have the processes of factorisation been described or discussed. Precisely how varied data from multiple sources has been factorised is, therefore, unknown. This is a surprising omission on the part of Farrington and others as publishing this information could strike at one of the most vehement objections to RFR. That this information has not been published does, however, lead one to question whether publication would, in fact, assuage the critics. The problem is, we cannot judge and this is not in the interests of science or the advancement of knowledge. The suspicion is, of course, as Farrington conceded, many of the measures used were in fact 'inadequate' and these inadequate measures have been translated, somehow, into quantifiable and testable constructs. The distance travelled between social reality and artefactual risk factors may, indeed, be great.

Designing a study and collecting the data are, of course, only part of the research process. Data must be analysed to produce results and these results must be interpreted to produce findings which convey the ultimate contribution to knowledge resulting from the research. It is at this point that theory and methodology collide. It would have been perfectly possible, for example, for Farrington to analyse his data to explore the cumulative effect of risk factors over the life course for offending behaviour – and who knows what results would have been obtained? As a developmental psychologist, however, Farrington has privileged statistical tests which examined the relationship between early childhood risk factors and offending behaviour to the exclusion of other potentially explanatory theories. His results, therefore, and the interpretation of his results have been in accord with the theory that informed the development of the research. This is, of course, an entirely normal and appropriate process. As a developmental psychologist/criminologist, Farrington is perfectly justified, even obliged, to analyse his data in terms of his developmental theoretical underpinnings and to evaluate and interpret his findings in this manner. There is a further obligation, however, on Farrington and others, to place these findings in their own and a broader context in order to evaluate the contribution they make to understanding.

Are the results sufficiently strong and robust to support the theory and justify its continued use? Is the theory itself strong and robust enough to make sense of all the results? Are there other research results which cause us to modify or mitigate use of the theory? In the case of the Cambridge Study: the results, as they have been presented, are unequivocal. On the other hand, Farrington's theoretical position that the factors present in early childhood determine behaviour in adolescence, for many people, stretches credibility. Indeed, there now exists a body of research evidence counter-factual to this crash test dummy thesis that, at the very least, urges extreme caution in generalising the basic conclusions from the Cambridge Study.

The question arises – has the Cambridge Study actually restricted the development of RFR by introducing and exacerbating a series of method-ological paradoxes? For example, the simplicity of its findings and conclusions has been, in part, a product of an overriding confidence in the definitive developmental influence of childhood risk factors on adolescent offending. This simplicity and confidence has led to a widespread acceptance of a relatively short, limited and determinate list of risk factors considered to be predictive of offending. However, the emphasis on early childhood risk factors has been restrictive because it references the developmental philosophy almost to the total exclusion of the possibility that risk factors identified at a later stage of the life course may be influential on offending (see Webster *et al.* 2006). Indeed, the very representation of 8–10 years of age as 'early childhood' is a potentially problematic foundation for the developmental strand (certainly one that has yet to be adequately acknowledged or explored) because it has served as an artificial cut-off, excluding the examination of risk factors present, *inter alia*, before that age (e.g. from birth – see Moffitt 2006).

The simplistic oversimplification of the Cambridge Study findings has also resulted from the pervasive factorisation of complex risk data central to the methodology and analyses. This factorisation has washed away any qualitative benefits of the data and stripped it of any utility beyond the statistical. Nowhere has this oversimplification been more evident than in the use of complex multivariate analyses to reduce 150 risk factors (obtained using multiple measures of risk from multiple sources over long periods) to six predictive risk factors measured at a specific age in childhood and replicated thereafter in the Study. Armstrong (2004) has asserted that the identification of predictors of offending in the Cambridge Study has been 'too easy' and that the study was empirically-limited. This was exemplified in the conclusion that the study was unable to predict offending in the majority of actual subsequent offenders (Katz 1988). Consequently, Armstrong (2004) has questioned the validity of making predictions of offending on the basis of the Cambridge Study findings.

Indeed, there are deeper methodological and analytical reasons for questioning the predictive validity and utility of the Cambridge Study. The aggregation of data employed to facilitate ready comparisons between two broad groups (offenders and non-offenders) has perpetuated the methodological shortcut of aggregation introduced into RFR by the Gluecks. Thus the primary form of analysis of the Cambridge Study data has been to identify 'between-group' differences in the prevalence of risk factors (offenders versus non-offenders) and to rely on these to help explain delinquency, rather than a detailed and sensitive within-individual analysis which explains (changes in) the behaviour of an individual. Without this within-individual analysis, 'causal' or 'predictive' risk factors can only be identified at group level and are, therefore, not necessarily applicable to any individual member of that group – thus reducing the validity of the research in providing an explanation of delinquency. Between-group analyses and within-individual analyses are very different constructs, with the former being much weaker than the latter in terms of being able to explain behaviour, particularly the behaviour of specific individuals. It is thus much easier to find (or replicate) common risk factors across groups of young people, yet these risk factors are inherently unrepresentative of the individual sample members. This raises an important question: if identified risk factors cannot actually predict the behaviour of a specific young person then should they really be viewed as predictive or explanatory risk factors at all? Similarly, if the researcher has little or no control (other than statistical control) over the variables being measured (and not being measured), which is particularly likely in real world social research, then are the childhood risk factors linked to future offending actually explanatory in any substantive, conclusive sense, or must explanations be inevitably based on imputation?

The Cambridge Study in Delinquent Development has been the theoretical and empirical driving force behind longitudinal (and some cross-sectional) RFR in England and Wales and beyond. It has evolved RFR methodologically and consolidated developmental understandings of the influence of risk factors, notably in psychosocial domains, by interpreting the outcomes of regression analyses of the statistical links between risk factors in childhood and offending in adolescence. The predictive risk factors identified within the study have exerted a powerful influence over virtually all subsequent RFR. It is these early childhood findings that have inspired risk factor researchers and found their way into the consciousness (and hence policy making) of politicians and senior government policy makers, who have been attracted by the longevity of the Cambridge Study, the commonsense nature of its findings and the confidence with which Farrington has reported on their replicability and ostensible validity (see Chapter 6 for fuller discussion). However, the degree of confidence in, and acceptance of, the findings and conclusions of the Cambridge Study by present-day researchers and policy makers is deeply concerning. Whilst exemplifying some robust methodological developments (notably a prospective longitudinal design and the use of multiple data sources), the study has been:

- weak and inhibited in its theoretical underpinnings – notably the adherence to developmentalism;

- unduly influenced by researcher bias – notably in a selective reading of previous research, assumptions about the nature of the risk-factor–offending relationship and in sampling from a restricted population likely to evidence developmental deficits;

- uncritically pragmatic – notably in arbitrarily choosing 8–10 year olds as providing the baseline for the measurement of developmental risk factors;

- analytically relatively unsophisticated – notably the excessive use of crude factorisation, using multivariate analysis to identify a restricted range of predictive risk factors for offending and an over-reliance on between-group comparisons.

These weaknesses have been exacerbated by the alacrity with which simplistic conclusions have been drawn and promoted to ease communication and comprehension (Farrington 2000), when these have been neither justified nor sustained by the research. Overall and taken together, the critical review presented here makes it impossible to agree with the statement that: 'the benefits of this project in advancing knowledge have greatly outweighed its costs'. The costs are too great and the evidence base is simply too weak to support the popular conclusions of the Cambridge Study.

The Offending, Crime and Justice Survey

The Home Office-commissioned Offending, Crime and Justice Survey (OCJS) began in 2003. The aim of this longitudinal survey has been to measure 'levels and trends in youth offending, antisocial behaviour and victimisation amongst young people aged from ten to 25 living in the general household population in England and Wales' (Wilson *et al*. 2006: 12). The OCJS authors have also stated a particular interest in obtaining data 'to identify the risk factors associated with the onset and continuation of offending and drug use, and factors associated with desistance' (Budd *et al*. 2005a: 1).

It is quite difficult to characterise the OCJS and to place it within the overall development of RFR. On the one hand, the study has adopted a longitudinal design (which is capable, at least in theory, of identifying causal or predictive relationships between risk factors and offending), yet on the other hand, the authors have claimed only to be interested in identifying risk factors *associated* with offending (a weaker and more restricted form of analysis typical of cross-sectional research). Neither characteristic is, however, justified or explained. What the research will do has been described by the authors, but why and for what purpose has been left unexplained. Moreover, the OCJS reports do not situate the research within any particular strand of RFR. Is it developmentally based (cf. Farrington) or life-course based (cf. Sampson and Laub) or something else? The authors do not discuss these matters or explain their influences. The original OCJS report (Budd *et al.* 2005a) does make reference to what it sees as important RFR, particularly the longitudinal studies in Cambridge and Edinburgh (see Smith and McAra 2004) and the cross-sectional Peterborough Youth Study (Wikström and Butterworth 2006), Youth Lifestyles Survey (Flood-Page *et al.* 2000) and the International Self-Reported Delinquency survey (Junger-Tas *et al.* 2003), but it stops short of any explicit statement about its reference point – thus making it difficult to properly situate and evaluate the research. Reading between the lines, however, and focusing on those studies referred to and those left out, a deference to developmentalism and developmentally identified risk factors may be imputed. Indeed, such a developmental focus is perhaps unsurprising as Farrington conducted the initial scoping/literature review that informed the study. The prioritisation of the developmental studies cited suggests, by omission, that the OCJS has been less influenced/ interested in the social development perspective, life-course or constructivist RFR – but this can only be inferred as the authors have neglected to address such issues.

In terms of developing the content of its questionnaire, the OCJS appears to have been heavily influenced by the Cambridge Study (indeed, Farrington served as a peer reviewer for the original OCJS questionnaire). The OCJS seems to have uncritically accepted and adopted the definitive list of risk factors for offending produced by the Cambridge Study, supplemented by administrative, Home Office-driven, concerns such as 'attitudes to the police'. Again, however, these can only be inferences as the authors were not explicit on such matters. Indeed, overall, the OCJS reports generally fail to situate the research within the wider context of RFR, to address the sorts of issues or research questions one might expect of longitudinal RFR or to explain the purpose of the research beyond the fairly bland statements reported above. The research, therefore, has been theoretically and empirically under-developed and somewhat pragmatic, uncritical/ill-informed and unsophisticated.

The OCJS methodology

An original nationally-representative sample of 5,000 young people aged 10–25 years was divided into sub-groups based on age (10–15 years old and 16–25 years old) and the sample members have completed questionnaires annually in 2003 (Budd *et al.* 2005a), 2004 (Budd *et al.* 2005b) and 2005 (Wilson *et al.* 2006). These questionnaires have addressed self-reported offending and other self-reported problem behaviours (drug use, alcohol use, antisocial behaviour) and contact with and attitudes to the Criminal Justice System. Additionally, individual and social background factors (reported as 'risk factors') have been measured in the 2004 and 2005 questionnaires and have been focused on the domains of:

- *Perceptions of local area* – attitudes to local area, disorder problems, trust in police;

- *Lifestyle and behaviour* – antisocial behaviour, offending, drug taking, alcohol use, victimisation, impulsivity, attitudes to offending;

- *Family and friends* – relationships with, been in trouble with the police, household income, attitude to antisocial behaviours, parenting skills;

- *School* – standard of teaching, affection for, suspension/expulsion.
    (see Budd *et al.* 2005b; Wilson *et al.* 2006)

Offending, other problem behaviours (e.g. drug use) and exposure to risk factors have been measured by the annual OCJS questionnaire in terms of their occurrence in the previous 12 months. Offending has been measured as a dichotomous variable (offended in the past year – yes or no) from responses to an inventory of 20 core offences. *Frequent* offending has been measured as having committed six or more different offences in the past year (although this is more a measure of versatility than frequency) and *serious* offending measured as the young person having committed any one of six serious offences on the inventory (vehicle theft, burglary, robbery, theft from person, assault resulting in injury, selling class A drugs). Measures of risk factors have been generally derived from a number of constituent statements; for example, the factor *perception of parenting skills* consisted of five sub-factors/statements:

- my parent(s) usually praise me when I have done well;

- my parent(s) usually listen to me when I want to talk;

- my parent(s) usually treat me fairly when I have done something wrong;

- my parent(s) usually want to know where I am when I am not at home;

- my parent(s) often argue or fight with each other.
    (Budd *et al.* 2005b)

In the OCJS questionnaire, there has been significant variability between the number of constituent statements for each so-called risk factor, the size of the response scale used and the method of coding the total scores for each factor as either risk or protection (although this tended to be through simple dichotomisation – see below). For example in the *family and friends* section, the number of constituent statements, size of response scale and scoring of totals differed for:

- *Perceptions of parents' parenting skills* – four statements, each coded either one (good) or two (bad). From the total scores across the statements, a dichotomous variable was created, with scores of 5–6 labelled as 'good' parenting skills (a protective factor), whilst seven and above indicated 'poor' parenting skills (a risk factor).

- *Parents' perceived attitude to certain behaviours* – four statements, each using a three-point response scale (1 = 'parents would mind a lot' through to 3 = 'parents would not mind at all'). A dichotomous variable was created within which scores of 4–6 indicated attitudes not favourable to delinquency (protective factor) and scores of 7–12 indicated attitudes favourable to delinquency (risk factor).

- *Gets/got on with parents when aged 10–16 years* – three statements using a yes/no response scale, with scores recoded as 'gets/got on well with parents' (protective) or 'gets/got on badly with a least one parent' (risk).

- *Time spent with parents* – one question with five possible responses (all, most, some, little, none), recoded and dichotomised as 'spends all or most free time with parents' (protective) or 'spends some, little or no time with parents' (risk).

There has been an evident insensitivity in coding and analysis due to the persistent dichotomisation of responses into positive and negative categories, with no opportunity to record responses that may be neutral, scaled (e.g. quite good, very bad), context-dependent, contingent or variable/ dynamic. To compound the insensitivity of the dichotomisation of total scores for each factor, the range of scores obtained by the OCJS has been simply and crudely split in half, such that there may only be a one point difference between a score coded as indicating risk and one coded as indicating protection. No attempt has been made to conduct a more sensitive form of dichotomisation, such as splitting the range of scores into quarters and making statistical comparisons between the top and bottom quarter of scores (a process employed elsewhere in RFR – see, for example, Anderson *et al.* 2001).

The OCJS findings and conclusions

Having totalled and dichotomised risk factor scores, regression analyses have been used to examine the statistical correlations between risk factors and offending. The 2004 and 2005 rounds of the OCJS have identified factors 'independently statistically associated' (Wilson *et al.* 2006) with a conflated category of 'serious and frequent offending' (in the past 12 months) amongst both age groups (Budd *et al.* 2005b; Wilson *et al.* 2006). The following factors have been statistically associated with offending for both age groups (10–15 years and 16–25 years) in both 2004 and 2005:

- having been a victim of personal crime in the last year;

- committing antisocial behaviour in the last year;

- having friends or siblings in trouble with the police;

- taking any drug in the last year.

Other reported statistical associations between risk factors and offending were: 'being drunk once a month or more in the last year' (associated with offending by both age groups in 2004 and by 10–15 year olds in 2005) and 'most likely to think that criminal acts are OK' (associated with offending by both age groups 2004 and by 16–25 year olds in 2005).

Several other factors were associated with offending by young people in the 2004 OCJS, notably 'suspension or expulsion from school' and 'not trusting the local police' (associated with offending by both age groups). In addition, for 10–15 year olds in 2004, 'gets/got on badly with parents', 'perceptions of poor parenting skills', 'spends little/no free time with parents' and 'parents' attitudes favourable to delinquency' were all associated with offending. These results, however, were not replicated in the 2005 study.

The OCJS as RFR

Some fairly major problems with the OCJS have already been set out above. It is, paradoxically, quite difficult to evaluate and critique a piece of research that is so bland and lacking in detail concerning its central purpose (which some suggest was to offer a measure of self-reported offending to complement the victimisation focus of the British Crime Survey – Hine, personal communication). Researchers need to state and justify their aims in order to fully permit any critical review of their actual achievements. However, setting aside, as much as is possible, the issues raised above, the OCJS claimed to be interested in 'identifying the risk factors associated with the onset and continuation of offending and drug use, and factors associated with desistance' (cf. Budd *et al.* 2005) and this claim must now be evaluated.

As the first longitudinal RFR study of a nationally representative sample of young people in England and Wales, the OCJS has a number of clear potential strengths. For example, like all longitudinal RFR, the OCJS has the potential to conduct within-individual analysis to explore the causal or predictive influence of risk factors on the pathways and criminal careers of individual young people. The breadth and scope of the sample could also enable more sensitive analyses of the salience of these factors for young people of different ages, genders and ethnicity – groups that have been relatively neglected by traditionally aggregated, androcentric and ethnocentric RFR. However, the potential methodological advantages of the longitudinal survey have been largely overlooked in the OCJS. Rather than cumulatively exploring the influence of risk factors on offending behaviour by building on successive data collection episodes and subjecting the data to a cumulative and reflexive evaluation in terms of specific age groups, genders, types of offence etc, the OCJS has simply repeated the same survey of crudely factorised and dichotomised psychosocial risks each year with two broad age groups (who may not necessarily contain the same members each time). Crude implementation has reduced a longitudinal research design into a cross-sectional study which is incapable of addressing questions of causality. For example, on the basis of their findings, the authors could correctly assert that asking young people about offending and risk factors from the previous 12 months of their life has produced results that are 'live' and relevant to the young people who have reported them. However, their utility as explanatory constructs is highly questionable, as the nature and direction of the relationship between these crude, dichotomised (risk) factors and homogenised measures of offending cannot be established from the narrow cross-sectional methodology used – an approach which has not explored issues of temporal precedence between the appearance of 'factors' in the past year and offending in the past year. Therefore, the OCJS has been unable to establish whether the factors associated with offending have any actual causal or predictive influence on offending or, indeed, whether they are 'risk' factors at all.

Furthermore, the analytical power of the OCJS has been limited by the decision to conflate the categories of serious offending and frequent offending into an holistic measure of 'offending'. These distinct categories of serious and frequent offending are not comparable nor even necessarily compatible, thus any risk factors statistically linked to a generalised measure of offending lack sensitivity. There is thus not only a reduced ability to show which factors are related to which outcomes – serious or frequent offending, but statistical analysis is more likely to produce correlations between independent and dependent variables when the dependent variable is so widely and loosely defined. Lack of confidence in the explanatory utility of the OCJS is the inevitable result.

The OCJS also makes extensive use of aggregation. Despite its alleged longitudinal design, this research has yet to be used to attempt any within-individual analysis (e.g. measurement of within-individual change), preferring instead to report on general trends in offending and risk factors for offending within two aggregated age groups. The 5,000 young people who have been purportedly tracked across the separate administrations of the questionnaire have not necessarily even been the same young people each time, as the OCJS has adopted a rotating panel survey design which has replaced lost sample members with new members each year. For example, approximately 2000 young people dropped out of the original 2003 sample, necessitating their replacement by new sample members in the 2004 OCJS and in 2005, 817 new sample members were added to replace dropouts from the previous year. Consequently, the risk factors identified in each round of the study have not necessarily been predictive of offending even at an aggregated group level because the makeup and nature of each age group has changed each year.

Moreover, the two broad age ranges (10–15 years and 16–25 years) employed in analysing aggregate results have been crudely treated as though they were homogenous groups, with all young people across each age group sharing common characteristics etc – as opposed to broad and varied groups of young people with potentially important physical, psychological, social, cultural and economic differences between their respective members. For example, can it possibly be valid to assert in an uncritical fashion that ten year olds share the same risk factors with 15 year olds or that the behaviour of young people aged 16 years is influenced in the same way by the same factors that influence 25 year olds?

The OCJS has exemplified the methodological paradoxes of RFR. The authors have been definitive about the risk factors for offending identified within the two broad age groups, but have relied on the crude factorisation of risk and have been unable to explain the nature of these risk factors, offending or the relationship between the two – particularly for the individual young people within each sample. The authors have been confident about the advantages of their longitudinal design, boasting that it will enable them to 'examine the development of offending 'careers' and identify factors that contribute to onset, continuation and desistance' (Budd *et al.* 2005a: 5). However, the authors have failed to acknowledge the limitations of factorisation, dichotomisation and aggregated analysis (as opposed to within-individual analyses), failed to consider the impact of the attrition of sample members and the addition of new members and produced results typical of a repeated cross-sectional study. At the theoretical level, the study has drawn on developmentally identified risk factors, but explored them in a cross-sectional manner in relation to their current influence in the lives of older young people – belying the lack of theoretical understanding and failure of the researchers to situate their study within the wider research literature. The OCJS has prioritised statistical control (e.g. representative sampling, avoiding sampling error, statistical weighting, multivariate analysis) over methodological validity, putting process over purpose and ultimately losing sight of its goal. The authors have proffered a range of simplistic, definitive and allegedly representative conclusions regarding the risk factors for offending by 10–25 year olds, yet these conclusions have been predicated on oversimplified, indefinite, aggregated and possibly confused understandings of risk factors derived from homogenised samples of young people and homogenised, overly-broad measures of offending.

Social Contexts of Pathways Into Crime

In 2003, the ESRC provided £2.1 million to the Social Contexts of Pathways Into Crime (SCoPIC) partnership. The SCoPIC partnership consists of three prospective longitudinal studies, each focused on a different developmental stage in the life course: The Childhood Study (led by Terri Moffitt), The Peterborough Adolescent Development Study (led by Per-Olof Wikström) and Sheffield Pathways out of Crime Study (led by Tony Bottoms). According to SCoPIC Network Director Per-Olof Wikström:

Too often different approaches – the study of social factors and individual characteristics, for instance – have been dealt with separately in research, and this problem has been reflected in crime prevention initiatives with similar limitations. We need a more integrated approach, understanding how different factors interact and how these interactions vary in different times and places.

(Wikström, www.scopic.ac.uk)

Therefore, the three SCoPIC studies have, whilst standing alone, each taken an ecological perspective on RFR by considering the influence of social context and its interaction with psychosocial risk factors for youth offending and desistance. The central aims of the SCoPIC network have been:

- to shed light on the interactions between individual characteristics and social context in producing offending behaviour;

- to assist in the development of improved public policies reducing criminality and enhancing individual's life chances, particularly in disadvantaged urban areas.

(Wikström, no date)

The Childhood Study

SCoPIC has funded The Childhood Study, a neighbourhood-based study of children and families already participating in, but extending, the ongoing Environmental Risk (E-Risk) Longitudinal Twin Study (Moffitt and the E-Risk Study Team 2002), which itself has been funded by the Medical Research Council. The E-Risk Study and the Childhood Study are coordinated by Terri Moffitt, a psychologist at Kings College, London. The E-Risk Study has focused on the genetic and environmental factors related to disruptive behaviour in a quest to better understand the nature–nurture debate. Of particular interest to the E-Risk study has been the interaction between individual and environmental risk factors in producing disruptive behaviour. For this purpose, the study has drawn on 1,116 families in England and Wales who had same sex twins born in 1994–1995. Data was collected when the child was aged five years using maternal interviews, life history calendars, teacher questionnaires, experimental tasks, observations and interviews/tests with children to assess cognitive functions, IQ and social behaviour, plus measures of neighbourhood structural characteristics such as socio-economic disadvantage, poverty and unemployment (Moffitt and the E-Risk Team 2002).

Based on the methodology of the E-Risk Study, Moffitt and her colleagues founded the Childhood Study in order to test two competing hypotheses regarding the nature of the relationship between genetic and environmental characteristics in explaining the behaviour of children:

• neighbourhood characteristics have a causal influence on child development and are correlated with problem behaviours in childhood;

• neighbourhood characteristics are correlated with problem behaviours because neighbourhoods reflect the genetic risk characteristics of the families within them. In other words, genetic risk factors serve as risk factors for neighbourhood characteristics, which then function as risk factors for offending.

(Moffitt, www.scopic.ac.uk)

The Childhood Study methodology

Moffitt (2006) and her team (Candice Odgers, Barry Milne, Lisa Cheung, Tim Matthews) collected a range of *official* data measuring environmental context – OFSTED school data, UK census data (based on family postcode), poverty indicators, measures of parenting skills and social support levels, home visitors' ratings and reports of abuse and emotional and mental health problems for the parents in 1,116 families taking part in the E-Risk Study. These official measures have been supplemented by a qualitative 'life history calendar' (a grid completed by mothers that facilitates the recall of the nature, timing and duration of life events and changes in family structure). Official data and the life history calendars have been supplemented by a one-off 'neighbourhood survey questionnaire' administered to 15 neighbours of each family. The survey has measured what the researchers called 'neighbourhood-based risk factors' experienced by each family, including: criminality in the local area, levels of antisocial behaviour, inter-group conflict, adult surveillance of young people, community cohesion, community norms and feelings of safety. Using ratings from at least three of the child's neighbours, Moffitt and her team have drawn a measure of 'neighbourhood collective efficacy' for each sample member that refers to the degree of social cohesion between neighbours and their willingness to intervene in neighbourhood affairs for the common good (Moffitt and Odgers 2007).

The Childhood Study findings and conclusions

Statistical analyses of the factorised data from the Childhood Study indicated that the level of neighbourhood collective efficacy experienced by children in the sample had a significant relationship with offending, when family and neighbourhood structural factors are controlled for. Neighbourhood collective efficacy was found to be lower in poverty-stricken neighbourhoods and therefore said to function as a risk factor for offending by sample members living in those neighbourhoods (Moffitt and Odgers 2007). At this very early stage, Moffitt and Odgers (2007) claim to have emphasised the crucial role of neighbourhood *processes* (as opposed to structural factors) on the development of offending in children (Moffitt 2006). However, at such an early stage in the research, it is extremely difficult to evaluate the veracity of these claims as the Childhood Study team have published only very limited details of their methods and findings (mainly confined to the SCoPIC website).

The Childhood Study as RFR

The Childhood Study authors have utilised a prospective longitudinal design to track the behaviour of a large sample of children over a long period using multiple data sources. The intensive focus on neighbourhood (structural characteristics and processes) resonates with the ecological strand of RFR. The exploration of macro-level risk factors (e.g. neighbourhood structural characteristics) and the potentially complex processes by which risk factors operate has broadened the narrow psychosocial foci and restricted deterministic understandings of risk factors within traditional longitudinal RFR. The investigation of genetic risk factors has further broadened the psychosocial focus of RFR, whilst their measurement from the age of two years onwards has broadened the focus on childhood (particularly 8–10 year olds) that was established within the Cambridge Study.

However, there have been attendant methodological issues which have yet to be resolved. The investigation of the genetics–neighbourhood relationship has arguably been oversimplified. The first genetic measures were taken when the children were aged two years, yet the single neighbourhood collective efficacy measure (the neighbourhood survey questionnaire) was taken when the children were aged ten years, thus precluding exploration of a possible influence of neighbourhood collective efficacy (not to mention an interaction with genetics) at an earlier age in the child's life. It is notable, therefore, that even the pursuit of a broader and more complex understanding of risk factors within the Childhood Study has been oversimplified; reliant on imputation regarding the nature of the risk-factor–offending relationship and beholden to the deterministic interpretation of young people as passive recipients of risk rather than active constructors of risk factors. The latter point is clearly demonstrated by the study's failure to directly engage with the sample members at any stage of the research thus far, in favour of eliciting measures of genetics and neighbourhood from other sources (e.g. official statistics, mothers, neighbours). In fact, the Childhood Study is not yet in a position to detail exactly how neighbourhood processes result in offending, or even if this is indeed the direction of the relationship. Moffitt and Odgers (2006) have stated that future work will explore the direction of the neighbourhood–offending relationship in terms of whether neighbourhoods cause offending or simply reflect the genetically influenced risk characteristics of their families. However, this definitive ambition would appear to overestimate the researchers' ability to identify causality through the control of risk factors as variables. The presumption is that statistical control will replace experimental control in this endeavour.

The Peterborough Adolescent Development Study

The longitudinal Peterborough Adolescent Development Study (PADS), coordinated by Per-Olof Wikström, emerged from the cross-sectional Peterborough Youth Study, which itself spawned the Situational Action Theory and its evolution into DEAT. In Situational Action Theory and the DEAT, youth offending is seen as the product of an interaction between individual risk factors and behavioural contexts, mediated by the young person's decision-making processes (Wikström 2006a; Wikström and Butterworth 2006; see previous chapter for a more detailed discussion of these theories). The PADS was designed to further explore and test this hypothesis. The overall intention has been to investigate the social mechanisms linking risk to offending, to examine whether these mechanisms vary with community context and age and to explore how these mechanisms interact with young people's decision-making processes (Wikström 2006a).

The PADS methodology

PADS has accessed a sample of 707 young people who were aged 12 years in March 2003, using interviews with parents/carers and taking 'new measures' (within RFR) of neighbourhood disadvantage and individual decision making, young people's perceptions of alternative behaviours and day-to-day routines. At present, as with the Childhood Study, there has been a paucity of detailed information published regarding the methodology, analysis and findings from PADS and this is reflected in the rather brief methodological and finding sections provided here and in the tentative evaluations offered.

The PADS findings and conclusions

Initial findings from this relatively young study have indicated the importance of environmental risk factors associated with youth offending by highlighting that most youth offending takes place with peers outside of the family and school contexts. Wikström (2006a) has formulated the concept of 'collective efficacy' (an elaborated version of Moffitt's 'neighbourhood collective efficacy'), which adds a measure of 'moral context' to the amount of social cohesion and informal social control experienced by young people in their environment/neighbourhood. He has argued that time spent unsupervised with peers in areas of low collective efficacy and high environmental risk is a major risk factor for offending, but only for young people with an existing high propensity to offend (the notion that low morality weakens self-control) and only if that time is spent with delinquent peers. Exposure to environmental risk is itself influenced by poor parental monitoring and truancy from school.

The PADS as RFR

The PADS, according to Wikström, contributed to criminological explanation by addressing tensions between causes and correlates, individual and ecological levels of explanation and development and change (see Wikström 2005) through the provision of data to validate Wikström's integrated DEAT. The DEAT is intended to explain how the propensity to offend activates in a given situation, thus offering a more complex and 'scientific realist' understanding of risk factors as a series of mechanisms and processes that interact with individual agency and situational influences (see Wikström 2008). The PADS data has allegedly enabled Wikström to explore 'what puts the risk into risk factors' in the current lives of young people (e.g. low morality and low self-control generate a high propensity to offend). At this point in the research, Wikström (2006a) claims to have identified an interaction between the individual and their environment and to have explored how this can precipitate offending in individuals with an existing high propensity to offend. Wikström also notes that, at this early stage, PADS has been unable to effectively explain offending by individuals with a low propensity to offend or offending in areas with high collective efficacy. As yet, however, it appears that there has been little exploration of the aetiology of morality and self-control, particularly in relation to whether each of these risk factors has their own set of risk factors which themselves may have a causal relationship with offending (i.e. multi-stage and proxy risk factors), what Wikström himself calls 'causes of the causes' (2008: 133). However, it must be stressed that without further detail or publications forthcoming from the PADS research team, any confident and definitive claims made by the authors, not to mention any methodological criticisms made here, cannot be properly evaluated or substantiated.

Perhaps the biggest issue for PADS concerns its origins and intentions. The study has been established to test and validate the DEAT and this objective has informed and dictated its content, methods and analysis. However, the dynamic DEAT has been reliant on imputation and extrapolation from cross-sectional data (from the Peterborough Youth Study – see Chapter 2) that (in the form it was collected) should have precluded many of the original conclusions regarding causality and process. Consequently, any post-hoc validation of the DEAT could be self-fulfilling and specious.

Sheffield Pathways out of Crime Study

The retrospective-prospective longitudinal Sheffield Pathways out of Crime Study (SPOOCS) began in November 2002. The authors set out with the intention of exploring the individual and 'social contextual' factors relating to desistance from offending (Bottoms *et al.* 2004) – a much-neglected area within RFR. Much like its sister studies within the SCoPIC partnership, SPOOCS began with a clear theoretical framework that it intended to test – namely the continuous interactions between structure (e.g. Sampson and Laub's [1993] 'turning points') and agency (e.g. Maruna's [2001] 'cognitive transformation processes') and between developmental factors and current context, and how these interactions may influence desistance from adolescent offending in the early 'adult' years. The 'interactive framework' to be explored by SPOOCS was to consist of five interrelated concepts:

- *Programmed potential* – the quantifiable and measurable risk of reoffending indicated by assessment of demographic characteristics: (e.g. age, gender) and past behaviour (e.g. previous offending).

- *Structures* – external social structures that can limit or enable action (e.g. serve as risk or protective factors), such as employment and job stability.

- *Culture and habitus* – cultural contexts/social worlds (closely linked to structures) wherein individuals share beliefs, attitudes, behaviours (see also Bourdieu 1977).

- *Situational contexts* – the contexts, occasions and situations that may encourage or inhibit offending. For example, entering a meaningful relationship could discourage further offending (see Laub and Sampson 2003).

- *Agency* – the individual's understandings of their own actions and 'personal conceptions about the past and future' (see Laub and Sampson 2003: 146).

(see Bottoms *et al.* 2004)

The SPOOCS methodology

In order to explore the interaction between structure and agency, the SPOOCS team drew a sample of 300 adults aged around 20 years old (born in 1982–1984) and living in Sheffield, England. The criteria for inclusion in the sample was having received at least two official convictions, with the rationale that less frequent offenders were less suitable targets for a study of desistance because low-rate offending in adolescence is normative (see Laub and Sampson 2001). The age of 20 years was chosen on the basis that the well-established 'age-crime curve' has indicated a rapid decrease in offending when young offenders reach their early twenties (Bottoms *et al.* 2006; Bottoms *et al.* 2004). The sample members mostly originated from socially disadvantaged areas of Sheffield, most had a 'volatile housing history' (frequent moves or changes in location of accommodation, poor standard of housing) and most were unemployed. The researchers have interviewed sample members at nine month intervals to assess their current circumstances and lifestyle, childhood and upbringing, community belonging, employment, self-assessment of future prospects and the impact of life events and developmental transitions.

In accordance with the other SCoPIC studies, to date, few publications have been made available that have reported the methodology and findings of the SPOOCS study, so substantiation and evaluation of the authors conclusions is a potentially premature, limited and extremely difficult exercise.

The SPOOCS findings and conclusions

Preliminary dissemination of the interview findings (Bottoms *et al.* 2006) has indicated a strong link between early disadvantage in a social context and future offending. This early disadvantage has been particularly evident in terms of having unsupportive parents (offering little or no advice, protection or financial support) and an unsettled lifestyle (drug addiction, prison, sleeping rough). The SPOOCS team have also identified a link between psychological risk factors (excitement, boredom, peer pressure and perceived lack of alternative actions) and offending. The psychological factors that have appeared to encourage desistance from offending have been changing self-perceptions, moral pressure from partners, parents and peers and becoming a parent (Bottoms *et al.* 2006). However, SPOOCS has not found a link between neighbourhood collective efficacy and offending, despite this link being evident within the

SCoPIC partnership studies focused on other developmental stages, namely childhood (Moffitt 2005) and adolescence (Wikström 2006a).

The SPOOCS as RFR

From the information provided to this point, a potential strength of SPOOCS lies in its much needed exploration of desistance within RFR, which brings with it a welcome focus on protective factors within an area of study traditionally dominated by risk. SPOOCS has explored these neglected foci through an innovative mixed longitudinal methodology of:

- retrospective longitudinal analysis of the developmental impact of childhood risk factors;

- prospective analysis of current risk factors.

The retrospective-prospective SPOOCS methodology is ostensibly innovative within RFR in that it has been seldom employed in a body of longitudinal RFR more inclined towards either/or choices between the two (with the notable exception of the early studies of the Gluecks). The SPOOCS authors appear committed to a more holistic interpretation of desistance that incorporates social structures, culture, situation and agency – aspects regularly overlooked by a developmental RFR literature more concerned with validating the deterministic influence of factorised versions of psychosocial childhood influences. However, the strength of SPOOCS in this regard could also be a weakness. In their evolution of the restricted foci and understandings of traditional RFR, the SPOOCS team have appeared to disregard (rather than supplement or downplay) the potential impact of psychosocial risk factors on 'programmed potential' (typically constituted by static risk factors such as gender) and desistence from offending in favour of socio-cultural, situational and agentic explanations. However, until further publications are forthcoming, it will remain unclear as to whether Bottoms and colleagues intend to ascribe any explanatory utility to psychosocial risk factors – considered by much RFR to be the most important building blocks in the development of RFR.

The scope of SCoPIC conclusions

The longitudinal RFR studies in the SCoPIC partnership have yet to yield full, substantive results or to widely disseminate their empirical findings and conclusions, so it is somewhat premature to evaluate them in the overall context of longitudinal RFR in England and Wales. However, despite the nascent state of each study and a dearth of transparent and detailed dissemination of methods and findings thus far, the researchers have not been tentative or guarded in making claims (or pre-conclusions) from their ongoing work regarding, for example, the developmental link between certain psychosocial risk factors experienced in childhood (e.g. low neighbourhood collective efficacy – Moffit and Odgers 2007, low morality and self-control – Wikström 2006a, early social disadvantage – Bottoms et al. 2006). These claims have typically been predicated on pre-existing theories of risk factor influence generated in previous research, be it Moffitt's theory of genetic-environment interaction from the E-risk study (Moffitt and the E-Risk team 2002), Wikström's DEAT (Wikström 2005, 2006a) from the Peterborough Youth Survey or Bottoms's interactive theory of desistence. However, to date, the published results do not yet justify such conclusions.

It is not too early, however, to acknowledge the intentions of the SCoPIC studies. For example, the partnership has pursued advancements in RFR by exploring neglected sites of risk factor influence (e.g. neighbourhood structural characteristics, collective efficacy, genetics and morality) and by attempting to understand how risk factors become activated/deactivated in a given situation (e.g. through a focus on agency, process and mechanisms). These foci should augment RFR, which has been traditionally concerned with measuring psychosocial risk factors as static developmental variables (see also Pitts 2003a). Methodologically, however, there has remained a focus on the oversimplification of complex understandings of risk factors through factorisation. This widespread quantification of data facilitates simplistic statistical analyses and the promulgation of definitive conclusions but it contemporaneously restricts the degree to which the researchers could qualitatively explore and understand the rich nature and complexity of the concepts being investigated (e.g. risk, neighbourhood collective efficacy and desistance). The SCoPIC studies, thus far, seem to have sought to understand risk factors and risk processes as artefacts and as amenable to explanation and understanding through statistical relationships – a process which may ultimately reduce the explanatory utility of these studies.

Pathways Into and Out of Crime: Risk, Resilience and Diversity

A pathways strand of longitudinal RFR (France and Homel 2007) emerged in the late 1990s and early 2000s, which supplemented the traditional focus on quantitative risk profiling and identification of statistical relationships between risk factors and offending with more qualitative, in-depth explorations of how risk can be socially constructed by young people and significant others in their lives and how young people can actively experience and negotiate their pathways into and out of crime in different socio-structural contexts. The qualitative focus of this strand of RFR has been exemplified in England and Wales by a major research network established in 2003: Pathways Into and Out of Crime: Risk, Resilience and Diversity (Hine 2005). This ESRC-funded (£1.4 million over four years) partnership consists of five longitudinal surveys spanning six UK universities (Sheffield, De Montfort, Nottingham, Newcastle, Essex and Glasgow Caledonian).

The ongoing projects within the Pathways Into and Out of Crime partnership have sought to apply and test the pathways approach by refocusing RFR away from the developmental determinism of early childhood psychosocial factors acting on passive and helpless young crash test dummies and towards a deeper consideration of how young people interpret and choose to respond to risk in their current lives and how their ability to negotiate risk is affected by others. Three main aims have been stated for the partnership:

- to expand our understanding and knowledge of the relationship between risk factors and children and young people's pathways into and out of crime;

- to gain a fuller understanding of how children and young people who are identified as being 'at risk' of being future offenders negotiate pathways into and out of crime;

- to understand the social processes of protection, resilience and resistance that mediate between risk factors on pathways into and out of crime.

(Hine 2006)

The Pathways Into and Out of Crime partnership studies have challenged longitudinal RFR that has been based on psychosocial models of risk and focused on the individual. The studies have preferred to examine how 'risk' can be socially constructed, how young people interact and negotiate with their social worlds and how gender, ethnicity, culture and social experience can shape the nature of young peoples experiences (Hine 2006).

The Pathways Into and Out of Crime methodologies

Several of the partnership projects have employed methodologies with strong qualitative elements to engage with so-called 'hard to reach' and 'minority' groups of young people who have been under-represented in the mainstream school samples that have dominated much RFR. The partnership projects are:

- Risk and resilience in children who are offending, excluded from school or have behaviour problems – An investigation of the 'factors that enhance or reduce risk', critical turning points and pathways into and out of crime for first-time offenders working with Youth Offending Teams, young people permanently excluded from school and young people with statements of special educational needs (Hine et al. 2007).

The study methodology consisted of interviews with young people and key professionals.

- Risk, protection and resilience in urban Black and Asian culture – A project utilising video stimuli created by young people and focus group discussion with researchers to examine young people's experiences, constructions and negotiations of risk in their area and 'the combination of risk and protective factors which can lead to resilience or susceptibility' in Black and Asian young people (see Haw 2007).

- Risk, protection and resilience in the family life of children and young people with a parent in prison – An exploration of the factors, experiences and processes related to risk, protection and resilience for children with a parent in prison, using questionnaires, pre- and post-release interviews with imprisoned parents and interviews with children and young people (Walker and McCarthy 2005).

- Young people, social capital and the negotiation of risk – A study of the influence of social and material resources (social capital) on perceptions, experiences and negotiations of risk, decision-making (risk choices) and risk-taking behaviour by young people from secondary schools, Youth Offending Teams and community groups (see Boeck et al. 2006). The study has employed survey questionnaires, interviews and focus groups with young people.

- Risk, protection and substance misuse amongst young offenders – An examination of the relationship between substance use and offending, using structured questionnaires, with a particular focus on the 'relationships between substance misuse, offending and personal and social risk factors' (Hammersley et al. 2003).

The projects have attempted to explore and elaborate the relationship between risk factors and problem behaviours to gain a greater understanding of *how* risk and offending interact and to address gaps in knowledge regarding how established risk factors link to pathways into crime. The projects have eschewed the replication of basic descriptions of *what* risk factors link statistically to offending. The scope and achievements of the Pathways partnership to date may best be illustrated by three partner studies which have taken weak, moderate and strong constructivist perspectives respectively (see Kemshall et al. 2007).

Substance use and offending (weak constructivist)

In a joint project between Glasgow and Essex Universities, Richard Hammersley and his research team (Hammersley et al. 2003) set out to study the 'common causal configurations' of risk factors allegedly underpinning substance misuse and offending. The research team have explored the relationship between psychosocial factors, substance misuse and offending/desistance and evaluated the extent to which substance use acts as a mediator between psychosocial risk factors and offending behaviour. The study has adopted a weak constructionist perspective through its focus on the immediate situational contexts of a sample of young offenders and the pathways into and out of substance use and offending that result from the decisions made in these contexts.

Methodology (Hammersley et al. 2003)

The researchers began with an opportunity sample of 293 young offenders from 11 Youth Offending Teams across England and Wales; each of which had previously participated in the Home Office Drugs Research Programme in 2002. A second wave of data collection (funded by the ESRC through the Pathways Into and Out of Crime partnership) was carried out 18 months after the Home Office-funded research with 102 (34 per cent) young people from the original cohort. Data was collected through structured questionnaires measuring substance use and offending in the past 12 months (using the UK version of the ISRD inventory – Graham and Bowling 1995). So-called 'risk' factors were assessed through interview self-reports of exposure in current life (precise time of exposure not measured) to factors relating to personal traits and experiences (coping mechanisms, self-esteem, school affiliation, sociability), plans and expectations for the future (planned qualifications and earning, expectations of being in trouble again by the age of 25 years), parenting (perceived parenting style, perceived parental control) and life problems (e.g. mental health problems, pregnancy, homelessness, serious injury, being beaten up, long-term relationship break-up, depression, exclusion from school).

Each factor was a composite of several sub-factors/statements, each of which were factorised (typically using Likert scales of different lengths), totalled and converted into a dichotomous risk/protection indicator. For example:

- *Coping style* – a combination of scores indicating strength of agreement on a three-point Likert scale ('not at all', 'a little bit', 'more than a little') for ten statements relating to coping mechanisms in the face of problems (e.g. 'I do something about it', 'I pretend that it hasn't really happened').

- *Self-esteem* – measured using Rosenberg's ten item self-esteem inventory containing yes/no responses. Scores of above three were coded as indicating low self-esteem and therefore risk.

- *School affiliation* – four related items (enjoy(ed) school, do/did well, feel/felt school work is important, play(ed) truant a lot) using five point Likert scales (from strongly agree to strongly disagree).

- *Parenting* – a combination of two factors, perceived parenting style (composed of five sub-statements) and perceived parental control (composed of four sub-statements), with each sub-statement using a five point Likert response scale ('strongly agree' to 'strongly disagree').

- *Life problems* – an inventory of 11 life problems requiring yes or no responses.

Findings and conclusions (Hammersley *et al.* 2003)

Following multivariate analysis of the two waves of data collection (wave one funded by the Home Office; wave two funded by the ESRC) by the research team, the authors identified four key 'predictors' of both offending and substance use: the number of life problems experienced in the past two years, expectation to be in trouble again by the age of 25 years, low positive coping style and low school affiliation. It was also asserted that substance use predicted offending. From this multivariate analysis, Hammersley *et al.* (2003) concluded that the psychosocial factors measured in the structured questionnaire were more predictive of offending than they were of substance use and that substance use appeared to act as a mediator between 'risk' factors and offending (although exactly how this happened was not explained), rather than as a risk factor for offending in its own right.

From a social constructivist perspective, the researchers argued that there was a need to understand risks and risk factors within cultural and historical contexts (Kemshall *et al.* 2007) rather than assuming that risk factors are static and causal in a deterministic sense, although the current (weak constructivist) study offered little to address this (strong constructivist) aim.

Methodologically, the Hammersley *et al.* study offers yet another example of RFR which has assumed that factors associated statistically with offending are necessarily predictive and therefore constitute 'risk' factors, without having established their temporal precedence over offending (e.g. the precise date/time of first exposure to factors relative to episodes of offending behaviour). The study has also exemplified the recurrent limitations of factorising and dichotomising risk and the inherent insensitivity of using quantified and aggregated procedures to represent and analyse complex phenomena of risk for individual young people. Group-based associations between variables, for example, say little or nothing about the actual lives of real young people.

Social capital and risk taking (moderate constructionist)

At De Montfort University, Hazel Kemshall, Thilo Boeck and colleagues (see Kemshall *et al.* 2007; Boeck *et al.* 2006) resolved to investigate the relationship between social capital and young people's constructions and negotiations of risk and protection and their related risk decisions and risky behaviour. Based on the dual premise that social capital promotes positive outcomes and reduces risk, and that risk decisions are often made in groups/social networks, Boeck et al. examined risk in terms of a continuous interaction between agency and structure (a moderate constructivist approach) and the influence of social capital on offending.

Methodology (Boeck et al. 2006)

The social capital study drew an opportunity sample of 589 young people (458 from schools and youth groups, 131 from Youth Offending Teams and Youth Inclusion Projects) aged 11–19 years from the Midlands area. Amongst these 589 young people, the De Montfort team administered 500 individual and group-based questionnaires, conducted 24 interviews and ran 17 focus groups to explore perceptions, negotiations and decisions related to risk and protection, including expectations and perceived ability to influence the future, leisure time pursuits, social networks, self-identity, sense of belonging and structural barriers to opportunity. Following qualitative analysis, the 'most important' risk findings (although it was not specified how this judgement was made) were then re-examined using interviews with 12 persistent offenders.

Findings and conclusions (Boeck et al. 2006)

Boeck and his colleagues identified two distinct groups of young people from their qualitative analysis (the details of which have not been disseminated in any depth). One group existed in *tight networks* centred on their immediate localities (e.g. the street, local park, home) and was typified by a static nature and a restricted range of activities such as 'hanging around'. This group was more likely to be members of the Youth Offending Team/Youth Inclusion Programme sample. The tight network group was characterised by *risk stagnation*, a state of unwillingness to extricate themselves from their current situation, network and localities. The second group existed in *extended networks* which were more dynamic, involved participation in more after-school activities and associations and connections with other networks beyond their immediate locality. Members of this group were more commonly found in the school/youth group sample and were seen as existing in a state of *risk navigation* whereby they participated in diverse and far-reaching networks and had a more focused and active view of life when compared to the hopeless, more fatalistic perspectives of young people in tight networks.

From a constructivist viewpoint, Boeck and his colleagues concluded that networks functioned as a complex factor that could indicate both risk and resilience in particular forms, dependent on how restricted/diverse and closed/linking these networks were. The identification of the states of risk stagnation and risk navigation were seen to exemplify the continuous interaction between agency and structure that had been overlooked by traditional, oversimplified understandings of risk factors and thus 'highlighting that the role of (the) traditional risk factor is highly complex' (Kemshall *et al.* 2007: 99). The research team concluded that enhanced social capital was a very promising route out of crime and that dynamic social capital (i.e. social capital experienced in extended networks) 'allows young people to "navigate" and ultimately have the resources to cope, manage and make informed choices and act on them' (Kemshall *et al.* 2008).

Exploring young people's perspectives on school exclusion (strong constructionist)

A project examining the risk and resilience in children who are offending, excluded from school or have behaviour problems, based at Sheffield University, has examined critical pathways into and out of offending and how young people who have offended, been excluded from school or have behaviour problems manage, negotiate and resist risk in their lives – notably in interactions with professional agencies. The project has adopted a strong constructionist position that has focused on how the school as an institution can construct risk through exclusion rates and arbitrary processes of exclusion (see Hine *et al.* 2007; Kemshall 2007).

Methodology (Hine et al. 2007)

The research team studied an opportunity sample of 110 young people (83 boys, 27 girls) over a two-year period. This sample was obtained from three cohorts: young people who have been permanently excluded from school, young people who have had contact with Youth Offending Teams early in their lives and young people who have a statement of special educational needs relating to emotional and behavioural difficulties. Individual interviews were conducted with sample members (110 in year one, 54 follow-up interviews 6–9 months later), along with life history case studies (with 13 young people) and interviews with key stakeholders (Youth Offending Team staff, head teachers in schools and pupil referral unit, education welfare officers and police officers). The interviews with young people were intended to provide a better understanding of young people's risk- and protection-related experiences, perceptions and processes, whilst the stakeholder interviews sought to explore the impact of professional decision-making and official interventions on these experiences, perceptions and processes.

Findings and conclusions (Hine et al. 2007)

Preliminary findings have highlighted a diverse range of experiences and perspectives of school exclusion as reported by young people. Interview findings have illustrated the complexity of school exclusion as a potential risk factor and how this factor can be differently constructed and experienced by different young people (Hine 2005; see also Kemshall *et al.* 2007). In particular, young people's reports implicated 'the importance of context in determining whether a factor is risk or protection' (Hine *et al.* 2007). For example, some sample members believed that they had been victimised by the school exclusion processes (e.g. they were in the wrong place at the wrong time) in relation to other pupils who had escaped punishment for similar behaviour, whilst for other sample members, exclusion had been protective in that it had removed them from exposure to other risk factors (e.g. peer pressure, academic underachievement).

In a review of this study that mirrored the original researchers' strong constructivist standpoint, Kemshall concluded that it is too simplistic to assume that school exclusion operates as a causal or predictive risk factor for offending because 'the direction of causality is unknown (and) . . . the precise mechanisms through which the relationship between school experiences and offending is mediated require explicating' (Kemshall *et al.* 2007: 95).

The Pathways Into and Out of Crime studies as RFR

According to Hine (2006), the Pathways studies have demonstrated that for young people there are 'substantial differences between the reality of their everyday experiences and the theory presented within the dominant current policy framework for interventions'. Thus, within the pathways strand, risk has been conceived and examined as an interactive and dynamic *process* that is complex, multi-faceted and sometimes bi-directional – contra the artefact-based model of RFR which views risk as static and uni-directional.

Thus far, the main conclusions from the pathways projects have been:

- context can be important in determining whether a factor is associated with risk or protection. Circumstances assumed to signify risk (e.g. school exclusion) may actually be protective;

- young people's responses to risk can depend on community context, peer group, family context (e.g. relationships with family) and their relationship with professionals;

- resilience to risk factors and negative influences can be promoted by family and peers;

- 'risk stagnation' can occur when young people are unable or unwilling to remove themselves from their current situation due to feeling hopeless and fatalistic.

(Hine 2005, 2006)

What has been lacking from the (dearth of) published material relating to the Pathways Into and Out of Crime partnership studies thus far is a detailed, comprehensive dissemination of the methods employed to collect, code and analyse data (although the Hammersley *et al.* substance use and offending study is a notable exception to this). For example, there has been limited information offered regarding exactly what questions have been asked and in what form, how the responses were coded, what form of analysis underpinned the conclusions and what this analysis can demonstrate about the nature of the relationship between risk, protection and offending. To this point, the methods and analyses of all bar one of the pathways projects have been less transparent and explicit than those of artefact RFR studies such as the Cambridge Study and the OCJS. Of course, it is entirely possible that the qualitative, subjective, non-standardised, non-generalisable and occasionally ethereal nature of the methods and analyses employed have been much less suited to precise and systematic explication than their quantitative counterparts. This being the case, it is no surprise that the more quantitative study by Hammersley *et al.* has been able to be more transparent and detailed regarding its methods and analyses than the other Pathways projects. However, further information could be provided by each of the partnership studies regarding, for example, questionnaire content, interview and focus group schedules, secondary data analysis, data coding and thematic analysis. Without full details and a comprehensive understanding of exactly what each study has done, the legitimacy and validity of subsequent con-clusions and the ability of the outsider to subject these studies to detailed scrutiny and evaluation is undermined and artificially restricted.

Methodologically, the prioritisation of qualitative, consultative methods and analyses has augmented a RFR movement traditionally dominated by quantitative, prescriptive methods and analyses (particularly the factorisa-tion and analysis of adult-prescribed judgements of risk) and has encouraged a focus on the marginalised issues of protection and resil-ience. However, the studies have yet to fully explore the potential benefits of the longitudinal designs they have aspired to. For example, there has been a paucity of within-individual analysis that could explain individual changes and possible causal influences on a specific young person's behaviour. There has also been a preference for one-off, follow-ups (similar to repeated cross-sectional designs) at the expense of iterative rounds of data collection that could explore the cumulative implications of risk for specific individuals.

The pathways approach has reconceptualised RFR through interpretive understandings that treat 'risk' as an everyday reality for young people that they make meaning of and negotiate. These conceptions of the young person as an agentic, active negotiator of their own pathways into and out of crime, with their meanings, negotiations and choices being influenced by social, cultural, political and historical context, have been antithetical to the conceptions of statistical risk factors influencing young people's lives deterministically from childhood that have permeated Government policy and practice (Hine 2006; Armstrong *et al.* 2005). The Pathways Into and Out of Crime projects have challenged overly-simplistic and deterministic understandings of risk as a readily quantifiable, 'factorisable' and predictable concept that is located within the individual and determines their future behaviour – replacing this view with a messier view of active, agentic young people from different minority groups trying to make sense of their exposure to a rapidly changing and unpredictable 'complex' of risk in a variety of social contexts. Much of this risk is less readily measurable, if indeed it can be measured at all.

The constructivist interpretation of risk factors espoused within the pathways strand of RFR, supported by the findings of the Pathways Into and Out of Crime studies, has understood that risk is not a quality of the individual, but of the social situation an individual finds themselves in – some individuals are better able and/or better enabled to manage their situation and to realise different outcomes. However, in order to produce findings of practical utility and to avoid 'evolving' (or some would say 'devolving') into a post-modern and ethereal theoretical exercise, the partnership has fallen into some of the methodological paradoxes of RFR. For example, it could be argued that the studies have overestimated and been overly-definitive regarding the extent to which young people are able to understand, negotiate and respond to risk and the extent to which both young people and researchers are able to measure the construction of risk, based on an indefinite and imprecise understanding of risk itself. The conclusions of the Pathways Into and Out of Crime partnership thus far may have 'over-egged the pudding' somewhat in an attempt to assert young people's active role in constructing their own lives. Young people may not be fully aware of or able to measure the extent or nature of the risk in their current lives; nor is it likely that they are able to adequately negotiate or feasibly respond to every aspect of this risk. An irony has emerged that by ascribing the young person too much capability to influence their own lives, they may be set up for failure and blame if they cannot tackle risk. It is as if the constructivist interpretations of risk that have both fed and emerged from the Pathways Into and Out of Crime studies have not been deterministic enough and have rejected out of hand that young people may be irrevocably influenced by risk factors in certain situations in much the same way as they can influence risk factors in others.

The Teesside Studies

Three interrelated studies have been conducted at Teesside University under the supervision of Robert Macdonald. The Teesside Studies have taken a constructivist perspective of how young people experience risk in particular socio-structural contexts and how their resultant perceptions and decisions affect their transitions into adulthood. In *Snakes and Ladders: Young People, Transitions and Social Exclusion* (Johnston *et al.* 2000), 98 young people aged 15–25 years from the same neighbourhood, social class and ethnic background were interviewed about their transitions into adulthood. In *Disconnected Youth? Growing Up in Britain's Poorest Neighbourhoods* (McDonald and Marsh 2005), 88 young people aged 15–25 years living in socially disadvantaged neighbourhoods were interviewed as a means of examining the relative merits of underclass theories and how ideas of social exclusion connected to the 'lived realities' of these young people. The initial Teesside studies were followed up by *Poor Transitions: Young Adults and Social Exclusion* (Webster *et al.* 2004), which set out to examine where youth transitions had led members of the original two samples once they reached adulthood. It is this final study that has had the most explicit focus on examining the influence of risk on offending pathways.

The Poor Transitions: Young Adults and Social Exclusion methodology

The central data collection episode consisted of interviews with 185 young people living in the North East of England, aged 16–25 years. The young people were asked to recall their biographies back to childhood as a way of investigating how individual risk factors interacted at different stages with the structured opportunities and barriers they faced (e.g. employment opportunities, low wages, lack of affordable social provision). Webster *et al.* then re-interviewed 34 original members of the *Snakes and Ladders* and *Disconnected Youth* samples (16 males, 18 females) who were then aged between 23–29 years. The *Poor Transitions* study utilised retrospective biographical interviews with these individuals, along with a re-analysis of the biographical interviews in the two previous Teesside studies, in order to 'sketch out the *nature* and *shape* of criminal careers' (MacDonald 2007: 115).

The Poor Transitions: Young Adults and Social Exclusion findings and conclusions (Webster et al. 2004)

From the interviews, the researchers made what they called rough 'approximations' of the influence of risk factors on offending (Webster *et al.* 2006), although it was not made clear how these approximations were reached. These approximated risk factors for offending were identified as:

- early and frequent truancy;
- living in a single-parent family;
- having no educational qualifications;

- living a troubled, traumatic life;

- domestic violence;

- having a parent in prison;

- acrimonious parental divorce;

- living in care;

- socioeconomic deprivation.

(Webster *et al.* 2006: 9)

Emphasising how RFR has tended to individualise risk and 'ignore the role of neighbourhood influence and context in the emergence of risk factors', Webster *et al.* (2006: 12) drew particular attention to the risk-related role of *social capital* – the commitments to the social networks in which the young people lived and operated. The *Poor Transitions* study distinguished between *bonding* social capital, the connections young people had with their families and close friends, and *bridging* social capital, which were associations beyond the immediate circle of family and friends (similar to the tight and extended networks within the Pathways Into and Out of Crime study of Kemshall and colleagues). The authors concluded that young people who offended appeared to have been constrained by the inherent limits of bonding social capital and the restricted socio-economic opportunities within social networks limited to families and friends.

In a review of the Teesside studies, MacDonald (2007) concluded that despite the unrepresentative nature of the samples used, the biographical accounts obtained helped the Teesside team to gain an overview of the nature and shape of the criminal careers of their sample members. In particular, MacDonald highlighted two key 'movements' that appear to consolidate serious and long-term offending:

- *the hardening up of school disaffection* – full-blown educational disengagement, typically demonstrated by frequent and persistent truancy, along with a simultaneous engagement with 'street corner society', which contributed to the development of oppositional identities;

- *the influence of cheap heroin* – the key motivator behind exclusionary transitions that distanced young people from their families, functional lifestyles and the labour market and enmeshed them within chaotic lifestyles.

Through a detailed analysis of the historical, cultural and socio-economic conditions of neighbourhoods, coupled with 'approximations' of risk factors garnered from interviews, the Teesside Studies (particularly *Poor*

Transitions) highlighted that the biographies of young people had been influenced by living in a region that had recently experienced a sharp increase in poverty and multiple deprivation, combined with rapid deindustrialisation and economic restructuring. This had resulted in lower wages for local young people, fewer benefit entitlements and a rapid decline in opportunities for employment and training. This 'myriad' of structural risk could not have been predicted by artefact-based approaches that neglect historical, socio-economic and geographical context (Webster *et al.* 2006). The authors concluded that the relationship between risk factors and offending is complex and multifaceted rather than unproblematically causal and predictive, as depicted in traditional RFR. For example, the relationship between truancy and offending is not straightforwardly-causal (Webster *et al.* 2006). Rather, the causal process may be the 'hanging around' with delinquent peers and the building of masculine identities that can accompany truancy – so the important consideration is how truancy time is spent (e.g. the process of developing certain forms of deleterious relationship with others). Truancy and hanging around may be, for example, a search for masculine identity or constructive use of leisure time, so in this case, the risk-factor–offending relationship may not be as simplistic as it is often portrayed (MacDonald 2007).

The Teesside biographies also suggested that unpredictable critical moments in young people's lives (e.g. experiencing rape, suffering a road accident) could increase or decrease the likelihood of future offending by increasing their vulnerability or resistance to future risks and stressors. In particular, the Teesside research team identified a significant degree of *resilience* against offending and substance use amongst the high risk members of the sample, which indicated support for a constructivist understanding of risk.

The Teesside Studies as RFR

MacDonald (2007: 118–20) has offered five key conclusions from the Teesside Studies:

- There is a need to avoid deterministic, reductionist and positivist assumptions of 'a tight, causal fit between particular risk indicators and later, or concurrent, behaviour'. Instead, the relationships between risk and offending should be understood as 'associations'.

- It is infeasible to predict with confidence which specific young people will offend in the future. Despite the Disconnected Youth study confirming 'the link between having experienced risk factors and being a frequent offender' (Webster 2005: 5) it also showed that young people experiencing high risk do not necessarily offend.

- There are inherent difficulties in establishing which risk factors are most significant for different young people at different points in their life and in different contexts.

- Large-scale quantitative studies are less able than qualitative RFR studies 'to get close up to social actors' own subjective, complicated accounts and life stories'.

- RFR has overemphasised individual-level risk and relatively neglected the influence of historical and spatial contexts (e.g. deindustrialisation, poverty, the influx of cheap drugs).

(MacDonald 2007: 118–20)

The Teesside Studies have explored an understanding of risk and protection in one highly specific sample of socially deprived and socially excluded young people in one disadvantaged area of England. Indeed, the assumption that the risk–offending relationship is generalisable (or even predictable) would be anathema to qualitative and nuanced understandings of risk generated by the Teesside Studies; studies that were seeking illumination rather than representativeness in their understandings of risk. The paradox of unconstructive constructivism embodied by the Teesside Studies is that the pursuit of a broader, yet at the same time more young person-specific, understanding of risk has highlighted how little researchers can control and predict risk and protection processes, how little is understood of the full complexity of the relationships between risk, protection and offending and how daunting a prospect it really is to plan and implement holistic and valid preventative interventions based on overly simplistic and determinative notions of risk. Constructivism may be unconstructive (compared to artefact RFR) but it may be a closer approximation to reality.

Conclusion: longitudinal risk factor research in England and Wales revisited

The key longitudinal RFR studies in England and Wales have varied significantly in terms of the strand of RFR/theoretical model of risk that has underpinned their aims, methods, findings and conclusions. The earliest and most influential study, the Cambridge Study in Delinquent Development, pursued and evolved a *developmental* understanding of (psychosocial) risks as factors that could be identified in childhood, quantified and statistically-linked to offending in adolescence and adulthood. The OCJS adopted an equivalent developmental and artefactual view of risk, although not one that was ultimately justified or substantiated by the methodology and analyses employed. The SCoPIC partnership studies each maintained an *ecological* view of the relationship between risk and offending by focusing on the interaction between risk factors in the individual and those in the neighbourhood. Risk was conceived as an artefact/factor, but the concept of agency was added to move RFR away from traditional deterministic understandings of risk factor influence. A further move away from determinism was evident by the Pathways Into and Out of Crime partnership and the Teesside Studies. Each contributory study within these partnerships adopted a constructivist pathways perspective of risk and protection as negotiated processes with potential for a multiplicity of outcomes as opposed to uni-deterministic factors.

Taken together, the key longitudinal RFR studies in England and Wales have exhibited several demonstrable methodological strengths that have challenged and evolved the field. In particular, the prospective measurement of multiple factors from multiple data sources using standardised methodologies has facilitated simplistic and confident conclusions regarding the predictive validity and replicability of different childhood and adolescent risk factors for offending. More recent studies sponsored by the ESRC (SCoPIC, Pathways Into and Out of Crime) have expanded the foci of longitudinal RFR beyond investigations of deterministic psychosocial risk factors in childhood to a more detailed examination of macro-level structural, socio-cultural, economic and historical risk factors, along with investigations of current lives in terms of situational influences, individual agency and young people's capacity to construct risk. The intention of these more holistic, multifaceted and less deterministic studies has been to evolve an understanding of the previously neglected issue of how risk is constructed and becomes animated in offending behaviour.

The overriding question to emerge from the studies discussed is: have they fulfilled the potential benefits offered by their longitudinal designs? Indeed, to what extent have these studies actually been longitudinal at all? Moreover, what has longitudinal research in England and Wales contributed to the resolution of the methodological weaknesses of RFR? A somewhat pessimistic response, for example, would be that the methodological paradoxes of simplistic oversimplification, definitive indefinity and replicable incomparability that emerged in the work of the Gluecks have been exacerbated and promulgated to a much wider audience through the Cambridge Study and that these paradoxes have been further embedded within the psyche of risk factor researchers in England and Wales in the methodological confusion of studies such as the OCJS. For as much as the ESRC-sponsored studies have attempted to redress the methodological shortcomings of artefact RFR through innovative longitudinal designs and more complex analysis of interactions, mechanisms and processes in current life, these studies have also mirrored several of the weaknesses of their predecessors. Notwithstanding their longitudinal designs, few studies have explicitly drawn on the findings from previous data collection episodes to inform data collection and analysis at successive stages, despite this dynamic and reflexive facility being a major potential benefit of longitudinal research. More fundamentally for longitudinal research designs, few studies have conducted within-individual analyses of the data in order to identify and attempt to explain the potentially causal influence of risk factors at the level of the individual young person. Consequently, any conclusions drawn have been inevitably based on aggregation, imputation and extrapolation from the data and have not necessarily been valid or applicable to any of the research participants.

The extended study period afforded by longitudinal designs has been under-utilised in England and Wales (even within the Cambridge Study, which has preferred self-replication to the iterative identification of new risk factors). For example, artefact RFR studies have tended to prioritise childhood (typically eight years of age and onwards) as their starting point and have terminated the study in adolescence or early adulthood. This has largely been due to the preference for developmental understandings of the influence of risk factors, which has led to a subsequent neglect of risk factors across the life course. The extended measurement period has been particularly under-utilised in terms of the sensitive measurement of the temporal ordering of risk and offending behaviour in terms of, *inter alia*, the onset, duration and intensity of exposure to risk relative to the onset, duration and intensity of offending behaviour (both self-reported and officially-recorded). Even when the temporal precedence of risk over offending has allegedly been established, there has been insufficient attention paid to exploring the potential mechanisms and processes of influence that may explain how exposure to risk leads into offending behaviour.

The inductive potential of prospective longitudinal designs to generate and explore new theories and insights into the development and nature of risk factors for offending and risk as a dynamic, complex process has been largely overlooked by studies more concerned to test and validate existing theories that have been generated in previous research. Despite its scope and longevity, the Cambridge Study has remained wedded to replicating the methodology, findings and conclusions of the Gluecks' early developmental work. Similarly, the OCJS was strongly informed by the Cambridge Study to the point of conducting a quasi-replication of its content and analyses, regardless of their validity or applicability. The SCoPIC studies have each prioritised the validation of a nascent theory formulated by their main author, whether it be Moffitt's hypothesis of genetic-environmental interaction tested within the Childhood Study, Wikström's DEAT within the PADS or Bottoms's interactional theory of desistence within SPOOCS. Where this deductive validation of a priori theories has not been conducted, for example, within the Pathways partnership, the studies have privileged the exploration and validation of existing understandings of risk and risk factors (rather than identifying new, original risk influences). Indeed, the Pathways partnership studies have been so focused on the present day construction of risk and the limitations of predicting and generalising the influence of risk factors, that the very necessity for a longitudinal design has been brought into question.

The ostensible replicability across longitudinal studies of a small group of psychosocial risk factors, whose influence on offending has been explained in largely developmental terms, has overlooked the methodological limitations within, and discordances between, the individual studies that have constituted longitudinal RFR in England and Wales. Studies have differed in relation to their contexts (e.g. historical, political, geographical), the demographic characteristics of their samples (e.g. in terms of age, gender, social class) and the representativeness of these samples within the youth populations from which they were drawn. When these considerations are placed alongside the emerging body of pathways RFR, the implication is that the replication of risk factor findings across different studies does not indicate generalisability or comparability in how these risk factors could or should be interpreted.

The most prominent longitudinal RFR studies in England and Wales have, therefore, typically under-exploited the methodological potential of the longitudinal design and perpetuated a series of methodological paradoxes that undermine the utility and validity of RFR. Longitudinal RFR in England and Wales has tended to adopt a partial and restricted methodology that has relied on overly-simplistic, factorised conceptions of risk feeding into deterministic statistical understandings of the relationship between childhood risk factors and offending. These understandings have, in turn, encouraged definitive, generalised conclusions based on the aggregation of data from unrepresentative samples on the one hand and highly complex, specific and unrepresentative understandings of risk and protection as negotiated and (often) unpredictable processes on the other. Studies have largely failed to adopt an iterative, reflective methodology that identifies new, age- and context-specific factors and processes at each data collection stage (rather than simply replicating the same childhood risk factors each time) and have neglected within-individual analyses and investigations of temporal precedence that could have explored the potentially causal and predictive influence of risk. This partial, restricted and simplistic methodology has served to distort the social phenomena under investigation and has produced findings and conclusions that fail to adequately describe the relationship between cause and effect in understanding youth offending and that certainly do not bear the weight of prediction.

Chapter 4

Cross-sectional risk factor research in England and Wales – achievements, limitations and potential

The UK government, under pressure from the general public and the media to 'do something' about the youth crime 'problem' in the insecure and unpredictable 'risk society', has desired easily digestible, unequivocal and (perhaps most crucially) speedy conclusions from research (see Wilcox 2003). Cross-sectional research has been deemed fit for purpose in this regard. Cross-sectional designs typically utilise surveys to obtain a 'snap shot' of the state of affairs in a population *at one point in time* (see Robson 2002). Cross-sectional studies are able to gather, analyse and disseminate data from large populations more quickly and with lower attrition rates than longitudinal designs, producing a faster turnaround of results and increasing the chances of obtaining 'up-to-date', relevant data that can, for example, offer relevant, live targets for policy and intervention strategies. Cross-sectional research is also comparatively less expensive, less resource intensive and less time consuming than other methodologies. Furthermore, the facility to more easily access larger, more nationally- and statistically-*representative* samples of young people enables researchers to more confidently generalise results.

There is, however, a major difference between longitudinal and cross-sectional designs, which limits the *explanatory* potential of cross-sectional RFR. In contrast to the longitudinal tracking of behaviour over extended periods, cross-sectional RFR has typically collected data on the so-called independent variable (risk factor) and the dependent, target variable (offending) at a single point in time or over the same general period of time (e.g. the past 12 months). Any statistical analysis is, therefore, limited to identifying correlations/statistical associations between the two variables. In other words, cross-sectional research is not a research method suited to exploring issues of causality between variables. As Farrington has said:

it is impossible in cross-sectional surveys to establish what came first, and what caused what. (Farrington 1996: 7)

However, Wikström (2008) has disputed such claims, arguing that establishing the temporal precedence of certain factors over offending, therefore establishing them as 'risk factors', *is* feasible within cross-sectional designs if measurement is sensitive to the exact point in time that the individual was first exposed to a factor relative to their first episode of offending. For example, it is possible for cross-sectional research to establish that, in the past year, a factor was experienced in January and offending began for the first time in December. In this way, data can still be collected at a single point in time and relative to the same time period (e.g. 12 months), but measurement of risk and offending can be temporally sensitive. Thus, if temporal precedence is established in cross-sectional research then imputations of causality are, indeed, possible. However, cross-sectional RFR, to date, has failed to evidence such a degree of sensitivity in its methods. For this reason, researchers conducting cross-sectional surveys have, in the main, shied away from characterising the identified risk factors as *causal* of offending. However, risk factor researchers have not been shy in asserting that factors statistically *associated* with offending are actually *predictive* of offending – thus imputing a temporal precedence and predictive influence that cannot and should not be concluded through snapshot, one-off survey designs that have measured risk factors and offending contemporaneously or over a generic 12 month period. The cross-sectional methodologies employed in RFR have been simply unable to explore the nature (e.g. causal direction) of the interaction between (risk) factors and offending beyond identifying correlations and statistical associations. Any conclusions that go beyond this (even, indeed, use of the term 'risk factor') illustrate a definiteness born of indefinity and a limited and over-simplified understanding of the relationship being asserted.

The nature, quality and validity of the evidence of risk that has emerged from cross-sectional RFR in England and Wales requires evaluation. It is particularly important to explore the contribution of cross-sectional RFR to the evolution of our understanding of risk and the potential utility of the policy and practice these understandings have informed. Furthermore, it is necessary to consider whether cross-sectional methods and findings have been employed in an inappropriate fashion that has belied their limitations and overlooked the substantive differences with longitudinal RFR. A range of important theoretical and methodological questions must be asked of the largely government-sponsored body of cross-sectional RFR studies in England and Wales:

- What has been the theoretical basis of the main studies and has this been compatible with the research design employed?

- How have data been analysed and what conclusions have been made regarding the prevalence, extent and nature of relationships between 'risk' factors and offending by young people?

- Have these conclusions been justified/legitimised by the methodology employed, the quality of the data and the nature of the analyses?

- Have cross-sectional designs offered a sensitive, flexible and valid method of evolving RFR and our understanding of the concept of risk?

A selection of the most important and high profile cross-sectional RFR studies in England and Wales will be outlined and explored in order to engage with these questions and to evaluate the legitimacy, validity and achievements of cross-sectional research within the RFR movement.

The Home Office Youth Lifestyles Survey

The 1992 House of Commons Home Affairs Select Committee established an enquiry into youth offending in England and Wales and the Criminal Justice System's alleged failure to deal adequately with it (House of Commons Home Affairs Committee 1993). The Committee questioned whether official statistics accurately reflected the true extent of youth offending and highlighted the need to identify the causes of youth crime in order to inform crime prevention policy and practice. As a result, the Youth Lifestyles Survey (YLS) was commissioned to explore the extent and nature of youth offending in England and Wales and, more importantly, to inform policy responses by pinpointing the reasons why young people began offending in the first place and ceased offending once they had started.

The first YLS authors (John Graham and Benjamin Bowling) reviewed existing information on factors that encouraged the onset of youth offending. They immediately identified the psychosocial-developmental, criminal careers research of Farrington (especially the Cambridge Study in Delinquent Development) as their theoretical basis and as the basis of the family, school and peer group risk factors they were to measure (Graham and Bowling 1995).

The YLS-I methodology

The YLS was first run in 1992/93 (Graham and Bowling 1995) with 1,721 young people aged 14–25 years obtained from a random sample of households in England and Wales, supplemented by a booster sample of 808 young people from ethnic minorities. Young people were interviewed in their own homes about their offending behaviour – using questions adapted from the International Self-Reported Delinquency (ISRD) inventory developed by the Dutch Ministry of Justice (Junger-Tas *et al.* 1994). A UK-version of the ISRD was created (Graham and Bowling 1995), altering the wording of several questions to better reflect definitions of criminal offences in England and Wales (e.g. adding 'without the owner's permission' to the question of 'did you ever take away a car?'). A total of 23 offences were measured, covering the categories of expressive property offences (e.g. criminal damage, arson), acquisitive property offences (e.g. various types of theft, trespass, fraud) and violent offences (e.g. various types of assault, threatening with a weapon, public disorder). Young people were asked to report (yes or no) whether they had ever committed any of these offences (the measure of *lifetime* offending) and whether they had committed any of the offences in the last year (defined as *active* offending). If they reported 'yes' to any offence, they were asked at what age their offending began (*onset* of offending) and how many times it had been committed (*frequency* of offending – 1–2, 3–5, 6–10, 11 or more).

Young people were asked questions regarding 'their social and demographic backgrounds and their experiences at home and at school ... to ascertain which background factors are closely associated with offending (and desistance from offending)' (Graham and Bowling 1995: 31). The purpose of this central element of the study was to attempt to explain the onset of offending. On the basis that previous studies had established that most young people begin offending in their early teens, the YLS research team only asked young people about the presence of these background factors at the ages of 14–15 years. Consequently, 14–15 year olds were asked about their current lives, whereas those aged over 15 years provided information on background factors retrospectively. The family and school-based factors measured were:

- *Socio-economic group* (standard five-point classification of occupational group).

- *Family structure* (both natural parents, single-parent or natural parent plus step-parent).

- *Family size* (no siblings, one, two or three siblings).

- *Attachment to family* (strong or medium/weak).

- *Parental supervision* (high or medium/low).

- *Siblings in trouble with the police* (siblings in trouble or no siblings in trouble).

- *Friends in trouble with the police* (friends in trouble or no friends in trouble).

- *Attachment to school* (high or low).

- *Standard of schoolwork* (above average or average/below average).

- *Truanted from school* (truanted or did not truant).

- *Temporarily excluded from school* (excluded or not excluded).

- *Permanently excluded from school* (excluded or not excluded).

(Graham and Bowling 1995)

Multivariate analysis (logistic regression) was employed to examine the statistical links between the dichotomous measure of ever offending (yes or no) and the (typically dichotomous) quantified measures of background factors. Logistic regression was used to analyse the relative (independent) effect of each of the background factors when controlling for the statistical effects of all other factors.

Following the first interview stage, life history interviews were conducted with 21 young people (ten males, 11 females) who had reported ever offending, but who were no longer active offenders (thus labelled as *desisters*). Qualitative interviews explored a series of factors identified in previous empirical research as contributing to young people's personal and social development and desistance from offending (e.g. Sampson and Laub 1993). These social development variable/factors were:

- completing full-time education;

- stable employment;

- leaving home;

- getting married/stable relationship;

- staying at home to look after children;

- taking responsibility for self and others.

(Graham and Bowling 1995: 53)

Reflective of the onset of offending analysis, the social development variables were dichotomised 'to simplify the analysis and presentation of this information' (Graham and Bowling 1995: 53) and to enable multivariate analysis of their relative influence on offending. Overall, these analyses were intended for YLS-1 'to establish the reasons why some young people start to offend, and what influences those young offenders who desist from offending to sustain a non-criminal lifestyle' (Graham and Bowling 1995: ix).

The YLS-1 findings and conclusions

The factors considered to be most strongly associated with the onset of offending across all members of the sample were parental supervision, association with delinquent peers and truancy from school. In gender-specific terms, having delinquent siblings and having been excluded from school were the strongest correlates with onset for males, whereas low attachment to the family and school were the strongest correlates for females.

The life history interviews highlighted that a successful transition from childhood to adulthood underpinned desistance from offending and that males lagged behind females in completion of this transition. Male desistance was identified as influenced by living at home in their twenties, academic success and avoiding criminogenic influences (e.g. association with delinquents). Males reported that the positive influence of peer group, finding a sense of direction in their lives and learning the consequences of their actions were most likely to lead to desistance. Therefore, Graham and Bowling (1995) characterised the factors linked to desistance as 'protective factors' that reduced the likelihood of future offending. In contrast to males, female desistance was found to be abrupt and conscious, encouraged by 'protective factors' such as completing full-time education, leaving home, leaving school, forming partnerships and having children.

Graham and Bowling confidently asserted that their questionnaire findings provided 'a basis for explaining why some young people start to offend while others do not' (Graham and Bowling 1995: xi), whilst the interviews enabled them to 'identify the influences, conditions and circumstances which ultimately led to desistance from offending' (Graham and Bowling 1995: xiii). They concluded that these findings strongly suggested that youth policy should prioritise interventions aimed at 'preventing individuals from ever starting to offend and ... finding ways to encourage offenders to desist' (Graham and Bowling 1995: xiii).

The YLS-2 methodology

In 1998/99, a second sweep of the YLS was run with 4,848 members of a broader age group, 12–30 year olds obtained from a random sample of households in England and Wales (Flood-Page *et al.* 2000).

The YLS-2 attempted to gain a 'more complete picture' of youth offending than the first YLS (Flood-Page *et al.* 2000) by extending the range of socio-developmental factors measured in YLS-1 with the addition of 'widely-replicated' factors that were believed to 'influence' offending (taken from the 1998 Rutter *et al.* summary of international RFR – see Chapter 5) in the domains of:

- *Individual* – IQ, temperament, cognitive impairment, hyperactivity, impulsivity.

– family structure, family size, relationship with parents.

⌐*chool* – low achievement, truancy, exclusion, disaffection.

- *Lifestyle* – substance use, leisure activities, peer groups.

(Flood-Page *et al.* 2000: 31)

As in the first sweep of the YLS, the vast majority of these 'influences' were measured as dichotomised variables, for example: parental supervision (poor or not poor), attachment to school (disaffected or not disaffected), school achievement (above average or below average/average), bullied others (yes or no), family or friends in trouble with the police (yes or no) and drug use in last 12 months (yes or no). The remaining variables were not dichotomised, but were nevertheless quantified using rating scales, for example, family structure (two natural parents, lone parent, step-family, other) and truancy (truanted at least once a month, truancy less often, non-truant). Unlike in the first sweep, the background factors were measured in terms of exposure in current lives/in the past year (with some school factors such as truancy and exclusion measured retrospectively for the 18–30 age group) rather than in terms of their presence at age 14–15 years.

As in the YLS-1, the quantified background factors and dichotomised measures of offending were analysed using logistic regression. For the purpose of analysis and reporting, the sample was divided into two age groups: 12–17 year olds and 18–30 year olds.

The YLS-2 findings and conclusions

Multivariate analysis identified the main correlates of serious and persistent offending in the YLS-2 sample to be:

- both age groups – regular drug use, association with delinquent friends;
- 12–17 year olds only – disaffection from school, truancy, poor parental supervision, hanging around in public;
- 18–30 year olds only – regular alcohol use, having no qualifications on leaving school.

The research team concluded that each of the factors statistically associated with serious and persistent offending actually constituted 'predictors of offending' and 'risk factors' and that their identification served to emphasise the importance of risk-focused preventative intervention programmes targeting these factors (Flood-Page *et al.* 2000). At the same time, however, the researchers cautioned that 'as it is cross-sectional, the YLS cannot unravel whether adverse background factors themselves lead to offending, or whether offending itself exacerbates adversity' (Flood-Page *et al.* 2000: 56).

The Youth Lifestyles Survey as RFR

The replicability of findings between both rounds of the ostensible apparent methodological strength. The auth reports have concluded that family background and rela ship groups, educational experience and lifestyle fact correlated with offending' (Graham and Bowling 199~. ~+, anu uiese factors, therefore, function as 'risk factors' and 'predictors of offending' (Flood-Page *et al.* 2000: 43). Both studies have concluded with claims that the YLS has helped to quantify and underscore the influence of 'socially-based' risk-related factors on the onset, prevalence and development of offending and their important role in informing the content of preventative interventions with young people. For example, according to Flood-Page *et al.*, 'the breadth of these risk factors underlines the importance of programmes that address a wide range of factors' (2000: 56).

Both sweeps of the YLS have uncritically transposed the content and conclusions of the longitudinal Cambridge Study in Delinquent Development into a cross-sectional design. This transposition has signified a simplistic oversimplification of the central tenets of Farrington's research, which sought to examine the *developmental* influences of childhood risk factors on later behaviour rather than the active and contemporaneous influences of risk factors during the same period in which offending behaviour takes place. Longitudinal and cross-sectional designs are simply incompatible in this regard as they are measuring different forms of relationship between psychosocial factors and offending. Longitudinal designs have been commonly used in RFR to explore causal and predictive relationships in order to support developmental understandings of 'risk' factors for offending, but cross-sectional designs have been limited (by the researchers who have designed them) to identifying correlations between factors and offending at a single point, with no investigation of temporal precedence and the direction of these relationships and no consequent, definitive understanding of psychosocial background factors as causal or predictive 'risk' factors at all. The cross-sectional methodology employed by the YLS has, however, oversimplified the necessary complexity of measurement and analysis required to fully explore the causal and predictive nature of the risk-factor–offending relationship. For example, the YLS-1 authors claimed to have identified risk factors that provided 'a basis for explaining why some people start to offend' (Graham and Bowling 1995: xi). However, this definitive conclusion was based on statistical relationships (correlations) between dichotomous measures of background factors taken at the average age of offending onset within the sample (14–15 years old). This aggregated and over-simplified measure has neglected analysis of the temporal links between background factors and the actual age of onset for each individual young person who reported having offended (even though this sure was actually taken in the study). It was therefore possible that a young person's initial exposure to particular background factors actually post-dated the onset of offending or occurred concurrently, so these factors should not have been considered predictors or risk factors at all. Although Flood-Page *et al.* (2000) touched on this problem in the YLS-2, it did not stop them also from asserting that the background factors they had linked statistically to offending (i.e. as correlates) represented risk factors.

The findings from the YLS have been limited by their oversimplified depiction of risk engendered by the factorisation of the survey data (even factorising qualitative interview data regarding desistance), which has reduced potentially complex, multi-faceted and qualitative characteristics, behaviours and attitudes to crude dichotomised insensitive statistical variables that can be readily entered into multivariate analysis. Thus, an oversimplified, crude set of 'factors' have substituted for qualitative understandings of what risk means to individual young people. These factors have been entered into statistical analyses to produce similarly crude and limited understandings of the relationship between risk factors and offending.

The definitiveness of the conclusions from the YLS has been based not only on the uncritical application of longitudinal findings within cross-sectional designs and the overly-simplistic factorisation of risk information, but also on the aggregation of data obtained from broad age groups and from generic measures of offending. This process has lacked specificity and sensitivity on a least two fronts. Firstly, it has been based on the assumption that the respective age ranges (14–25 year olds and 12–30 year olds) in each survey and the categories of offending measured (e.g. ever, active, serious and persistent) were homogenous. This erroneous assumption precluded any detailed examination of individual differences within and between the samples in each survey. Moreover, there was no exploration of potential differences within the broad categories of offending measured (e.g. 'ever', 'active', 'serious', 'persistent') even though these over-generalised and insensitive categories do not necessarily contain similar behaviours that can be conflated with any degree of validity. Secondly, the process of aggregation has favoured the easy production of correlates based on group-level analyses and has therefore precluded within-individual analysis of background factors, so none of the factors identified in either study should be viewed as predictive/explanatory of or even correlated with the offending of any specific individual.

The methodologies of the two sweeps of the YLS have embodied and perpetuated the paradoxes that drive RFR: the simplistic oversimplification of risk through factorisation, the definitiveness of conclusions regarding the risk-factor–offending relationship in the face of indefinite and partial information, confident claims to replicability despite incomparability (between the two studies) and the unrepresentativeness of the aggregated and homogenised findings to any individual participant. An overriding question, therefore, is whether or not these methodological paradoxes exert an invalidating influence on the findings and recommendations for risk focused interventions that have emerged from the YLS. Undoubtedly the answer is yes. Both sweeps of the YLS have imported inappropriate lists of risk factors, employed crude forms of measurement and factorisation, utilised insensitive group-based forms of analysis and failed to properly take account of the limitations of cross-sectional methodologies for the conclusions reached. It would be inadvisable, indeed, to use the findings of the YLS to try to understand youth offending and inadvisable to act on the resulting recommendations.

Youth at Risk: the Communities that Care National Youth Survey

The Communities that Care (CtC) registered charity originated in the USA in 1992 and was established in the UK in 1997 with financial support from the Joseph Rowntree Foundation. CtC is now an established international organisation in the UK, the Netherlands, Ireland, Australia and over 600 communities in the USA. CtC UK (since 2006 part of the Rainer charitable foundation) has national offices in Wales, Northern Ireland, Scotland and England. CtC is a social development programme that supports (typically socially disadvantaged and high crime) communities in conducting local (often school-based) risk audits/assessments and subsequent planning of interventions based on the risk audit (Hawkins and Catalano 1992). CtC has been designed and implemented to give practical expression to the Social Development Model (see Catalano and Hawkins 1996; see also Chapter 2).

The CtC Youth Survey

At the heart of the CtC process is the Youth Survey, a questionnaire administered in secondary schools that measures self-reported problem behaviours and identifies a series of psychosocial 'risk' factors for communities to target through risk-focused interventions. The CtC Youth Survey contains 17 of the allegedly most significant 'risk' factors for offending and six of the most significant 'protective factors'. These factors have been identified through systematic reviews and statistical meta-analyses of longitudinal research conducted in the UK (e.g. Farrington 1996) and across the industrialised Western world (e.g. Rutter *et al.* 1998) over the past 50 years. These factors are located in the domains of:

- *Family* – poor parental supervision and discipline, family conflict, family history of problem behaviours, parental involvement/attitudes condoning problem behaviour, low income and poor housing.

chool – low academic achievement (beginning at primary school), aggressive behaviour at school, including bullying, lack of commitment to school (including truancy) and school disorganisation.

- *Community* – community disorganisation and neglect, availability of drugs, disadvantaged neighbourhood, high population turnover and lack of neighbourhood attachment.

- *Individuals friends and peers* – alienation and lack of social commitment, attitudes that condone problem behaviour, early involvement in problem behaviour and friends involved in problem behaviour.

- *Protection* – social bonding, healthy standards, opportunities for involvement, social and learning skills, positive recognition and praise for positive behaviour.

(Beinert *et al.* 2002: 5–7)

The Youth Survey measures these risk and protective factors in terms of their existence in the current lives of young people. The currency of the risk factors was indicated by the content and phrasing of a series of statements to which young people report their agreement or disagreement on a four-point scale: NO! (disagree strongly), no (mostly disagree), yes (mostly agree), YES! (strongly agree). For example, in terms of the family risk factor known as family conflict, young people were asked for their strength of agreement with the following statements:

- people in my family often insult or yell at each other;

- people in my family have serious arguments;

- we argue about the same things in my family over and over again;

- adults in my home sometimes try to hurt me, for example, by pushing, hitting or kicking me;

- adults in my home sometimes try to hurt each other, for example, by pushing, hitting or kicking each other.

(Beinert *et al.* 2002: 22)

The Youth Survey also takes measures of young people's involvement in 'problem behaviour' as a baseline against which to assess the statistical influence of the psychosocial factors that represent risk and protection in the survey. Accordingly, young people are asked to indicate whether they have offended in their lifetime (ever) and in the past year (active), whether they have used different substances (drugs, alcohol and cigarettes) over their lifetime and recently (in the past four weeks), whether they have ever been excluded from school and if they have ever been pregnant.

For analysis purposes, factor scores are dichotomised into the categories of yes (strongly or mostly agree) and no (strongly or mostly disagree). Measures of offending and substance use are aggregated across, *inter alia,* school year, age group and gender. Bivariate analysis is then employed to statistically link the presence of each psychosocial background variable (yes/no) to the presence of problem behaviours (yes/no). These results are then used to shape local intervention strategies designed to reduce risk and enhance protection. Overall, Beinert *et al.* have summarised the CtC process in the following manner:

> CtC takes the research evidence concerning risk factors and applies it in a workable programme, intended to strengthen communities and enable children and young people to achieve their potential. (Beinert *et al.* 2002: 9)

Youth at Risk: the CtC national survey

In 2000–2001, CtC UK ran the Youth At Risk study, administering the Youth Survey to a nationally representative random sample of 14,445 young people aged 11–16 years in 89 secondary schools (themselves randomly selected from local authority areas) in England, Wales and Scotland (Beinert *et al.* 2002). The tripartite aims of the Youth at Risk survey were to measure:

- levels of youth crime, truancy, smoking, drug and alcohol use among children and young people of secondary school age;

- levels of exposure to associated risk and protective factors;

- the strength of the relationship between individual risk and protective factors in the CtC model and the range of measured problem behaviours.

(Beinert *et al.* 2002: 48)

Following bivariate analysis of the findings from their national survey, Beinert *et al.* produced the generalised conclusions that:

> there was a statistically significant relationship between exposure to risk and the levels of involvement in problems and problem behaviour reported by young people (and) ... significant association between each protective factor, as measured, and a reduced likelihood that young people would report involvement in crime. (Beinert *et al.* 2002: 48)

Nothwithstanding that this result (and particularly their conclusions about protective factors) is inevitable given that they have analysed a dichotomised set of variables, the authors concluded that the findings from the Youth at Risk study provided 'strong evidence that supports the validity of the CtC model' (Beinert *et al.* 2002: 48) and that these findings could be used to inform communities in their planning of community specific 'risk and protection-focused crime prevention' interventions with children and young people.

The CtC process and its evidential bases (the Youth Survey and Youth at Risk study) is theoretically underpinned by the processes of risk influence hypothesised by the Social Development Model (Hawkins and Catalano 1992; Catalano and Hawkins 1996). However, the Youth Survey and the Youth at Risk study are cross-sectional in design. Thus, in seeking to provide an evidential basis for CTC, notions and findings from longitudinal research have been uncritically transposed into cross-sectional surveys and assumptions have then been made about the nature of the risk-factor–offending relationship and notions of causality and preventative utility. However, the temporal insensitivity of the cross-sectional CtC design (e.g. measuring background factors and problem behaviours concurrently) does not enable an exploration of the direction of the relationship between these background factors and offending. Thus, any factors correlated with offending should not have been labelled 'risk factors', because to do so implies that they have temporal precedence over offending. Cross-sectional research of the type used by CTC is, in fact, incapable of evidencing the processes theorised in the Social Development Model and incapable of showing anything more than statistical associations between different features or aspects of young peoples' lives.

Beinert *et al.* (2002) acknowledged the limitations of cross-sectional RFR in passing, but also concluded that repeated administrations of the Youth at Risk survey (yet to be undertaken) would open the way for an analysis of time trends in the risk-factor–offending relationship. Such a claim is feasible (given certain preconditions such as repeat administration of the questionnaire to the same sample), but at this stage, definitive statements regarding the risk-factor–offending relationship should have been limited to the realms of correlation, which would befit the cross-sectional nature of the design.

Taken another way, it could be argued that the goal of the CtC process should not be a criminological mission to validate the Social Development Model, but a tool directed towards social policy concerns. Seen in this way, the CtC process is concerned with the identification of active factors and problem behaviours experienced in the current lives of young people in specific communities as way of informing the relevant and timely development of general policy and practice. The CtC Youth Survey has the potential to empower communities and to inform locally-sensitive problem-focused policy and practice that targets locally specific concerns relevant to the current lives of local young people, but it cannot validate the Social Development Model or provide any direct evidence of causality.

When applied to local communities, the relevance and currency of the factors identified through the Youth Survey are clear benefits to a CtC process seeking to identify locally-relevant psychosocial factors and problem behaviours, as opposed to factors/behaviours identified in nationally representative samples and then applied uncritically to local youth populations. These factors and behaviours, therefore, can serve as promising targets for local policy and practice formations as they are relevant and salient to young people in a specific community at a given time. This is an important development in RFR as it represents an eschewing of the prediction of individual behaviour and the targeting of individualised interventions, in favour of identifying and recommending locally-specific, community-level interventions.

There are, however, some problems with the CtC process and the Youth Survey. Risk has been measured in the Youth Survey and converted rather crudely into quantitative factors for ease of statistical analysis. This factorisation distorts and misrepresents the quality of the variable being assessed/measured and inevitably desensitises and over-simplifies the complexity of the phenomena of risk and its potential function as a dynamic process influencing offending or other behaviours in a myriad of possible ways. Likewise, the concept of protection within the study has been factorised and, further still, has been over-simplified to solely represent the dichotomy of a risk factor, rather than conceiving of protective factors and processes as exerting an influence on behaviour independent of risk factors.

The statistical analysis used to animate the CtC process has been somewhat crude and poorly understood. For example, CtC have tended to produce homogenised findings across broad age groups, treating 11 year olds as if they were the same as 16 year olds, paying scant attention to age-specific factors related to problem behaviours and the relation of different factors to the onset, frequency, duration and intensity of these problem behaviours. Statistical analyses where there are a broad range of independent and dependent variables and where these variables are broadly defined (and crudely dichotomised) are highly likely to show significant correlations, but the variables so correlated are unlikely to have any kind of real relationship outside of the statistical test. The identification of promising targets for preventative interventions through the CtC process is, therefore, too sweeping and possibly erroneous.

Finally, factors identified as correlated with offending at the local level may well be useful targets for local policy and practice, but they may not be the *most* appropriate targets for intervention when the baseline list of factors has been generated from factors generated by research from around the world or a nationally representative survey. Firstly, pre-existing research may generate factors of no relevance to a particular local community whilst missing those that are relevant and secondly, may (and, in fact does) restrict the domain of independent variables to psychosocial variables at the expense of locally specific, but highly relevant, structural factors. Not only does CtC fail to capture locally specific factors and exclude additional potentially important structural factors, it also fails to engage local communities and young people specifically in defining the scope and range of factors to be investigated in the local study. CtC is guilty, therefore, of being an overly pre-programmed process which is at odds with its stated intentions.

The Promoting Prevention evaluation

Promoting Prevention is a cross-cutting, multi-agency partnership approach to youth crime prevention developed in Swansea, UK and led by a partnership of representatives from across the local authority (e.g. social services, education, youth services, housing, community safety, training centres), South Wales Police, the probation service, the local health authority and numerous voluntary agencies. The Promoting Prevention approach is based on the principles of educational, economic and social inclusion and is underpinned by the principles of youth consultation and empowerment (see City and County of Swansea 2001), in line with the United Nations Convention on the Rights of the Child (UNICEF 1989) and in the context of the Welsh Assembly Government policy documents Better Wales (National Assembly for Wales 2000) and Extending Entitlement (National Assembly Policy Unit 2002). Therefore, within Promoting Prevention, provision and policy is structured around entitlement to a range of services designed to promote the attainment and development of all young people (see also National Assembly Policy Unit 2002). The initiative contains a range of corporate, strategic and restorative interventions that are both targeted (e.g. alternative curriculum provision, mentoring, family group conferencing, anger management, detached youth work, reparative activities) and universal (e.g. drugs education, careers guidance, Youth Action Groups, peer education schemes).

The Promoting Prevention evaluation methodology

The Promoting Prevention partnership has been allocated a dominant role in determining the nature of the solution to local youth offending, informed by the findings of an independent evaluation conducted by Swansea University from 2002–2004 (see Case and Haines 2004; Haines and Case 2005) and co-funded by the Youth Justice Board and the local authority. The aims of the evaluation were: (1) to assess whether existing Promoting Prevention provision reflected the nature of risk expressed by local young people; (2) to indicate promising areas on which to focus an inclusive, promotional social policy approach to working with local young people. Consequently, the Promoting Prevention evaluation was underpinned by a self-reported offending and risk factor questionnaire administered to an opportunity sample of 1,278 young people (657 males, 621 females) aged 11–15 years drawn from five local secondary schools.

Active self-reported offending (yes/no in the last year) was measured using the UK version of the ISRD instrument (Graham and Bowling 1995). Active risk factors (experienced in current life) were measured in the psychosocial risk factor 'domains' of family, school, neighbourhood/community, lifestyle and personal/individual factors using statements adapted from the CtC Youth Survey instrument (Case 2004; see also Beinert *et al.* 2002). Young people responded on a five-point Likert scale (strongly agree–agree–neither agree nor disagree–disagree–strongly disagree) to a series of risk-related statements such as:

- I do not get along with my parent(s);

- I do not do as well as I should at school;

- I feel stressed and worried.

The Promoting Prevention evaluation findings and conclusions

Logistic regression was employed to identify statistical associations between risk factors and the dichotomised measure of active offending. Particular attention was paid to identifying risk factors specific to each gender and each age group sampled, leading to the following findings:

- *Family* – sibling drug use and parental criminality were associated with active offending for the whole sample, whilst parental drug use (reported by 12–13 year olds only) and unclear parental rules (reported by 13–14 year olds only) were statistically-correlated with offending for these subgroups in the sample.

- *School* – having a poor relationship with teachers was associated with offending for the whole sample, whereas being a bully (females) and academic underachievement (11–12 year olds only) were associated with offending in these particular subgroups.

- *Neighbourhood* – wide availability of drugs (whole sample) and lack of attachment to neighbourhood (13–14 year olds only) were the neighbourhood factors correlated with offending.

- *Lifestyle* – antisocial behaviour (whole sample), having antisocial peers (whole sample), alcohol/drugs problems (males only), having criminal peers (females and 12–13 year olds only), positive attitudes to drugs (13–14 year olds only) and participating in few positive activities (14–15 year olds only) were lifestyle-based factors associated with offending.

- *Personal* – rule breaking attitudes, risk taking behaviour and sensation seeking were statistically-identified as associated with offending for the whole sample, whilst impulsivity (males only), self-harm (females only), inability to defer gratification (males and 13–14 year olds only), stress (12–13 year olds only) and feeling sad/miserable (13–14 year olds only) were all statistically-associated with active offending in these sub-groups.

    (Case 2004; see also Case and Haines 2004; Haines and Case 2005)

It was emphasised that the more detailed analysis of gender and age in risk profiles and the locally specific nature of the study enabled the subsequent planning of services and interventions that were more sensitive to difference than previous studies and their implicit homogenisation of results (see Haines and Case 2005).

The Promoting Prevention evaluation as RFR

The Promoting Prevention evaluation retained several of the common methodological weaknesses of RFR, particularly an inherent reductionism demonstrated by factorisation, psychosocial bias, temporal indefinity and aggregation – resulting in an inevitable indefinity regarding what was discovered and what could be concluded. The evaluation questionnaire, adapted as it was from the CtC Youth Survey, analysed correlations (not causal relationships – although this was never claimed) between factorised and aggregated measures of risk located in psychosocial domains and a measure of offending taken over a broad period ('in the last year'). The evaluation team had no way of understanding the direction of the relationship between risk and offending because of the temporal ambiguity surrounding exactly when young people experienced risk and offended relative to one another (i.e. which came first).

The Promoting Prevention evaluation questionnaire (in line with the CtC Youth Survey that underpinned it) exemplified the uncritical and inappropriate transportation and application of childhood risk factors identified in developmental, longitudinal RFR into a cross-sectional form of RFR that was actually measuring the influence of risk in the current lives of adolescents. Furthermore, despite the gender and age sensitive nature of the analysis, any statistical correlations identified could not be attributed to any individual young person in the study due to the extent of aggregation that took place. However, the methodological weaknesses of the study (identification of correlations only, temporal indefinity, inappropriate importation of developmental factors, aggregation) were mitigated to the extent that the research was intended to inform local policy and service review rather than seeking to identify deterministic risk factors to inform individualised, risk-focused preventative interventions based on a deterministic, developmental premise.

The On Track Youth Lifestyles Survey

In 1997, the Labour government established the Home Office Crime Reduction Programme. A key element of the Programme was the On Track Early Multiple Intervention Programme, for which £30 million was allocated (originally from the £250 million Crime Reduction Programme; later part of the £960 million Children's Fund). The On Track programme funded local authority projects in neighbourhoods categorised as high deprivation/high risk to provide services to young people aged 4–12 years (and their families) to reduce offending through early intervention. Local authorities in England were invited by the Home Office to bid for On Track funding on the basis of proposed delivery plans that demonstrated a 'risk approach' (see Hine 2005) to reducing risk and youth offending in their area. The overarching goal of On Track was:

> to reduce children's risk of offending and involvement in antisocial behaviour as well as enhancing those prosocial factors that counteract the impact of risk. (Armstrong *et al.* 2005: v)

In each area receiving On Track funding, a range of risk-focused 'evidence-based preventive services' (e.g. parent training, home-school partnerships, pre-school education, home visiting, family therapy) was developed (Armstrong *et al.* 2005). Each project was managed by a local partnership, which included members from relevant child-focused agencies (e.g. local authority educational and social service departments, youth offending teams, police and voluntary sector organisations).

As part of the multi-strand evaluation of On Track, a repeated cross-sectional On Track Youth Lifestyles Survey (not to be confused with the Home Office Youth Lifestyles Survey which was a completely separate piece of work) was commissioned by the Home Office to measure changes in levels of risk and youth offending in On Track areas. The survey was administered in primary and secondary schools in On Track areas in 2001 (Armstrong *et al.* 2005) and 2004 (Bhabra *et al.* 2006a, 2006b). The aim of the On Track Youth Lifestyles Survey was to 'collect baseline data about risk factors, protective factors and self-reported involvement in problem behaviours' and to conduct repeat surveys in order to 'identify changes in the patterns of self-reported problem behaviour, allowing the evaluation to assess the impact of On Track strategies' (Armstrong *et al.* 2005: 1). The On Track programme was based on a set of definitive beliefs espoused by the Home Office (not necessarily by the evaluation team):

- the (developmental) belief that risk factors found to be present in individuals at an early age were predictive and causal of offending in later years;

- that these risk factors could be targeted and changed by focused interventions;

- that levels of offending would decline as a result;

- that levels of risk factors would be lower in adolescence than in childhood;

- that measuring the prevalence and frequency of developmental risk factors in adolescence would provide a reliable measure of the impact of the programme.

(Hine 2005: 118)

The On Track Youth Lifestyles Survey methodology

The On Track Youth Lifestyles Survey employed a repeat cross-sectional survey design to:

- access children's self-report of problem behaviour;

- measure levels of risk and protection within the sample population; and

- provide a base-line for comparison with repeat surveys of the On Track school population

(Armstrong et al. 2005: 3)

The 2001 sweep of the research was conducted with all (consenting) primary and secondary schools in each of the high deprivation, high crime areas in England and Wales that were participating in the On Track programme: accessing a total sample of 18,184 primary schoolchildren and 13,365 secondary schoolchildren. The second sweep in 2004 took a random stratified sample of 7,433 children in primary schools and 12,682 young people in secondary schools in On Track areas.

In the period between the two sets of surveys, funding cuts were made to the evaluation (hence the smaller sample in 2004) and the On Track programme was transferred from the Home Office Crime Reduction Programme to the Children and Young People's Unit, which was then integrated into the Department for Education and Skills. In this time, the original research team (Armstrong et al.) was replaced by a new team (Bhabra et al.) and there was little subsequent contact between the two teams (Hine 2008). However, the authors of the second round of surveys restated the aim of the On Track Youth Lifestyles Survey 'to investigate the characteristics of the school aged population in On Track areas, in terms of a constellation of risk and protective factors' (Bhabra et al. 2006b: 1).

Both studies utilised two questionnaires which were known as the 'Primary School Survey' and the 'Secondary School Survey' – both of which were based on the theoretical model of CtC and its ready-made, validated Youth Survey, but with the addition of a range of questions regarding victimisation and bullying (Armstrong *et al.* 2005). Consequently, the questionnaire contained psychosocial risk and protective factors mainly drawn from the established developmental list, plus some ecological factors relating to 'community'. Theoretically, 'risk factors' were conceived as 'characteristics or attributes of an individual, family, social group, or community that increase the probability of certain disorders or behaviours arising at a later point in time' (Bhabra *et al.* 2006b: 3), whilst 'protective factors' were seen to 'inoculate' or 'mitigate' risk factors and to promote resilience – 'positive functioning in the face of adverse circumstances' (Bhabra *et al.* 2006b: 3). The 'risk and protective factors' measured in the questionnaires focused on:

- *Family* – poor parental supervision and discipline, family conflict, siblings involved in problem behaviour, parental attitudes condoning problem behaviour, a positive relationship with parents, family attachments.

- *School* – lack of commitment to school, opportunities for prosocial involvement in school, positive feelings about school, high school expectations of behaviour.

- *Community* – community disorganisation and neglect, lack of neighbourhood attachment, easy availability of drugs, positive relationship with adults.

- *Individual/Peers* – attitudes condoning problem behaviour, friends involved in problem behaviour, individual conflictual attitudes, being a victim of crime, bullying.

(Armstrong *et al.* 2005: 32)

Offending and antisocial behaviour, as a conflated category, was assessed by a self-report inventory of offences/antisocial behaviours – subsequently categorised by the research team into *minor* (shoplifting, vandalism, buying/handling stolen goods, antisocial behaviour) and *major* (theft, burglary, assault, carrying a weapon). Offending/antisocial behaviour was measured in terms of having been 'committed over the past year'.

In each sweep of the study, each 'risk factor' was measured in terms of its presence in current life, although the precise length of this measurement period was not made clear and it was, instead, left to the respondents to interpret temporally-generic questions such as 'the rules in my family are clear' and 'I like my neighbourhood'. Each risk factor was derived from 'composite scales measuring different 'constructs' or dimensions of risk, created by combining related questions' (Bhabra *et al.* 2006a: 18). The statistical relationship between the individual questions in each composite scale were originally identified through a statistical technique known as cluster analysis in the first sweep (Armstrong *et al.* 2005) and adopted uncritically by the authors of the second sweep. For example, the 'family conflict' risk factor consisted of the sub-questions 'people in my family often insult or yell at each other', 'people in my family have serious arguments' and 'we argue about the same things in my family over and over again'. Every factor was given a risk level score depending on how the individual responded to each of the constituent questions on a four-point Likert rating scale (YES, yes, no, NO). Young people were considered 'high risk' on a specific factor if they responded positively (YES or yes) to over half of the constituent questions, 'moderate risk' if they responded positively to less than half and 'no risk' if they answered in the negative to all the sub-questions. Constructing composite factors allegedly enabled the researchers 'to capture the "bigger picture", allowing [them] to explore differences between sub groups without (we hope) getting too lost in the minutiae of the data' (Bhabra *et al.* 2006a: 18).

In order to identify 'risk factors' for offending, the research team used logistic regression, a multivariate analysis technique that 'takes account of interrelations between the variables included in the analysis and predicts the likelihood of someone with that characteristic being involved in offending' (Armstrong *et al.* 2005: 43).

The On Track Youth Lifestyles Survey findings and conclusions

The risk factors significantly associated with offending/antisocial behaviour across the two surveys (2001 and 2004) were:

- positive attitudes to antisocial behaviour, sibling antisocial behaviour, peer antisocial behaviour, conflict at home, truancy, challenging behaviour (both primary schoolchildren and secondary schoolchildren);

- disruptive behaviour at school, bullying and victimisation (primary schoolchildren only);

- school exclusion, challenging attitudes, alcohol misuse, parental drug misuse, smoking, negative perceptions of neighbourhood (secondary school children only).

Analyses also identified the following factors as 'protective' against reporting offending/antisocial behaviour across the two surveys:

- parental warmth/involvement, parental supervision/discipline and satisfaction with school (both primary school children and secondary school children);

- positive perceptions of neighbourhood, constructive use of leisure time (primary school children only);

- school involvement/participation, good relationship with parents, social support, clear school rules (secondary school children only).

In the second report, Bhabra *et al.* (2006a, 2006b) focused on the *changes* in levels of reported risk factors in each age group between the two studies (analysed using t-test and chi-square) as a means of (allegedly) enabling the authors to measure change in risk levels between the two administrations. Following statistical comparisons between the 2001 and 2004 surveys, the 'risk factor' of positive attitudes to antisocial behaviour was found to have significantly decreased (in statistical terms) for both primary and secondary school samples, disruptive behaviour at school decreased amongst primary schoolchildren and sibling antisocial behaviour, peer antisocial behaviour, truancy, school exclusion, challenging attitudes and alcohol use decreased amongst secondary schoolchildren. However, the risk factors of truancy and challenging behaviour increased amongst both sample groups.

Increases in measured levels of protection between the samples in the two studies were reported for constructive use of leisure time (primary school children) and clear school rules (secondary school children), but there were statistically significant decreases in reported levels of parental warmth/involvement, parental supervision/discipline, satisfaction with school (both samples), positive perceptions of neighbourhood (primary school children) and school involvement/participation (secondary school children).

Following the first sweep of the On Track Youth Lifestyles Survey, Armstrong *et al.* concluded that 'risk factors are significantly related to problem behaviour and multiple interventions with young people and their families are likely to impact positively in reducing risk and the likelihood of offending' (Armstrong *et al.* 2005: v). Bhabra *et al.* (2006a, 2006b) consolidated this conclusion following the second sweep by maintaining that they had identified risk and protective factors that were dynamic (not fixed) concepts that can change over time and that these risk factors exerted a cumulative influence (more factors, more risk, more offending). However, they stressed that the difficulty in establishing causal relationships between risk factors and offending/antisocial behaviour raises particular problems for policy makers and practitioners in targeting risk-focused interventions appropriately. Armstrong *et al.* also cautioned that 'to fully understand the nature of problem behaviour in any given context it is necessary to be aware of the social and cultural variables that influence that behaviour and the construction of specific risks and protective factors within communities and other social settings' (Armstrong *et al.* 2005: 56).

The On Track Youth Lifestyles Survey as RFR

The repeated cross-sectional design of the On Track Youth Lifestyles Survey has enabled the same questions to be asked in each survey and has thus enabled the identification and replication of a small set of psychosocial 'characteristics of school aged children' across the two sweeps of data collection and analysis. However, the information obtained has offered little to elucidate the 'constellation of risk and protective factors' experienced by sample members, largely due to five key reasons:

1. The absence of analysis of the temporal ordering of background characteristics and offending means that any characteristics/factors statistically-linked to offending/antisocial behaviour should only be seen as correlates rather than risk and protective factors *per se*.

2. The factorisation of characteristics taken to indicate risk and protection and measurement of these factors within broadly-phrased 'catchall' categories has engendered the inevitable (statistical) replication of the 'old faithful' – the narrow body of psychosocial risk factors that drive developmental RFR.

3. The homogenisation and aggregation of broad samples of young people between and within each sweep means that any relationships identified between characteristics and offending/antisocial behaviour do not necessarily apply to any particular individual in the study samples.

4. The uncritical acceptance in sweep two of the composite factors identified in sweep one (rather than a fresh analysis of the validity of these factors for the 2004 sample) potentially invalidates any comparisons between the two surveys.

5. The repeated cross-sectional design rendered it impossible to establish whether the same group of young people have been surveyed in both sweeps. Any reported differences in risk/protection between the two sweeps may, therefore, have simply reflected differences in the characteristics of both groups and not anything related to the On Track interventions.

In a manner increasingly typical of cross-sectional RFR, the On Track Youth Lifestyles Survey offered an over-simplified and partial exploration of risk and protection. The snapshot design and two-stage factorisation process could not facilitate exploration of the nature of the relationship between psychosocial characteristics in current life and offending/antisocial behaviour in the past year beyond the identification of statistical correlations between the two. This type of methodology should only enable researchers to conclude that it is statistically probable that young people who report exposure to certain factors in their current life will also report having committed an offence/antisocial behaviour. Whilst relationships may be statistically significant, they do not necessarily exist in any real or practical way. The factors identified may even have been statistical artefacts with no relationship to offending, certainly no influence on it, outside of a statistical test. For example, conclusions that the On Track Youth Lifestyles Survey had identified 'risk factors' that were 'predictive' of offending/antisocial behaviour simply cannot be justified by the analyses. By extension, Bhabra *et al.*'s recommendations for multiple risk-focused interventions as the most promising responses to the survey findings cannot be substantiated because the analyses within the On Track Youth Lifestyles Survey have not been able to determine whether factors predated or exerted any dynamic influence on offending.

The claim that different factors changed in prevalence and extent over time is ill-informed – offering little in the way of valid comparison between the two different samples accessed and nothing by way of a qualitative understanding of this change, if indeed it even existed beyond the statistical sampling model applied. The second sweep of the On Track Youth Lifestyles Survey demonstrated particular weaknesses in its attempt to analyse 'trends' and 'changes' in risk and protection levels over the life of the study. Bhabra *et al.* made an insufficient effort to acknowledge and address the substantial sampling differences between the two rounds of the Youth Lifestyles Survey. The two survey sweeps were not necessarily (or even probably) conducted with the same young people (as they would have been in a longitudinal study) – some young people who participated in 2001 may have become too old to fall within the primary or secondary school age ranges by 2004; others would not have been chosen again by the random sampling procedure in 2004. Therefore, any changes in the extent and nature of the 'risk factors' reported were, by definition, between groups, so any 'changes' may have been due to the measurement or influence of pre-existing differences between samples and not necessarily the product of On Track interventions. Indeed, even if specific individuals were included in both samples and did demonstrate changes in levels of risk, protection and offending, these changes may not have been attributable to On Track because the young person did not necessarily receive On Track interventions, they were simply a pupil at a school in a recipient area.

The On Track Youth Lifestyles Survey researchers have apparently taken for granted the alleged predictive influence of 'risk factors' espoused in the research that inspired their work and have been content to test for their existence and influence in a new sample, regardless of the methodological and theoretical incompatibility between cross-sectional designs and the developmental, deterministic and positivistic strand of RFR.

Conclusions as to the predictive validity of 'risk' factors in the On Track Youth Lifestyles Survey, indeed, even labelling these elements as 'risk factors', have in large part relied on imputing the nature of the relationship between risk and offending – rather than statistical correlates identified through a static cross-sectional design. Similarly, 'risk' factors have been identified through comparisons between broad, aggregated and homogenised groups of young people so, despite their ostensible replicability, the findings were not necessarily representative of any individuals involved in the study. In essence, the authors of the On Track Youth Lifestyles Survey (especially the authors of the second sweep, who made far-reaching statistical comparisons between the two studies) have offered definitive conclusions on the basis of factorised, aggregated and inconsistent/incompatible data, statistical analysis of correlations and imputed causal linkages which are not sustained by the methodology employed.

The Youth Justice Board Risk and Protective Factors review and the Role of Risk and Protective Factors study

> in order to develop interventions that can successfully prevent youth crime, it is essential to identify and understand the risk and protective factors associated with it. (YJB 2005a: 4)

The Risk and Protective Factors review

In order to identify the risk and protective factors associated with youth crime and to inform the development of risk assessment tools for use in the Youth Justice System (see Chapter 6), the Youth Justice Board (YJB) commissioned a team through CtC (Barry Anderson, Sarah Beinert, David Farrington, Jonathan Longman, Pat Sturgis and David Utting) to review 'the extensive research literature on youth crime' (YJB 2005a: 31). The YJB was particularly interested in understanding 'why is it that some children, as they grow up, become involved in criminal activity, while others stay out of trouble and respect the law?' (YJB 2005a: 5).

The Risk and Protective Factors review methodology

For the purposes of the review, the authors defined risk factors as 'correlations that distinguish between the lives and backgrounds of offenders and those of non-offenders' (YJB 2005a: 5), whilst protective factors were viewed as 'signifying the opposite or absence of risk, [factors that] protect children and young people against involvement in crime [and] moderate the effects of exposure to risk' (YJB 2005a: 23). The authors stated a methodological preference for prospective longitudinal RFR (thereby privileging developmental RFR) for inclusion in the review because prospective longitudinal designs allegedly avoid retrospective bias and can examine in young people 'how earlier aspects of their lives relate to the most recent outcomes' (YJB 2005a: 5). It was also noted, as in the Understanding and Preventing Youth Crime review (Farrington 1996 – see Chapter 5), that the largest and most important RFR studies have been conducted in the UK, Scandinavia, the US and New Zealand. Beyond these general statements, however, the authors provided little additional information regarding how RFR studies were selected for review or what methodologies the studies had employed to identify risk and protective influence.

The Risk and Protective Factors review findings and conclusions

A distinct psychosocial bias was evident in the findings of the review, with the identification of the most commonly-replicated risk and protective factors restricted to the familiar and convenient domains of:

- *Family* – prenatal and perinatal complications, having a young mother, poor parental supervision and discipline, family conflict, family history of criminal activity, parental attitudes condoning antisocial and criminal behaviour, low income, poor housing and large family size, parental neglect, parental conflict, disrupted family life.

- *School* – low academic achievement, aggressive behaviour (including bullying), lack of commitment to school (including truancy), school disorganisation.

- *Community* – living in a disadvantaged neighbourhood, availability of drugs, lack of attachment to neighbourhood, availability of firearms (in the US only).

- *Personal or individual* – hyperactivity, impulsivity, cognitive impairment, low intelligence, alienation and lack of social commitment, attitudes condoning offending and drug misuse, membership of a delinquent peer group.

- *Protective factors* – female gender, resilient temperament, outgoing disposition, high intelligence, self-efficacy, social bonding, prosocial attitudes (including within the family and community), clear expectations for behaviour by role models (e.g. parents, teachers, community leaders), opportunities for involvement in constructive activities and recognition for achievement.

(YJB 2005a: 7–27)

The Risk and Protective Factors review as RFR

The Risk and Protective Factors review exemplified the self-perpetuating and reductionist nature of developmental RFR by identifying a narrow range of psychosocial risk and protective 'factors' from a partial body of RFR, which drew heavily on selective previous reviews, particularly *Understanding and Preventing Youth Crime* (Farrington 1996) and *Antisocial Behaviour by Young People* (Rutter *et al.* 1998). These reviews were supplemented throughout the report by the findings from the Cambridge Study in Delinquent Development, despite the authors having cautioned that 'the classic British longitudinal studies of offending are many years old, highlighting a need for more modern evidence' (YJB 2005a: 5). The Risk and Protective Factors review was conducted with such a degree of psychosocial, developmental and artefactual bias, by a group of individuals with evident vested interests that it was always destined to uncritically replicate previous developmental RFR findings, rather than providing a genuinely open review of the available evidence.

The review replicated the inherent methodological weaknesses of much developmental RFR, particularly the self-serving psychosocial bias and the definitive indefinity that has surrounded conclusions relating to the risk–offending relationship. The confident conclusions that the study had met its aim to 'identify and understand the risk and protective factors associated with (offending)' (YJB 2005a: 4) mask the near-sighted partiality of this identification process and the lack of understanding regarding how these factors actually relate to offending (or not) and the unwillingness to address research findings which present contradictory or different views. Although the authors freely admitted that 'the relationship between risk and protective factors and the precise ways in which they interrelate and react is uncertain (YJB 2005a: 27) and that risk factors may only be correlates/associates with offending, they still concluded that risk factors can exert a causal influence on offending. Ultimately, the Risk and Protective Factors review merely confirmed the established hegemonic developmental body of psychosocial early childhood risk factors for offending without ever questioning the evidence-base – the review is, in fact, as much of a crash test dummy as the children portrayed in developmental RFR.

The Role of Risk and Protective Factors study

Following the Risk and Protective Factors review, the YJB commissioned Oxford University Probation Studies Unit (Alex Sutherland, Simon Merrington, Sarah Jones, Kerry Baker and Colin Roberts) to carry out 'an exploratory examination of the risk/protection paradigm' (YJB 2005: 43). This examination took the form of empirical research into the relationship between 'risk' and 'protection' (notably the commonly-identified factors from the previous review), particularly whether this relationship is *interactive* (i.e. protective factors mediate the effects of risk factors) or *cumulative* (i.e. overall levels of risk are more important than specific factors). This research, known as the Role of Risk and Protective Factors study, aimed to:

- investigate what is already known about protective factors;

- collect data on risk/protective factors, using two distinct samples of young people, in two consecutive sweeps;

- establish a profile of risk/protective factors for each sample, and identify the factors which differentiated the two groups;

- explore the relationship between risk/protective factor domains;

- explore how risk/protective factors relate to self-reported offending.

(YJB 2005: 13)

The Role of Risk and Protective Factors Study methodology

Due to delays in beginning the fieldwork, combined with information technology difficulties, the initial plan to conduct two data collection sweeps with both samples was abandoned in favour of a single data collection episode, such that 'only a retrospective analysis of the relationship between risk, protection and offending could take place' (YJB 2005: 43). An opportunity sample of 1,283 young people aged 8–16 years was drawn from two groups across England and Wales – a 'School/College' group (three secondary schools, one college) and an 'Agency' group consisting of 'hard-to-reach' young people accessed through 11 Youth Offending Teams (YOTs), two Pupil Referral Units (PRUs), one children's home, one Young Offender Institution (YOI), one secure training centre, two Shelter projects (a charity for homeless people) and four Youth Inclusion Programmes.

In order to assess the nature of the relationships between risk and protection, the Role of Risk and Protective Factors study team formulated a three stage research process of literature review, questionnaire and interview:

A *literature review* of prospective longitudinal (developmental) RFR studies, mainly conducted in Britain, Scandinavia, the US and New Zealand, was conducted because these provide 'the most reliable research information' (YJB 2005a: 5). The review was also interested in empirical studies relating to protective factors and resilience, as a way of establishing working definitions of risk and protective factors (see YJB 2005a). Particular attention was paid in the review to the Cambridge Study in Delinquent Development (West and Farrington 1973) and the *Antisocial Behaviour and Young People* review (Rutter *et al.* 1988; see also Chapter 5).

Questionnaires were administered to all sample members to measure self-reported offending and levels of 'risk' and 'protection'. Self-reported offending (*ever* and *recently* – in the past month) was measured using yes/no responses to an offence inventory equivalent to the UK-version of the ISRD instrument (Graham and Bowling 1995). Risk and protection levels were measured using a four-point Likert scale assessing strength of agreement ('not like me', 'a bit like me', 'quite like me', 'just like me') with a series of statements relating to exposure to risk in the domains of:

- your family and where you live;

- school and work;

- your lifestyle and the area where you live;

- smoking, drinking and drugs;

- your health;

- how you think and behave;

- what you think about your future.

(YJB 2005a: 59–65)

Every risk/protection domain contained a series of sub-statements, each of which constituted a potential risk factor. For example, the school and work section asked young people for their strength of agreement with statements such as:

- like (or liked) going to school/college;

- want help with reading and writing;

- always try their hardest with school or work;

- often stay (or stayed) away from school without permission;

- have been bullied at school or at work.

(YJB 2005b: 59)

In the first instance, reported levels of agreement with the statements were analysed statistically using a Chi-square to test for significant differences between the School/College and Agency groups in (aggregated) reported risk and protection levels. For each statement, statistical comparisons were made between the percentages of young people in each response category ('not like me', 'a bit like me', 'quite like me', 'just like me'). Only factors that statistically distinguished between the two sample groups were entered into further Chi-square analysis to investigate any statistical relationships with self-reported ever and recent offending; an analytical method with the potential to exclude risk factors if they were pertinent to *both* groups. So, for example, when asked in the smoking, drinking and drugs questionnaire section if they 'have friends who often use drugs', 60 per cent of the School/College group responded 'not like me' compared to 27 per cent of the Agency group, whereas 12 per cent responded 'just like me', compared to 40 per cent of the Agency group. These differences were found to be statistically significant, indicating that members of the Agency group were significantly more likely to have friends who often used drugs. In this case, therefore, 'having friends who often use drugs' was retained as a factor for subsequent analysis of association with offending.

Interviews were conducted with an opportunity sample of 139 young people – 118 drawn from the Agency group, 15 from the college sample and six from secondary schools. The interview schedule covered the themes addressed in the questionnaire, namely: home and family life, education, neighbourhood and lifestyle, friends, personal (relationship, drug use, drinking, offending) and an extra section (for the Agency group) about experiences of working with the YOT (YJB: 2005b). The three main stated aims of the interview element of the study were to 'give examples of interesting protective factors that have been reported, to 'look at young people's coping strategies [and to] explore the interaction of risk and protection as described by young people' (YJB 2005b: 112).

The Role of Risk and Protective Factors study findings and conclusions

In accordance with the aims of the study, the YJB was interested in the significant risk factors for, and differences in risk levels between, both the School/College and Agency groups.

The Agency group was reported to be significantly more likely than the School/College group to self-report offending and to agree with statements that indicated exposure to the following 'risk' factors:

- *Family* – stay away from home without asking, living with others who get into trouble with the police, don't see much of father.

- *School* – regular truancy, being a victim of bullying.

- *Lifestyle and local area* – high crime neighbourhood, wide availability of drugs in neighbourhood, delinquent peers, not much to do in neighbourhood, dangerous behaviour.

- *Smoking, drinking and drugs* – drug using peers, spend a lot of money on cigarettes, alcohol or drugs, have offended when under the influence of alcohol or drugs, have offended to get money for drugs.

- *Health* – doing things which they know will be bad for their health.

- *Thinking and behaviour* – get into trouble because it's exciting, commit crimes because friends do, anger management problems, restlessness.

- *Thoughts about the future* – will offend in the near future, see themselves as criminals.

(see YJB 2005b)

The School/College group was reported to be significantly more likely than the Agency group to agree with statements that indicated higher levels of 'protective factors' in terms of:

- *Family* – do jobs around the house.

- *School and work* – affection for school/college, try hard at school or work.

- *Lifestyle and local area* – can talk to friends about problems.

- *Health* – feel good about themselves.

- *Thinking and behaviour* – think that religion is important, feel that they have a say in what happens in their life.

- *Thoughts about the future* – to sort out the problems, want to stay out of trouble.

(see YJB 2005b)

Subsequent Chi-Square analysis identified the following factors as 'risk factors' for ever offending, recent offending or for both forms of offending by the Agency group (YJB 2005):

- *Family* – stay away from home without asking (both forms of offending), don't see much of their dad (recent offending only).

- *School and work* – like (or liked) going to school/college (both ever and recent offending), always try their hardest at school or work (both ever and recent offending), often stay (or stayed) away from school without permission (both ever and recent offending), have been bullied at school or at work (ever offending only).

- *Lifestyle and local area* – live in places where there is lots of crime (both ever and recent offending), live in places where it's easy to get drugs (both ever and recent offending), have lots of friends who get into trouble (both ever and recent offending), live in areas where there is not much to do (ever offending), do nothing in their spare time (both ever and recent offending), do things they know are dangerous (both ever and recent offending).

- *Smoking, drinking and drugs* – spend a lot of money on cigarettes, alcohol or drugs (both ever and recent offending).

- *Health* – do things which they know will be bad for their health (both ever and recent offending).

- *Thinking and behaviour* – get into trouble because it's exciting (both ever and recent offending), commit crime because their friends do it (ever offending), feel guilty when they do something bad (ever offending), can't control their anger and have to lash out (both ever and recent offending), fidget a lot and can't sit still for long (ever offending).

- *Thoughts about the future* – think they will offend in the near future (both ever and recent offending), think of themselves as criminals (both ever and recent offending), want to stay out of trouble (recent offending).

(see YJB 2005b)

Analysis of the interview data (using an analytical procedure that was not made explicit in the study report) apparently enabled several, more in-depth conclusions regarding how young people felt able to respond to risk and enhance protection. For example, young people reported that, at times, they were unaware of how risk factors influenced their behaviour. The young people interviewed reported several factors that they believed exerted a protective influence on their behaviour in terms of, *inter alia*, minimising the impact of risk, reducing their likelihood of offending and increasing their chances of desistance. These 'protective factors' were *consequential thinking* (the ability to consider the positive and negative consequences of their actions), *empathy* (awareness of the feelings, thoughts and reactions of victims, friends and family), *coping strategies* (e.g. self-isolation, substance use, exercise, talking to others, self-harm) and *peer relationships* (positive and negative peer influence, including the offending-related attitudes and behaviours of peers). Thus, the authors concluded that:

- protective factors could be 'obscured' by immediate and pressing risks;

- young people could be resilient to offending even if they were exposed to multiple risk factors, notably through using 'coping repertoires' to handle life events;

- 'offending thresholds' dictated what young people were prepared to do or not do in response to risk and why (linked to reasons, motivations, feelings);

- risk and protection are 'interwoven' in young people's lives.

(see YJB 2005b)

Based on both questionnaire and interview findings, the YJB Role of Risk and Protective Factors study reported an *interactive* relationship between risk and protection. It was concluded that risk factor domains were inter-linked and that risk factors were dynamic concepts operating on a continuum that could change over time. The report concluded with recommendations for further exploration of offending thresholds, coping repertoires, general resilience and individual differences in risk levels by age, gender and ethnicity (all of which may affect the effectiveness of generic interventions), notably through 'case-specific analysis' of risk in individual young people (YJB 2005b). When evaluating their cross-sectional study, the researchers asserted that 'the snapshot obtained from this exploratory research provides a useful starting point for considering the relevance of interactions between factors and explanations of offending behaviour' (YJB 2005b: 8).

The Role of Risk and Protective Factors study as RFR

The authors of the Role of Risk and Protective Factors study have claimed that their findings support the *interactive* model of risk and protection, claiming to have demonstrated the interconnectedness, interdependence and dynamic nature of relationships between different risk and protective factors. However, it is difficult to see how such confident conclusions can be justified on the basis of the cross-sectional design employed and the nature of the data collected – even if the quantitative (factorised) questionnaire results were supplemented by qualitative, retrospective interviews. There was, for example, no attempt to establish the temporal precedence of the factors (experienced in current life) over offending behaviour carried out at some unmeasured point in time (ever) or in the last month (recent). Certainly many 'ever' offending episodes would have preceded the measurement of risk and even a 'recent' measure of offending was insufficient to establish the temporal precedence of factors and thus to implicate them as 'risk' or 'protective' factors because the precise timing of exposure relative to episodes of offending behaviour was not established, either in the quantitative questionnaire or in the retrospective qualitative interviews. Therefore, the study did not meet its key aims to 'collect data of risk/protective factors' or to 'explore how risk/ protective factors relate to self-reported offending' because factors were measured and analysed in such a limited manner that neither temporal precedence nor the (predictive or causal) direction of their relationship with offending could be established. This should have restricted analysis and conclusions to the identification of factors as statistical correlates with offending.

Even if it were accurate (which it cannot be) that the factors measured (in the questionnaire particularly) exemplified risk and protective factors with a substantive relationship to offending, the depth and scope of the analysis has been reductionist. Firstly, analysis was artificially restricted to only those factors that were reported at significantly higher levels by one of the sample groups compared to the other, thus precluding the opportunity to explore factors that may have constituted risks for both groups. Secondly, analysis was limited to factorised, statistical investigations of psychosocial influences, to the neglect of socio-structural factors or any consideration of risk and protection as constructed and negotiated mechanisms and processes. The interviews did attempt to address this latter point and did produce information from the much-neglected perspective of young people on the much neglected subject of dynamic interactions between risk and protection in everyday life. However, even this ostensibly progressive element of RFR was prone to psychosocial bias because the researchers worked to a prescribed interview schedule that was underpinned by a literature review of developmental RFR and a questionnaire with an equivalent psychosocial, developmental bias.

Any progressive and innovative foci of the study were further restricted by the limited conception of the nature of a 'protective' factor. The idea that a factor is protective 'when its impact on a young person contributes to a positive outcome (i.e. not offending)' (YJB 2005b: 7) is insensitive and over-simplified. Protective factors (if the term is to have any real meaning) have the potential not only to prevent the onset of offending or encourage desistence from offending once it has begun, but also to have dynamic relationships with a range of positive outcomes. Therefore, the study presented a static and limited/partial interpretation of the relationship between generic (risk-dependent) protective factors and non-offending at a single point in time, without being able to discriminate between non-offenders and offenders in terms of the dynamic influence of protective factors over time.

The cross-sectional Role of Risk and Protective Factors study has attempted to explain the interaction between risk and protective factors and their relationship with offending by relying heavily on questionnaire data that has encouraged the post-hoc animation of static factors and the liberal use of imputation and extrapolation. The content of the question-naire (which was based on the CtC Youth Survey and was thus underpinned by the tenets of the Social Development Model) was avowedly socio-developmental and this developmentalism was reflected in conclusions regarding the predictive and deterministic influence of 'risk' factors on offending. However, the factors within the questionnaire were originally identified in longitudinal, developmental RFR that tracked their development from childhood and linked them to offending in adolescence and young adulthood, as opposed to identifying them as statistical correlates of active offending (as did the Role of Risk and Protective Factors study). However, any dynamic effects, directional influence or temporal precedence related to risk and offending can only be imputed on the basis of the static cross-sectional design employed. Importing factors from longitudinal, developmental RFR in this way makes a set of methodological assumptions, namely:

- that 'risk factors' adopted from developmental RFR are valid measures of risk in themselves;

- that factors measured in childhood and identified as predictive of offending in adolescence are necessarily appropriate and valid measures of risk in the current lives of adolescents;

- that transporting so-called predictive risk factors into cross-sectional designs and statistically linking them to current offending enables researchers to impute that their predictive influence (itself debatable in the original longitudinal research) is relevant and appropriate for the current sample.

However, these methodological leaps are reliant on imputation and erroneous extrapolation rather than any inherent internal or external validity. The authors did not explore the full potential of their data, for example, individual differences in the influence of different risk factors (e.g. for different age groups within the 11–16 year old age range, for males compared to females, for different young people within and between the School/College and Agency samples). Instead, results were aggregated across the age range and for each sample group. Such aggregation, although common in RFR, is insensitive to individual, cultural and local differences and is necessarily unrepresentative of any single individual within a sample group. It seems that the quest to provide simple, definitive conclusions has encouraged a level of abstraction in analysis that undermines the conclusions. So distant has the analysis (especially the quantitative analysis) become from the actual lives of real young people that, at best, it has provided a thin glaze covering a rich oil painting. Similarly, the homogenisation of such broad groups has been inadvisable as, for example, it cannot be methodologically valid to assume compatibility between the behaviours of, and influences on, 11 year olds compared to 16 year olds or between the different sub-groups that made up the Agency sample. These processes of aggregation in independent variables are also evident in the dependent variable – offending. Thus different aspects of offending behaviour (e.g. seriousness, frequency and duration) are conflated into general categories of *ever* and *recent* offending. Aggregation like this is not only much more likely to result in statistically significant findings, but it washes out anything the research might usefully have to say about between group differences. The result is insensitive analysis and weak conclusions that bear little weight.

The legacy of the Risk and Protective Factors review and the Role of Risk and Protective Factors study is that of an over-simplified and methodologically-confused body of RFR that has drawn superficial and unsubstantiated conclusions on the basis of a partial (limited and biased) understandings of risk and protection generated by a superficial literature review. It remains unclear whether these studies actually set out to develop better understandings of the relationship between risk, protection, youth offending and the relationship between the three or whether, in reality, the studies were an exercise in validating and perpetuating a select, established group of psychosocial risk and protective factors that have been privileged by the YJB. Notwithstanding the methodological biases, limitations and weaknesses of the Role of Risk and Protective Factors study and the similar failings of its precursor, the Risk and Protective Factors review, the YJB has proffered the invalid, unsubstantiated and startlingly-unreflexive conclusion that:

together, these pieces of research represent the most up-to-date and accessible source of information on risk and protective factors, the relationship between them, their link to offending, and how this knowledge can be applied within the youth justice system. (YJB 2005a: 4)

Conclusion: cross-sectional risk factor research in England and Wales revisited

Cross-sectional RFR offers one major advantage over its longitudinal counterpart – the potential to collect data and turn around results over a condensed period. Cross-sectional designs also have the potential to identify 'live' factors with larger samples (often random and even nationally representative) than have been accessed by the more time and resource intensive longitudinal approaches, which have tended to utilise smaller opportunity samples that are not representative of the demographic groups from which they were drawn. Longitudinal RFR has typically produced these non-generalisable findings slowly and sporadically; findings which are often inevitably dated by the time they have been disseminated and addressed within policy and practice. Indeed, this datedness is an inevitability of longitudinal RFR and its need to track factors over long periods to establish their ultimately predictive effect on future offending. In contrast, cross-sectional designs have the potential to focus on ostensibly 'active' risk factors in the current lives of young people (cf. Wikström 2008), which serve as live and relevant targets for policy and practice. However, weak cross-sectional methodologies have failed to exploit this potential and any statistically significant factors are exclusively correlates with offending rather than actual predictors or causes. Indeed, even the use of the term *risk factor* in the cross-sectional research studies discussed above is inappropriate as it implies a causal and/or directional relationship which the methodologies that have been used cannot sustain. Any attempts to explain the mechanisms and processes that operate in the 'black box' between risk factor and offending or offer prescriptions for risk-based interventions are beyond the scope of existing cross-sectional research.

There are a range of weaknesses, indeed flaws, common to cross-sectional RFR in England and Wales, including:

- *Temporal indefinity* – the temporal precedence of so-called risk factors over offending (and protective factors over desistance) has not been explored, despite being possible within cross-sectional designs (see, for example, Wikström 2008). Instead, measures of social background factors in current life (or in the past 12 months) have been assumed to predate and predict offending in the past year when they are, at best, indicators of and correlates with offending (i.e. not 'risk' factors at all).

- *Uncritical importation of developmental risk factors* – all too often, cross-sectional RFR instruments (typically questionnaires) have adopted measures of risk that have been originally identified in samples of children and tracked into adolescence and adulthood through longitudinal RFR. Not only has this process assigned a validity to developmental risk factors that may be moot, but it has also rested on the questionable assumption that factors measured in childhood exert an equivalent influence in the *current* lives of the adolescents surveyed in cross-sectional studies to the exclusion of other, as yet unidentified, current factors.

- *Psychosocial bias and reductionism* – a knock-on effect of the wholesale acceptance and adoption of developmental risk factors and the consequent drive to validate and replicate them has been the privileging of psychosocial factors above potential socio-structural factors (a psychosocial bias). Just as the field of potential risk factors studied has been artificially narrowed and desensitised through this psychosocial bias, so have understandings of risk and protection through their methodological and analytical reduction to statistical artefacts (reductionism). Such reductionism has come at the expense of exploring potential influences as mechanisms and processes of change that can be constructed and resisted by young people.

- *Homogenisation and aggregation* – the large samples accessed and the large amounts of data collected in cross-sectional studies have offered the potential to investigate exposure to different factors relevant to, *inter alia*, age, gender, locality and different forms of offending. However, cross-sectional RFR in England and Wales has preferred to treat its broad, diverse samples and the different factors and behaviours measured in its survey instruments as if they were homogenous (e.g. by measuring risk, protection and offending as broadly-constituted concepts and categories). This homogenisation encourages the aggregation of data for the purposes of analysis which not only fails to capture differences between groups within samples, but the mere fact of this aggregation for the purposes of analysis may actually permit and facilitate statistical correlations. In other words, the number and strength of correlations between risk factors and offending are a direct product of analysing relationships between broadly-constituted concepts and categories. Thus researchers can be accused of privileging replicability (in the form of statistical reliability) over a detailed exploration of the validity (e.g. meaningfulness and existence in real life) of the risk factors that populate RFR.

- *Overriding policy-focus* – perhaps the most pervasive weakness of cross-sectional RFR in England and Wales, one which may explain (but not justify) the methodological shortcuts adopted, has been the overriding slavishness to the government policy focus. This focus appears to have encouraged the production of immediate, practical findings and conclusions from RFR at the expense of pursuing longer-term aetiological and explanatory goals. As such, sufficient time has not been taken to formulate original theories of risk factor influence or to evaluate the applicability of existing RFR theories for use in properly thought out cross-sectional designs.

- *Erroneous conclusions* – perhaps the most worrying of the weaknesses in cross-sectional risk factor research has been the extent to which researchers have been too quick to reach conclusions about risk factor influence which are simply not sustained by the methodologies employed. For a field of research which promotes itself as the 'appliance of science' (and, indeed, enjoys much credibility on this basis) to be so scant in its attention to basic principles of scientific research is cause for great concern.

Ultimately, it is debatable whether 'risk factor research' is an appropriate label for the studies addressed in this chapter, as they have largely attempted to translate developmental risk factors into a cross-sectional format that has not actually been capable of identifying 'risk factors' at all.

Chapter 5

Hunting for the universal risk factor

RFR in England and Wales has been limited in its attempts to progress understandings of the aetiology of offending and to inform preventative and ameliorative policy and practice due to a group of common, unresolved methodological paradoxes. Typically, definitive and simplistic conclusions have been drawn regarding the existence and nature of risk and the nature of its relationship with offending or antisocial behaviour, founded on methodologies and analyses too restricted to have supported such conclusions. Researchers conducting longitudinal and cross-sectional RFR have tended to convert potentially complex risk and protection information into quantifiable factors (in the case of protective factors, often simply dichotomised in relation to risk) which have been measured in relation to a generalised period of time (e.g. current life, the last 12 months, a specific developmental stage) and aggregated across large, homogenised samples of young people. This over-simplification and subsequent between-groups analysis has been preferred to measuring the onset and influence of risk relative to different forms of offending behaviour or by subjecting the data to analysis at the level of the individual young person. The body of factors measured have been labelled 'risk and protective factors' despite uncertainty about their temporal precedence over, or the nature and direction of their relationship with, offending and desistance. The factors created and analysed have reflected the psychosocial biases of the developmental strand of RFR and have largely overlooked socio-structural influences and constructivist explanations of risk and protection. This has resulted in a self-perpetuating artefact RFR literature seemingly intent on replicating a narrow group of psychosocial risk factors that are unrepresentative of the scope and complexity of risk influence or the characteristics and behaviours of the groups from which they have emanated. In contrast to the simplistic and practical (yet methodologically-flawed) artefact-based RFR, constructivist explanations of risk (e.g. the pathways approach) have appeared unconstructive, ethereal, impractical (although possibly more 'real') and unappealing to policy makers and practitioners seeking clear, simplistic and achievable solutions to youth offending. Thus RFR in England and Wales remains dominated by developmentalism and 'artefactualism'.

It is necessary, therefore, to look further afield towards the rapidly expanding corpus of international RFR to evaluate the extent to which the methodological limitations and biases demonstrated in England and Wales have been addressed and resolved, or simply exacerbated and further entrenched within RFR across the globe.

A series of theoretical and methodological questions must be asked of the most mainstream and widely-cited international RFR studies conducted by researchers with the highest profiles and reputations in the RFR field; questions which reflect those employed to evaluate the achievements of RFR studies in England and Wales:

- What has been the theoretical basis of the main studies and has this been compatible with the research design employed?

- How have data been collected and analysed, and what conclusions have been made regarding the prevalence, extent and nature of relationships between risk factors and offending by young people?

- Have these conclusions been justified/legitimised by the methodologies employed, the quality of the data and the nature of the analyses?

- Have the designs of RFR studies across the globe offered a sensitive, flexible and valid method of evolving RFR and our understanding of the concept of risk and risk factors?

Farrington (2000, 2007) claims that there has been a 'globalisation' of risk factor knowledge which has proliferated and facilitated cross-fertilisation between academics, policy-makers and practitioners from many different countries, such that RFR has become a prominent, if not the dominant, approach to explaining and preventing youth offending in, for example, England and Wales, Scotland, the US, Canada and New Zealand. An overarching question that must be addressed in this chapter, therefore, is to what extent this globalisation has relied on a theoretical, methodological, analytical and interpretive uniformity in order to identify the factor(s) that underpin offending by young people in all countries and that would provide a 'unified explanatory edifice' (D. Smith 2006) for youth offending. Has there been, as Case (2007) suggests, a tangible quest amongst risk factor researchers in the Western world to hunt down the 'holy grail' of the globalised, *universal* risk factor?

The pervasive influence and theoretical hegemony of developmental understandings of risk at the global level has been exemplified in two large scale reviews of international RFR: *Understanding and Preventing Youth Crime* (Farrington 1996) and *Antisocial Behaviour by Young People* (Rutter *et al.* 1998). Each of these ostensibly 'extensive' and 'comprehensive' reviews has privileged developmental studies of quantified psychosocial risk factors measured in childhood and allegedly predictive of later offending. These artefactual and psychosocial biases have emerged, in part, from the limited availability of alternative forms of RFR from which to select (creating an unavoidable selection bias), but they have also been a product of the developmental, psychological preferences of the authors.

Understanding and Preventing Youth Crime

The *Understanding and Preventing Youth Crime* review of empirical RFR in the Western world, conducted for the Joseph Rowntree Foundation in the UK by David Farrington, presented 'knowledge about the development, causes and prevention of youthful offending' (Farrington 1996: 46). The review was focused on what Farrington himself perceived to be the most 'methodologically adequate' RFR studies, which typically were those that utilised prospective longitudinal designs (particularly studies using several data sources, such as child, parent, teacher and peers). Farrington's methodological choices were made to enable him to explore a developmental view of the influence of childhood risk factors on future offending, on the basis of the assumption that 'there is no shortage of risk factors that significantly predict offending and antisocial behaviour' (Farrington 1996: 7).

Although Farrington defined a risk factor as that which predicts an increased (statistical) likelihood of later offending, he did not clarify whether longitudinal studies were chosen for review on the basis of an empirical demonstration of the predictive influence of risk factors. He did state, however, that the (static) variables of gender and ethnicity would not be reviewed 'because such factors have no practical implications for prevention' as they cannot be changed (Farrington 1996: 7). Cross-sectional studies were also excluded from the review on the basis that they were less able than longitudinal designs to measure the development of risk and protective factors over time and were more prone to 'mistaken assessments' that could not be resolved at a later stage in the study through repeated contacts that 'help to maximise validity' (Farrington 1996: 7). However, no other details were provided in the report regarding how many studies were reviewed, how they were chosen (e.g. what other criteria were used to assess a study to be 'methodologically adequate') and how different risk factors and offending had been defined, measured and analysed in each study (e.g. whether the methodologies and analyses were internally robust and externally comparable).

Understanding and Preventing Youth Crime findings and conclusions

Despite an absence of methodological and analytical detail, Farrington concluded that the most commonly-identified risk factors in his review were *predictive* of future offending and could be grouped into five domains:

- *Family* – prenatal and perinatal factors (e.g. teenage motherhood), poor parental supervision and discipline, low social economic status, parental conflict and separation.

- *School* – negative school influences (e.g. bullying), academic underachievement.

- *Neighbourhood/Community* – negative community influences (e.g. neighbourhood disorganisation, household overcrowding, physical deterioration of neighbourhood).

- *Peer group* – association with delinquent friends.

- *Individual* – personality (impulsivity, hyperactivity, restlessness), low intelligence and attainment.

(see Farrington 1996)

The review concluded that British longitudinal studies of delinquency had produced findings that were consistent with methodologically-comparable studies in North America (e.g. McCord 1979), Scandinavia (e.g. Pulkkinen 1988) and New Zealand (e.g. Moffitt and Silva 1988), as well as with British cross-sectional surveys (e.g. Hagell and Newburn 1994; Graham and Bowling 1995). However, Farrington qualified his conclusions by cautioning that the risk-factor–offending relationship remained only partially understood because:

> identifying which risk factors are causal and which are merely predictive or symptomatic of an underlying antisocial personality can be problematic . . . a further problem is that most risk factors tend to coincide and be interrelated. (Farrington 1996: 26)

Understanding and Preventing Youth Crime as RFR

The Understanding and Preventing Youth Crime review consolidated the growing internationalisation of RFR by identifying a series of ostensibly globally-applicable and universally-replicated risk factors for youth offending. This widespread replication of risk factors through studies with allegedly robust methodologies (e.g. multiple data sources, large community samples, prospective longitudinal designs) was an apparent validation of the risk factors that had been identified in developmental and ecological RFR since the early work of the Gluecks.

However, Farrington provided insufficient detail in his review to substantiate or enable a full evaluation of many of his conclusions regarding the universalism of risk factors. For example, little detail was provided regarding:

- the choice of studies to review;

- how the methodological robustness of these studies was analysed and evaluated;

- whether studies measured the temporal relationship between factors and offending;

- whether measurement of temporality was robust enough to substantiate conclusions regarding the predictive nature of risk factors;

- to what extent the replicability of findings across different studies, samples and countries indicated a comparability and universalism in the definitions of risk and protection, definitions of offending employed (indeed, whether offending was the target behaviour at all or whether measures of 'antisocial behaviour' or 'delinquency' were used) and the nature of the risk-factor–offending relationship.

Differences and ambiguities in any of the above areas must seriously limit the validity and reliability of any conclusions that certain risk factors have been universally-replicated and that they influence youth offending in an equivalent manner across the globe.

There were further omissions and biases that raise issues as to the validity of the conclusions drawn and the comprehensiveness of the review itself. For example, the range of factors investigated was limited by the psychosocial and developmental focus of much RFR to that point. Consequently, whilst psychosocial risk factors in the family, school, peer group and the community (an emerging focus within ecological RFR at that time) received comprehensive coverage, the impact of socio-political, legal, socio-structural, economic, historical and cultural factors and contexts, all of which were likely to vary greatly across different countries, were crucially neglected by the review. This is not to say, necessarily, that the psychosocial risk factors identified were not predictive of offending in different countries for different samples of young people, but rather that their influence may have been mitigated, moderated or usurped by the presence and analysis of these other neglected factors.

An important omission in the review was the failure to consider research that suggests the possibility that risk and protection operate as mechanisms and processes (as opposed to deterministic factors) with complex relationships to offending in different contexts at different times for different groups of young people. Farrington (1996) presented risk in a psychosocial reductionist manner and as a developmental concept (reflected in the studies reviewed), thus oversimplifying the nature of risk and the risk–offending relationship. The result was an over-generalised, mechanical representation of how risk and offending interrelate, with limited actual understanding of, or ability to explain, *how* risk and risk factors may encourage offending behaviour.

Farrington's confident conclusions that predictive risk factors have been globally-replicated gave rise to similarly confident recommendations for appropriate preventative interventions, notably based on the CtC programme (Farrington 1996). However, these recommendations animate and exacerbate the existing methodological weaknesses of the review and the studies within it. If factors prevalent at age eight years are causal or predictive of later offending then there is a logic to preventative interventions conducted with young people when they are eight years old. CtC, however, is a social development programme implemented in the teenage years and the logic of targeting causal or predictive factors prevalent at age eight years when the young person is, say, 14 years old, no longer has credibility. Thus, a generalised, biased and partial understanding of the risk–offending relationship inevitably promoted a similarly-flawed and unsubstantiated 'understanding' of how risk-focused interventions could prevent offending.

The studies highlighted in Farrington's review appear, therefore, to have been too restricted to allow a comprehensive review of RFR. The studies reviewed reflected a selection bias (which may have been due, in part, to Farrington's own developmental, psychosocial leanings) that precipitated an oversimplification of the nature and extent of risk factor influence and produced definitive conclusions that were only partially informed and over-generalised. Further to the alleged global predictive validity of the 'risk factors' identified in the review, there was insufficient information provided of the methodologies and analyses employed to identify risk factors to enable an assessment of whether the relationship between factors and offending had been adequately explored in each study. For example, it was unclear whether issues of temporality had been fully addressed in each study in a comparable manner. There was also a lack of sensitivity as to whether risk factors had been explored relative to age, gender or ethnicity. The homogenisation of samples and aggregation of data across groups of young people in different studies meant that the replicated risk factors were identified on the basis of 'group' analysis which is inherently less sensitive and accurate than within-individual analysis and not necessarily representative of/applicable to any specific individual participating in the studies reviewed. Similarly, there was no concession that the general, homogenised categories of 'offending' against which risk factors were measured in each study could have been too broad and insensitive to fully capture the essence of the risk-factor–offending relationship, particularly as risk factors may vary according to, *inter alia*, the nature of offending (e.g. active versus lifetime, property versus violent, first-time versus persistent), its frequency, seriousness and duration. Neither was there any discussion that definitions of offending can vary greatly across different countries, which questions the validity of any conclusions regarding replicable risk factors because the same risk factors may actually be linked to different measures of offending behaviour (see also O'Mahony 2008). Overall, Understanding and Preventing Youth Crime has promoted developmental and deterministic, globalised conceptions of risk that are, in fact, partial and unsubstantiated by the evidence.

Antisocial Behaviour by Young People

Funded by the UK government's Department of Health, Michael Rutter and colleagues conducted a review of empirical studies across the Western world that examined the relationship between risk factors and youth antisocial behaviour. The review, published as *Antisocial Behaviour by Young People* (Rutter *et al.* 1998), updated and extended a similar review conducted 15 years previously (Rutter and Giller 1983) on the basis that, since the original review 'there has been a substantial increase in empirically based knowledge on the nature of delinquency, its causes, factors that influence its perpetuation into adult life, and its prevention and treatment' (Rutter *et al.* 1998: 2). Antisocial behaviour was the behavioural measure preferred over delinquency/offending because it was seen as crucial to investigate behaviour that was problematic, yet which could lie 'outside the realm of the law' (Rutter *et al.* 1998: 1).

The Antisocial Behaviour by Young People methodology

The Antisocial Behaviour by Young People review incorporated large scale prospective longitudinal studies conducted across the Western world, on the basis that this form of RFR represented 'the most useful research' according to a set of methodological criteria that were perceived to increase the reliability, validity and comprehensiveness of the data collected and the analysis conducted. Studies were selected if they:

- used *prospective longitudinal designs*, which were considered necessary to study causaility;

- accessed *large samples* of the general population of young people throughout childhood, adolescence and early adulthood;

- accessed 'young people' aged 10–19 years;

- collected data from *multiple sources* in order to account for biases and to enable the triangulation and validation of findings and conclusions across different sources;

- attempted to *measure causality* on at least one of five criteria: individual differences in liability to engage in antisocial behaviour, the translation of that liability into the actual committing of illegal acts, differences over time or between places in the overall levels of crime, situational variations in delinquent activities and persistence or nonpersistence of antisocial behaviour as individuals grow older.

(see Rutter *et al.* 1998: 15)

The Antisocial Behaviour by Young People findings and conclusions

Rutter *et al.* separated the risk factors they identified into risk *mechanisms* ('causal' risk factors) and risk *indicators* (factors associated indirectly with the causal process). These risk mechanisms and indicators were placed into three distinct categories: *individual, psychosocial* and *societywide* and reported by Rutter *et al.* (1998) as follows:

- *Individual* – the factors of cognitive impairment, temperament (impulsivity, sensation seeking, lack of control, aggression) and distorted social information processing were all identified as risk mechanisms. Genetics was found to function as both a risk mechanism and risk indicator. Hyperactivity was considered to be a risk indicator, most likely to be associated with poor social functioning.

- *Psychosocial* – risk mechanisms included poor parenting (coercive or hostile, abusive or neglectful, ineffective, poor supervision), association with delinquent peers (supporting the hypothesis that 'birds of a feather flock together') and unemployment. Risk indicators in the psychosocial domain were family structure (teenage parenthood, large family, broken home) and family poverty and social disadvantage, both of which were linked to the risk mechanism of poor parenting.

- *Societywide* – the risk mechanisms of mass media (e.g. exposure to TV or film violence) and gender were identified, but found to have a limited evidence base. School factors (truancy, school ethos, teacher behaviour, clear management, make-up of pupil body) were also identified as risk mechanisms, but it was concluded that they were, as yet, under-researched and that there was insufficient understanding of exactly how they operated on antisocial behaviour. Ethnicity was highlighted as a factor more likely to be a risk indicator (linked to the risk mechanisms of poor living conditions and unemployment). Area differences (e.g. the architecture of the area) was considered to be a potential risk indicator linked to the risk mechanisms of style of policing and population make-up in different areas.

Rutter *et al.* concluded that individual risk factors were the most common form of risk mechanisms for antisocial behaviour, particularly for young people who persistently offend across their life course. The authors further concluded from the international literature (with particular reference to the work of the Gluecks and the follow-up study of Sampson and Laub (1993) – see Chapter 2 for a fuller discussion of this research) that risk mechanisms can serve as pre-existing dispositions towards antisocial behaviour by interacting with life experiences in a cyclical and cumulative way. Whilst this hypothesis illuminates the potentially criminogenic interaction between risk factors and life events, it was suggested that it also allows for the possibility of young people escaping/breaking out of (i.e. desisting from) patterns of antisocial behaviour at key turning points in their life.

Rutter *et al.* (1998) claimed that they had been able to consider a 'wide range of possible influences' on antisocial behaviour, from wider society to 'personal social contexts' (such as family, school, peers) to the individual. They also asserted that the 'systematic epidemiological testing of causal hypotheses' reviewed in their book was highly instructive in its ability to examine within-individual changes in risk factors over time (see also Farrington 2007), particularly if the individual's prior behaviour and social circumstances were taken into account at the same time. With regard to the studies' attempts to measure causality using any of the five causal dimensions, Rutter *et al.* suggested that 'what works in one of these categories may not be a factor in another ... (because) causal processes are neither simple nor unidirectional' (Rutter *et al.* 1998: 378). They concluded their report by claiming that the development of a multi-disciplinary international community of risk factor researchers has contributed to the more effective dissemination of risk-focused methods, more robust analyses and stronger conclusions as to the influence of different risk factors for antisocial behaviour by young people.

Antisocial Behaviour by Young People as RFR

Like Understanding and Preventing Youth Crime before it, the Antisocial Behaviour by Young People review made a significant contribution to the internationalisation and globalisation of RFR through its confident claims that universal risk factors had been identified and replicated in international RFR and that these factors were globally applicable across countries, samples and contexts. The review took a less simplistic approach to examining the causal influence of factors in comparison to other RFR reviews, particularly through the use of five distinct causal hypotheses as criteria for inclusion of studies in the review and by making the analytical distinction between risk mechanisms and risk indicators. Unlike much of the dominant RFR literature, the review did not rely entirely on a psychosocial focus (although this did dominate), instead including limited coverage of neglected areas of risk influence such as life events and socio-structural factors (which were labelled 'societywide' factors). However, the authors acknowledged the psychosocial bias to the studies available for selection, noting that 'this is where much recent research has been concentrated' (Rutter *et al.* 1998: 379). Rutter and colleagues, however, drew heavily on the developmental RFR of Farrington, citing over 40 of his publications at length during the course of the review and making reference to many of the studies reviewed in *Understanding and Preventing Youth Crime.*

Due to the inherent limitations and biases of much of the RFR evidence reviewed, the legitimacy of the confident and broad conclusions made by Rutter and his colleagues is debatable. Although the concept of a risk factor was less simplistic than in previous studies due to the focus on imputed risk mechanisms that could explain the causal influence of risk on offending, the studies reviewed made only limited attempts (if at all) to evidence this putative causal influence in favour of imputing causal processes and concluding causation on the basis of post-hoc statistical manipulations. Furthermore, it is frequently unclear in the book as to which studies reviewed actually attempted to measure exposure to risk relative to the onset and development of antisocial behaviour, so the existence of temporal precedence and the consequent predictive and causal influence of risk factors are difficult to evaluate from the information presented.

Rutter *et al.* (1998) acknowledged their conscious decision to exclude qualitative, ethnographic studies from the review (as these apparently rendered the measurement of risk mechanisms problematic). However, this exclusion ultimately resulted in a focus on survey-based RFR that had been underpinned by the reductionist factorisation of risk and that had ignored constructivist explanations of how risk influences offending. The restricted scope of their review, therefore, not only limited the range of possible conclusions, but it was based on research which itself was limited in scope and which had a tendency towards over-simplified and over-exaggerated claims.

Perhaps most debilitating to the validity of the conclusions of universality in *Antisocial Behaviour by Young People* was the lack of critique of, and reflection on, potential cross-cultural differences in the definition of antisocial behaviour, which is a notoriously ambiguous, subjective and dynamic measure (perhaps even more so than its counterpart 'offending'). Unacknowledged disparities in definitions of this core behaviour between the countries and studies in the review render valid comparisons difficult and could illegitimate the definitiveness of any conclusions drawn regarding replicable, universal risk factors.

Any conclusions of causality (let alone universal causality), simply cannot be unequivocal in the face of the limitations of the Rutter *et al.* review and the studies included in the review. Even if common 'global' risk factors for antisocial behaviour could be identified (and this is highly doubtful given differences in definitions, measurement, factorisation and analysis used across the various studies), the nature of the relationship of these risk factors and antisocial behaviour is far from universally established or clear. Despite claims to have identified 'findings that do generalize across samples and across social contexts' (Ruttter *et al.* 1998: 13), replication of lists of factors across the studies does not necessarily indicate that risk factors were operating in an equivalent, comparable fashion (e.g. functioning as 'risk' factors for antisocial behaviour) for different groups in different countries, particularly when the disparate definitions of antisocial behaviour across studies, contexts and the cultures are considered.

Globally flawed?

The Farrington and Rutter *et al.* reviews have represented international RFR and offered a series of positive conclusions about the methodologies employed and the utility of the data for developing understandings of the extent and nature of risk factors and their relationships with offending and antisocial behaviour. Most notably amongst these conclusions has been support for putative globally applicable, universal risk factors, which have been viewed as the products of comparative (ostensibly comparable) methodologies and replicated findings across different groups of young people in different contexts and countries. Whether such far-reaching conclusions have been (or could ever be) justified by the methodological and analytical quality of the studies included in these reviews is questionable. This is of enormous concern, as the support for the universal risk factor as a measurable, feasible, practical concept that has been engendered by these reviews has rapidly accelerated the popularity and application of (artefactual, developmental) RFR across the globe. It is entirely possible, therefore, that such widespread support for globalised RFR amongst researchers, politicians, policy makers and practitioners has been grounded in developmentally-biased, methodologically-dubious and incomparable studies that have dramatically over-inflated their collective conclusions beyond the scope and potential of their data and analysis.

The review of both longitudinal and cross-sectional RFR in England and Wales conducted in this book (see Chapters 3 and 4) has reached conclusions which are seriously at odds with the conclusions of the Farrington and Rutter *et al.* reviews. Attention now turns to evaluating some of the most notable RFR studies (such as those utilised by Farrington and Rutter *et al.*) from around the world to further explore the validity of the concept of a universal risk factor.

The International Self-Reported Delinquency study: standardised RFR and universal risk factors

The cross-sectional ISRD study was founded in 1990 by the Dutch Ministry of Justice, under the direction of Josine Junger-Tas. The study's main aim was to examine 'cross-national variability in patterns of correlates of self-reported delinquent behaviour' (Junger-Tas *et al.* 2003: 11). The authors emphasised that this aim could be most effectively achieved by using a standardised methodology (e.g. a common measuring instrument) to enable 'valid international comparisons' (Junger-Tas *et al.* 2003: 3).

In order to address the aim of making international comparisons between the correlates of delinquency, a working group of researchers from 13 participant countries was established to devise a standardised questionnaire. This working group was comprised from six government-linked centres (in the Netherlands, England and Wales, Finland, Northern Ireland, Portugal and New Zealand) and seven universities (in Belgium, Germany, Spain, Italy, Greece, Switzerland and the US). The ISRD-1 instrument contained questions regarding delinquency, social reactions to the young person's delinquency, socio-demographic variables relating to the young person and 'a small number' of theoretical variables relating to the central features of Social Control Theory – attachment to, commitment to, involvement in, and belief in, the formal and informal institutions of social control, particularly the family and school (see Hirschi 1969). Social Control Theory was chosen as the explanatory basis for the first ISRD (ISRD-1) because the theory was considered to have a 'universal character' and a robust empirical base in a 'great number of countries' (Junger-Tas *et al.* 2003). The research team 'hypothesized that the way these bonding variables operate would be similar across countries' (Junger-Tas *et al.* 2003: 9) – comparable to the concept of the universal risk factor. However, details regarding what informed the selection of the individual constructs used in the questionnaire have not been forthcoming.

ISRD-1 has been followed up by ISRD-2, a study based on a similar but expanded questionnaire and an extended number of (mainly European) countries – 33 in total. Only the methodology and results from ISRD-1 will be discussed here as the results from ISRD-2 (which commenced 2003–2005) were not available at the time of writing.

The ISRD-1 methodology

From 1991–1992, the ISRD-1 accessed five *national* and six *city-based* multistage, random samples of 14–21 year olds. The target age range was chosen by the working group to reflect what they considered to be the mean age of onset of youth offending (14 years old) and also to include younger adults in the sample (up to 21 years of age) who may have desisted from offending. The national samples were drawn from the Netherlands, Spain, Switzerland, Portugal and finally England and Wales (where a non-multistage, random sample was taken) and six city samples were taken from Germany (Mannheim), Northern Ireland (Belfast), Italy (Sienna, Genoa and Messina), Finland (Helsinki), Belgium (Liege) and the US (Omaha). The New Zealand city sample (Dunedin) was excluded as it was a longitudinal cohort sample using a modified survey instrument (see later in this chapter for further discussion of the Dunedin Study), whilst the Greek study was excluded because precise sampling details were not provided.

Delinquency amongst sample members was measured using a bespoke self-reported inventory of acts that were agreed by the working group to represent offences in the countries participating in the ISRD-1. Young people were asked whether they had ever committed any of the offences (*lifetime* prevalence). If they responded 'yes', they were asked if this offending had occurred in the last year (*current* prevalence) and how many times it had occurred (*frequency*). Young people were considered to be offenders if they self-reported having committed at least one of the offences on the inventory. A sub-measure of *serious* delinquency consisted of acts judged by the working group to indicate serious offences – theft, car theft, robbery, burglary, extortion, beating someone up, injuring with a weapon and selling drugs.

The correlates of delinquency were assessed in two main domains:

- *Socio-demographic variables* – gender, age, family composition, socio-economic status, education level, school attendance, leisure activities;

- *Social control constructs* – parental supervision, relationship with parents, attachment to school, commitment to school, academic achievement, relationship with peers.

(Junger-Tas *et al.* 2003: 22)

Questionnaire variables/constructs were measured using a mixture of yes/no and (more often) Likert-scale response formats. For example, the construct 'parental supervision' required young people to indicate their strength of agreement with two statements ('parents know with whom you are' and 'parents know where you are') on a dichotomous yes/no response scale. In contrast, 'relationship with parents' was assessed with the statement 'get along with mother/father' and a three-point Likert scale for responses ('well', 'quite well', 'not very well at all').

The ISRD-1 was designed to test 'cross-national variability in patterns of correlates of self-reported delinquency [which] may be socio-demographic in nature, or related to school, family, leisure, or peers' (Junger-Tas *et al.* 2004: 28). However the authors noted 'several drawbacks' in making direct statistical comparisons between the results from each participating country, particularly that:

the cultural, social, economic and political differences among the 11 individual countries are too many to enumerate, which makes interpretation of international differences in delinquency in terms of macro-level variables problematic. (Junger-Tas *et al.* 2003: 28)

Consequently, the authors decided to adopt what they termed a 'middle course strategy' of grouping the countries and cities into three regionalised clusters to reflect similarities in macro-level cultural, political and socio-economic characteristics (precise details of which were not provided). These clusters were:

- *Anglo-American* – England and Wales, Northern Ireland (Belfast), US (Omaha).

- *North West European* – Netherlands, Switzerland, Finland (Helsinki), Germany (Mannheim), Belgium (Liege).

- *Southern European* – Spain, Portugal, Italy (Sienna, Genoa, Messina).

The ISRD-I findings and conclusions

For ease of presentation, the statistically significant relationships between social control constructs and delinquency at the levels of region and gender that were identified by the study team (Junger-Tas *et al.* 2003) have been set out in a table below. Statistical links between socio-demographic variables (other than gender) and delinquency were marginalised in the study analyses, presumably (although this is not explicitly discussed in a report) because their static nature offered less explanatory utility in comparison to social control constructs.

Table 5.1 demonstrates the replicability found within- and between-regions in the ISRD-1 in terms of statistical correlations between social control constructs and different measures of delinquency. For example, the school-based constructs of 'attachment to school' ('like school') and 'truancy in the last year', along with the family-based construct 'get along with mother' were statistically related to delinquency for both males and females across each of the three regions, whilst 'get along with father' was correlated with general delinquency for all groups apart from Anglo-American females. By way of another example, in the family domain, 'parents know where you are' was correlated with general delinquency for both genders throughout the Anglo-American and North West Europe regions and was correlated with serious delinquency for males in these regions and for males in South Europe. Other constructs were not replicated as widely across the regions but demonstrated replicability within specific regions (each of which were composed of samples from a least three countries) and for specific groups (e.g. 'going out with family' was correlated with serious delinquency by Anglo-American males and general delinquency by North West European females).

Table 5.1 The relationship between social control constructs and delinquency

	Anglo-American		North West Europe		South Europe	
FAMILY	M	F	M	F	M	F
Get along with father	X		XO	XO	X	X
Get along with mother	X	XX	O	X	X	X
Going out with family	O			X		
Parents know where you are	XO	X	XO	X	O	
Parents know with whom you are	XO	X	XO			
SCHOOL						
Like school	X	X	X	X	X	X
Work hard at school	X					
Held back	X					
Truancy in last year	X	X	X	X	X	X

M = male, F = female.
X = statistically correlated with general offending, O = statistically correlated with serious offending.

The authors acknowledged that 'comparisons between countries and country clusters are rather crude. This means that we cannot in all fairness make well founded and explicit policy recommendations' (Junger-Tas *et al.* 2003: 143). However, notwithstanding this, Junger-Tas *et al.* saw fit to 'speculate' about the methodological and policy implications of their work, namely that:

- all family control variables in the study show a clear decline with age (n.b. a conclusion relating to the reported levels of each variable rather than their age-specific relationship with delinquency);

- in all countries there was tighter control on females than males;

- the social control variables selected had a strong association with delinquency;

(see Junger-Tas *et al.* 2002)

Junger-Tas *et al.* (2003) concluded that social control constructs had been replicated across the participating countries and, therefore, could be considered to be universally-applicable correlates with delinquency:

It seems clear that biological, cultural, socialization and environmental factors all play a role in the prediction of delinquent behaviour. (Junger-Tas *et al.* 2003: 368)

However, the authors qualified their generalised conclusions by acknowledging that further work was needed to explore the cross-national applicability of social control constructs in relation to specific contexts and cultural settings.

The ISRD-I as RFR

In the foreword to *Delinquency in an International Perspective*, the full report of ISRD-1, David Farrington heralded the ISRD-1 as 'a unique, highly significant and path-breaking research project', insisting that 'the authors should be commended for their heroic attempts to compare both individual countries and groups of countries' (Farrington, in Junger-Tas *et al.* 2003: ix). For their part, the authors have maintained that the project's central component, namely the *standardisation* of delinquency measures and social control constructs across different countries, has been 'quite viable' and offered a 'huge advantage of assuring comparability across varying samples and contexts' (Junger-Tas *et al.* 2003: 145).

Meanwhile, the authors have acknowledged that their cross-national comparisons were 'rather crude' and did not facilitate 'well-rounded and explicit policy recommendations' (Junger-Tas *et al.* 2003: 143). They drew particular attention to discrepancies in the sampling techniques and sample compositions in the participant countries, which resulted in 'varying claims to representativeness' and variations in core questionnaire content between countries. However, despite these caveats and the tentativeness of some of the ISRD-1 conclusions the study is problematic in a number of important respects.

A cross-national, comparative study of 'risk' correlates with offending that ignores or marginalises potential socio-economic, cultural, political and legal differences between- and within-countries can only, at best, present a partial picture. Despite such macro-level differences being viewed as 'enumerable' at a between-country level, there was no discussion of their potential influence within-countries (e.g. between different localities spread across the national samples), their capacity to change over very short periods (e.g. due to significant socio-economic or political changes in a given country) or, perhaps most importantly, the relative influence of these macro-level factors on the social control constructs at different times in different places on different groups of young people.

In the ISRD-1, the reliability of cross-national comparisons appeared to rest on the aggregation of social control data and its relationship with delinquency across the target age range, across genders, across cities, across countries and even across multiple countries within the three regions analysed. This aggregation involved an homogenisation of the demographic make-up and responses obtained from regions, nations, cities, age groups and genders, each of which were potentially broad categories containing disparate individuals. The aggregation and homogenisation employed may, therefore, have resulted in the over-generalisation and desensitisation of findings and conclusions to the point that they do not represent any actual relationship between a given construct and delinquency beyond one that has been statistically-manu-factured.

There are also concerns in ISRD-1 about the chosen measure of delinquency. Table 5.1 (above) shows the statistically significant relation-ships between a range of factors and delinquency (indicated by X) – where delinquency was measured by one (or more) positive responses to the self report inventory. This is a particularly blunt measure of delinquency and one which is highly likely to produce a larger number and range of positive statistical associations than a more refined notion of a delinquent. Thus, when a slightly more stringent definition of delinquency is employed (serious offending, O in Table 5.1), the statistical correlations between factors and offending drop away. It must be said that even the measure of serious offending is not very sharp as it may include just one 'serious' offence and not be indicative of a young person with a delinquent lifestyle. ISRD-1, therefore, has poorly operationalised its measure of delinquency and seriously over-estimated the reported links between a range of factors and offending.

Finally, whilst the ISRD-1 authors were generally careful to point out that their study could not address issues of causality but was concerned to explore a range of cross-national correlates with delinquency, they did conclude that a range of factors all play a part in *predicting* delinquency. Whilst this might have been simply a 'slip of the pen' it is a serious error and one which is reflected much more widely in a cross-sectional RFR literature which is given to misrepresentation.

The ISRD-1 researchers should be congratulated for their attempts to conduct a single international research project, but their methodology and analysis do not sustain any claim to have identified cross-national patterns of correlates of self-reported delinquent behaviour.

The Causes and Correlates Studies: universalised risk across the US

The Office of Juvenile Justice and Delinquency Prevention in the US began the Causes and Correlates studies in 1986. The overarching aim of the project was 'to improve the understanding of serious delinquency, violence, and drug use by examining how youth develop within the context of family, school, peers, and community' (Browning et al. 1999: 1). The project has consisted of three prospective longitudinal studies: the Rochester Youth Development Study (Thornberry 1994; Thornberry et al. 2003), the Denver Youth Survey (Huizinga and Espiritu 1999; Huizinga et al. 2003) and the Pittsburgh Youth Study (Loeber and Hay 1997; Loeber et al. 2003). From the outset, all three projects were designed to investigate the causes, correlates and consequences of delinquent behaviour, especially serious and chronic delinquency. Since their inception, the partner studies have each expanded to incorporate the investigation of additional and associated issues of concern, including the antecedents of both prosocial and antisocial behaviour, teenage parenthood, transitions into adulthood and patterns of work (see Thornberry and Krohn 2003).

A central feature of the Causes and Correlates *studies* has been the use of a 'similar research design' to aid comparability between the studies (Browning *et al.* 1999) and, as a consequence, to identify risk factors that could be generalised (universalised) across the studies. To this end, the three research teams initially worked together closely to develop a set of core measures, including a shared inventory of self-reported delinquent behaviour (adapted from the National Youth Survey Self-Reported Delinquency Scale, Elliott *et al.* 1985) and risk-focused questions relating to demographic characteristics, drug use, involvement with the juvenile justice system, family and educational experiences, peer relationships, community characteristics and attitudes and values.

The Rochester Youth Development Study

Led by Terence Thornberry, the Rochester Youth Development Study (RYDS) began in 1988 with the aim 'to investigate the causes and consequences of adolescent delinquency, with a particular focus on serious, chronic offenders' (Thornberry *et al.* 2003: 11), although this original aim has subsequently 'expanded into a broader investigation of both prosocial and antisocial development across the life course' (Thornberry *et al.* 2003: 11). The RYDS has been theoretically-underpinned by Interactional Theory (Thornberry 1987) and Social Network Theory (Krohn 1986):

- *Interactional Theory* – according to Thornberry, risk factors and offending function within a relationship of reciprocal causal influence (which varies at different developmental stages and for young people with varying levels of structural disadvantage) and weak social controls, especially attachment to family, commitment to school and association with delinquent peer groups (similar to the Social Development Model's fusion of social control, differential association and social learning – see Catalano and Hawkins 1996) – hence the link to . . .

- *Social Network Theory* – Krohn suggests that delinquency occurs when the individual becomes 'enmeshed' in networks that promote antisocial behaviour, particularly if these networks (e.g. peer groups) are multiple, overlapping, dense, stable and contain members demonstrating equivalent antisocial attitudes and behaviours (Krohn 1986).

The RYDS methodology

Due to the intended focus on serious delinquency, the RYDS research team decided to sample only young people perceived to be at 'high risk' of demonstrating this behaviour. The team chose to sample only young people from public (i.e. non-selective) schools in Rochester (New York) and only those in the seventh and eighth grades (aged 12–14 years old – widely considered to be the peak age of offending onset). From this sampling frame, males were 'over-sampled' to constitute 75 per cent of the final sample and similar oversampling took place in areas of Rochester with the highest arrest rates – the assumption being that males in these areas are the group most likely to commit serious delinquency.

The RYDS team conducted interviews on a biannual basis from 1988–1992 and on an annual basis from 1994–1997 with 1,000 boys and girls who were aged 13–14 years old when the study commenced. Biannual and annual interviews over the same periods were also conducted with parents/carers of the sample members.

Delinquency in its active form (i.e. committed currently or recently) was measured using an inventory of 36 delinquent acts derived from the National Youth Survey's Self-Reported Delinquency Scale (Elliott *et al.* 1985), the shared measure of delinquency within the Causes and Correlates studies. Responses were subsequently categorised into *general offending* (e.g. status offences, vandalism, minor property crimes), *serious property offending* (e.g. burglary, arson) and *serious violent offending* (e.g. attacking someone with a weapon, throwing rocks or bottles at someone). The self-reported delinquency data was supplemented by official records of arrests obtained from the Rochester Police Department (youth offending data) and the New York State Division of Criminal Justice Services (adult offending data).

Interviews with both young people and parents/carers focused on the 'wide range of environmental, social, and psychological forces' (Thornberry *et al.* 2003: 18) that allegedly contribute to delinquency and substance use. The environmental, social and psychological forces measured were grouped into six categories:

- *Family* – socio-demographic characteristics, parent-child relations, attachment to parents, maltreatment parental stressors;

- *School* – commitment to school, academic achievement;

- *Area characteristics*;

- *Peer group relationships* (e.g. association with delinquent peers);

- *Social networks*; and

- *Individual characteristics* (e.g. beliefs).

(Thornberry *et al.* 2003: 18)

A structured interview schedule collected data on different elements of risk, with over half of the items measured derived from the core measures agreed by the Causes and Correlates partners at the outset of the study, including:

- *Child Behaviour Checklist* – a 112 item questionnaire measuring problem behaviours such as anxiety, depression, oppositional behaviour and hyperactivity, using a three point response scale of 'not true', 'somewhat or sometimes true' and 'very true or often true';

- *Revised Diagnostic Interview Schedule for Children* – a measure of the child's psychopathology;

- *Attitude Towards Delinquent Behaviour Scale* – a 15 item measure of attitudes towards delinquency, antisocial behaviour and substitutes;

- *Child's Relationship with Parents/Siblings Scale* – 30 items measuring the boys' perceptions of their relationship with their mother and father;

- *Positive Parenting Scale* – measuring boy's perceptions of positive parental responses to their behaviour;

- *Peer Delinquency Scale* – a 15 item measure of the proportion of boys' peers engaged in delinquency.

(Loeber *et al.* 1998)

In each scale, the environmental and psychosocial forces were converted to a numeric variable (i.e. factorised). For example, on the Child's Relationship with Parents/Siblings Scale, 'attachment to parents' was a composite of 11 statements measuring how often ('never', 'seldom', 'sometimes', 'often') young people felt that they got along well with, respected and enjoyed being with their parents, felt anger, violence, trust or pride towards their parents and felt that their parents lacked understanding, were too demanding and interfered with their activities (Thornberry *et al.* 1991: 34).

At the time of writing, 12 waves of interview data had been collected – up until the sample members were aged 22 years. Data from the interviews has been supplemented with official data from school (e.g. truancy and exclusion data), police (e.g. arrest records), probation departments, family court and social services.

At a general analytical level, the researchers 'tried to examine the various conceptual premises that underlie interactional and network theories ... for example ... bidirectional causal influence, developmental changes in causal effects, and how family and peer networks coincide to produce delinquency and drug use' (Thornberry *et al.* 2003: 20). Two forms of bidirectional/reciprocal relationship between risk and delinquency were outlined prior to analysis (Thornberry *et al.* 1991):

- *Instantaneous/contemporaneous* 'causal links' between factors and offending at the same point in time;

- *Lagged/cross-lagged* mutual causal relationships that develop over time.

Due to the potential for 'multicollinearity' between the two models (i.e. they may be measuring the same factors and relationships) and the inability of the instantaneous model to examine the 'temporal and causal ordering' of factors and delinquency (Thornberry *et al.* 1991: 20), only the lagged model has been explored. To do so, the RYDS has measured risk factors and delinquency contemporaneously at each data collection stage/wave, but analysed the relationship between the two sets of variables across data collection waves, typically analysing measures of risk taken at time A (e.g. wave one) against changes in levels of delinquency between time A and time B (e.g. wave two).

The RYDS findings and conclusions

Following analysis of the interview data, the researchers hypothesised an influence on delinquency of the following environmental, social and psychological 'forces':

- *Family* – parental perceptions of low attachment to their child and the young person having a negative perception of involvement with and control by their parents were exacerbated (statistically) by the exogenous factors of economic hardship and single-parent family structure (Smith and Krohn 1995).

- *School* – low commitment to school and low academic achievement were statistically-correlated with an increased likelihood of self-reporting delinquency, whilst high levels of commitment to school and high academic achievement correlated with non-delinquency (Thornberry *et al.* 1991; Thornberry and Krohn 1995).

- *Neighbourhood* – living in a disadvantaged neighbourhood exerted an indirect statistical effect on delinquency by being linked to an increased likelihood of reporting exposure to negative socio-structural and neighbourhood factors such as economic hardship and lack of social support. These factors were then statistically-linked to low levels of attachment to parents, parent-child involvement and parental control over their child (Thornberry *et al.* 2003).

- *Peers* – gang membership was strongly associated with delinquency, whilst association with delinquent peers had an indirect statistical effect on delinquency through the reinforcing effects of the peer network. In turn, delinquent behaviour was linked to the increased likelihood, frequency and intensity of associations with delinquent peers (Thornberry *et al.* 1994).

- *Individual* – positive beliefs about drug use were associated with an increased probability of young people reporting delinquency.

The RYDS authors have interpreted their findings as offering support for the existence of the 'bidirectional causal influences [and] developmental changes in causal effects' that their theoretical model predicted (Thornberry *et al.* 2003). For example, Thornberry *et al.* (2003) have concluded that:

- the child's individual characteristics and the parent's inept parenting style are likely to become causally interwoven. Bidirectional, reciprocal influences (positive correlations) between the child's temperamental qualities and the parent's child management style can be observed as early as toddlerhood;

- neighbourhood characteristics affected delinquency indirectly, for example, through the impact of poverty and social disadvantage on risk factors such as parental supervision, attitudes to parents, association with delinquent peer groups and social isolation;

- association with delinquent peers indirectly affected delinquency through the 'reinforcing environment' of the peer network. In turn, delinquency increases associations with delinquent peers;

- isolation in deviant peer networks, coercive behavioural styles and academic failure, all influenced in part by earlier antisocial behaviour, lead to continuing involvement in delinquency during adolescence.

The RYDS as RFR

The RYDS has been ostensibly better able to address the nature of the relationship between risk and delinquency than previous examples of RFR due to its explicit focus on the temporal ordering of the two measured variables. However, there is a possibility that the temporal precedence of factors over delinquency has been imputed rather than empirically demonstrated. Just because the measurement of risk pre-dated the measurement of delinquency and thus allowed the interpretation of a time-lagged (predictive) relationship between the two, this does not necessarily mean that the two variables were causally related. It could be, for example, that delinquency actually occurred beforehand or concurrently, but simply was not measured, self-reported or officially recorded at that time. Of course, the multi-method approach and lagged model analysis minimises the potential influence of such confounding variables. However, even if the data collected was accurate, the conclusion of a predictive relationship may not be a true reflection of reality. Any measured relationships between risk at point A and (changes in) delinquency at point B may have been entirely statistical (artefactual), rather than existing in any real sense. It is equally likely that changes in delinquency between measurement time A and B are not attributable to the presence of particular risk factors in the intervening period. That is not to say that risk factors cannot influence delinquency causally, but such conclusions should not even be considered without further exploration of potential explanations of this causal influence, the precise temporal episodes of exposure to, or onset of, risk and offending and more detailed investigation of the purported processes of behavioural changes fostered by exposure to risk. With this in mind, the extent to which the risk factors identified as predating offending could be definitively concluded to be *causes* was overestimated by the study, which of course affects (reduces) the capacity to identify bidirectional causal influences. There is a significant sense that the results were interpreted selectively to fit Thornberry's original theoretical framework and that alternative explanations of the findings have not been explored.

Even if it were assumed that issues of temporality and causality were settled and agreed, would the conclusions of the RYDS stand up to scrutiny? The answer is undoubtedly no, for a series of cogent methodological reasons. For one thing, even if the risk constructs measured in the RYDS could be uncritically accepted as having a causal influence, their factorisation deprived the researchers of any qualitative depth and detail with which to explore the nature and operation of this causality as a mechanism, process or explanation. The crudity and reductionism of the risk measures were compounded by their aggregation across a single broad group of young people, with no sensitivity to potential individual differences and a disregard for within-individual analysis, which could better support explanations of individual behavioural change based on exposure to risk. The RYDS conclusions, already underpinned by uncritical reductionism and broad-brush generalisations, were further undermined by the developmental and psychosocial biases of the data collection instruments; partialities that seriously question the explanatory scope and breadth of the factors measured and the conclusions drawn.

The Denver Youth Survey

The prospective longitudinal Denver Youth Survey (DYS) aimed 'to identify social conditions, personal characteristics, and developmental patterns that are linked to sustained involvement in delinquency and drug use [particularly] risk and protective factors that may initiate, sustain, terminate, or, perhaps more importantly, prevent delinquency and problem drug use across the lifespan' (Huizinga *et al.* 2003: 47). The DYS research team, under the supervision of David Huizinga, stated that their study was based on an integrated theoretical model that synthesised strain, social control and social learning perspectives (see also Elliott *et al.* 1985) and that this model has been expanded to account for the effects of 'neighbourhood social disorganisation, biological history including perinatal events, childhood experience and socialisation, personality and mental health, formal and informal secondary (external) controls, and rational choice' (Huizinga et al. 2003: 49).

The DYS methodology

In order to assess young people considered to pose the highest risk of carrying out the target behaviours (delinquency and drug use), the research team sampled randomly from households in 'high risk neighbourhoods' in the target area, Denver. Neighbourhoods were chosen as high risk if their official crime rate was in the top third across Denver and if they had accompanying population and housing characteristics considered to be criminogenic such as a high proportion of ethnic minorities and low socio-economic status amongst residents.

The DYS team conducted annual interviews (from 1988–1992 and from 1995–1999) with 1,527 boys and girls who were aged either seven, nine, 11, 13 or 15 years old when the study began. Young people in the seven and nine year old groups were re-interviewed in 2003 when they were aged approximately 22 years.

Delinquency over the past year and the age of onset were measured using a Self-Reported Delinquency Scale: an inventory of *serious property offences* (e.g. robbery, burglary, car theft, arson), *serious violent offences* (e.g. serious assault, gang fights) and *minor offences* (e.g. public disorder, theft under five dollars, minor property crime). For younger children (aged seven and nine years), the Self-Reported Antisocial Behaviour Scale was used, wherein age-inappropriate acts such as joyriding were removed from the Self-Reported Delinquency Scale. Drug use and the age at which it began (onset) were recorded in relation to alcohol, marijuana and 'hard' drugs.

The interview foci were located in the biopsychosocial risk domains of family (parenting, attachment, marital discord, domestic violence, parental criminality), neighbourhood social characteristics (including family integration and support within the neighbourhood), school (involvement in education, educational strain) involvement in activities (community, religious, work, peer group delinquency), personal and psychological characteristics (of the young person and their parents) and medical history. Each factor was a composite of several sub statements with which young people had to indicate their strength of agreement ('never, seldom, sometimes, often'). For example, 'positive parenting' was measured as:

When you do something your parents approve of how often do they – 'give you a wink or a smile?', 'say something nice about it?', 'give you a hug?', 'give you a reward?', 'mention it to someone else?' (Huizinga et al. 1991: 106)

Multivariate regression analysis examined statistical relationships between the psychosocial factors measured in the interviews and delinquency measured at a later date. The factors linked to delinquency/non-delinquency were viewed as 'risk' factors and were also labelled 'explanatory' and 'causal' variables. Subsequently, cluster analysis was conducted to identify the risk factors that were particular to delinquents in two distinct developmental groups: childhood (aged seven to nine years) and youth (aged 11–15 years). The intention was to identify multiple aetiological (causal) pathways ('personal typologies' of risk) into delinquency rather than to uncritically assume that the same constellation of risk factors was responsible for delinquency in all young people. Huizinga and colleagues were clear that their 'orientation is not atheoretical. Our search is structured in data reflecting a general developmental model' (Huizinga *et al.* 1991: 86).

The DYS findings and conclusions

The key risk factors for delinquency in the DYS were identified (using multivariate statistical analysis) as:

- *Family* – criminality of family members, parental drug use and the family claiming welfare benefits were all statistically-associated with self-reported delinquency by males. Multiple changes to family structure was considered to be a risk factor for both males and females. Parental monitoring, home curfew rules, having a stable two-parent family and high levels of parental discipline were linked to non-delinquency by males and females.

- *School* – academic achievement, being in an age-appropriate school grade and graduating from high school were all hypothesised to increase resilience to and protect against delinquency due to their statistical relationship (association) with self-reported non-offending. Low academic achievement was associated with an increased likelihood of reporting delinquency (Huizinga *et al.* 2003).

- *Neighbourhood* – living in a disadvantaged neighbourhood was theorised to exert an indirect (statistical) influence on delinquency through its significant statistical relationship with socio-structural and neighbourhood factors, which themselves were linked to lower levels of attachment to parents, parent–child involvement and parental control over their child (Thornberry *et al.* 2003). Neighbourhood social control, social bonding and normative consensus on values and behaviour were found to mediate the effects of neighbourhood social disorganisation (poverty, mobility, single parent families, ethnic diversity) on delinquency (Huizinga *et al.* 2003).

- *Individual* – psychological problems (low self-esteem, social isolation, positive attitudes to delinquency, low guilt, lack of perceived opportunities in the future) were statistically-associated with self-reported delinquency. In contrast, high self-esteem and high self-efficacy were statistically-related to reports of non-delinquency (Huizinga 1997).

- *Individual delinquent typologies* – Huizinga *et al.* concluded that 'there is typological diversity among the child and youth samples in etiological or explanatory variables' (Huizinga *et al.* 2003: 75). In both the child and youth samples, having a more positive home life and a prosocial orientation were significantly more likely amongst *non-delinquents* compared to *low-level* or *high-level* delinquents. In contrast, the delinquent groups identified were more likely than non-delinquents to have pro-delinquent attitudes and beliefs, to have delinquent friends and to be impulsive/hyperactive (Huizinga *et al.* 1991). When the developmental typologies were explored for gender differences, Huizinga *et al.* (1991) discovered that delinquent personality, weak prosocial beliefs and the use of neutralisation techniques (making excuses for delinquency) were stronger influences on delinquency for males, especially in mid-adolescence and young adulthood, compared to females at the same developmental stage. The most important predictors of delinquency across both genders and all developmental stages were association with delinquent peers and psychological problems in adolescence.

The authors concluded that the integrated theoretical model that underpinned the data collected had enabled them to identify 'typological diversity ... in etiological or explanatory variables', multiple 'etiological pathways' to delinquency and different developmental sequences related to the onset and maintenance of, as well as desistance from, delinquency (Huizinga *et al.* 2003: 75). The main conclusions from the DYS have been that there is not one specific 'constellation of variables' that produces delinquency at all times within all individuals and that much greater attention should be paid to the asserted 'typological diversity' in risk factor influence – with the implication that the integrated theory that underpinned the study would be the ideal explanatory device for this purpose in future studies.

The DYS as RFR

The DYS conclusion of multiple 'etiological pathways' adds a layer of complexity and sensitivity to the traditionally over-generalised and universalised conclusions of RFR. The definitiveness of this innovative aetiological conclusion is not, however, fully substantiated by the evidence from the study. The causal influence of risk factors assumed by the notion of 'etiological pathways' has been premised on crude, desensitised, factorised measures of risk, aggregation of data across homogenised developmental groups (with little detailed consideration of age or gender differences) and a presumed control over the measurement of variables in the real world. There has, for example, been very limited analysis of the relative influence of different risk factors (or groups of risk factors) for specific age groups (as opposed to the broad child and youth age groups) and for different forms of delinquency in the DYS. Moreover, the conclusion that risk factors operate in dynamic 'pathways' and pre-date delinquency has been implicated from the repeated measurement of statistical associations, not causal relationships, and the assumption that risk has temporal precedence over delinquency, despite measures of each being taken concurrently (risk measured in current life, delinquency in measured over the past year), with no exploration of the precise timing of exposure to either. Unlike the RYDS, the DYS has attempted to address the explanatory influence of risk through measuring the age of onset of delinquency. However, devoid of an equivalent measure of the *onset* of risk, temporality has been dependent on the measurement period rather than actual exposure to risk relevant to delinquent behaviour. However, even if it could be established that the onset of a risk factor predates the onset of delinquency, this does not necessarily imply any explanatory/ causal relationship between the two at that point in time (although this relationship could have existed at that time or at some point in the past or subsequently). In this case, once again, risk factor researchers have been restricted to explanation based on statistical measurement rather than a developed understanding of how risk explains delinquency at a specific point in time or over a given period.

The Pittsburgh Youth Study

Managed by Rolf Loeber, the Pittsburgh Youth Study stated the key aims 'to investigate and describe developmental pathways to serious delin- quency ... [and] the risk and protective factors that influence the development of serious offending' (Loeber *et al.* 2003: 94). The Pittsburgh Youth Study (PYS) set out to address the 'adevelopmental' nature of most theories of youth offending (citing the Social Development Model and the work of Farrington as notable exceptions) by expanding on developmental criminology with a broader and more detailed account of the 'causal processes' that underpin the development of offending from childhood into adulthood (Loeber *et al.* 2003). In particular, the authors noted the paucity of RFR focused on preadolescent samples, such that 'it is often impossible to gauge whether the measured onset of delinquent acts (e.g. in the previous year) was truly an onset or a mere repetition of earlier behaviour' (Loeber *et al.* 2003: 93).

The Pittsburgh Youth Study methodology

In order to access young people considered most at 'at risk' of committing serious offences, the PYS team drew a random sample of 1,517 'preadolescent' boys from public schools in inner-city Pittsburgh. Sample members were aged 5–6, 8–9 or 11–12 years old when the study began. From 1992 onward, annual interviews were conducted with the youngest sample (five and six year olds) and oldest sample (11–12 year olds). At each interview stage, parents/carers of the sample members were interviewed. The middle age group (those aged eight and nine years old when the study began) were re-interviewed when they were aged 22 years.

The interviews at each successive administration utilised a range of quantitative behavioural scales and questionnaires, many of which were shared measures across the causes and correlate partnership (e.g. Positive Parenting Scale, Peer Delinquency Scale – see Loeber *et al.* 1998) to obtain data from sample members. The PYS is notable, therefore, for the way in which it has utilised pre-existing validated research instruments for data collection although this does not signify a move away from the established concerns of developmental risk factor researchers concerning the domains where risk is held to originate:

• the individual (impulsivity, guilt, intelligence and IQ, personality, attitudes);

• family (interactions with parents, parental discipline, parental anxiety and depression, communication with parents, family transitions – including; divorce, parental separation, relationship with parents);

• school (e.g. academic achievement); and

• socio-economic status (neighbourhood status, welfare dependency, living in a disadvantaged neighbourhood, broken homes, unemployment, low level of education).

Loeber *et al.* considered that each of these domains contained and constituted potential 'risk factors' that represented the 'causes or correlates of delinquency' (2003: 108). Each potential risk factor was a 'construct' or composite of several sub-factors derived from ratings scales and Likert-scale responses. For example, the construct of 'parental discipline' was a composite of non-persistent discipline, counter-control, physical punishment and parents disagreeing on discipline. The construct relating to 'friends' was a composite of having few friends, having bad friends and having poor relationships with peers (Loeber *et al.* 1998).

Official delinquency was measured using official court records. Self-reported delinquency and drug use were measured with a 33 item Self-Reported Antisocial Behaviour Scale (Loeber *et al.* 1989) for the youngest and middle samples and the Self-Reported Delinquency Scale and 16 item Substance Use Scale (Elliott *et al.* 1985) for the older sample. A sub-measure of *serious delinquency* was taken that consisted of car theft, breaking and entering, strong-arming, attacking to seriously hurt or kill and forced sex. On the self-reported delinquency questionnaire, young people were asked to indicate if they had ever committed any of the delinquent acts listed and, if so, at what age they had committed them the first time (the onset of delinquency).

So-called 'explanatory factors for delinquency' (Loeber *et al.* 1998: 97) in each age range were identified using logistic regression analysis to measure the statistical relationship between factors and dichotomised measures of general and serious delinquency in concurrent (rather than time-lagged) measurement periods. The research team acknowledged the limitation of this analytical procedure in passing when admitting that 'we will often refer to "predictors", while realising that analyses are essentially correlational' (Loeber *et al.* 1998: 97).

The Pittsburgh Youth Study findings and conclusions

At each wave of data collection, the correlation between different risk factors and delinquency was assessed for each of the age-related samples in order to develop a profile of which correlations increased and decreased with age. The risk factors that were statistically-associated with self-reported juvenile delinquency in the PYS samples were:

- *Family* – in the youngest and middle samples, low socioeconomic status of the family, living in a small house, father's unemployment, having a poorly-educated mother, coming from a broken home, high levels of maternal stress, substance use problems, anxiety/depression were associated with early onset and serious delinquency, as were unhappy parents (youngest sample only) and parental anxiety/depression (middle sample only) (Farrington and Loeber 1999). Poor parental supervision was the family-based 'risk' factor linked most strongly to an increased likelihood of reported delinquency by boys in each of the three samples (Loeber *et al.* 1998).

- *School* – in each age group, low academic achievement was statistically linked to self-reported delinquency, whereas high academic achievement was associated with reports of non-delinquency.

- *Neighbourhood* – across all three samples, living in a disadvantaged neighbourhood (measured using census variables) was correlated with an increased likelihood of reporting exposure to the family-based factors of low socioeconomic status and poor parental supervision (Stouthamer-Loeber *et al.* 2002).

- *Individual* – cognitive and behavioural impulsivity and high ADHD (youngest and middle samples) and depressive mood (boys in the youngest and oldest samples) were all linked to delinquency (Loeber *et al.* 1998). Certain individual factors were hypothesised as having an indirect effect on delinquency through their statistical relationship with other risk factors. For example, it was hypothesised that low IQ could be linked to feelings of frustration, failure and humiliation at school, which were themselves statistically-linked to alienating experiences, a factor with a significant statistical relationship to delinquency (Lynam 1993). Conversely, it was speculated that students with high IQ may experience better relationships with teachers and enjoy the rewards of education above those offered by delinquent behaviour.

- *Protective factors* – high accountability, trustworthiness, ability to feel guilt, motivation at school and living in a non-disadvantaged neighbourhood all reduced the statistical probability of the PYS sample members reporting delinquency (Stouthamer-Loeber *et al.* 2002).

- *Age-group factors* – school problem behaviours, deviant peers and positive attitudes to deviancy were more predictive of delinquency as young people got older. In contrast, physical aggression and social withdrawal decreased in their ability to predict delinquency as young people aged.

Loeber *et al.* (2003) hypothesised that individual risk factors dominated the causal processes that lead to early onset offending (an original focus of their study) and that 'from childhood to adolescence, children are introduced to factors in their peer group and neighbourhood, which for most did not exist in their early childhood' (Loeber *et al.* 2003: 120). They went on to conclude that psychosocial factors (in the family, school and neighbourhood domains) were primarily responsible for late onset offending. On the basis of the PYS results, Loeber *et al.* concluded that:

> offending by most juveniles results from forces within the individual and forces in the individual's social environment (parents, siblings, and peers) in different social contexts (family home, school, neighbourhood). (Loeber *et al.* 2003: 129)

The PYS researchers claimed to have addressed the 'adevelopmental' nature of many theories of delinquency by focusing on operationalising and investigating the main developmental elements of youth offending (Loeber *et al.* 2003). The research team has stressed that unlike most theories that have emerged from RFR, which have focused on correlations between risk factors and offending, they have been able to produce information about the 'causes' that differentiate young people who escalate into serious offending (Loeber *et al.* 1998). The research team has further claimed to have contributed:

empirical knowledge . . . based on the life course of individuals rather than the usually weak relationships between variables, while recognising that knowledge about relationships between variables can inform knowledge about types of individuals. (Loeber *et al.* 2003: 130)

Theoretically, the key conclusion from the PYS (reflecting a key conclusion of the entire Causes and Correlates project) has been that similar risk factors affect all young people, but that the causal influence of these factors is different at different ages. The claims and conclusions of Loeber and colleagues, however, do not stand up to critical scrutiny.

The Pittsburgh Youth Study as RFR

Certainly, when compared to the single age group studied in the RYDS and the aggregated age group data of the DYS, the accelerated longitudinal design of the PYS (analysing factors related to delinquency for different age groups over the same time period) had more potential to explore the different causal processes for different elements of the delinquent career (onset, escalation, desistance) and for young people at different developmental stages; which could have offered a first tentative step towards specific theories of the developmental pathways into delinquency (as claimed by Loeber *et al.* 2003). However, despite this potential advantage in analytical complexity and sensitivity over its Causes and Correlates partner studies, the PYS has produced definitive conclusions regarding the causality of risk factors that are invalidated by the partial and methodologically-crude understanding of the risk-delinquency relationship provided in this study. As in the other Causes and Correlates studies, the measurement of risk and the risk-delinquency relationship has been over-simplified in the PYS by the factorisation of standardised risk constructs and further reduced by the psychosocial bias within these standardised measures. There has been an equivalent uncritical imputation of (and consequent failure to reflect upon the detrimental impact of) the lack of methodological control over the variables measured, the aggregation of risk factor data across a broad and inappropriately homogenised age groups (thus ignoring individual differences) and the consequent absence of within-group, within-individual analyses. Although analysis of temporal ordering has been attempted, it has relied on measuring the onset of delinquency without an accompanying measure of the onset of risk, which even in itself would be insufficient to evidence a relationship between risk and delinquency without a robust explanation of the processes by which risk can influence delinquency.

Perhaps most damningly, however, the authors imputed the developmental influence of risk by comparing their results for different ages across the sequential administrations of their questionnaires. However, such developmental conclusions are misplaced as the authors have reduced their longitudinal design (and the potential to carry out powerful within-individual analysis) to a simple repeat cross-sectional study by choosing to only analyse the relationships between variables collected in the same annual sweep. It is difficult to understand or explain why the authors did this, but it means, of course, that they cannot say anything definitive about causality. The results and conclusions, therefore, reported by Loeber *et al.* above, are simply not sustained by the analysis they employed and should be regarded as spurious.

The Causes and Correlates studies revisited

The triumvirate of Causes and Correlates studies has attempted to develop multiple theories of serious delinquency by identifying so-called explanatory, causal risk factors and pathways that are shared by young people across different cities in the US, with the resultant imputation that these factors are universally-applicable. Do these collective, replicated findings, therefore, take RFR forward? The Causes and Correlates project has been heralded by the authors of the three studies as 'the largest and most comprehensive investigation of the causes and correlates of delin-quency ever undertaken' (Thornberry *et al.* 2004: 1). The project has, through an intensive exploration of the nature of the risk factor-delinquency relationship (particularly by examining the temporal preced-ence of risk factors), claimed to have contributed to RFR through the systematic exploration of developmental pathways into delinquency. In this respect, the partnership has begun to address (intentionally or otherwise) Farrington's concerns that there has been an absence of understanding of the 'processes or developmental pathways that inter-vene between risks factors and outcomes' (Farrington 2000: 7). However, the artefactual nature of the methodologies and analyses employed have provided little to validate risk as a dynamic process (rather than as a static factor) or to begin to explain or evidence the actual processes that link factors to outcomes at different points in time.

In contrast to claims that the studies covered 'a wide range of factors', the developmental aims of the Causes and Correlates studies, guided by some of the most prominent developmental criminologists within the RFR field, have inevitably privileged the investigation of psychosocial risk factors and the exploration of universally-applicable, deterministic, pre-dictive relationships between risk factors and delinquency. This bias has been reflected in the use of a set of standardised psychosocial measures (e.g. the Child Behaviour Checklist), demographically-biased samples (high-risk samples from high-risk neighbourhoods), and common analyti-cal techniques (multivariate regression measures to identify correlations between risk at time A and delinquency at time B). Consequently, with an equivalent body of 'risk' factors measured in an equivalent way in each study for equivalent groups of high-risk young people, it was inevitable that a degree of replicability and universalism would emerge. This replicability is, therefore, likely to be the product of standardisation of methodology (the same restricted set of questions, targeted on artificially constructed samples and crudely, often cross-sectionally, analysed between groups) (D. Smith 2006). In the words of Case (2007: 92) 'if you do what you've always done, you'll get what you've always got'.

The Causes and Correlates studies have been an intensive, yet self-fulfilling exercise in validating the tenets of developmental RFR. The identification of different developmental pathways and their portrayal as causal and explanatory has been reliant on statistical control, imputation and face validity – extrapolating dynamic and causal processes from the identification of statistical correlates and analyses of quantified and aggregated variables which cannot be experimentally controlled or isolated in the real-world context. As such, the interpretive leap involved in understanding correlates as causes has been unjustified in the light of the methodological and analytical limitations of the participant studies.

Sex Differences in Antisocial Behaviour: exploring risk from birth

The Dunedin Multidisciplinary Health and Development Study, or the Dunedin Study as it has come to be known, began in 1972 in Dunedin, New Zealand. The study set out to conduct 'a longitudinal investigation of the health, development and behaviour of a complete city-wide cohort of births between 1 April 1972 and 31 March 1973' with the central aims of:

• the prediction of childhood correlates of future health and behaviour outcomes;

• the developmental study of continuity and change in health and behaviour;

• the epidemiological study of the prevalence and incidence of health problems and behaviour problems.

(Mofitt *et al.* 2001: 10–11)

Moffitt *et al.* (2001, 2006) have pursued their third aim through a specific study of 'the developmental epidemiology of sex differences and antisocial behaviour during the first two decades of life ... [with a] focus on antisocial behaviour during adolescence both as the prime outcome of childhood risk and as an important predictor of subsequent adult outcomes' (Moffitt *et al.* 2001: 2–3). The methods, results and conclusions from this study have been mainly disseminated in a book entitled *Sex*

Differences in Antisocial Behaviour: Conduct Disorder, Delinquency and Violence in the Dunedin Longitudinal Study (Moffitt *et al.* 2001).

The Sex Differences in Antisocial Behaviour methodology

The Dunedin Study sample represented a complete cohort of children born between 1 April 1972 and 31 March 1973 in Dunedin, New Zealand. Sample members have been assessed on 11 occasions thus far – at age 3, 5, 7, 9, 11, 13, 15, 18, 21, 26 and 32 years.

Data for the Sex Differences in Antisocial Behaviour study has been collected from multiple sources (sample members, observers, parents, teachers, partners, peers, police, courts) using multiple, 'age-appropriate' methods (e.g. observation, behavioural problem checklists, cognitive tests of memory and reading, diagnostic interviews, official records) and multiple measures of antisocial behaviour (Moffitt *et al.* 2001: 14):

- *Psychometric ratings* of difficult temperament (at age three and five years).

- *Teacher and parent ratings* of antisocial behaviour problems using the Rutter Child Scale (at ages five, seven, nine and 11 years) and the Revised Behaviour Problem Checklist (at ages 13 and 15 years).

- *Diagnostic scales* measuring conduct and personality disorder (age 11, 13, 15, 18 and 21 years).

- *Self-reported delinquency* measured using the Self-Reported Early Delinquency interview (Elliott *et al.* 1983) (at ages 13 and 15 years) and the Self-Reported Delinquency interview (Elliott *et al.* 1985) (aged 18 and 21 years), both of which are standardised instruments measuring self-reported 'illegal' activity in the past 12 months.

- *Official records* of police arrests (age 11, 13 and 15 years) and court convictions (age 13, 15, 18 and 21 years).

- *Peer reports* of 'delinquent reputation' (age 18 and 21 years), asking whether the sample member has problems with aggression, offending, alcohol use and drug use.

- *Self-report and partner report* of domestic abuse (age 21 years).

From the multiple sources of data collected, a 'dependent variable' of *adolescent antisocial behaviour* was formulated as a composite of standardised measures taken at seven separate points: parent reports (at age 13 and 15 years), teacher reports (at age 13 years), self-reports (at age 13, 15 and 18 years) and peer reports (at age 18 years). The aggregated, composite measure of adolescent antisocial behaviour was constructed to provide a single dependent variable against which to measure the statistical impact of the so-called risk predictors. According to the authors:

> Aggregation is not always appropriate, of course, but in the service of obtaining more reliable estimates of risk and protective factors in development, investigators are better off creating aggregated scores by combining, within specified developmental periods, several measures of the same construct. (Moffitt *et al.* 2001: 93)

In terms of independent 'risk' variables, the researchers focused on what they saw as 'the most important risk factors for antisocial behaviour' discerned from large scale reviews of RFR (e.g. Rutter *et al.* 1998). They labelled these risk factors as 'risk predictors' and measured them in the 'most important domains' of risk factor influence at a range of different ages (based on suppositions about when different factors are most likely to be relevant or active at different times in the child's life):

- *Parental (maternal)* – young motherhood (measured at birth of sample child), low maternal IQ and poor maternal reading skills (when sample members were aged three years), poor maternal mental health (age seven, nine and 11 years), mother's neuroticism (when sample members were aged three years), maternal criminality (when sample members were aged 21 years).

- *Family* – deviant (negative, inappropriate) mother–child interaction (when sample members were aged three years), harsh discipline, inconsistent discipline, family conflict (all measured when sample members were aged seven and nine years), number of caregiver changes (when sample members were aged 11 years), number of residence moves (measured when sample members were aged five, seven, nine and 11 years), family socioeconomic status (averaged across the first 15 years of the study), relationship with parents (when sample members were aged 13 and 15 years).

- *Cognitive and neurological* – neurological abnormalities (when sample members were aged three years), intelligence (when sample members were aged three years), low neuropsychological memory scores (when sample members were aged 13 years), poor reading achievement (when sample members were aged seven, nine and 11 years), low resting heart rate (when sample members were aged seven, nine and 11 years).

- *Behavioural (individual)* – difficult temperament (when sample members were aged three and five years), hyperactivity (when sample members were aged five, seven, nine and 11 years), internalising problems (when sample members were aged five, seven, nine and 11 years).

- *Peer relationships* – peer rejection (when sample members were aged five, seven, nine and 11 years), peer attachment (when sample members were aged 13 years), peer delinquency (when sample members were aged 13 years), lack of involvement in school activities (when sample members were aged 15 years).

With the exception of five variables measured at age 13 and 15 years (relationship with parents, attachment to peers, peer delinquency, involvement in school, neuropsychological memory scores), the measurement of so-called *risk predictors* pre-dated the measurement of adolescent antisocial behaviour (as assessed between the ages of 13 and 18 years). Thus, most of the supposed predictive relationships identified are really only indicative of a temporal precedence in the measurement of risk factors (i.e. they were measured some years before the offending measure was taken), rather than necessarily indicating precedence in their onset and/or position in the relationship with offending. Even when the five variables were measured contemporaneously with offending, which would have enabled analysis of the direction of their relationship with offending, there was no examination of their age of onset relative to offending onset, so predictive relationships were not explored.

The first stage of analysis examined correlations between the risk predictors and adolescent antisocial behaviour. Subsequently, multiple regression was employed to establish 'whether the effect of the risk predictor on adolescent antisocial behaviour varies as a function of the Study member's sex' (Moffitt *et al.* 2001: 101).

Although the authors provided brief explanations of how each risk factor may influence antisocial behaviour, they stated that an 'extensive review' of the presumed risk-factor–antisocial behaviour relationship in each case was beyond the scope of the book (Moffitt *et al.* 2001). Such a conclusion illustrates what is implicit throughout the Moffitt *et al.* study, namely that the authors' primary interest was the exploration of sex differences in exposure to risk factors rather than a detailed exploration of the existence, extent and nature of any relationships between risk factors and offending for young people of both sexes.

The Sex Differences in Antisocial Behaviour findings and conclusions

Correlational analysis identified that every *maternal* risk predictor was significantly associated with antisocial behaviour by both males and females (except for mother's neuroticism, which was not associated with female antisocial behaviour). The multiple regression analysis identified no significant gender differences, indicating that maternal risk factors exercised similar levels of (statistical) influence on antisocial behaviour for both genders.

Similarly, all of the *family* risk predictors were significantly correlated with male and female antisocial behaviour, except for 'number of residence moves' (which was not correlated with female antisocial behaviour). The authors found that most of the family risk predictors had stronger effects on male antisocial behaviour than female antisocial behaviour.

In terms of *neuro-cognitive* risk predictors, most were significant predictors of male and female antisocial behaviour, although 'neurological abnormalities' and 'low resting heart rate' had very modest correlations with antisocial behaviour. The predictor of 'intelligence' was found to be more significantly associated with antisocial behaviour for males than females.

Every *behavioural* predictor was significantly correlated with antisocial behaviour by both genders, apart from 'child internalising problems', which was unrelated to antisocial behaviour for either gender. Multiple regression discovered that, in particular, 'difficult temperament' and 'hyperactivity' were more predictive of antisocial behaviour among males than females.

The *peer-relationships* risk factors found to link to antisocial behaviour in boys and girls were 'rejection by other children' during primary school years, 'affiliation with delinquent peers' and 'feeling marginalised from school and conventional peers'. 'Peer rejection in childhood' was more predictive of male antisocial behaviour than antisocial behaviour by females. However, the authors cautioned that unlike in the other domains, peer-relationships risk factors were measured at the same time as antisocial behaviour. Consequently, the direction of the relationship between the two could not be established and thus correlations should be taken to taken to indicate peer-related risk *factors* rather than risk *predictors*.

The authors concluded that:

- the same risk factors predict antisocial behaviour in both males and females, no replicable sex-specific risk factors for antisocial behaviour were identified;

- female antisocial behaviour does not require special attention within aetiological research;

- the risk measures selected from the Dunedin Study archive accounted for most of the variation in antisocial behaviour by males and females;

- temperament, hyperactivity, peer relationships and personality traits can account for most of the sex differences in antisocial behaviour amongst young people;

- developmental contexts are crucial to understanding the influence of risk factors across the life course.

(see Moffitt *et al.* 2001)

Sex Differences in Antisocial Behaviour as RFR

The Sex Differences in Antisocial Behaviour study aimed to contribute to developmental RFR by exploring the influence of risk factors measured from birth – more than satisfying the recommendations of certain developmental risk factor researchers (e.g. Richard Tremblay – see the Montréal Longitudinal and Experimental Study below) that longitudinal RFR begin at earlier ages. This has enabled measures of risk to be obtained several years before measures of antisocial behaviour, enabling the authors to test a wider range of factors (e.g. the under-explored potential of biological/neurological factors – although how much the authors have actually done this is moot) over a longer period and to have more confidence in their temporal precedence and predictive validity than has been possible in other RFR.

Beyond this important difference between the Sex Differences in Antisocial Behaviour study and other developmentally-biased RFR, the study exemplified the methodological weaknesses of its sister studies (psychosocial reductionism, crude factorisation, developmental static determinism etc). However, there are two further matters that strike at the heart of the quality of the Sex Differences in Antisocial Behaviour study that require sustained attention, namely: assumptions of causality based on temporal precedence and the validity of the statistical correlations between risk predictors and antisocial behaviour.

Firstly, the developmental emphasis of the authors has led them to impute predictive relationships between psychosocial variables and anti-social behaviour on the basis of a temporal precedence in the *measurement*, rather than the *onset*, of risk relative to the measurement of antisocial behaviour (an equivalent imputation to that found in the Causes and Correlates studies). The emphasis on measurement periods as indicative of the temporal relationship between risk and antisocial behaviour overlooks the possibility that antisocial behaviour was present in young people's lives prior to age 13 years and, as such, may have pre-dated, overlapped or even become conflated with several of the early childhood risk factors measured from age three to 11 years. In other words, there is no direct link between the presence (measurement) of a risk and the behaviour it is supposed to cause – they are simply measured sequentially and implied to be causally related. The mere statistical identification of temporal precedence of risk predictors over antisocial behaviour does not necessarily indicate an actual relationship between the two beyond the statistical – although this relationship is imputed and used to form the basis of the conclusions of the study (cf the 'psychosis of positivists'). The simple identification of exposure to risk in childhood and an episode of antisocial behaviour in adolescence does not indicate unequivocally that one led to or can explain the other. For example, even if a factor (e.g. harsh parental discipline) was first measured prior to antisocial behaviour, specific episode of/exposure to the factor may have had no actual impact on antisocial behaviour *at that point* (except for statistically) and may actually have been predicted/caused/exacerbated/reintroduced by antisocial behaviour at a later stage or have predicted or caused antisocial behaviour when manifesting itself again later in life. In the absence of detailed temporal and qualitative data, the statistical correlational techniques used in the Sex Differences in Antisocial Behaviour study can only highlight superficial relationships, rather than having any capacity to explain them. Much greater methodological sophistication, than was evident in the Sex Differences in Antisocial Behaviour study, is needed to show that temporal precedence and causality are both present and linked.

Secondly, the uncritical use of aggregation of multiple measures/constructs has produced a dependent variable (antisocial behaviour) so broadly-defined and non-discriminatory that multiple risk factors are inevitably correlated with it, particularly when explored superficially through basic correlational analysis. Although they argue that their approach was justified, Moffit *et al.* artificially constructed the dependent variable of antisocial behaviour so broadly that, in fact, almost every variable in their study was positively correlated with it. Consequently, it is very difficult to read their results as anything other than the crude and simplistic product of weak methodology and an extreme lack of statistical sophistication. Thus the Sex Differences in Antisocial Behaviour study actually contributes little or nothing to our understanding of risk factors and their relationship to antisocial behaviour.

The Montréal Longitudinal and Experimental Study: childhood risk and risk-focused intervention

Originating in 1984, the Montréal Longitudinal and Experimental Study (MLES) aimed 'to study the development of antisocial behaviour from kindergarten to high school with a specific focus on the role of parent–child interactions' (Tremblay *et al.* 2003: 205). The MLES authors espoused an explicitly developmental and psychosocial theoretical basis to their understanding of the impact of risk factors on antisocial behaviour, citing the theoretical influences of the Cambridge-Somerville Youth Study and the Cambridge Study in Delinquent Development. The study's central thesis was that boys with a low socio-economic status (due to their parents' occupations and/or the neighbourhood they live in) who show disruptive behaviour at kindergarten age are most 'at risk' of frequent and serious antisocial behaviour in the future compared to other children from the same environment (Tremblay *et al.* 2003). To examine this thesis, the MLES focused on the impact of parent–child interactions, psychological problems (hyperactivity, anxiety), substance use, school performance, poverty and 'physical factors' (e.g. health, nutrition, pre-natal complications, maturation, hormone levels).

The MLES methodology

In the first year of the study, a purposive sample of 1,161 boys aged six years was taken from kindergartens in 53 schools in 'low socioeconomic status' areas of Montréal, Canada. To control for cultural effects, boys in the sample had to have biological parents born in Canada and had to speak French as their first language. The behaviour of each of the sample members was rated by their teachers using the Preschool Behaviour Questionnaire (Tremblay *et al.* 1987), a 13 item checklist containing indicators of disruptive behaviour: bullying, kicking, biting, hitting, fighting, being disobedient, blaming others, irritability, being destructive, restlessness, being inconsiderate, lying, being 'squirmy', not sharing and being unpopular. The 125 boys rated above the seventieth percentile on the disruptive behaviour scale were classified as 'disruptive'. From this group, 82 boys were allocated to a longitudinal group receiving intensive observation from which 43 were allocated to an experimental intervention/treatment group, which would receive a preventative intervention consisting of parent training and social skills training. A further 41 'non-disruptive' boys (defined by falling below the seventieth percentile on the disruptive behaviour scale) from the original sample constituted a control group against which the findings from the experimental intervention would be evaluated.

On an annual basis, all boys in the three sample groups (control, longitudinal and treatment) were interviewed to investigate (largely psychosocial) factors relating to family relationships, parenting, attitudes to school, peer relationships, leisure time, personality and the impact of life events. These interviews were supplemented by annual questionnaires with mothers that collected information on family background, family relationships, parenting, social support, life events and the child's delinquency over the past 12 months.

Serious delinquency and the frequency of delinquency were measured annually from the ages of ten to 17 years and once again when the boys were aged 20 years. The MLES employed a self-report inventory of 27 delinquent acts, with the boys required to report how often they had committed delinquent acts in the past 12 months, using a four-point Likert-scale: 'never, once or twice, often, very often'.

The annual rounds of interviews have been augmented at various stages in the study by *ratings of behaviour* (physical aggression, opportunism, conduct problems, anxiety, inattention, hyperactivity, prosocial behaviour) by mothers and classroom peers (when the boys were aged ten, 11 and 12 years), *psychiatric interviews* with boys and mothers (when boys were aged 15 years), *direct observation of social interactions* in school, home and in a laboratory setting (between the ages of 7–15 years) and *physiological and neuropsychological tests* with sub-samples of boys (between the ages of 7 and 20 years old).

Logistic regression analysis was conducted to identify ('predictive') statistical relationships between psychosocial factors measured at each data collection episode and delinquency measured in later data collection episodes (Nagin and Tremblay 2005), with the implication being that temporal precedence in the measurement of risk factors equated to (i.e. enabled imputation of) the temporal precedence of risk factors in their relationship of influence with delinquency (i.e. risk factors could be interpreted as predictive and/or causal).

The MLES findings and conclusions

A series of key findings have emerged from the MLES regarding the predictive influence on delinquency of the psychosocial factors measured through the different data collection episodes, in particular:

- *Kindergarten disruptive behaviour* – teacher ratings of physical aggression, hyperactivity and non-prosocial behaviour (but not anxiety or inattentiveness) predicted self-reported delinquency during the transition from childhood to early adolescence (Pulkkinen and Tremblay 1992).

- *Kindergarten personality* – teacher ratings of high levels of impulsivity, low anxiety and lack of regard for others, predicted delinquency during the transition from childhood to adolescence, irrespective of the deviant characteristics of peers (Tremblay *et al.* 1994).

- *Family poverty* – boys from families experiencing economic hardship scored lower on measures relating to learning, physical health, emotion, family and environment. Family poverty predicted serious delinquency (breaking and entering, arson, theft of objects over $100, vandalising a car, beating someone up) but did not predict other types delinquency (e.g. petty theft).

- *Parenting process* – low levels of parental monitoring (e.g. poor supervision, lack of rule-setting in the home) was associated with an increased risk of self-reported serious delinquency.

- *School failure* – there was an association between not being in an age-appropriate classroom at the age of 16 years and delinquency at that age, which suggested a 'significant relationship between academic failure and delinquency'.

(see Tremblay *et al.* 2003)

In relation to the original study aim of exploring the development of antisocial behaviour from kindergarten to school, the authors concluded that the factors they identified were *associated* with delinquency, not causal of this behaviour. Tremblay and colleagues stated that factors were not 'causal' because, 'longitudinal studies are still only correlational studies, and the strong association between a predictor variable at time A and an outcome variable at time B does not necessarily imply a causal relationship. In fact, most time A–time B correlations are probably not causal' (Tremblay *et al.* 2003: 224). However, they did argue that these factors do play a predictive role in either sustaining or reducing antisocial behaviour.

There has been somewhat limited dissemination of the factors identified in the experimental portion of the study, Tremblay *et al.* (2003) reported that three years post-intervention, when most boys were in their final year of elementary school (nine to ten years old), self-reported delinquency amongst members of the treatment group had decreased, as had (teacher- and peer-rated) levels of disruptive behaviour and association with disruptive friends. More members of the treatment group were in an age-appropriate classroom and had fewer disruptive friends than the longitudinal group and this was considered to exert a positive impact at that time and on into high school on different aspects of development such as self-esteem, positive attitudes to school and reduced delinquency (see Vitaro and Tremblay 1994). The frequency of self-reported delinquency was significantly lower in the treatment group compared to the control group three to six years later between the ages of 13 and 16 years, a finding that the authors attributed to the effects of the intervention.

It was concluded by Tremblay and colleagues that 'the importance of the beneficial impact (of the intervention) on elementary school adjustment should not be overlooked' (2003: 232) and that 'comparative changes in delinquent behaviour and the significantly higher levels of academic adjustment observed in youngsters from the experimental group may be attributable to the treatment' (Tremblay *et al.* 2003: 235). However, the authors noted that this positive impact at age ten years had apparently disappeared by the age of 15 years, exemplified by the finding that the majority of the experimental group boys (59 per cent) were not in an age-appropriate classroom by that time. Tremblay *et al.* attempted to explain this 'disappointing' finding by offering a pessimistic conclusion that seems contradictory to their support for the efficacy of the preventative experiment:

> Given that poor school adjustment at age 15 is the norm for this sample of boys from low SES environments, it was unlikely that an intervention directed at disruptive behaviour would have enabled disruptive kindergarten boys to have more success in high school than the majority of their peers. (Tremblay *et al.* 2003: 232)

Notwithstanding their pessimism regarding the potential of the experimental intervention, the authors interpreted (imputed) their findings as suggesting that improvements in parental practices and in the child's social competence/social skills, which were both apparently encouraged by the intervention, were operating as 'protective factors' that discouraged the onset of delinquency and encouraged desistance from delinquency.

The MLES authors recommended the continued use of longitudinal designs within RFR on the basis that correlational (cross-sectional) studies can continue to correlate putative causal variables, assessed at a given point in time, with antisocial behaviour assessed at another point in time (Tremblay *et al.* 2003: 242). Indeed, the study's authors have claimed that their findings highlighted the need for more valid and potentially practical longitudinal exercises 'to start earlier than school entry to understand and prevent the development of antisocial behaviour' (Tremblay *et al.* 2003: 236). Indeed, the authors go on to claim that:

> The MLES still appears, at the beginning of the twenty-first century, to be the largest longitudinal and experimental study specifically designed to understand the development and prevention of delinquency with subjects first assessed before Grade 1. (Tremblay *et al.* 2003: 208)

The MLES as RFR

The MLES design has been, to a point, typical of longitudinal, developmental RFR, in that 'risk' factors have been measured in early childhood and their 'predictive' power has been analysed in adolescence (similar to the approach taken by the Causes and Correlates studies, for example). Where the MLES has sought to be different has been in beginning to measure 'preadolescent' risk (beginning at age six years), so exploring developmental pathways of risk for a longer period (albeit still terminating the main study at 20 years). The MLES has also acknowledged clearly that its attempt to measure the temporal ordering of risk and delinquency has not identified risk factors that can be considered 'causal'. However, risk has been interpreted as predictive of (i.e. prefiguring) delinquency. Stating that factors are predictive of delinquency is a less strong, although more accurate, conclusion to draw than claiming causal relationships. Consequently, the research findings should be interpreted with a lower level of confidence or certainty in the expressed linkages between factors and outcomes than a study which demonstrated causality.

In an attempt to demonstrate the strength of these predictive linkages between childhood developmental risk factors and adolescent outcomes, the MLES adopted an experimental design – with a treatment group receiving interventions targeted on pre-established risk factors. The outcomes of this experiment were, however, mixed, with some benefits in outcomes being enjoyed by the treatment group in the pre-teen years, but these improved outcomes were not evident at age 15 years. How can these results be explained? There are a number of different and sometimes competing possible explanations:

- *Imprecision* – that the imprecise (e.g. aggregated, homogenised, factorised) measurement and imputations of temporal precedence (rather than precise measurement of the timing of risk and offending) inevitably produced multiple correlations that could be interpreted selectively, but which had no validity or explanatory utility for individual young people. For example, the temporal precedence of risk was imputed in the absence of definitive information that the sample boys had not committed delinquent acts before the age of ten years (the first time at which delinquency was measured). Such behaviour may have prefigured, even caused, the onset of risk, but neither preadolescent delinquency nor the age of onset a risk was measured. Furthermore, the psychosocial bias in the MLES has become psychosocial reductionism due to the widespread factorisation of risk, the quantitative, statistical analysis (and consequent deterministic interpretation) of the relationship between risk and delinquency and the portrayal of protective factors as risk-dependent – all to the detriment of more in-depth exploration of risk and protection as processes that can explain delinquency and/or that can be explained and constructed by the young people who commit delinquent acts.

- *Psychosocial reductionism* – that the study actually failed to measure/ assess the most relevant factors in early childhood. The developmental focus of the MLES has induced a psychosocial bias within the data collection, to the neglect of, for example, socio-structural factors, thus perpetuating an over-simplified and restricted view of the scope and nature of risk in young people's lives. For example, family poverty (measured by economic hardship) was taken to distinguish young people who were actually poor from those who just lived in the poor/low socio-economic status neighbourhoods (measured by average family income) from which the sample was taken. However, there was little exploration of the specific characteristics of these poor neighbourhoods or the effects of these characteristics on individual risk factors. It was as if low neighbourhood socio-economic status was ascribed the status of a demographic variable/static risk factor (like gender or ethnicity) that could be taken for granted and did not warrant further investigation.

- *Flawed theory* – that the simple developmental model is actually flawed and a young person's life is more shaped by their current circumstances and/or agency than childhood developmental deficits.

- *Invalidity* – that there is, in fact, no causal relationship between factors and outcomes.

235

- *Artefact* – that the predictive relationship between factors and outcomes exists only in the results of the statistical tests used and not in the real world.

- *Misdirection* – that the interventions targeted the wrong factors (because they did not emerge from study of the group who were actually submitted to them but from prior research) or the interventions themselves were not effective in remedying the attributed deficits.

The MLES set out to utilise its longitudinal design and developmental preconceptions in order to 'test causal hypotheses and identify effective interventions' (Tremblay *et al*. 2003: 230). However, the results actually tell us very little about risk factors and their relationship to delinquency. Although Tremblay *et al*. produced lists of factors that they considered 'predictive' of future delinquency, the test of the validity and relevance of these factors in causing delinquency showed no discernable relationship. It seems likely, therefore, that on the basis of these results that the predictive factors were not predictive at all. Therefore, Tremblay *et al*.'s implication that young people are crash test dummies on an inevitable developmental pathway to delinquency does not bear the weight of much confidence. It is arguable that the MLES actually promulgated a 'black box' (see Porteus 2007) approach to understanding he relationship between both risk factors and delinquency and between risk-focused interventions and the prevention of delinquency. Therefore, the MLES has contributed little substantive knowledge of the risk factors that may predict delinquency, what is happening inbetween intervention and outcome (i.e. delinquency or decreases in delinquency) or *how* the intervention may have changed behaviour (if it did so at all) beyond existing differences between the samples compared, the unmeasured influence of life events or the young person simply growing out of crime.

The Seattle Social Development Project: childhood risk factors, risk-focused intervention and the Social Development Model

In 1985, the prospective longitudinal Seattle Social Development Project (SSDP) was established under the guidance of David Hawkins, the originator of the Social Development Model. The SSDP set out to understand and prevent youth crime and violence by conducting a panel study and by implementing a linked risk-focused intervention. Both the risk factor study and the risk-focused intervention were constructed to test the tenets and constructs of the Social Development Model (Hawkins and Weis 1985); a distinct strand of RFR that 'organises a broad range of risk and protective factors into a model specifying causal hypotheses to capture key elements of socialization' (Hawkins *et al*. 2003: 279). Through a synthesis of various explanatory theories, the Social Development Model has hypothesised parallel and developmentally-specific processes producing prosocial and antisocial behaviours (see Chapter 2). For Hawkins and his colleagues, an empirical investigation into the constructs of the Social Development Model was necessary – for two main reasons:

- the Social Development Model had been established as a hypothetical model with a limited evidential basis;

- the theoretical constructs of the Social Development Model (social control theory, social learning theory and differential association theory), when taken in isolation, could not fully account for the aetiological processes of delinquency, nor were they able to adequately explore delinquency across different developmental stages (see Hawkins *et al.* 2003).

The SSDP methodology

The SSDP drew a purposive, multi-ethnic sample of 808 children aged ten years old from schools in high crime neighbourhoods in Seattle, US. Sample members and their parents were regularly interviewed in the first 12 years of the project (sample members nine times; parents six times). In addition, the children's teachers completed the Child Behaviour Checklist (Achenbach and Edelbrook 1983) for the first five years of the project (1985–1989). Interviews at each data collection point obtained data relating to psychosocial 'risk and protective factors' for offending that overlapped with social development constructs (see Chapter 2), with the measurement of new items relating to sexual activity, work, marriage, pregnancy and parenting being added when the children were over 16 years of age. The factors measured were:

- *Involvement, interaction and perceived rewards/costs* – in relation to school, family, neighbourhood, peer, work and intimate relationships.

- *Skills* – social, academic and work-related.

- *Bonding* – commitment and attachment to school, parents and peers, intimate/marital relationships.

- *Belief in the moral order/antisocial opportunities* – drug availability, antisocial behaviour of others, parental and peer substance use, parental attitudes favourable to drug use.

- *Exogenous variables* – position in the social structure (income, economic deprivation, living arrangements, ethnicity, gender, age), external constraints (parenting, neighbourhood characteristics, victimisation) and individual constitutional factors (cognitive functioning, temperament, factors relating to: school, family, peer network, work and relationships).

The individual variables of aggression, anxiety and depression were measured and factorised through teacher ratings on the Child Behaviour Checklist. Family, school and peer factors were measured in interviews through dichotomous (yes/no) measures of agreement with a series of sub-questions/statements. For example, 'attachment to parents' was a composite of:

- Would you like to be the kind of person your mother is?
- Do you share your thoughts and feelings with your mother?
- Would you like to be the kind of person your father is?
- Do you share your thoughts and feelings with your father?

The factor 'school commitment' was a composite of agreement with two statements:

- I do extra work on my own in class;
- When I have an assignment to do, I keep on working on it until it is finished.

Whereas, the 'low neighbourhood attachment' factor was an aggregation of yes/no responses to three statements:

- I know many people in my neighbourhood;
- I like my neighbourhood;
- I feel safe in my neighbourhood.

(Chung *et al.* 2002: 85–6)

Frequency and seriousness of *delinquency* was measured from age 13 with a self-report inventory asking the children if they had committed any of a series of offences (and if so, how often), namely: vandalism/criminal damage, theft/robbery, assault/violence, use of weapons, selling drugs, being in trouble with the police, traffic offences, white-collar crime, gambling, gang involvement and domestic violence. Offences were broken down into minor, moderate and serious categories (see Chung *et al.* 2002). For example, assault was recorded in terms of picking fights or throwing objects at people (minor), hitting parents, hitting teachers or hitting someone with serious intent (moderate) and using force to get money from people (serious). Similarly, theft was divided into taking things worth less than $5 (minor), taking things with more than $5 but less than $50 (moderate) and taking things worth more than $50 (serious).

The SSDP has collected additional psychosocial risk data from a range of sources, notably *official records* from *schools* (information regarding test scores, special educational needs and disciplinary proceedings collected annually until 1991), the *police* (arrest records collected annually until 1993) and the *courts* (annual collection of sentencing records until sample members were aged 21 years).

Critical of the way in which other studies have adopted crude and/or homogenised offending outcome measures (that, for example, do not offer anything more specific than 'offender' or 'non-offender'), Hawkins *et al.* (2003) were concerned to be more specific in measuring their target outcomes. The authors emphasised the importance of understanding the different developmental trajectories of offending, rather than making oversimplified and generalised comparisons between aggregated groups of 'offenders' and 'non-offenders'. They believed that 'there are distinctive groups that follow distinctive trajectories of offending with distinctive etiologies ... [so] different causal mechanisms and pathways may be needed to understand distinct patterns of criminal behavior over time' (Hawkins *et al.* 2003: 265).

Group-based statistical modelling (Chung *et al.* 2002) identified five groups of young people, each with their own developmental trajectory of offending between the ages of 13 and 21 years:

- *non-offenders* (never offended);

- *late onsetters* (offended after age 13 years);

- *desistors* (had offended at age 13 or older, but were not offending at age 21 years);

- *escalators* (were offending more at age 21 than at age 13 years);

- *chronics* (were offending at equivalent levels at ages 13 and 21 years).

The so-called psychosocial 'predictors' of delinquency for the full sample were measured by using logistic regression to analyse the statistical relationship between risk factors measured at time A (e.g. at ten years old) and a dichotomous (yes/no) measure of delinquency taken at time B (e.g. 18 years old). For each of the developmental trajectory groups, risk factors measured at age 10–12 years were analysed against delinquency measured at 13 years of age and beyond. For example, once the 'late onsetter' group had been established, the psychosocial risks reported by these individuals at age ten years were analysed against their subsequent offending at the age of 13 years and any statistical links were taken to indicate risk factors for these group.

The SSDP findings and conclusions

The psychosocial risk factors and social development model constructs identified as significantly-related to offending in the study were:

- *Family* – positive external constraints imposed by the family (e.g. consistent rules, clear behavioural boundaries) were associated with the absence of delinquency during adolescence (Kosterman *et al.* 2000). However, bonding to the family was *not* statistically-linked to non-delinquency (Hill *et al.* 2002), in opposition to a central tenet of the Social Development Model that family bonding exerts a protective influence. That said, the authors acknowledged that because they did not ensure that the bonding measured was to prosocial family members, the SSDP analyses failed to account for the existing criminality, violence or antisocial attitudes of family members, which themselves could have been modelled by sample members, in accordance with Social Learning Theory (Hawkins *et al.* 2003).

- *School* – low academic achievement measured at age 12–13 years predicted delinquency at age 15–16 years (Herrenkohl *et al.* 2000), whilst high academic achievement was linked to the absence of delinquency (Ayers *et al.* 1999). A lack of bonding to school was also a risk factor for later delinquency (Ayers *et al.* 1999) and violent behaviour at age 18 years (Herrenkohl *et al.* 2000), especially when combined with low academic achievement.

- *Peer group* – association with delinquent peers (along with delinquent siblings and adults) statistically-predicted future delinquent behaviour, notably serious delinquency at age 12–13 years (O'Donnell *et al.* 1995).

- *Individual* – having poor social skills at age 12–13 years was predictive of delinquency at age 15–16 years, whilst young people with higher levels of social skills and substance use refusal skills were significantly less likely to report delinquent behaviours between the ages of 12 and 14 years than young people without these interaction skills (Ayers *et al.* 1999).

- *Developmental trajectories* – according to Chung *et al.* (2002), late onsetters at age 13 years were significantly more likely than non-delinquents to report individual risk factors (especially aggression, anxiety and de-pression) at age 10–12 years, whereas escalators from age 13 years were more likely than desisters to report peer, school and neighbourhood factors (especially lack of attachment/bonding to school, availability of drugs in the neighbourhood and antisocial peers) at age 10–12 years. Chung *et al.* (2002) went on to analyse risk factors (measured at age 10–12) for each offending trajectory group in relation to the seriousness of their offending. They found that poor family management was a risk factor for minor offending by the late onsetter group only, aggressive behaviour was a risk factor for both minor and serious offending amongst the late onsetter and chronic offender groups, whilst having antisocial peers, low academic achievement, low school bonding, low

neighbourhood attachment and availability of drugs in the neighbourhood were all risk factors associated with minor and serious offending
amongst the escalator, desister and chronic offender groups.

Hawkins and colleagues concluded that their analysis of the interview
data and additional data sources had enabled them to pinpoint the
'indicators of major psychosocial risk factors for crime' (Hawkins *et al.*
2003: 257) and to establish the large degree to which social development
model constructs are able to predict delinquency. The authors also
concluded (from the identification of developmental offending trajectories) that early intervention was crucial in order to prevent the development of delinquency and other problem outcomes (e.g. violence) and
multiple interventions should be prioritised as responses to the multiple
pathways into delinquency. Most importantly, it was concluded that
'developmental trajectories do not require different etiological theories.
Constructs from the social development model can account for somewhat
different factors contributing to different behavioral trajectories' (Chung *et
al.* 2002: 82).

The linked SSDP intervention

In order to explore experimentally the influence of the psychosocial risk
factors identified (see above) and their malleability within risk-focused
intervention, students in the SSDP sample were assigned to one of four
groups: a *control* group that received no interventions, a *parent-training
only* group (parents received training when the child was in grades 5–6,
i.e. aged 10–11 years), a *late intervention* group (the child received a social
development intervention and parents received parent training when the
child was in grades 5–6 only) and a *full intervention* group (which received
social development intervention and parent training when the child was
in grades 1–6, i.e. aged 4–11 years).

The SSDP evaluation compared the effect of risk and protective factors
on delinquency once sample members had been exposed (or not exposed
in the case of the control group) to the type(s) of interventions offered to
their group, which consisted social development and/or parent training:

- The *social development intervention* 'sought to reduce specific risk factors
  and to increase protective factors for adolescent health and behaviour
  problems specified in the social development model' (Hawkins *et al.*
  2003: 284). Particular focus was given to risk factors in the domains of
  family (clarity of parental norms and rules for behaviour, consistently
  enforced behavioural expectations, poor family management practices,
  favourable parental attitudes towards problem behaviour, family conflict, family bonding), school (academic failure, attachment and commitment to school) and peers (delinquent and antisocial peer influence).

Classroom teachers were trained in proactive classroom management, interactive teaching and co-operative learning techniques, combined with giving social skills training to students. In particular, the teaching interventions aimed to increase the protective factors of clarity of school behavioural norms and rules, consistently enforced expectations for behaviour, academic achievement and attachment to school. The social skills element was focused on increasing resistance to delinquent peers.

- The *parent training* consisted of parenting evenings for 'developmentally-adjusted' training in effective parenting skills and supporting children's success – in order to enhance the alleged protective efficacy of effective family management, bonding to the family, avoiding/dealing with family conflict and constructive parental attitudes to problem behaviour.

The SSDP intervention results

Two years following completion of the interventions, the full intervention group (compared to the control group) demonstrated significantly lower levels of delinquency and aggression, but significantly higher levels of family management, involvement with family, attachment to family and attachment/commitment to school (Hawkins *et al.* 1991). These findings remained consistent at age 18 years, six years following the interventions (Hawkins *et al.* 1999). At the age of 18 years, young people who had been in the full intervention group were significantly more likely than control group members to be more attached and committed to school, to have demonstrated higher academic achievement and to display lower levels of delinquency and violence.

According to Hawkins *et al.* (2003), the SSDP demonstrated an intervention 'dose effect', with greater reductions in offending and more positive outcomes evidenced in the full intervention group, followed by the late intervention group, then the parent training only group and finally the controls. The authors concluded that risk and protective factors were equivalent to 'causal processes' that should be addressed using multiple interventions, because there are multiple direct and indirect paths to offending and violence. They emphasised the importance of intervening early in the development of delinquent pathways and the need for a dual focus on interrupting negative pathways and promoting positive pathways (Hawkins *et al.* 2003). Moreover, the risk and protective factors identified in the SSDP were considered to be viable foci for preventative interventions in childhood and adolescence because 'interventions that change the course of development during childhood can have long-term positive effects in promoting prosocial bonding and reducing violence' (Hawkins *et al.* 2003: 303).

The SSDP as RFR

Hawkins and his colleagues do not appear to be developmentalists in the traditional sense (i.e. advocates of childhood risk factors leading to adolescent offending). Their focus has been on identifying influential risk *processes*, including those leading to *pro*social behaviour, and their strand of RFR is not as reductionist and oversimplified as much extant RFR, largely due to the attempts to identify different developmental trajectories ranging from adolescence through to young adulthood. However, a degree of reductionism has remained which has undermined the depth and complexity of the resultant understandings of risk that have been produced. The major limitations of the ongoing SSDP have been (and continue to be) the pervasive psychosocial bias that results in the authors pre-empting the most important risk factors to measure, along with the factorisation and aggregation of potentially complex and multi-faceted risk and social development constructs that are specific to individual young people; procedures that wash away much of the dynamic, qualitative and nuanced nature of both constructs. This bleaching out of complexity has been exacerbated by the aggregation of risk data across a series of broadly-framed groups (i.e. the experimental intervention groups and the developmental trajectory groups) such that the mooted antisocial and prosocial pathways are not representative (or necessarily relevant to) any specific individuals in the study sample. Furthermore, the different offending trajectories identified and explored actually emerged from a single, 'general' measure of offending which, as the authors acknowledged, lacked sensitivity to the potentially-diverse aetiologies of different forms of offending (Chung *et al.* 2002).

A central weakness in the SSDP research conclusions was the overly-basic and literal use of temporal precedence to indicate the predictive effects of risk factors and social development constructs. Information relating to risk and social development was collected annually from when the sample members were aged ten (i.e. Time A), whilst offence data was not collected until sample members were aged 13 (i.e. Time B). Subsequently, predictive relationships between risk factors/social development constructs and offending/offending trajectories were identified on the basis of temporal precedence (i.e. that measures taken at Time A predated those taken at Time B). However, as has been discussed at length previously, basic temporal precedence such as this does not necessarily indicate predictive influence, nor does it tell us anything about causal relationships or dynamic processes, the latter of which was claimed by the study authors. All that was established conclusively by the SSDP research was that risk factors/social development constructs could be measured prior to offending and statistically associated with different offending trajectories and differing levels of offence seriousness, with no consideration that (unmeasured) offending episodes could have pre-dated and therefore influenced the onset of risk factors/social development constructs and no definitive explanation as to how, if at all, risk factors/social development constructs were related to offending. There was certainly little evidence provided to support the claim that risk factors are 'causal processes' in the pathways to offending. This final point suggests a criticism of the conclusions from the intervention element of the SSDP; the forming of confident conclusions based on a lack of available empirical evidence to explain (as opposed to impute) how, if at all, the different interventions were related to and/or influenced risk factors/social development constructs and ultimately brought about changes in offending.

The SSDP offered some bold claims as to the positive and independent effects of its interventions on offending pathways (with the potential influence of extraneous factors not even acknowledged), but there were weak links between the breadth of these conclusions, the findings from the research element of the study and the design of the project. Therefore, the supposed validation of the Social Development Model constructs in the SSDP research and intervention elements appears to have rested on the replication of traditional developmental risk and protective factors and the apparent success of the social development interventions, rather than on any validated, definitive understandings of substantive relationships with offending or the actual processes of change precipitated by risk and protective factors/social development constructs.

The Edinburgh Study of Youth Transitions and Crime: towards a synthesised, integrated explanation of risk

The prospective longitudinal Edinburgh Study of Youth Transitions and Crime was co-directed by David J. Smith, Lesley McAra and Susan McVie in the School of Law at the University of Edinburgh. The Edinburgh Study, as it has become known, began in 1998 with funding from the ESRC (1998–2002) and has been subsequently funded by the Scottish Executive (2002–2005) and the Nuffield Foundation (2002–2005). Although Scotland is part of the UK, this Scottish research is included in the international chapter partly because the focus of much of this book is on England and Wales, but for other reasons too. Scotland has a distinctive culture, legal system, criminal justice system and polity which is reflected in the study's design and intention to speak to an international audience. The Edinburgh Study was 'not concerned with early childhood influences, but with transitions and personal transformations during adolescence and adulthood' (Smith and McVie 2003: 169–70) on the basis that earlier RFR had demonstrated the predictive ability of childhood risk factors, but with a worrying number of 'false positives' (children predicted to offend in the future who did not), which highlighted the significance of *adolescent* influences on offending. Thus the authors set out explicitly to build on but go beyond existing research. The research team's desire to broaden the scope and ambition of traditional RFR by addressing previously-neglected foci was reflected in their statement of the key aims of the Edinburgh Study:

Unlike previous studies, it focuses in particular on explaining gender differences, and on the mechanisms leading to serious, long-term, and frequent offending. It aims to assess the influence of contact with the official systems on subsequent criminal careers. Finally it integrates explanations at the level of the individual and local community. (Smith and McVie 2003: 169)

Therefore, the study team sought to extend RFR by formulating an holistic, integrated understanding of risk influence that could be applied to the study of youth offending universally in different contexts for different samples of young people. Accordingly, the Edinburgh Study deliberately adopted a broad and comprehensive methodology. The study team was particularly interested in exploring individual development (i.e. developmental strand of RFR), young people's interactions with formal and informal agencies of control (compatible with the Social Development Model and the life course strand of RFR), how young people negotiated their pathways into and out of offending (cf. the pathways approach) and the interactions between individualised, psychosocial (risk) factors (e.g. personality, family) and socio-structural neighbourhood factors (e.g. social controls in the community, physical environment) such as those typically explored by ecological RFR. By integrating knowledge and perspectives drawn from across the disparate strands of RFR, the Edinburgh Study aimed to better 'understand the causes of youth crime and how offending emerges in the process of development from childhood to adulthood' (Smith and McAra 2004: 14).

The Edinburgh Study methodology

The Edinburgh Study cohort consisted of 4,317 young people aged between 11 ½ and 12 ½ years who entered Edinburgh secondary schools in autumn 1998. In total, 40 of the 49 secondary schools in Edinburgh participated (including all state-funded mainstream schools and most of the independent sector and special educational schools) in the six annual sweeps of data collection from 1998–2003. Data has thus far been collected from multiple sources using multiple methods:

- *Pastoral teacher questionnaire* (1999 only): an abbreviated version of the Goodman's Strengths and Difficulties Questionnaire (Goodman 1997), which measures problem and prosocial behaviour by 4–16 year olds by rating young people on ten statements about their behaviour and emotional state.

- *Parent/carer survey* (2001 only): assessed family structure, relationships, conflict, parental supervision and discipline, parental contact with the school, knowledge of the child's leisure activities and offending behaviour.

- *Official records*: collected from the local Social Work Department (1998–2006), Children's Hearings system (1998–2005), police (2001–2002), schools (1998–2003) and Scottish Criminal Records Office (2006).

- *Neighbourhood information*: police recorded crime data, census data such as migration and high youth population statistics (indicating neighbourhood instability) and rates of unemployment, overcrowding, renting and single-parent households (indicating economic deprivation), and information collected from a community survey of Edinburgh residents carried out in 2001. Overall, the Edinburgh team categorised 91 local neighbourhoods based on six census characteristics producing indicators of levels of social stress and official (police-recorded) offending statistics.

The main data collection instruments have been:

- *Young person questionnaire*: measuring prevalence and frequency of self-reported offending and a set of 'explanatory' factors seen as increasing the 'risk' of offending. These factors were identified following 'extensive consultation with researchers in the UK and those involved in longitudinal studies of crime and young people in the US and New Zealand' (D.J. Smith *et al.* 2001: 10).

- *Young person interview*: individual qualitative interviews following up the questionnaires by measuring a range of more specific issues, including reasons for involvement in, and desistance from, offending.

In the questionnaire, active delinquency (i.e. in the past 12 months) has been measured using an inventory of 18 offences. From sweep three onwards, the general delinquency category was sub-divided into *broad* delinquency (having committed any of the offences on the inventory) and *serious* delinquency (having committed any serious delinquent act – joyriding, carrying a weapon, robbery with force or threats, car breaking, arson).

Explanatory factors in the questionnaire have been measured in terms of:

- *Family* – parental supervision, autonomy/parental trust, conflict with parents, parental discipline, activities with parents;

- *School* – attachment to school, parents' commitment to school, misbehaviour at school and punishment, truancy;

- *Neighbourhood* – cohesion (being friendly with people in the neighbourhood), problems (e.g. vandalism, selling drugs, fighting), policing;

- *Lifestyle* – experience of bullying and victimisation, hanging around the streets, substance use, contact with the police;

- *Peers* – peer pressure, friendship groups and relationships, peer delinquency and substance use;

- *Individual* – self-esteem, alienation, impulsivity, moral reasoning, future aspirations, worries and coping strategies.
(see D.J. Smith *et al.* 2001; Smith and McVie 2003)

Each 'explanatory' element was a composite measure of responses to a set of sub-statements (covering the past 12 months) with which young people had to indicate their strength of agreement on a Likert-scale, with high scores indicating a high level of that (risk) factor. For example, 'parental supervision' was a composite of four items (how often your parents know where you are going, who you are with, what time you will be home and whether you came back on time) scored on a four point scale of 'always', 'usually', 'sometimes' or 'never'. The same scale was used to factorise 'parent/child conflict', which was a composite of responses to the question 'how often do you argue with your parents about' followed by a series of issues ('how tidy your room is', 'what you do when you go out', 'what time you come home', 'who you hang about with', 'your clothes and appearance'). On the other hand, 'police contact' (measured as yes or no), has been a conflation of children's hearings records of police referral for 15 year olds, whether the young person self-reported being charged by the police before age 15 years (yes or no) and number of times in trouble with the police in the last year (from none to 11 and above).

At sweeps one and two (when the young people were aged 12 and 13 years), baseline measures of delinquency and explanatory factors were taken and simple correlations between the two were examined statistically using binary regression (D.J. Smith *et al.* 2001). From sweep three onwards 'the study provided the first real opportunity to carry out more sophisticated analysis of the data, making use of the longitudinal design of the study and testing the effects of explanatory and potentially causal factors on later delinquency' (McVie 2003: 24). Consequently, multivariate analyses have been employed to investigate relationships between factors measured at earlier ages (e.g. during sweeps one and two) and delinquency (general and serious) measured at a later stage and to 'estimate the effect of each of the explanatory variables as a predictor of delinquency, after taking into account the effect of all of the others' (Smith and McAra 2004: 17).

The Edinburgh Study researchers were also interested to explore the potential for system contact to amplify deviance. In the Scottish context,

247

the 'system' comprised contact with the police (stage one of the system), referral by a police Juvenile Liaison Officer to the reporter (stage two) and reporter referral (stage three) to a children's hearing (a welfare-based, needs-orientated decision-making system predicated on early and minimal intervention). At sweep four of the study (with young people aged 14½–15½ years – the peak age of referral to the reporter in the study and nationally across Scotland), binary logistic regression was used to identify the psychosocial characteristics of young people referred to each stage of the system. To control for selection effects and to highlight the characteristics of young people moving through the system, propensity score matching was conducted, whereby individuals in the system were statistically-matched with a comparable (control) group from the original Edinburgh sample who were not in the system (McAra and McVie 2007).

The Edinburgh Study findings and conclusions

In relation to the *family*, poor parental supervision and parent/child conflict at both sweeps one and two was significantly correlated with later delinquency (D.J. Smith *et al.* 2001). Smith and McAra (2004) discovered that parenting style and family functioning (parents tracking and monitoring behaviour, child's willingness to disclose information, parental consistency, parent/child conflict, excessive punishment) measured at age 13 years (sweep two) predicted delinquency at age 15 years (sweep four), which 'demonstrates that parenting had a genuine causal influence on the later behaviour of teenagers' (Smith and McAra 2004: 3).

In terms of *school*: attitudes to school, relationships with teachers and school-based misbehaviour were all closely correlated with delinquency in the first two sweeps of the study (D.J. Smith *et al.* 2001). Attachment to school (particularly attachment to teachers and the belief that school success will bring later rewards) measured at age 13 years was predictive of delinquency at age 15 years, as was parental commitment to school, which suggested that 'there is a role for schools in preventing the development of delinquent behaviour' (D.J. Smith 2006: 4).

There were significant correlations between different indicators of deprivation in the *neighbourhood* and delinquency in sweeps one and two (D.J. Smith *et al.* 2001). This finding was reinforced at sweep five (when young people aged 16 years), which used ordinal regression to identify correlations between concurrent measures of delinquency and measures of neighbourhood deprivation (high unemployment, dense local authority housing, dissatisfaction with the neighbourhood, living in a disorderly neighbourhood), as opposed to measures of individual deprivation (e.g. separation from parents, unemployment (D.J. Smith 2006). In contrast, young people who reported delinquency at age 12 years were more likely to have desisted by the age of 17 years if they lived in a socially advantaged neighbourhood and reported bonding with parents and teachers and parental involvement in school in the intervening period (D.J. Smith 2006).

The main *peer-* and *lifestyle*-related factor highlighted was gang membership, which predicted delinquency at age 17 years when measured at age 12 years (Bradshaw and Smith 2005). Contact with the police and local criminal justice agencies was also significantly-correlated with continued delinquency (D.J. Smith 2006; McAra and McVie 2007).

At the *individual* level, impulsivity (measured at age 16 years) was more strongly-correlated with delinquency measured at the same age than was neighbourhood deprivation (D.J. Smith 2006).

At sweep four, a detailed analysis of gender-specific explanatory factors (using ordinal regression to measure the explanatory variables and delinquency concurrently) concluded that 'the pattern of findings were similar for boys and girls, suggesting that for the most part the same model of explanation for delinquency is likely to apply to both' (Smith and McAra 2004: 16).

The system contact/deviancy amplification element of the study initially identified ten variables (experienced in the past year) that statistically predicted selection at each stage of the system, namely: gender (male), non-two parent family, free school meal entitlement (a measure of poverty), drug use, hanging out most days, truancy, neighbourhood deprivation, early police contact, number of times in trouble with police and volume of serious offending (McAra and McVie 2007: 331), which suggests that system contact and progression through the system was the product of particular decision-making processes. The most notable finding was that although the self-reported serious offending of both groups (those in the system and matched controls) decreased between sweeps four and five, young people exposed to children's hearings at sweep four were significantly more likely to report serious offending one year later. This suggested to the authors that 'repeated and more intensive forms of contact with agencies of youth justice may be damaging to young people in the long-term' (McAra and McVie 2007:333) due to, *inter alia*, labelling, creating a master status of offender, exacerbating socio-structural factors already outside of the young person's control (e.g. family structure, social deprivation, gender) and targeting intervention on the family and education rather than on the individual and the offence (McAra and McVie 2007).

The Edinburgh Study as RFR

The Edinburgh Study has most assuredly *not* been atheoretical, as other RFR studies have claimed to be (cf. Glueck and Glueck 1950; Farrington 1988). It has been an ambitious project that has explicitly aimed to incorporate and evaluate several different strands of RFR in one comprehensive study. The authors have set out to develop more comprehensive 'explanatory models' of how risk factors operate (e.g. with reference to a broader set of micro-and macro-level influences) than have been explored in more restricted forms of RFR. For example, the integrated Edinburgh approach has moved beyond typical ecological considerations of neighbourhood 'collective efficacy' (Sampson *et al.* 1997), community functioning and neighbourhood socio-economic status (Wikström and Loeber 1998) to explore broader and much-neglected socio-structural factors (e.g. gender, family structure, social deprivation) and deleterious impact of contact with criminal justice agencies, using official data sources, self-reports and innovative statistical techniques such as propensity score matching.

A key conclusion from the Edinburgh Study has been that the 'explanatory variables' for broad and serious offending form 'explanatory models' which can be used to guide policy and practice with young people. However, what are these explanatory models and, if they exist, what are they actually explaining? The Edinburgh Study has addressed the temporal ordering of risk and delinquency through regression analyses of risk measured at time (sweep) A and delinquency measured at time (sweep) B and supplemented this procedure with multivariate analysis of the individual influence of each factor when controlling for the effects of all others. However, like other longitudinal RFR studies, the Edinburgh Study has not measured the onset of risk in relation to the onset of delinquency, so conclusions of temporal precedence and explanatory power have been restricted to imputations based on the temporal ordering of *measurements* of risk and delinquency rather than any necessary *actual* real world relationship. Therefore, the researchers have been unable to demonstrate or model any definitive real-world (non-statistical) relationship between the two, unable to demonstrate the direction, intensity and duration of any relationships and unable to offer detailed, evidenced, qualitative explanations of the processes by which factors may impact on delinquency or vice versa.

Indeed, this explanatory problem is common to much RFR. For the most part the Edinburgh Study researchers are sensitive to this issue. For example, they have employed ordinal regression techniques to produce explanatory 'models' which they have acknowledged to be 'contemporaneous models (the explanatory and the outcome variables described the same time period) not longitudinal models showing the effects . . . on later delinquency' (Smith and McAra 2004: 17). However, again in common with much RFR, the slip to claims of causality is never far away (cf. Smith and McAra 2004: 3). The problem of demonstrating causality between risks and outcomes (and the associated imputed strength of relationship between variables) is endemic to artefactual RFR. On the other hand, demonstrating statistically predictive relationships between factors and outcomes is a realistic product of RFR, but it must be recognised that the strength of these relationships is far from certain. The strength, even of predictive relationships and the degree of confidence we can place in them is dependent on a range of additional matters. Quality of measurement, specificity of factorisation, clear temporal precedence and the appropriate use of statistical tests are all issues shown to have an impact on the veracity of findings and conclusions from RFR. So too, theoretical influence, researcher bias and the age-related collection of data, plus the types of data collected (psychosocial, structural etc) all have an impact on the confidence that should be placed in the findings from the Edinburgh Study.

The Edinburgh Study was explicitly designed and developed to address the known weaknesses of much previous RFR, but as yet, success has been limited. The focus on socio-structural influences and the influence of system contact has been a welcome challenge to the reductionist psychosocial bias of much artefact RFR. However, the Edinburgh Study has retained a predominantly psychosocial, factorised and cross-sectional view of risk in line with the limitations of much previous developmental and artefactual research.

A vast amount of data has been collected within the Edinburgh Study and it should be recognised that to date the analysis of this data remains in its early stages. Befitting their comprehensive strategy and the critical, reflexive approach the authors say they are taking, they have eschewed a simple developmental hypothesis in analysing the data and have stated a desire to test different theoretical models and hypotheses using increasingly complex statistical modelling techniques, even employing a designated statistician for this purpose. However, this remains a nascent process and results to date remain limited.

The explanatory models in the Edinburgh Study have been extricated from a patchwork of theories and methodologies from across the gamut of RFR; research that has been characterised by a theoretical, methodological, analytical and interpretive diversity. Therefore, it is debatable as to whether these various strands are able to hang together in a coherent and consistent integrated model, particularly one intent on factorising complex risk measures and fitting diverse theoretical explanations into a developmental paradigm for analysing and interpreting the 'predictive' and 'explanatory' power of these 'risk factors'. Consequently, it is difficult to evaluate whether the Edinburgh Study represents an evolution of RFR through a coordinated and internally valid approach or whether it is merely a collection of loosely-connected theories and approaches within a study, each examining different aspects of risk within a methodology that remains devoutly developmental in orientation (although having its origins in adolescence rather than childhood) and interpreting findings through the post-hoc application of 'relevant' theories or whether the study has set out to 'test' the validity and veracity of different models, but has not done so as yet. The diverse, disparate theoretical foci have, to an extent, robbed the research of a clear and coherent theoretical identity and have had their central tenets over-simplified by a reductionist approach to measurement and analysis, which has limited the definitiveness with which conclusions can be supported.

The universal risk factor: hunted down or created?

RFR has certainly become a global enterprise (see France and Homel 2008); at least if 'global' is taken to mean spanning the industrialised 'Western' World. From its origins in the US in the work of the Gluecks, through to the hugely influential Cambridge Study of West and Farrington in the UK and beyond, RFR has spread to many, if not most, Western countries. RFR studies across the globe have made use of longitudinal and cross-sectional research designs, typically consisting of survey methods (questionnaires and interviews) followed by the factorisation and statistical analysis of psychosocial background factors and factors in current life as a way of understanding and explaining youth offending. Perhaps quite naturally, even inevitably, as this disparate body of international research findings has emerged, researchers have looked at the overall body of knowledge and drawn out commonalities in their findings. However, has the widespread global replication and apparent commonality of risk factors in (largely developmental) RFR ignored or disregarded the vast 'contextual and cultural variations' between (and within) different countries (Hargreaves 2007: 5), not to mention individual differences in relation to age, gender, ethnicity, locality and type of offence?

The global enterprise of RFR that has replicated largely the same body of psychosocial risk factors across time, place and sample and fostered claims to generalisable, universalised risk factors has not been an entirely homogenous, coordinated international research effort, but rather a series of heterogeneous studies informed by divergent theoretical underpinnings and a range of aims and objectives. However, substantive homogeneity has been evident in the narrow range of psychosocial risk factors measured, the pervasive (often crude) factorisation of risk and the use of statistical analyses to impute temporal precedence – the majority of which have encouraged developmentalist conclusions regarding the predictive validity of risk factors and their existence as potential globally-applicable 'universal truths' (D. Smith 2006). The consistent replication of developmental understandings of psychosocial measures of risk across location, context, developmental stage, sample and time has fuelled claims of the existence of universal 'risk factors', which are typically understood as present in childhood and exerting a deterministic, predictive and comparable impact on offending in adolescence for all young people. Subsequent 'successful' risk-focused intervention programs (e.g. MLES, SSDP) have reinforced and valorised developmental understandings of how risk factors influence offending universally – sometimes against the evidence.

However, in reaching these conclusions, the international RFR movement has uncritically assumed that replicability across countries implies *comparability*, in the face of differences between- and within-studies in terms of, *inter alia*:

- sample composition and age range;

- socio-political context (which impacts on diverse definitions of offending, delinquency and antisocial behaviour in different countries);

- constructions of risk and protection by young people;

- constructions of risk and protection by researchers choosing the factorisation processes and standardised instruments with which to measure and interpret risk;

- the precise timing of data collection episodes and analyses;

- the theoretical bases that have informed the study;

Subsequent conclusions regarding the efficacy of risk-focused interventions have simply compounded the extant limitations and weaknesses of RFR by imputing explanations for successful outcomes, equivalent to how much RFR has imputed the nature of the relationship between risk factors and offending.

Farrington (2002) has maintained that if cross-national differences are evident in RFR then criminologists need to identify the 'active ingredients' that explain them (e.g. social, cultural, legal, or criminal justice processes in different countries). However, researchers simply have not looked for these ingredients and have preferred to impute any causal/explanatory linear influence of risk and risk-focused interventions using superficial statistical manipulations and the uncritical acceptance of temporal ordering as a basis for the developmental influence of risk on current behaviour and developmental pathways. There has been little consideration that factors may actually *post-date* and *be caused by* offending/delinquency/antisocial behaviour, occur concurrently to these behaviours (either maintaining a relationship with them or not at that time) or *pre-date* the target behaviours but have no influence on them at the time of their measurement (e.g. the factor causes offending during exposure at a later point, possibly when exposure is more intense and/or over a longer duration).

A global RFR movement has attempted to identify risk factors as universal in influence and replicable across the globe. However, standardised cross-sectional RFR and longitudinal replications of generalised, developmental and artefactual understandings of risk have eschewed analysis of the validity of risk factors in young people's lives and has arguably washed away the cultural, political, social, national and local differences that impact on:

- different constructions and understandings of 'childhood', 'youth', 'gender', 'ethnicity' and 'offending';

- the definitions and interpretations of risk that influence how they are responded to by young people, families, communities and countries;

- the ability of different groups of young people to resist, negotiate and influence risk at different stages in their lives.

Studies have, therefore, largely ignored 'the historical and social context and ... the importance of diversity and local knowledge rather than only searching for universal relationships' (Pearce 1996: 682). International RFR has demonstrated a similar insensitivity to between- and within-individual differences in the risk–offending relationship relating to, *inter alia*, age, gender, ethnicity, type/seriousness/duration/frequency of offending and the intensity, duration and frequency of exposure to risk and protection. Therefore the 'universalism' of understandings of risk has been artificially restricted by the psychosocial bias, reductionism and determinism inherent to the hegemonic developmental strand of RFR. Much international RFR has been oversimplified by its 'developmentocentric' and positivistic nature, which has understood risk and protection through crude factorisation, aggregation and imputation. Across the Western world, a dominant form of largely developmental RFR has privileged the investigation of childhood factors and their predictive influence on offending in adolescence over the influence of these or other factors in current life.

International RFR has characterised the risk-factor–offending relationship as predetermined at an early age, implying that children are crash test dummies inextricably bound for deleterious outcomes in the absence of risk-focused intervention at earlier and earlier ages. Neither the methodological validity of these deterministic conclusions, nor the validity of measuring the salience of childhood risk factors in the lives of older children and young people, has been adequately questioned or evaluated by developmentalists. A developmental determinism has attained clear hegemony in the field, reflected in and perpetuated by the predominance of developmental studies within major reviews of international RFR. However, the chosen studies, the selected definitions of 'risk' factors and the preferred interpretations of the relationship between these factors and offending included in these reviews have been dictated by two of the most prominent developmental risk factor researchers since the inception of the paradigm (David Farrington and Michael Rutter). This inherent bias has been overlooked and the reviews have become established as ostensibly independent and comprehensive depictions of the state of RFR knowledge.

The global 'movement' of RFR has been typified by a mismatched power struggle between high profile developmental research and a small, almost invisible body of qualitative, ethnographic studies, predominantly in England and Wales (e.g. the pathways studies discussed in Chapters 2 and 3). Developmental devotees committed to the (often government supported) investigation of globally applicable, universal risk factors in the form of clinical (e.g. 'objectively' measured, amenable to treatment), psychosocial *variables* have established proprietary rights over RFR. The mid-1950s hegemony of sociological, explanatory theories of the risk–offending relationship appears a distant memory. There is a clear theoretical and methodological hegemony of artefact-based models of risk 'factors' over qualitative understandings of risk *processes* of influence in a more complex relationship between young people and offending. The ongoing international agenda and dominant paradigm for RFR has been misguided – reflective of an aggressive attempt by psycho-developmentalists to dominate aetiological explanations of youth offending. However, the resultant 'explanations' have imputed and extrapolated more than they can explain through the over-simplified factorisation and aggregation of risk (largely confined to psychosocial domains), the over-generalised and unrepresentative analysis of statistical differences between-groups rather than within-individuals, the imputation that risk factors have temporal precedence over the onset of offending and the consequent imputation that these factors exert a causal or predictive influence on offending. The self-perpetuating developmentalism and artefactualism of much international RFR undermines any claims that explanations of risk, risk factors and risk-focused interventions are universally-applicable. More importantly, the biases and limitations of international RFR question the validity of the label of 'risk factor' on two levels:

- whether risk and its relationship with offending can or should be explored and understood quantitatively in terms of 'factors'?

- whether the factors identified in RFR actually indicate 'risk' of offending in any explanatory or predictive sense beyond the statistical?

If the answer to either question is no, then the feasibility, validity and appropriateness of the very notion of 'risk factor research' is open to question. Crucially, neither of these questions can be answered adequately with reference to the existing international body of RFR. The reason for this answer is, however, largely because the methodological and analytical quality of this research is so inconsistent and weak that it is impossible to make a reasoned judgement. Consequently, whilst the intention (at the outset of this chapter) was to investigate international RFR and to explore/evaluate the notion of the universal risk factor, what was discovered was a range of studies so flawed that, in fact, they preclude definitive conclusions because the research itself has not produced findings or conclusions robust enough to base conclusions on.

Chapter 6

Risk assessment in the Youth Justice System: application without understanding?

The application within youth justice policy and practice of understandings of risk and protection generated from RFR has grown exponentially in recent years, to the point that the assessment and targeting of risk (factors) now underpins all work with young people in the Youth Justice System of England and Wales. All young people who come to the attention of the Youth Justice System (YJS) are assessed in terms of their risk level: the risk that they present of offending and of reoffending if they are already offenders. However, upon closer examination, it becomes clear that the risk assessment processes promoted by the Youth Justice Board and particularly the risk assessment instruments that underpin these processes, have been founded on the mis-appliance of research findings and have exacerbated the methodological over-simplification, indefinity and imputation that undermine RFR. Indeed, the entire approach is based on research that has failed to provide solid evidence about risk and its relationship to offending or evidence of the validity of targeting risk in preventing or reducing offending.

In this chapter, the utility of risk assessment in the YJS will be evaluated in the light of the RFR methodologies, analyses and conclusions that have underpinned it. Following discussion of the development of New Labour's emphasis on risk and actuarial risk assessment, there will be a critical review of the risk assessment instruments (*Asset* and *Onset*) that have emerged from this political focus. Particular critique will be offered regarding risk assessment's ambiguity of purpose, use of crude factorisation, inappropriate application of developmental risk factors, imputation of the temporal precedence of risk over offending, the general lack of knowledge as to what precisely constitutes risk, enduring uncertainty about the relationships between so-called risk factors and offending behaviour and unfounded definitive confidence in the ability of risk-focused interventions to address risk. The chapter concludes by exploring these methodological weaknesses in the context of the *Scaled Approach* to youth justice and risk-focused preventative intervention. Throughout the chapter, the over-riding critical theme will be the nature and extent to which the existing methodological and analytical weaknesses of RFR have been exacerbated through misappropriation and misapplication within risk assessment, thus raising questions over the theoretical and methodological validity of youth justice practice in England and Wales.

The risky shift: New Labour and the politics of risk

In 1992, the then Shadow Home Secretary Tony Blair set about wresting the 'party of law and order' mantle away from the Conservative Party by confidently proclaiming that his Labour Party would be 'tough on crime and tough on the causes of crime'. When they came to power in 1997, the Labour government's policy documents and 'get tough' rhetoric employed the language of risk to emphasise the apparent danger and threat posed by young people to others and the urgent need for the state to intervene in the lives of problematic young people in order to protect the public. In the words of one commentator, 'New Labour would be tough on risk and tough on the causes of risk' (Porteous 2007: 260).

The emerging *risk factor prevention paradigm* (see Hawkins and Catalano 1992) was ideally suited to meet New Labour's risk-focused aims. This model was originally imported from the fields of medicine and public health where it had been used to identify 'risk factors' for physical illnesses (e.g. high cholesterol diet and lack of exercise as risk factors for heart disease) and 'protective factors' that mediated against these illnesses (e.g. healthy, low-cholesterol diet and regular exercise to protect against the onset or exacerbation of heart disease). These identified risk and protective factors were then employed to inform preventative interventions (e.g. health promotion) targeting 'high risk' or 'at risk' groups; those scoring high in risk factors and low in protective factors. The epidemiological nature of this model and its purported ability to identify and reduce risk in a clinical, evidence-based manner, offered a common sense, practical and readily understandable approach that proved almost irresistible to some politicians, policy makers, practitioners and researchers working in the youth offending field. The transfer of the risk factor prevention paradigm (RFPP) to youth offending seemed straightforward. The logic of this dynamic in relation to youth offending has been very clearly articulated by Farrington:

> The basic idea ... is very simple: Identify the key risk factors for offending and implement prevention methods designed to counteract

them. There is often a related attempt to identify key protective factors against offending and to implement prevention methods designed to enhance them. (Farrington 2007: 606)

The RFPP has had particular appeal to youth justice policy makers and practitioners working in a risk-averse political climate of increasing managerialism, audit-focus, accountability, transparency, defensible practice and cost-effectiveness. It has provided a paradigm to enable the collection of actuarial, quantitative and empirical 'evidence' from RFR to drive policy and practice that is both evidence-based and defensible (Stephenson *et al.* 2007; Bateman and Pitts 2005). To reiterate Farrington's assertion:

A key advantage of the risk factor prevention paradigm is that it links explanation and prevention, fundamental and applied research, and scholars and practitioners. Importantly, the paradigm is easy to understand and to communicate, and it is readily accepted by policy makers, practitioners, and the general public. Both risk factors and interventions are based on empirical research rather than theories. The paradigm avoids difficult theoretical questions about which risk factors have causal effects. (Farrington 2000: 7)

New Labour – New Danger: the arrival of risk policy

One of the last substantive acts of the Conservative government in the 1990s was to commission a review of the youth justice system by the Audit Commission, an independent public body responsible for ensuring that government money is spent efficiently, effectively and economically. The review, entitled *Misspent Youth*, castigated the YJS for being inefficient, ineffective, uneconomical and comprised of agencies that worked very poorly together (Audit Commission 1996). *Misspent Youth* and its follow-up reports, *Misspent Youth: The Challenge for Youth Justice* (Audit Commission 1998) and *Youth Justice 2004* (Audit Commission 2004), strongly recommended, *inter alia*, that a new joined-up YJS should prioritise the prevention of youth offending through a focus on risk and early intervention.

The contested and political nature of *Misspent Youth* has been evidenced by comments from critics such as Pitts (2005), who described the review as a partnership between Audit Commission experts in socio-economic policy and 'psychologically-oriented criminologists' in the UK and US. Although the authors of *Misspent Youth*, Judy Renshaw and Mark Perfect (the latter of whom went on to be appointed by the then Home Secretary Jack Straw as Chief Executive of the Youth Justice Board for England and Wales), consulted fairly widely with academics and others (including the

National Association for Youth Justice). However, their work clearly benefited from a strong political steer (including from the Labour party which was 'preparing for government) and it drew heavily on 'psychologically-oriented criminologists'. New Labour needed *Misspent Youth* to herald a new era of youth justice policy and practice. Risk, with a ready made paradigm and body of evidence just waiting in the wings, provided the ideal vehicle.

Traditionally, youth justice debates, policy and practice (in the UK and around the world) have vacillated between approaches that are predominantly *welfare* or *justice* oriented. For New Labour, at the end of the 1990s, seeking a new 'third way', neither approach was a feasible option. Welfare was not an option in the third way politics of the Blairite government because universal provision, high levels of state support and notions of collective responsibility were anathema to the politics and economics of New Labour and to emerging models of governance (Haines 1999). Similarly, justice could not provide the way forward, if, for no other reason than, New Labour needed to break with the justice-based policies of the 1980s and 1990s as a crucial part of its arguments for the need for a new approach to youth justice. In practice, *Misspent Youth* provided this break – it ignored the achievements and successes of 1980s and 1990s juvenile justice (on which, see Haines and Drakeford 1998) and re-cast the era as one of 'doing nothing' about juvenile crime. In contrast, the new political imperative was to 'do something' about youth offending – but what and how?

Beyond the political imperative of 'doing something' about juvenile crime and the subsequent emergence of the mantra 'intervention, intervention, intervention', the key question/problem became: if neither welfare nor justice provided a rationale on which youth justice policy could be built, what did? For both the authors of *Misspent Youth* and the then Home Secretary Jack Straw, steered by his special advisor, Norman Warner (subsequently made the first Chair of the Youth Justice Board), *risk* became the answer and the subsequent driver of youth justice policy and practice in England and Wales.

The concept of risk offered huge potentialities. Focusing on risk obviated concerns with both welfare and justice. The concept of risk provided a qualitatively different third way and targeting risk provided a genuinely distinct objective from providing welfare or delivering justice for young people. Moreover, focusing on risk not only provided a ready justification for intervention (targeting those risks), but it opened up a whole new panoply of preventative interventions and policy options (the logic of intervening earlier and earlier to ameliorate risk). Thus, not only had a way of 'doing something' about youth offending been found, there was a ready made body of RFR ideally suited to animating this new evidence-based and common-sense strategy. More so, the political imperatives and RFR were ideally matched – not least to the extent that RFR provided the science to support political policies based on responsibilisation, individualisation and intervention – it was an idea whose time had come.

Many of the recommendations and policy proposals of *Misspent Youth* were consolidated and became law as part of the *Crime and Disorder Act 1998*, a broad restructuring and reformation of the Criminal Justice System in England and Wales. The primary aim of the YJS became the prevention of youth offending. To this end, the Crime and Disorder Act placed a statutory responsibility on local authority areas to form multi-agency Crime and Disorder Reduction Partnerships (known as Community Safety Partnerships in Wales) between the statutory agencies (local authority, probation, police, health) and voluntary organisations, to conduct local audits of crime and disorder and to formulate localised crime reduction strategies. A key regulatory component of these crime reduction strategies was 'intervention which tackles the risk factors associated with offending – personal, family, social, educational, health' (Home Office, Crime and Disorder Act 1998: Section 37). These interventions were to be focused on psychosocial risk factors because 'the implicit aetiology underpinning the Crime and Disorder Act [was] . . . derived from "developmental" theories of criminality' (Brown 2005: 100), themselves, of course, imbued with individual pathology and the avoidance of state responsibility. In particular, the developmentalism espoused within the Cambridge Study has been a guiding light for youth justice policy, as acknowledged by Farrington's claim that:

> the Cambridge Study has influenced the thinking of the British government about crime policy . . . From 1997 onwards, the new Labour government became more enthusiastic about risk-focused prevention. (Farrington 2003: 171–2)

The prioritisation within the Crime and Disorder Act 1998 of the prevention of offending and reoffending through targeting psychosocial risk factors indicated the government's over-riding faith in and commitment to the preventative utility of RFR as a means of tackling youth offending (see also Gray 2005). RFR and its logical corollary, the RFPP, have thus become jewels in the governmental crown – a practical, accountable, scientific and evidence-based methodology for tackling what are perceived to be serious social problems – youth offending and its new 'associate', youth antisocial behaviour.

Ensuring that developmental, psychosocial risk factors were addressed was to be the responsibility of the newly-formed, multi-agency YOTs in each local authority area. The practice of these YOTs would be overseen and co-ordinated by a new government quango, the Youth Justice Board for England and Wales. The role of the Youth Justice Board (YJB) was to collect data from YOTs, monitor their operation, disseminate 'effective' methods of responding to youth crime and to fund crime prevention initiatives (Home Office 1998: Section 41). Although originally quite modest, the YJB fairly rapidly extended its role to one of increasingly prescribing the nature and content of youth justice policy and, particularly, management and practice. This prescription has penetrated deeper and deeper into youth justice policy and practice and has been almost exclusively dedicated to establishing risk at the centre of the YJS.

Actuarial risk assessment and criminal justice managerialism

According to Porteous (2007), Westernised criminal justice systems had begun to place more emphasis on systemic rationality and managerialism in the late twentieth century, especially the actuarialist 'new technologies to identify and classify risk' (Feeley and Simon 1992: 454–5). Nowhere has this actuarialist turn been more evident than in the way that risk assessment has been rolled out across the YJS in England and Wales to the point that it increasingly underpins all responses to youth offending and so-called youth misbehaviour. The Labour Party has committed to an actuarial approach (the prediction of future offending behaviour from current assessments of levels of risk) to inform risk-based responses. Actuarialism has been promoted by new technologies (e.g. modern risk assessment/prediction instruments, advanced statistical tests) that have enabled new approaches to the management and control of young people by categorising them into subgroups with shared characteristics and similar quantified levels of 'risk'. This is *actuarial justice* – the statistical identification of high and low risk groups for the purposes of planning interventions and allocating criminal sanctions (see Feeley and Simon 1994). Proponents of risk assessment have argued that the techniques of actuarial justice have rendered decision-making more accurate and consistent by grounding decisions in a rigorously empirical framework based on data from a potentially wide range of information sources (see, for example, Grove and Meehl 1996) and have engendered a shift away from clinical or subjective judgements based on ideology or professional expertise (which is implicitly seen as either poorly applied or flawed). Taken positively, actuarial justice could be seen as a constructive way of standardising and raising the level of effectiveness of the YJS and youth justice practice. Seen critically, actuarial justice has been one element of a broader criminal justice managerialism intent of exerting increasing levels of centralised control over the YJS, YOTs and youth justice practitioners and, ultimately, the political management/manipulation of youth as a social problem (see, for example, R. Smith 2006).

A series of legislative acts in England and Wales, culminating in the Crime and Disorder Act 1998, have brought the findings of RFR and their application through the RFPP to prominence in work with young people who have either offended or who are considered to be 'at risk' of offending. The end of the 1990s witnessed the most radical set of youth justice reforms for 20 years (Haines and Drakeford 1998; Goldson 2000). The old 'juvenile justice' of the 1980s and 1990s was rapidly and comprehensively discredited and abandoned and a new system was put in place. This modernised 'new youth justice' (Goldson 2000) was managerialist, corporatist and prevention-focused, it offered not only a 'third way' risk-based alternative to the traditional youth justice concerns of welfare and justice but also new approaches to the management of youth justice. This new approach has been progressive and persistent. Whilst government and ministers have consistently and persistently pursued youth as targets of propaganda, rhetoric and psephological manipulation, the responsibility for driving through the new youth justice has been mainly discharged by the YJB – a responsibility it has embraced over its ten year life-span, with increasing alacrity and enthusiasm. It is here that modern managerialism and actuarial risk-based approaches become inextricably intertwined. The embodiment and driver of this fusion of managerialism and actuarialism has been the *Asset* risk assessment tool.

Asset: a common approach to risk and needs assessment

All children and young people entering the youth justice system should benefit from a structured needs assessment. The assessment process is designed to identify the risk factors associated with offending behaviour and to inform effective intervention programmes. The Youth Justice Board has developed the *Asset* common assessment profile for this purpose. (YJB 2004: 27)

In one of the YJB's first undertakings following the Crime and Disorder Act 1998, the Probation Studies Unit at the Oxford University Centre for Criminology was commissioned to develop *Asset*, a 'structured needs assessment' tool for use with all young people aged 10–17 years who enter the YJS (Baker 2005). What was required was:

a common approach to the process of assessment [that] can assist practitioners in planning their work, gathering appropriate and relevant information and analysing that information ... [as] the basis for arriving at judgements and making decisions which are clearly rooted in assessment outcomes and transparent to young people, their parents/carers and professional alike. (YJB 2003: 5)

Asset (the name of the tool, not an acronym) was seen as 'necessary for ensuring consistency of assessment practice in the emerging multi-disciplinary Youth Offending Teams' (Baker 2005: 107). The purpose of *Asset* was to assess the level of risk measured in different (mainly psychosocial) developmental domains of the young person's life in order to inform service development and intervention planning, thus reflecting 'not only concerns with more effective management of risk in terms of further offences, but also the impact of uncertainty and more challenging transitions in young people's lives' (Stephenson *et al.* 2007: 4). *Asset* was formulated to offer a practical, standardised and evidence-based method of targeting intervention based on measured risk of reoffending, the young person's perceived 'vulnerability' and their risk of serious harm to themselves and others (Baker 2005). *Asset* was thus concerned with both the management of risk and the targeting of risks.

The development of *Asset* was informed by earlier work by the Probation Studies Unit at Oxford University in designing and constructing the Assessment Case Management and Evaluation system for adult offenders (see Roberts *et al.* 1996). In order to build on this earlier research and to populate an assessment tool appropriate for use with young people, the Probation Studies Unit conducted 'a thorough review of the research literature relating to risk and protective factors for young people who offend and extensive consultation with practitioners, managers and specialists from a range of relevant services' (Baker 2005: 107). However, in actuality, this 'thorough review' privileged developmental models of risk, particularly the work of Farrington, Thornberry and Sampson and Laub that subsequently underpinned the APIS approach (see YJB 2003).

In April 2000, *Asset* was introduced as a structured risk and needs assessment tool for use with all young offenders (aged 10–17 years) along with explanatory notes to guide practitioners in completing the instrument (YJB 2000). Both National Standards for Youth Justice Services (YJB 2004) and risk assessment guidance to practitioners (YJB 2003) require the completion of a full *Asset* by YOT practitioners at the initial stage of contact with a young person and at assessment prior to sentencing for all young people subject to a community sentence or custody.

Asset takes the form of a questionnaire completed by YOT practitioners during and following interview with a young person. Practitioners are required to ask young people a series of questions relating to their current or recent exposure to so-called 'dynamic risk factors' in 12 psychosocial domains:

1. *Living arrangements* (e.g. living with known offenders, disorganised/chaotic arrangements, unsuitable living conditions).

2. *Family and personal relationships* (e.g. family/carers involved in criminal activity, substance abuse, adults failing to show care/interest, inconsistent supervision, experience of abuse, witnessing violence, bereavement).

3. *Education, training and employment* (e.g. regular truancy, underachievement, literacy difficulties, victim of bullying, poor relationship with teachers, lack of attachment, negative parental attitudes to school, lack of qualifications and skills, negative attitudes to training and employment).

4. *Neighbourhood* (e.g. signs of drug dealing and usage, racial tensions).

5. *Lifestyle* (e.g. associating with delinquent peers, lack of non-criminal friends, unconstructive use of leisure time, risky behaviour.

6. *Substance use* (e.g. detrimental effect on daily functioning, puts young person at risk, seen as essential to life).

7. *Physical health* (e.g. physical immaturity, delayed development).

8. *Emotional and mental health* (e.g. concerns about the future, mental illness, emotional or psychological difficulties, self-harm, suicide attempt).

9. *Perception of self and others* (e.g. difficulties with self-identity, low self-esteem, mistrust of others, lack of empathy for others, discriminatory attitudes).

10. *Thinking and behaviour* (e.g. impulsivity, need for excitement, inability to resist peer pressure, aggression, lack of understanding of consequences).

11. *Attitudes to offending* (e.g. reluctance to accept responsibility for behaviour, lack of understanding of impact on victims or own family, lack of remorse, belief that certain offences are acceptable).

12. *Motivation to change* (e.g. understanding of problematic behaviour, desire to deal with problems, understanding of the consequences of future offending, desire to stop offending).

In order to supplement what is known as the 'core profile' of *Asset*, four additional sections are completed relating to:

- *Positive factors* (e.g. positive attitudes, coping strategies, family support, neighbourhood facilities and services).

- *Indicators of vulnerability* (e.g. vulnerability to physical or emotional harm from others, from themselves or from life events/circumstances).

- *Indicators of serious harm to others* (e.g. evidence of actual harmful behaviour, current intentions and preparations to harm, specified potential victims).

- *What do you think* – where the young person is asked/invited to report their thoughts and feelings regarding issues 'about your life' (e.g.

family, school, work, friendship, substance use, health and emotion) and 'about your offending' (e.g. attitudes to offending, reasons for offending, views about desistance).

(see YJB 2007)

When practitioners have completed (yes/no) responses to each of the questions in a particular section, they are required to complete an evidence box in which they provide narrative evidence of the domain-specific risks and problems recorded. This narrative serves as the evidential basis for subsequent decisions and judgements (e.g. ratings of risk, recommendations for sentencing in pre-sentence reports to the court). Practitioners must then make a quantitative judgement on a five-point scale about the extent to which they feel the risk factors in each specific domain as a whole are associated with 'the likelihood of further offending': 0=no association, 1=slight or limited indirect association, 2=moderate direct or indirect association, 3=quite strong association, normally direct, 4=very strong, clear and direct association. When making these judgements, practitioners are instructed to consider several issues regarding the current and predicted relationship between offending and risk factors in that domain:

- Was the issue linked to past offending?

- Is there a direct or indirect link with offending?

- Is the link to offending consistent or occasional?

- Is the effect on offending likely to be immediate or over a longer period?

- Will the issue lead to offending on its own or only when other conditions exist?

(YJB 2000: 8)

The ratings for each psychosocial domain are totalled to give the young person an aggregate risk score out of 48 (12 domains, each with a maximum risk score of four). This aggregate score determines whether the young person is assessed as being a low, medium or high risk of being reconvicted in the 12 months following the assessment. National Standards for youth justice practice also dictate that *Asset* evidence of risk is reviewed by the practitioner to inform a risk management plan within which the level of proposed intervention should be related to the extent and nature of the risk measured (see YJB 2004). Accordingly, the young person's risk profile is to be re-visited every 12 weeks or otherwise adjusted if there are other significant events, new information or new offences that come to light that could affect the scoring and supervision plan that arises from it.

Asset and RFR: Reductionism and prescription

The content of the *Asset* risk assessment tool was based primarily on the findings from developmental RFR and was intended to provide youth justice practitioners with a practical, standardised and evidence-based approach to working with young people who offend. However, a reductionist and simplistic reading, interpretation and application of RFR 'evidence' has over-simplified the concept of risk and misapplied RFR findings and conclusions in an invalid and poorly-understood manner. In particular, an over-simplification of risk has been demonstrated by crude factorisation processes, developmental determinism and psychosocial bias within youth justice practice. Therefore, the introduction and widespread use of *Asset* as the cornerstone of youth justice practice both exacerbates and replicates the methodological weaknesses inherent within the flawed body of original RFR on which the tool is based.

Developmental determinism and psychosocial bias

What the evaluators of *Asset* have not explored is how practitioner prescriptions and interpretations of risk have been predicated on subjective, under-informed judgements which have been prescribed and limited by the YJB's preferred reading of RFR. The 'theoretical knowledge' of risk that practitioners have been required to apply to their assessment and planning of interventions has been the result of a narrow developmental reading of the RFR literature that has been prescribed by the YJB in an uncritical, totalitarian and under-informed fashion (as is discussed in the APIS section of this chapter). Even updated guidance recommendations to attend to the contextual influence of risk factors (YJB 2008) have privileged context-specific understanding of psychosocial risk factors rather than considering the potentially-independent influence of socio-structural contexts (e.g. low social class, ethnicity) on offending. Of course, *Asset* is meant as a guide to support practitioner expertise, but it has promoted a narrow, quantified, factorised and reductionist conception of risk factors and their relationship to offending. The body of risk factors made available for assessment in *Asset* have privileged psychosocial, childhood-related developmental understandings of the risk-factor–offending relationship. At the same time as emphasising how practitioners should avoid jumping to conclusions during assessments and 'relying on a favourite or fashionable theory' (YJB 2003: 103–4), the YJB has also dictated that practitioners' assessments of young people's risk of offending/reoffending must be informed by knowledge of RFR and an awareness of different explanations of offending behaviour and human growth and development, specifically:

- the *criminal careers model* of how psychosocial variables influence offending at different developmental stages (Farrington 1997);

- the *theory of age-graded informal social control*, which explores the influence of risk factors, transitions, turning points and life events at different developmental stages (Sampson and Laub 1993);

- the *interactional theory* of reciprocal causal relationships between risk factors and offending over the life course (Thornberry 1987; see also YJB 2003).

In particular, the Cambridge Study has achieved an hegemonic status and authority among policy makers (Leacock and Sparks 2002). Therefore, despite the caveats about avoiding a favourite or fashionable theory and jumping to conclusions, risk assessment guidance sets out conclusively the YJB's preference for the developmental strand of RFR and a bias towards explanations of how childhood-related psychosocial risk factors constitute developmental pathways into and out of offending over the life course. As such, alternative strands of RFR (e.g. constructivism, integrated approaches, ecological models examining the influence of structural factors on offending) and alternative risk factors (e.g. socio-structural, socio-political, economic) have been marginalised at the expense of a specific, deterministic understanding of the risk–offending relationship that has been generated and perpetuated through psychosocial reduction-ism and imputation. The YJB has been seemingly blind to (or dismissive of) the weaknesses of its own 'favourite and fashionable' developmental theories and has been myopic in recognising their limitations. Despite the YJB's claim that risk assessment offers 'comprehensive coverage of relevant risk and protective factors' (YJB 2008: 8), in *Asset*, a narrow body of psychosocial risk factors selected from a narrow body of developmental studies (each with their own theoretical and methodological weaknesses – see Chapters 2, 3 and 5 for critiques of each study) have been repeatedly measured with any and all young people who come to the attention of the YJS. Practitioners have been given little opportunity to explore risks that are not included on the *Asset* inventory, to examine risk as an experience or process that is constructed and negotiated by the young people, or, indeed, to conduct a detailed investigation of the meaning of different risk factors from the young person's perspective. An approach originally intended to improve the quality of assessments and interventions with young people, therefore, when mixed with modern managerialism and a cursory and/or biased knowledge and understanding about risk factors, has resulted in a highly prescriptive, yet ultimately reductionist form of risk-based policy and practice.

The manner of application in *Asset* of factors derived from developmen-tal, deterministic RFR is of concern. The risk factors in the original RFR that forms the basis of *Asset* were identified in childhood (e.g. 8–10 years old in the Cambridge Study) and statistically-associated with (yet con-sidered predictive of) offending in adolescence and adulthood. The inappropriate importation of developmental risk factors into the *Asset* instrument further highlights the incompatibility between *Asset* and the evidence base on which it rests. *Asset* has been, therefore, founded on a series of potentially-invalid assumptions relating to the acceptability of importing developmental risk factors (i.e. those identified in childhood as predictors of offending in adolescence and adulthood) into a tool that measures:

- risk factors in *current life*;

- risk factors for *adolescents*, typically 14–17-year-olds (the peak age range for officially-recorded youth offending – see Smith and McVie 2003);

- risk factors for *reconviction* (not offending or reoffending).

Along with these incompatabilities with the evidence base, there is also demographic diversity within the youth population on whom *Asset* is conducted, whereas the theoretical and empirical bases of *Asset* (criminal careers theory based on the Cambridge Study, interactional theory based on the Pittsburgh Study and the age graded theory of informal social control based on the early research of the Gluecks) were developed with samples that were ethnocentric, androcentric and living in different cultures (e.g. 1960's England, the US) several years before the introduction of *Asset*, therefore, identifying risk factors that may be outdated and/or irrelevant to a modern day sample. Surely then, the uncritical transfer in risk assessment of the methods, findings and conclusions from this research to a population with significant demographic, cultural and historical (temporal) differences can only serve to replicate and exacerbate the original methodological weaknesses and further undermine the validity of Asset and the risk assessment process in the YJS.

Factorisation and aggregation in Asset

The measurement of risk in *Asset* is based on crude factorisation – the reductionist conversion of potentially-complex and dynamic experiences, characteristics, circumstances, attitudes, behaviours, processes etc into a single, static, numerical value (0–4 in each domain) attributed by a YOT practitioner. These crude values are then further reduced into an aggregated risk score for each young person (out of 48), which is even further reduced to one of three aggregated categories: low, medium or high risk. This reductionism has reflected the YJB's desire for *Asset* to 'contribute to the development of the knowledge base through the collection of aggregated data' (YJB 2003: 5). However, such a sweeping, staged factorisation procedure cannot possibly produce measures of risk that represent the life of a young person in any valid, meaningful or comprehensive way, because too much quality, nuance and meaning is lost from the data at each step. Even superficial statistical relationships between risk factors and official measures of offending have been eschewed in favour of practitioner judgements of the face validity of relationships and the influence of risk; judgements that offer little of objective value to reflect, validate or explain any substantive, real-world relationships between risk and offending. Furthermore, *Asset* content is theoretically-and empirically-underpinned by a small group of developmental studies (see next section) that identified risk factors predominantly for a bending (rather than reoffending all reconviction) and used aggregator it risk data across groups of young people. Therefore, the *Asset* risk factors linked to the probability of reconviction for an individual young person were never intended to be explanatory or representative of the risks experienced by individuals; which problematises their use within *Asset*'s RFPP process of informing individually-targeted interventions.

Marginalisation of young people's perspectives

A source of bias in *Asset* risk assessment has been, therefore, the marginalisation of young people's qualitative perspectives and constructions of risk within an assessment tool reliant on factorisation and subjective practitioner-completion, albeit a consistent and technical form of completion that equates to a 'standardised subjectivity'. Insufficient attempt has been made to consult with young people and to integrate their qualitative views of risk into official risk assessment processes (see Case 2006). The adult neglect of young people's perspectives within *Asset* has led Case to bemoan a risk assessment and intervention planning process that provides 'a prescription without a consultation' (2006: 174). Although some young people do complete the small 'What do you think?' section at the end of the instrument, this is not required to be taken into account when practitioners make their judgements of risk. In any case, this section has been notoriously neglected, ignored or missed out entirely by practitioners (see Annison 2005). The paucity of investigation into young people's differing constructions of and responses to risk and risk factors and their differing conceptions of the relative salience of different risk factors (which may not accord with or even be addressed by the established quantitative, artefact-based RFR literature) casts doubt over the validity of the risk factors measured and targeted by risk assessment in the YJS. It would seem to make methodological, practical and ethical sense for practitioners pursuing 'effective practice' to complement quantitative risk assessments with the qualitative investigation of young people's perceptions and constructions of need, risk, risk factors etc (Case 2006), but such foci have been less than forthcoming in RFR and risk assessment tools.

The technicisation of practice

The evaluations of *Asset* have employed qualitative interviews to access practitioners' views of the tool's user-friendliness (e.g. inter-rater reliability) and utility in predicting reoffending and informing interventions. Practitioners have advocated for *Asset*'s ability to enhance diagnostic accuracy, to inform intervention planning (thus improving the efficiency of resource allocation) and to promote 'open and transparent practice (Baker 2005: 78). These benefits were championed in the YJB (2003) core guidance to accompany the completion of *Asset*, which argued that the tool promotes 'structured clinical assessment' that is standardised to avoid practitioner bias and that promotes consistent practice in multi-disciplinary YOTs. As a result, *Asset* has been lauded for providing detailed, structured, reliable, 'scientific' evidence to guide intervention and justify professional decision-making. The 'official' conclusion is that *Asset* has facilitated a breadth and depth of analysis not previously possible (see Baker 2005), has facilitated risk prediction and has guided crime reduction/prevention interventions through 'rigorous evidence-based assessment' (YJB 2003: 20).

However, these claims have been countered by criticisms of the tool's over-technical and actuarial nature (see Pitts 2003a; Annison 2005), Indeed, along with colleagues in 2002, Kerry Baker (a Research Officer in the Oxford University Centre for Criminology, now on secondment to the YJB) identified variability in how comprehensively and constructively practitioners completed the evidence boxes with detailed information that could inform transparent and practical interventions. In relation to intervention planning, *Asset* was 'often viewed by practitioners as an isolated piece of work and was not closely linked into other areas of practice such as pre-sentence report writing, reviewing the progress of an order or intervention planning' (Baker 2005: 77), which raises serious issues regarding the lack of fit between identified risk factors and the supposedly 'risk-focused' interventions that follow.

There is, therefore, an impasse between arguments that the standardisation and actuarialisation of risk assessment in the YJS has been beneficial to consistent, accountable, transparent, objective and efficient practice and contrary views that these processes have been used to control, neuter and deprofessionalise practitioners. Critics have accused *Asset* of reflecting an agenda to impose a uniform and unthinking approach to practice that has prioritised management targets and statistics over the needs of individual offenders (R. Smith 2006) and has encouraged a depersonalised, rigid tick box quality to assessments where 'risk factors become a 'checklist' of triggers to action' (Souhami 2007: 18). Critical youth criminologists in particular have characterised the risk assessment process within *Asset* as the 'technicisation', 'bureaucratisation' and 'routinisation' of youth justice practice (see Pitts 2001; Eadie and Canton 2002), which has deprofessionalised practitioners, robbing them of their ability to use discretion and experience when assessing risk and targeting interventions (see Robinson 2003). Pitts (2001) has labelled the *Asset* process 'korrectional karaoke'. Advocates have countered by claiming that this prescription may not have been a bad thing because practitioner discretion itself is not necessarily positive and can 'run counter to service users' interests' (Evans and Harris 2004: 874).

In response to these criticisms of *Asset*'s deprofessionalising and decontextualising influence, Baker (2005) has claimed that these accusations reflect a lack of familiarity with *Asset*'s design and content, a limited awareness of how the tool is actually used in practice and a failure to understand its potential to balance structure and autonomy. Baker (2005) has suggested that *Asset* is far from an automated tick-box exercise because it requires considerable practitioner expertise to 'apply theoretical knowledge to practical judgements' and to use the evidence box to contextualise the influence of psychosocial risk factors (see also YJB 2008). In this way, *Asset* is intended to be a valuable source of individualised risk information to complement other sources available to the practitioner – a guide to, but not a replacement of, practitioner judgement (see Baker 2005). For some, therefore, *Asset* has been celebrated as a method of enhancing diagnostic accuracy, promoting consistent and transparent decision-making (YJB 2005a, Baker *et al.* 2005). However, for other critical commentators (e.g. O'Mahony 2008; Pitts 2003a; R. Smith 2006), arguments that *Asset* is a comprehensive and valid risk assessment tool that enhances rather than automates youth justice practice and enskills rather than deskills practitioners, have reflected superficial and overly-optimistic interpretations of this risk assessment process.

In the light of the central arguments of his book, it is difficult to refute accusations that the content and manner of completion of *Asset* are technicised (e.g. factorised, aggregated) and prescribed. The desire to provide a 'welcome progression from invisible, idiosyncratic practitioner judgement' (Whyte 2004: 11) has encroached into the domains of theoretical and methodological prescription, running the risk deprofessionalising practitioners by reducing their ability to fully explore the extent and nature of the relationship between risk and offending for individual young people. Instead, *Asset* has introduced a technicised process of identifying and perpetuating a limited range of psychosocial risk factors based on an explicit, yet limited developmental knowledge base of risk and forcing practitioners to use 'evidence boxes' to make spurious and theoretically-biased guesses as to the predictive, developmental influence of risk factors on offending. Therefore, although the *Asset* risk assessment process has been couched in a language of autonomy and discretion, practitioners actually work under what could be seen as practical and theoretical duress.

Definitive indefinity in Asset: *Predictive utility or predictive futility?*

The oversimplification of risk measures (through factorised practitioner judgements) has fuelled oversimplified and definitive conclusions regarding the predictive nature of the relationship between risk and offending based on replicated statistical relationships between risk 'actors' and official measures of reconviction. However, a large degree of imputation has been required to draw such predictive conclusions, especially in the light of the definitional confusions and ambiguities of purpose that have characterised *Asset* risk assessment. It can be argued that the findings and conclusions of RFR have been applied within *Asset* in the absence of a definitive or even well-developed understanding of what is actually being measured, how and why.

In accordance with the government's need for 'evidence-based practice', *Asset* has been subjected to monitoring and evaluations of the evidence it has produced; evaluations conducted by the original developers of the tool at Oxford University. *Asset*'s original aims of identifying the 'risk and protective factors most closely associated with offending by young people' and obtaining 'an overall prediction of the likelihood of reconviction' (YJB 2000: 3) rested on the claims of developmental RFR and the purportedly predictive validity of the body of psychosocial risk factors identified within it. However, rather than conduct an evaluation of the validity and comprehensiveness of the theoretical and empirical bases of *Asset*, the evaluators have preferred to conduct a technical examination of the ability of *Asset* risk scores to predict official reconviction one and two years into the future (a measure of predictive validity). Consequently, the evaluations have identified the main benefit of *Asset* to be an impressive level of *predictive validity* (see Baker *et al.* 2002, 2005), as opposed to, for example, content validity.

Baker *et al.* (2002) examined the ability of *Asset* scores to predict reconviction (measured using police recorded juvenile crime data) after 12 months using a sample of 1,081 *Asset* profiles taken from an opportunity sample of 39 YOTs in England and Wales. The same research team followed up this study with an evaluation of predicted reconviction after 24 months in 2,233 *Asset* profiles (Baker *et al.* 2005). In both studies, the risk profiles were divided into *low score* (0–12) and *high score* (13–48). The level of predictive validity was assessed as the percentage of the low score group who were not reconvicted plus the percentage of the high score group who were reconvicted. *Asset* successfully predicted reconviction outcomes in 67 per cent of cases after one year (33 per cent of the overall sample were in the low score group and were not reconvicted, plus 34 per cent of the sample were in the high score group and were reconvicted) and 69 per cent of outcomes after two years (19 per cent low score-not reconvicted plus 50 per cent high score-reconvicted). This level of predictive utility, which actually increased over time, was consistent across sub-groups of the offending population (e.g. for females, black and ethnic minorities and age groups) and consistent in terms of predicting the occurrence, frequency and seriousness of offending over time (Baker et al. 2005).

In view of these levels of validity and reliability, Baker has claimed that 'ASSET enables more effective targeting of resources through increasing diagnostic accuracy' (Baker 2005: 108). An obvious counterpoint to this claim to high levels of predictive validity is that an overall score of 67–69 per cent successful prediction equates to a worryingly high rate of *false positives* – young people predicted to offend who did not and *false negatives* – those predicted not to offend who did. The evaluators have championed the reliability and validity of *Asset* on the basis of 'hit rates' of around two-thirds that 'out predict' equivalent risk assessment instruments used with adults (see Baker 2005), but is relative efficacy a justified measure of success? *Asset* incorrectly predicts the outcomes for one in three young people. Surely more should be expected from an instrument which carries such significant consequences for the way young people are treated. However, these instruments could themselves be potentially flawed in an unacknowledged way, so relative efficacy may be an unimpressive claim. In any case, through *Asset*, the reconviction outcomes of *one in three* young people have been wrongly predicted. As others have asked before (e.g. Annison 2005; Stephenson *et al.* 2007), what happens to these young people who have eluded and confounded *Asset's* supposedly impressive predictive capabilities? Are the false positive and false negative young people simply acceptable 'casualties of war' – with the positives allocated unwarranted, criminalising interventions and the negatives deprived of appropriate and valuable interventions because they did not appear 'risky' enough? On this basis, risk assessment in the YJS has contributed (in the case of a significant minority of young people) to a dichotomy of unwarranted intervention and unmet need (White 2008; Case 2007). As Smith has bemoaned:

Is routine error just an unfortunate by-product of scientistic logic? . . . do we consider it acceptable to 'get it wrong' sometimes in order to manage and control risk? (R. Smith 2006: 102)

Perhaps the best example of *Asset's* definitive indefinity has been the temporal indefinity and ambiguity inherent in the confident conclusions that risk measures have temporal precedence over offending. Simplistic, factorised measures of risk have been adopted uncritically from developmental RFR, have been associated with offending (through practitioner judgements) and have then been assumed (on the basis of this judgement, rather than statistical evidence to have temporal precedence and predictive influence over offending. However, there has been no explicit exploration of the direction of the relationship between *Asset* risk factors and measures of offending, for example, in terms of the onset of each measure or young people's relative exposure to risk and offending over a set period. *Asset* risk assessment simply requires young people who have recently offended to report to a practitioner whether they are currently and/or have recently been exposed to certain psychosocial risk factors. It could be, therefore, that offending has pre-dated exposure to risk (e.g. young people now have a poor relationship with their family because of their offending), which would accord with Thornberry's interactional model of the reciprocal risk–offending relationship, but would contradict the notions of risk factors as developmental predictors and triggers to offending that are promulgated by *Asset* risk assessment based on the deterministic conclusions of much RFR and which form the theoretical and empirical logic for risk-focused preventative intervention (i.e. the RFPP). However, if risk factors exist in a young person's life in the present day, then surely they are relevant to predicting reoffending and so are justified targets for intervention? Therefore, there may be an underlying problem regarding exactly what *Asset* is intended to do with a set of risk factors that were originally identified as predictive of initial offending.

Asset's identity crisis: Who am I? What am I?

So what is *Asset* risk assessment really for and what is it trying to do? A number of issues have emerged from a critical reading of risk assessment in the YJS which have illuminated an identity crisis within *Asset*; an ambiguity and inconsistency in *Asset*'s definition and purpose.

What is Asset's proposed function – actuarialism, clinical diagnosis or intervention planning?

Proponents of *Asset* (e.g. Baker *et al.* 2002, 2005) have claimed that the instrument has encouraged a synthesis of the benefits of actuarialism, clinical assessment and practitioner expertise. Critics (e.g. Pitts 2001) have counter-claimed that the stigmatising, desensitising and over-generalising effects of actuarialism have been accompanied by a technicisation of youth justice practice that has diluted the potential advantages of practitioner expertise and discretion. It remains unclear as to whether the tool is actually an actuarial instrument, as a clinical, diagnostic device, as an aid to practitioner expertise or whether the intention has been to fulfil all of these functions, as has been claimed (see, for example, Baker 2005).

Despite its presentation as a 'third generation' risk assessment tool combining actuarialism and clinical assessment (e.g. YJB 2003), *Asset* is clearly an actuarial tool. *Asset* 'provides aggregate data which can be used to inform decisions on resource allocation' (YJB 2003: 20) and structures risk assessments 'using descriptions of the characteristics of populations to predict the likelihood of reoffending of individual offenders' (R. Smith 2006: 49). *Asset* has been used to place young people into risk categories based on their measured level of risk and to allocate interventions accordingly – the fundamental characteristics/purpose of actuarialism (Silver and Miller 2002). Therefore, none of the interventions have been tailored to the risk profile of the individual young person to whom they have been administered and thus may not be valid responses to the specific needs and problems of the young offender in question.

According to Robinson, actuarial risk assessment instruments such as *Asset* simply 'cannot provide accurate predictions of risk in respect of individuals' (Robinson 2003: 116). Instead, the behaviour of individuals is imputed from that of the risk group into which they are placed following assessment; what Kemshall (2003) terms the 'actuarial fallacy'. These characteristics of *Asset* are endemic and necessary, but they are also at the root of the problem. The relative inaccuracy of *Asset* and the consequences that flow from it, such as enforcing standardised interventions on false positive young people, due to their membership of a statistical group (Kemshall 2003) questions its place as the central animating instrument of an entire structured youth justice system. Where *Asset* has been used to aid intervention planning (which, even according to the evaluators, has not been a consistent process – Baker *et al.* 2002, 2005), these interventions have been matched to aggregated risk profiles rather than to individual-ised risk profiles or the individual needs of the specific young people in receipt of the intervention. Farrington (2007) has acknowledged the methodological contradiction of prescribing individualised interventions to affect within-individual change predicated on the aggregation of risk factors at group level; a process that cannot identify causes or predictors of offending for individuals or offer credible individually-based, evidence-based interventions. Thus some have argued that aggregated risk profiling lacks sensitivity to individual needs and individual differences *within* sub-groups, resulting in the *decontextualisation* of risk and offending behaviour, which 'creates an arbitrary and ultimately unsustainable separation between the young person concerned and his/her social characteristics and needs' (R. Smith 2006: 197).

It is necessary to understand *Asset* as part of a much bigger system. Thus, an *Asset* assessment does not just lead to the allocation of a risk level for the young person and a corresponding level of intervention, it also leads to the application of largely pre-determined risk-focused interven-tions (e.g. an assessment of high risk linked to temperament issues, leads to an intensive level of intervention which takes the form of anger management programmes). *Asset*, therefore, only has a logic as a part of a much bigger system and the way in which it works is very specific to the system of which it is an integral part. *Asset* has been viewed as an abandonment of efforts to identify and treat the origins of offending, in favour of group categorisation and 'actuarial justice' and that prevention as the primary aim of the YJS, has been replaced by risk assessment (Silver and Miller 2002). Understanding *why* a particular individual behaves in a particular way (and can be treated) has been rendered irrelevant by actuarial risk assessment (Silver 2001) such as *Asset*. In this model, whether the risk factors measured are the right risk factors or even whether they are actually risk factors at all for a specific young person or a specific behaviour, has been rendered largely irrelevant – system managerialism now drives youth justice work (see also Goldson and Muncie 2006).

However, it seems likely that the extent to which some of these problems arise is at least partly a product of the poorly-explained and poorly-understood purpose of *Asset* and how it should be used. It is perfectly possible to argue, for example, that the attribution of an overall risk level to an individual via *Asset* is (and should be) limited to allocating an appropriate *level* of intervention based on an assessment of risk (of reoffending). Whilst one might question the accuracy, validity and reliability of *Asset* in this regard, the allocation of an individual to a group risk level is not intended to provide an individualised assessment of which risk factors are 'active' or what type of intervention should follow. Assessments about active risk factors and appropriate interventions are, thus, to be based on a deeper, professional, reading and interpretation of the more detailed individual contents of *Asset*. Whilst one might wish to also question the validity of the way in which *Asset* prescribes these contents and what is assessed, this argument does place limits around the impact of actuarial assessments and provides scope for professional individualised judgements. Accordingly, it can be concluded that *Asset* attempts to fulfil concurrent roles: actuarial, clinical and intervention planning. However, the feasibility and desirability of such a broad remit is moot. In particular, attempting to reconcile these multiple functions within a single assessment process appears to undermine and neuter the detailed, rigorous execution of any of the specific functions in their own right.

What does Asset seek to measure – risk, need or both?

Here, again, as above, there is some confusion about exactly what *Asset* is intended to measure: risk or need, or risk and need. McCarthey, Laing and Walker state: 'risk assessment and needs assessment are different, although they can often go hand-in-hand and can sometimes be confused' (McCarthy *et al.* 2004: 11). *Asset* has been presented by the YJB as a risk/needs assessment tool with the capability of informing interventions through the targeting of individualised needs. As the YJB have maintained, 'the first and most important function of *Asset* is to help Yots to assess the needs of young people and the degree of risk they pose and then to match intervention programmes to their assessed need' (YJB 2003: 31). Baker (2003) has championed the capability of *Asset* to afford practitioners a balance between risk and need. The YJB guidance to practitioners has attempted to clarify that once risk factors are identified through *Asset*, practitioners are charged with identifying the appropriate needs to address through intervention (YJB 2007a). Therefore, addressing needs takes the form of an identifiable, effective and available solution to a perceived problem – risks are indicators of problem outcomes whereas needs are sites for intervention to enable reductions in offending behaviour. The catch here, of course, is that these needs and sites for intervention are risk-dependent – addressing risk factors for offending that were identified within a body of RFR that depicted young people as a risk to themselves and others (see also Goldson and Muncie 2006; Case 2006).

Thus, *Asset* has been criticised for an over-emphasis on 'risk' and for introducing a 'focus on the criminal deeds of young people rather than their social or psychological needs' (Pitts 2005: 8). Evidence for this argument is to be found in the risk and criminogenic content of Asset and the types of interventions that flow from such restricted assessments. The emphasis on risk in *Asset* is striking. *Asset* contains only one explicitly needs-based section ('indicators of vulnerability') and one section focused on protective factors, compared to 14 risk-based sections (12 psychosocial sections, along with indicators of serious harm to others and the 'what do you think' sections). This risk bias, in combination with the plethora of risk-related judgements required of the practitioners in each section of *Asset*, practically dictates that assessment and subsequent intervention plans prioritise risk (see also Stephenson *et al.* 2007). Consequently, *Asset* has been criticised for its depiction of young people as simultaneously 'posing' risk and 'facing' risk, with their needs relegated to the background (Goldson 2005).

What do Asset risk factors actually predict – *offending, reoffending or reconviction?*

Perhaps the biggest ambiguity/indefinity within *Asset* risk assessment has been its own temporal precedence over preventative risk assessment tools targeting risk factors for initial offending (in line with much of the evidence base in RFR) as the government's chosen response to youth offending. The bulk of RFR and the central tenets of New Labour government policy have espoused a preventative ethos, prioritising the early identification and targeting of risk factors for initial episodes of offending by young people. However, the government's initial response to the needed to prevent offending was to commission the Centre for Criminology at Oxford University to construct a risk assessment instrument that measures risk factors experienced by existing offenders (i.e. risk factors for reoffending). The 'evidence-base' for *Asset* was imported from a body of RFR that identified risk factors that were predictive of a different behaviour (offending, rather than reoffending), indicating an incompatibility between the purpose of *Asset* and its evidence base.

Despite the expressed intention to predict the 'risk of (also referred to as the likelihood of) reoffending' (YJB 2008: 9), *Asset*'s aggregated risk levels are actually used to predict official *reconviction*, so tell us little about the risk factors that predict self-reported offending or about which risk factors actively contribute to officially-recorded *reoffending* and in what ways. Predicting reconviction does not equate to predicting reoffending (see Robinson 2003) and so risk factors for reconviction do not necessarily equate to those for reoffending. Conviction by the courts is by no means an accurate, valid and comprehensive measure of (re)offending, particularly as it excludes the dark figure of unreported, unrecorded and undetected crime. Most importantly from a methodological perspective, reconviction was never the outcome measure/dependent variable against which risk factors were identified in the RFR that underpins *Asset*. There has already been an uncritical acceptance and imputation within *Asset*'s development of a comparability between risk factors for offending and reoffending, an assumption that the seminal criminological RFR by the Gluecks would disavow. The use of reconviction as the dependent variable against which to assess risk factors serves to exacerbate both this invalidity and the degree of imputation needed to conclude predictive relationships between risk and offending. Reconviction is a partial measure of reoffending (let alone offending) and consequently a partial measure of the predictive utility of the risk factors measured in *Asset*. It may be, therefore, that there is a substantive, yet unmeasured, difference in the risk profiles of (officially) reconvicted offenders and young people who have reoffended, but who have not been reconvicted, raising questions as to the applicability of risk-focused interventions that have been originally 'evidenced' as addressing risk factors for reoffending. It could also be that conviction is, in itself, a risk factor for reoffending, rather than an outcome of exposure to risk (in line with Thornberry's interactional theory of a bidirectional relationship between risk and offending and early findings from the Edinburgh Study). For example, contact with official youth justice agencies could affect the level of risk experienced by a young person in a negative or positive way (e.g. the stigma could weaken family relationships; exposure to interventions could enhance resilience) or could even function as a risk factor in its own right (see Smith and McVie 2003; McCord 1978). Therefore, the young people assessed by *Asset* could already be at a huge disadvantage and thus be far more likely to be reconvicted because of the risk factors that brought them into contact with the YJS and/or due to this contact and subsequent exposure to interventions.

Asset has developed an identity crisis that has been reflected in its ambiguity and confusion of definition and purpose. *Asset* risk assessment in the YJS has reflected the methodological paradoxes of the RFR –

informing interventions through practical, simplistic and confident, yet narrow, over-simplified and fluctuating (even contradictory) understandings of the relationship between risk and a narrow measure of offending (reconviction) based largely on imputation and the invalid application of theory and findings from a small body of developmental RFR. Imputation has encouraged definitive conclusions to be drawn regarding the predictive influence, universal applicability and comparability of risk factors to all young people who offend. Although *Asset* may offer the scope for professional judgement when working with young people who have offended, this scope has been highly prescribed. The developmental shackles of *Asset* and the wider YJB-prescribed system it feeds are hard to shake off. The hegemonic developmental, risk-based paradigm that drives youth justice policy in England and Wales is animated by *Asset* risk assessment, a process which is rooted in the overall managerialism that binds the system together. However, factorisation of risk, technicisation, developmental determinism, psychosocial bias and imputing the nature of the risk-factor–offending relationship are all methodological weaknesses that bind the *Asset* risk assessment process together; thus aggravating the original flaws in RFR and perpetuating/animating them within contemporary youth justice practice.

The onset of risk assessment as early intervention: the pre-emptive strike

The Government's commitment to risk seems inexorable, as evidenced by the roll-out of risk assessment to encompass the measurement of risk of the onset of offending, to accompany the *Asset* focus on risk of reoffending/reconviction. It would appear that the government holds the view that the risk factors for reoffending are synonymous with those for the onset of offending, exemplified in the following claim by Bob Ashford, the YJB Head of Prevention:

> the risk factors for those on the cusp of entering the criminal justice system are, broadly speaking, the same as for those young people who have entered it. (Ashford 2007: 6)

Risk not only provides a third way philosophy for intervention in the lives of young people embroiled within the formal youth justice system, risk now provides the rationale and justification for a panoply of so-called preventative interventions. A whole range of ideas cluster around the nexus of risk-focused youth crime prevention:

- Young people present risks to other young people and wider society and any responsible government would want to reduce or manage these risks.

- Young people themselves contain risks and any responsible government would want to reduce or mitigate these to promote positive outcomes and minimise negative outcomes (including, but not limited to, offending) for young people and for the benefit of wider society.

- We know what the risks are that young people contain that predispose them to offending and other negative behaviours, so if we change them the outcomes will be changed.

- Prevention is much better than cure – why wait for something (bad) to happen before doing something about it, when it is possible to stop it happening in the first place?

- Intervention is a good thing (1) because government can be see to be doing something about a major social problem and topic of public concern and (2) because it will lead to better outcomes for more people.

- The earlier (and earlier) we intervene to prevent negative outcomes, the better it will be because we can 'nip problems in the bud', and prevent them from becoming more serious and entrenched and, therefore, more difficult (and costly) to change.

When all of these notions are put together, the logic of risk focused preventative intervention becomes inescapable – it is so obviously the right thing to do that it is a wonder no-one thought of it before! Such is the power and infallibility of this argument that when being interviewed by the BBC in 2006 about the government's preventative strategy and interventionist intentions, Tony Blair (as Prime Minister) said 'There is not going to be a solution [to the problem of youth antisocial behaviour] unless we are sufficiently hard-headed to say that from a very early age we need a system of intervention'. When it was put to Blair by the interviewer that he was clearly being advised that early intervention was the way to go and that this could mean when children were still in nappies, Blair replied 'or pre-birth even'! (see, http://news.bbc.co.uk/1/hi/uk_politics/5301824.stm). Thus, the logic of early preventative risk-focused intervention reaches its final and inevitable conclusion.

Whilst it is necessary to recognise that the government did not invent risk and notions of prevention or intervention, the political rhetorical value of usurping the advice it has been given to create a dynamic paradigm of youth crime prevention must be recognised and cannot be underestimated (see, for example, D. Smith 2006; R. Smith 2006). The *Misspent Youth* report (Audit Commission 1996), for example, made strong recommendations for an increase in investment in preventative activity within the YJS and recommended that this activity should be carefully targeted on 'at risk' young people and on the 'high risk' neighbourhoods in which these young people live. These recommendations for an enhanced focus on prevention were underpinned by evidence from developmental RFR and they have encouraged an emphasis on *risk-focused* early intervention. Notwithstanding the methodological and theoretical criticisms of *Asset*, the YJB has rolled out the risk assessment process in the form of *Onset* (see below) to inform risk-focused early intervention with young people who have not been officially convicted of an offence, but who can be readily identified through assessment as 'at risk' of offending in the future. Therefore, the government have asserted that:

> the 'flagging up' of early concerns about children's wellbeing and/or 'risk factors' have thus become central to government strategy and policy formation. (Chief Secretary to the Treasury 2003: 53)

Risk-focused early intervention in the YJS has been premised on developmental understandings of risk – seeking to address the predictive influence of risk factors for the onset of offending before any offending takes place – tackling *pre*-offending as opposed to reoffending. Populations and individuals are identified as, *inter alia*, 'at risk', 'high risk' or 'criminogenic', then targeted by risk-focused intervention at an early age and/or at what is viewed as an early stage in their offending career (i.e. when 'on the cusp' of offending behaviour). This form of 'nipping crime in the bud' has been considered to be effective, efficient and economical because risk factors can be tackled before they become entrenched and before they exert a negative influence on the young person's behaviour. Therefore, prima facie, risk-focused early intervention would appear to offer a highly practical, commonsense approach to the prevention of youth offending.

An issue emerges, however, regarding the purportedly empirical, evidential basis of risk assessment as early intervention; namely that the evidence base for its use and utility is actually scant. Loeber, Farrington and Petechuk have raised a related issue:

> A critical question from a scientific and policy standpoint concerning child delinquency is: 'How early can we tell?' It is difficult, however, to obtain a clear answer to this question . . . Few tools are available to distinguish those youth who will continue with behaviours that may lead them to become child delinquents. (Loeber *et al.* 2003: 8)

Risk factor researchers themselves have seldom made claims that targeting risk factors at an early age can reduce/prevent future offending. Several researchers have identified childhood risk factors and linked them to later offending, but have not attempted to change them, either due to deterministic beliefs that the influence of risk factors on offending is stable across the life course (e.g. Glueck and Glueck 1950; West and Farrington 1973) or due to having inherited a sample that were never subjected to intervention (e.g. Sampson and Laub 1993). Others have attempted risk-focused intervention with 'at risk' young people (e.g. Cabot 1926) and offenders (e.g. Tremblay *et al.* 2003; Hawkins *et al.* 2003; Bottoms and McClintock 1973), but with limited (if any) significant effects on offending. As Goldson (2005) has pointed out, there has been minimal evidence that risk-focused early intervention 'works' as a method of preventing general youth offending. Despite these concerns, official forays into delinquency prevention have proceeded apace – underpinned by a somewhat uncritical, unthinking and shallow adoption of the prima facie results and conclusions of RFR.

Onset: assessing the risk of offending

The YJB has explicitly responded to the *Misspent Youth* report's criticisms of insufficient focus on prevention by driving through an early intervention agenda, exemplified by the creation of two large-scale preventative programmes – *Youth Inclusion and Support Panels* and *Youth Inclusion Programmes*. Both programmes have been underpinned by a newly created risk assessment process known as *Onset*, which is 'the only specifically designed tool in use in early intervention/prevention programmes' (Walker *et al.* 2007: xiii)

Onset was introduced in April 2003 as a risk referral, assessment and intervention process for young people aged 8–13 years considered to be 'at risk' of offending in the future. The reason for choosing this age range is unclear, but a possible explanation for starting with eight year olds is that this mirrored the Cambridge Study age group with whom risk factors for future offending were first identified – risk factors that have informed and guided RFR for half a century and which have clearly had a significant impact on government thinking and policy. This assessment of risk factors for the *onset* of offending is what gives the instrument its name. Therefore, *Onset* focuses on risk factors for offending onset rather than for reoffending or reconviction (the focus of *Asset*) and has thus encouraged risk-focused early intervention (with 'early' taken to mean pre-offending and the prevention of offending onset), rather than risk-focused interventions seeking to 'prevent' the continuance or exacerbation of existing offending behaviour (see also Stephenson *et al.* 2007).

The *Onset* process begins with a referral to a Youth Inclusion and Support Panel (YISP) or Youth Inclusion Programme (YIP) by key stakeholder agencies such as the police, social services, education and health (both programmes are discussed later in the chapter). Initially, the *Onset referral and screening form* is completed by a practitioner from the referring agency. The form is divided into sections that broadly correspond to those in the *Asset* risk assessment instrument – living and family arrangements, statutory education, neighbourhood and friends, substance misuse, emotional and mental health, perception of self and others, thinking, behaviour and attitudes, positive factors, vulnerability and risk of harm by young person. In each section/risk domain, the practitioner is required to indicate (by ticking a box) whether they believe that the young person has been/is currently exposed to a series of risk factors. At the end of each section, there is a small evidence box for the practitioner to add a brief explanation of the evidence underpinning their assessments and how they consider risk factors to be linked to offending/antisocial behaviour.

The referral and screening form asks for the same information as the full *Onset* instrument (see below), but the risk factors are phrased slightly differently and include examples, in order to be 'more appealing and easier to understand for referrers' (YJB 2006a: 1). For example, in relation to the risk domain of 'living and family arrangements', the practitioner is asked to tick a (yes/no) box to indicate whether the following elements exist in the current life of the young person:

- is separated from either or both of his or her parents;

- lives in a deprived household;

- experiences inconsistent supervision at home;

- experiences harsh discipline in the home;

- family is known to be involved in crime/antisocial behaviour;

- is currently experiencing unstable accommodation.

(YJB 2006b: 3)

At the end of the form, practitioners are then asked to indicate their reasons for referring the young person to the YISP or YIP (the former of which requires that four or more risk factors be present in the young person's life) by highlighting aspects of the young person's behaviour that they are concerned about and the impact of this behaviour.

The full *Onset* risk assessment instrument was developed by the Oxford University Centre for Criminology (the developers of *Asset*). In the full instrument, which is completed at the point of referral and is reviewed at the midway point and closure of the (YISP or YIP) programme, practitioners are asked to rate 'the extent to which you think the following factors are associated with the young person's likelihood of offending or serious antisocial behaviour in the future' (YJB 2006c: 3). Practitioners are given equivalent guidance to that provided with *Asset* regarding how to rate evidence of an association between risk and offending/antisocial behaviour (i.e. on a scale of 0–4: 'not associated', 'slight/indirect association', 'moderate but definite association', 'quite strong association', 'very strong association'). Risk is measured within specific psychosocial domains, which mirror the *Asset* sections:

1. *Living arrangements* – e.g. living with known offenders or people who commit acts of serious antisocial behaviour, deprived household, accommodation unsuitable for his/her needs, absconding/staying away, no fixed abode, stable accommodation.

2. *Family and personal relationships* – e.g. family members involved in substance misuse or criminal activity, lack of interest shown in the young person, inconsistent supervision, domestic abuse, significant bereavement or loss, stable relationship with at least one parent or other family member, positive role-models.

3. *Statutory education* – e.g. any identified special educational needs, instances of exclusion, truancy or bullying, difficulties with basic literacy/numeracy, poor relationships with teachers, good at a certain subject, gets on well with teachers.

4. *Neighbourhood* – e.g. level of crime in the area, obvious signs of drug-dealing and/or usage, lack of age-appropriate facilities, isolated, location/lack of transport, racial or ethnic tensions, good opportunities for positive activities in the community.

5. *Lifestyle* – e.g. predominantly pro-criminal or disruptive peers, non-constructive use of time, lack of legitimate income, lack of age-appropriate friendships, involvement in reckless activity, has friends who are not offenders or antisocial.

6. *Substance misuse* – e.g. use of alcohol/tobacco/solvents/drugs, substance use which has a detrimental effect on education or relationships, offending to obtain money for substances, motivation to stop using.

7. *Physical health* – e.g. health condition that significantly affects everyday functioning, physical immaturity/delayed development, health put at risk through his or her own behaviour, not registered with a GP, regularly takes part in sports activities.

8. *Emotional and mental health* – e.g. problems coming to terms with significant past events, contact with mental health services, any suicide attempts or instances of self-harm, supportive family or other support networks.

9. *Perception of self and others* – e.g. inappropriate levels of self-esteem, general mistrust of other people, displays a lack of understanding for other people, discriminatory attitudes, displays a good understanding of the feelings of others – including any victims or their family/carers.

10. *Thinking and behaviour* – e.g. taking the young person's age into consideration – does not understand the consequences of actions, acts

impulsively, has a constant need for excitement, gives in easily to pressure from others, poor temper control.

11. *Attitudes to offending* – e.g. lack of understanding about the impact of offending on victim or their family/carers, lack of remorse, belief that certain offences are acceptable, sees becoming an offender as inevitable, does not see him/herself as an 'offender'.

12. *Motivation to change* – e.g. does not understand consequences of offending, cannot identify reasons to change behaviour, is unlikely to receive support from family/friends, is unwilling to fully co-operate and achieve change, goals for the future.

13. *Indicators of vulnerability* – e.g. the behaviour of others (bullying, abuse, neglect), events or circumstances (separation, loss), own behaviour (attempted suicide, self-harm, risk taking).

14. *Indicators of serious harm to others* – e.g. actual serious harm already caused, evidence of intent or preparation to harm, behaviour that could have harmed others.

(YJB 2006c: 1–10)

As with *Asset*, practitioners provide further explanation of their rating in an evidence box at the end of each section/risk factor domain. Practitioners are also given equivalent guidance to those completing *Asset* (see YJB 2006a) regarding the questions that they should ask themselves when rating evidence of risk (e.g. was the factor linked to past behaviour? is the link to offending direct or indirect? does the risk factor lead to offending on its own or in the presence of other factors?). The practitioner-completed sections are supplemented by an optional (to the practitioner) 'Over to you' section completed by the young person, which corresponds to the 'What do you think' element of *Asset* and which asks young people for their responses on a four-point scale ('not like me', 'a bit like me', 'a lot like me', 'just like me') to a series of questions regarding:

- *Your family and where you live* (e.g. I never stay away from home without asking).

- *School* (e.g. I need help with reading and writing).

- *Where you live and about your friends* (e.g. I live in areas where there is not much to do).

- *Smoking, drinking and drugs* (e.g. I have family or friends who use drugs).

- *Your health* (e.g. I worry about something that might happen in the future).

- *How you think and behave* (e.g. I rush into things without thinking).

(YJB 2006d: 1–3)

Following completion of the *Onset* assessment tool, practitioners produce an *Onset* intervention plan, which recommends an appropriate response to the risk presented by the young person and which should be linked to the risk profile that emerges from the assessment. For example, sections with ratings of 3–4 are considered by the YJB to be 'more closely linked to offending' than sections with lower ratings and therefore, these risk sections should be the priority for *Onset*-informed interventions. The *Onset* intervention plan has a short-term focus (e.g. three months) and is concerned with 'SMART' targets – specific, measurable, achievable, realistic and time-specific, in line with the YJB's managerialist.

Youth Inclusion and Support Panels: Onset *in action*

The *Onset* process was developed specifically for use by 'pre-crime, at-risk panels', later re-titled *Youth Inclusion and Support Panels* (YISPs). YISPs were originally established in April 2003 in 13 pilot areas and there are currently approximately 220 YISPs across the country. The majority of YISP funding in England and Wales comes from the YJB's YOT Prevention Grant, although in England, YISPs are joint-funded by the YJB and the Children's Fund (which sits within the Department for Children, Schools and Families). YISPs are multi-agency panels consisting of representatives from different agencies working with young people, in particular the statutory agencies of police, education, health and social services. The aim of these panels is to prevent offending and antisocial behaviour by 8–13 year olds (or 14–18 year olds in the case of the YISP+ programme) who have been identified by referring agencies (using *Onset*) as 'at risk' of offending and to ensure that these young people and their families can access mainstream services at the earliest possible stage (although participation is voluntary). Walker and colleagues have set out the origins and governmental objectives of the YISP project:

> using a matrix of the risk and protective factors which may lead young people into, or protect them from, crime, the YISPs were tasked with constructing a personally tailored package of support and interventions, summarised in an integrated support plan (ISP) designed to facilitate the kind of provision which will prevent the young person moving further towards crime. (Walker *et al.* 2007: ix)

In 2003, an independent evaluation of the 13 pilot YISPs was commissioned by the Department for Education and Skills from the Newcastle Centre for Family Studies and Newcastle University. The evaluation was subsequently extended in 2005 through co-funding with the YJB. The multi-disciplinary evaluation team set out 'to understand how YISPs targeted children and young people, assessed the risk and protective factors, developed integrated support plans and delivered multi-agency interventions' (Walker *et al.* 2007: x). A two-part evaluation was implemented to address these objectives:

- *Quantitative analysis* of initial, midway and closure *Onset* assessment scores in order to assess whether the YISP 'had a statistically significant impact on a measurable indicator of the risk of problematic behaviour' (Walker *et al.* 2007: xviii) amongst young people referred to the scheme.

- *Qualitative case studies* in four pilot areas in England and Wales using observations, discourse, narrative and documentary analyses and interviews with professionals, children and parents. The case studies explored perspectives of risk and were intended 'to identify the factors which might contribute to successful and unsuccessful delivery of interventions (and) outcomes as perceived by the providers and receivers of the interventions' (Walker *et al.* 2007: xi).

In carrying out their evaluation, the research team were hampered by incomplete data. Walker *et al.* (2007) found that there were serious gaps in the assessment data available from the YISP management information system (YISPMIS) that had been specially created to capture *Onset* assessment information. In the 13 pilot areas, 403 cases were available for analysis (from an unknown total of cases) that included *Onset* data for initial, midway and closure assessment scores. Following data cleaning and further tests of the completeness of this data, 229 of the 403 cases remained. Nevertheless, on the basis of the available data, Walker *et al.* (2007) saw fit to render a series of 'tentative' risk-related conclusions:

- risk factors related to education, neighbourhood, lifestyle and emotional and mental health were considered by practitioners to be the most important influences on offending and antisocial behaviour when making referrals to the YISP;

- higher levels of measured risk at referral offered the most potential for risk reduction over the course of the YISP;

- older children were less likely to demonstrate large reductions in risk levels;

- there were no gender differences in reductions in risk.

However, the evaluation team also concluded that the limitations and lack of representativeness of the quantitative data analysis meant that even more importance should be placed on the qualitative, explanatory case study element of the evaluation. Particular attention was paid to the perceptions of change (from time of referral to completion of the YISP intervention) elicited from 30 interviews with parents and 32 interviews with children, which focused on the risk domains of:

- *Family* – parents perceived overcrowding/poor housing conditions and children's attitudes and behaviour in the family home (e.g. destructiveness, aggression, disobedience) as serious issues at the point of referral, whilst young people reported complex and difficult family situations as a risk factor at referral.

- *Education/school* – parents reported that school problems presented significant risk factors for their child at the point of referral.

- *Community* – parent-reported neighbourhood/community risk factors at the point of referral included the child staying out late/overnight, criminogenic neighbourhoods, the child being drawn into drug cultures and the child gaining a bad reputation which could encourage police targeting.

- *Individual wellbeing* – several risk factors were reported by parents which related to the child's emotional and psychological wellbeing at referral, including self-harming behaviour, poor anger management, emotional and behavioural problems (e.g. attention deficit hyperactivity disorder), being a victim of bullying, low self-esteem and lacking social skills.

(Walker *et al.* 2007)

The majority of parents interviewed reported improvements in their child's behaviour in all risk domains following YISP interventions, including improvements in attitudes and behaviour at home and at school, improved school attendance, less harassment of parents by teachers, reduced involvement in offending and antisocial behaviour, no more hanging about on the streets, improved psychological health and reduced aggression (Walker *et al.* 2007). However, in all risk domains, parents were concerned that these improvements may not last once the intervention had ceased. Walker *et al.* concluded that YISP activities such as the one-to-one relationship with a key worker, constructive leisure activities, learning new skills, making new friends and providing parental support:

> may not themselves have had a direct impact on the children, . . . [but] some of the changes in circumstances may well have been facilitated by the fact that the child had been referred to YISP and members of the multi-agency panel had been able to commit resources to affecting change in the family's life. (Walker *et al.* 2007: 23)

From these admittedly tentative conclusions and on the basis of limited quantitative and qualitative data sets, the evaluation team advocated the systematic and rigorous risk assessment of children and young people, especially assessment targeting high-risk children and they championed the efficacy of 'delivering preventative services which address identified risk factors' (Walker *et al.* 2007: 159). It was concluded that 'assessing risk needs to be a continuous process ... [and that] there should be more consistency in the approach of professionals towards assessing children and young people' (Walker *et al.* 2007: 26). Whilst it is difficult to disagree with this conclusion to the extent that it supports the principles of assessment, clear planning and effective delivery of interventions in the YJS, to base these processes on risk (as currently conceived) is restrictive and highly spurious.

Youth Inclusion Programmes: Onset in action

Youth Inclusion Programmes (YIPs) were established by the YJB in 2000 in response to the demands of the *Misspent Youth* report for further investment in targeted preventative activity with young people identified through *Onset* as 'at risk' of offending and reoffending and those living in 'high risk' neighbourhoods. YIPs are tailor-made programmes for 8–17 year olds (Junior YIPs for 8–12 year olds, Senior YIPs for 13–17 year olds) living in 114 of the most socially deprived/high crime and therefore most high risk neighbourhoods in England and Wales (YJB 2006e). The YJB has outlined a series of key objectives for YIPs, particularly:

- to engage with those young people considered to be most at risk of offending and reoffending in a particular neighbourhood;

- to address the risk and protective factors identified by *Onset* assessments;

- to prevent and reduce offending through intervention with individuals, families and communities.

(YIP Managers' Guidance, YJB 2006e)

Guidance to YIPs Managers has set out the requirement for local agencies (the same agencies charged with referring young people to YISPs) to 'identify not only those who are offending, but also those at risk of future offending, social and educational exclusion' (CGE&Y 2002, in Morgan Harris Burrows 2003) and to refer them to the YIP through the *Onset* referral form. Practitioners working within the YIPs are confidently charged by the YJB to use the *Onset* core profile to identify their 'top 50' most at risk young people in the neighbourhood so that they can provide targeted intervention 'that will address their risk factors and prevent future offending' (see Morgan Harris Burrows 2003: 5).

YIPs managers are required to ensure that the most at risk young people identified are included in mainstream activities and are provided with targeted, dynamic and locally-based activities amounting to an average of ten hours of intervention per young person per week (CGE&Y 2002, in

Morgan Harris Burrows 2003). The activities/interventions offered typically include education and training, sport, arts, mentoring, drugs education, motor projects, family projects and outreach and detached youth work.

Once the first 70 YIPs had been established in 2000 (Senior YIPs only at that point), the YJB commissioned an independent evaluation of the impact of the first phase of the YIPs project (from 2000 until December 2002). The evaluation examined the impact of the YIPs on participating areas (59 in year one of the evaluation, falling to 57 in year two) and their impact on the 'top 50' young people in each area in terms of the YIP's three original objectives, which were:

- to reduce arrest rates by 60 per cent;

- to achieve a one third reduction in truancy and exclusions;

- to reduce recorded crime by 30 per cent.

(Morgan Harris Burrows 2003: 4)

Over phase one of the programme, the evaluation team analysed official statistics in each neighbourhood in relation to arrest rates, school truancy and school exclusion amongst the 'top 50' young people, along with overall recorded crime in the neighbourhood. It was concluded that in the two years since the implementation of YIPs:

- *Arrest rates* fell by 65 per cent for members of the top 50 (in each area) who had been 'actively engaged' (with engagement measured superficially as participation rather than as a deeper, qualitative or affective measure) in the programme since its inception and by 44 per cent for members who had not been actively engaged in the programme;

- *Unauthorised truancy* amongst the top 50 increased by 51 per cent;

- Temporary exclusions from school fell by 12 per cent for members of the top 50;

- *Permanent exclusions from school* decreased by 27 per cent for members of the top 50;

- *Recorded crime* increased by 3.6 per cent in participating neighbourhoods during the first year of the YIPs (29 neighbourhoods showed a decrease in crime, 30 showed an increase), increased by 7.9 per cent in participating neighbourhoods during the second year of the YIPs (14 neighbourhoods showed a decrease in crime, 43 showed an increase) and rose by 11.4 per cent across all participant areas over the course of the evaluation.

(Morgan Harris Burrows 2003)

Overall, the results of the quantitative phase one of the YIPs evaluation were clearly inconsistent, with general reductions in arrest rates and school exclusions, plus decreases in crime rates in some neighbourhoods being overshadowed by large increases in unauthorised truancy amongst the top 50 in each area and general increases in recorded crime in most YIPs neighbourhoods.

The quantitative evaluation of YIPs impact was supplemented by a qualitative evaluation of the *implementation* of YIPs. This part of the YIPs evaluation was conducted using a 'theory of change' model which hypothesised links between programme activities and outcomes using three criteria and made the following conclusions based on these criteria:

- *Programme rationale or 'plausibility'* – the evaluators rejected the notion that the less than impressive results could be due to 'theory failure' by strongly commending the programme rationale for being 'grounded in the emerging criminological evidence of the risk factors that increase the likelihood of offending and "what works" in addressing those factors' (Morgan Harris Burrows 2003: 15).

- *Programme delivery or 'doability'* – there was an alleged 'implementation failure' across the programme due to certain YIPs failing to routinely maintain records of 'at risk' young people and a paucity of evidence that YIPs interventions were directly addressing the risk factors identified.

- *Programme impact or 'testability'* – the possibility of 'measurement failure' was rejected on the basis that the scope of data concerning the top 50 young people had improved year-on-year and that recording personal characteristics (e.g. risk factors) and measuring intervention outcomes 'offers a huge potential to determine 'what works' in reducing crime and other antisocial behaviour' (Morgan Harris Burrows 2003: 18).

The evaluators' main conclusion accorded with the YIP's foundations in developmental RFR and the programme's faith in risk-focused early intervention, stating that that the key 'drivers of success' in YIPs neighbourhoods were 'identifying the most 'at risk' young people [and running] tailored and intensive interventions that directly address the risk factors of the young people involved' (Morgan Harris Burrows 2003: 138). However assistant and partial evidence from the evaluation simply does not support such a conclusion. Furthermore, the evaluators failed to even acknowledge the methodological invalidity of using *Onset* with existing offenders (YIPs target young people at risk of either offending or reoffending), in contradiction of the tool's (albeit sparse) evidential basis in RFR that identified risk factors for initial offending in order to target risk-focused interventions on the prevention of offending onset.

Onset *and* RFR: *reductionism, imputation and ambiguity*

Taken together, the *Onset* risk assessment process and the evaluations of the YISP and YIP programmes that it has underpinned have demonstrated much of the same methodological weakness and misapplication of RFR as *Asset*, which is unsurprising because *Onset* was essentially created to be *Asset's* little brother. For example, like its older sibling, *Onset* has embodied a reductionism of approach that has limited measurement of the complexity of risk (by using factorisation) and required imputation of the nature (e.g. the presence, direction, probability) of the risk–offending relationship because risk factors have been measured for young people who have yet to (and may never) of will offend. Therefore, *Onset* risk assessment has also mirrored *Asset* in its crude factorisation of risk and the developmental and psychosocial biases that have underpinned interpretations of the predictive influence and temporal precedence of risk over offending.

In *Onset's* defence, however, the risk factors it measures do, at least, reflect more closely those of the original RFR (e.g. the Cambridge Study) on which the instrument was based, as these original risk factors were identified for the onset of offending (rather than for reconviction, as is the case with *Asset*). Furthermore, the original risk factors were identified in childhood at ages that are broadly comparable with the age of young people who complete *Onset* (i.e. 8–10 year olds in the Cambridge Study compared to mainly 8–13 year-olds in *Onset*). As a defence of *Onset*, however, the strength of these arguments is mitigated by the extent to which RFR has actually established that certain factors are actually risks of/predictors of later delinquency in a statistical sense. Furthermore, the original risk factors were said to be predictive in a developmental sense (i.e. that childhood risk factors predict adolescent offending).

The predictive utility and accuracy of *Onset* risk factors and is therefore of the tool itself, has been assumed (imputed from previous RFR) rather than established (e.g. through evaluation of the tool), despite the YJB's insistence that all aspects of youth justice practice be 'evidence-based'. In this case, it appears that historical evidence from previous (not entirely compatible) RFR will suffice, rather than direct evidence that young people assessed as high risk by *Onset* actually progress to become offenders. The available evaluations of YISP and YIP have, however, demonstrated a developmental bias and imputation of efficacy that has created a self-serving evidence base for *Onset*. For example, the evaluators of YIP concluded that the programme and the use of *Onset* risk assessment were 'strongly grounded in the research evidence identifying the major correlates of offending behaviour by young people' (Morgan Harris Burrows 2003: 4–5). However, correlation does not indicate prediction, nor does it indicate that the onset of exposure to risk factors predates the onset of offending, which itself would indicate a predictive relationship between the two. Neither the (inconsistent) empirical evidence from programme evaluations, nor (sparse) empirical evidence from previous RFR, constitute a valid basis for the risk-focused early intervention approach embodied in *Onset*. Furthermore, the evaluators of YIP chose to attribute the less than impressive evaluation results to implementation failure, rather than to concede (or even to consider) that the developmental theoretical basis of *Onset* may be either at fault or inappropriate/invalid for measuring current risk factors amongst a more demographically-diverse (than the original RFR) population of young people. Instead, the evaluators assumed that their original developmental 'theory of change' (i.e. that risk factors predict offending and can thus be ameliorated by risk-focused intervention) was valid.

The YIP evaluation was supposed to provide an independent assessment and new evidence. The fact that the evidence did not fit the paradigm meant that the evaluators 'had to' situate their findings back into a paradigm they were supposed to be evaluating. A similarly self-fulfilling process was evident in the YISP evaluation. The limited and unrepresentative nature of the quantitative data collected was reconciled by the self-fulfilling conclusion that psychosocial risk factors were the key drivers of referral, with no acknowledgement that this was inevitable due to the psychosocial basis of the *Onset* referral form. The qualitative interview element of the evaluation perpetuated the psychosocial bias by confining its questions to parents and children to asking about risk in psychosocial domains. It comes as little surprise, therefore, that the evaluation was able to identify psychosocial risk factors for offending and to conclude that *Onset* and YISP were working in the most important risk areas, as identified by referrers, parents and children.

Onset has taken the YJB's uncritical acceptance of the developmental determinism of risk factors to new heights by widening the net of risk in which young people can be caught by the YJS to earlier and earlier ages and more behaviours that are not considered to be offences. *Onset* has become part of a complex that allows politicians, policy makers and practitioners to conclude definitively that exposure to certain specific risk factors prior to any offending behaviour will inevitably lead (crash test dummy-like) young people into offending unless certain risk-specific and risk-focused preventative intervention is put into place at an early stage in the child's life and/or early in their predicted pathway into offending. The positive conclusions from the evaluations of programmes underpinned by *Onset* have been eagerly adopted by politicians and policy makers, whilst the tentative nature of these conclusions and their accompanying methodological caveats have been overlooked. For example, the evaluators of YISP concluded that:

establishing causality between risk factors and offending behaviour has been difficult and, until recently, there has been limited

> understanding about the relationship of both risk and protective factors with later criminal or antisocial behaviour, and about the concept of risk itself. (Walker *et al.* 2007: 47)

> it is a considerable leap from assessing risk to being able to predict the future offending or antisocial behaviour. (Walker *et al.* 2007: 50)

If indeed the causal and predictive nature of the risk-factor–offending relationship remains only partially understood and largely imputed, then the promotion of risk-focused intervention on the basis of limited data addressing a limited body of poorly-understood factors would seem, at the very least, inadvisable. The YISP evaluation in particular has highlighted a common weakness within RFR: the drawing of definitive conclusions and recommending risk-based responses to youth offending on the basis of indefinite understandings of the central concepts (e.g. risk) and relationships (e.g. risk-offending, risk-focused intervention-offending) being targeted and the probable efficacy of this targeting.

Risk assessment by youth justice agencies has been presented as a coordinated and homogenised process utilising standardised methodologies and analyses to inform standardised forms of risk-focused intervention. However, the emergence of *Onset* as a tool of risk-focused early intervention has highlighted heterogeneous evidential bases and interpretations of the risk–offending relationship (i.e. developmental RFR) between the different risk assessment tools of the YJS, although this heterogeneity has been seldom acknowledged or addressed. The use of risk assessment to inform *early* risk-focused intervention activity has been underpinned by RFR (e.g. notably the Cambridge Study) that conducted statistical comparisons between offenders and non-offenders from the same general population. In contrast, *Asset* risk assessment has targeted risk factors for known offenders and informed clinical intervention/ treatment responses to prevent reoffending/reconviction. However, the risk factors for initial offending (measured in *Onset*) and the risk factors for subsequent reoffending/reconviction (measured in *Asset*) are not necessarily equivalent, yet risk assessment in the YJS has drawn on the same 'established' body of risk factors and RFR theories/strands to populate both instruments, interpreting and applying this RFR in equivalent ways in both tools. The potential incompatibilities between the risk factors for the onset of delinquency and those for reconviction have been brought into sharp focus by Farrington's assertion that whilst the retrospective prediction of offending (by known offenders) has been generally effective, so prospective prediction (of future offending by non-offenders) has been disappointing (Farrington *et al.* 2007). Therefore, compatibility of *Onset* with the content and purpose of its big brother *Asset* and the purported 'evidence base' of the prospective risk assessment tools of *Onset* and *Asset* has been questionable at the very least.

The multiple identities of the Onset early intervention process

Risk-focused early intervention driven by risk assessment is a nascent process within the YJS of England and Wales. Detailed scrutiny of risk-focused early intervention in the YJS unveils a series of ambiguities of definition and purpose that suggest an internal heterogeneity and contested nature that belies the confidence and definitiveness with which the government has championed this 'evidence-based' preventative approach. The extent to which the *Onset* risk assessment process has fed into the development of multiple personalities and foci for risk-focused early intervention in the YJS raises a series of issues such as:

- should risk-focused early intervention be targeted early in life or early in the pathway to offending (e.g. early in the development of risk factors)?

- should practitioners simply target early childhood risk factors and uncritically assume that these factors will have a deterministic influence on future offending unless they are addressed?

- should risk-focused early intervention be activated when young people show early indicators of risk (when they are 'high risk') or just before they develop these risk factors (e.g. when they may be 'at risk' or even 'at risk of risk')?

- should risk-focused early intervention be related to risk, age, behaviour or all of these? Consequently, are offenders eligible for risk-focused early intervention?

The concept, foci, objectives and methodologies of risk-focused early intervention have formed a movable feast. The evaluation of early intervention-based RFR and risk assessment has been fraught with difficulties because their identities, objectives and methodologies have been frequently ambiguous, amorphous and multi-faceted. What *has* been clear is that young people who have received interventions following *Onset* risk profiling have been unashamedly targeted on the basis of what they might do or what practitioners have judged them (statistically) likely to do, rather than what they have actually done, thus providing an artificial and self-fulfilling evidence base to support the aims of 'nipping crime in the bud' and being 'tough on the causes of crime'. Critical commentators have claimed that, in contrast to its espoused positive, commonsense goals, risk-focused early intervention has actually encouraged a pessimistic and fatalistic view of certain young people as 'high risk', 'at risk' and inevitably 'pre-criminal' (see Goldson 2005). This has allegedly engendered the pigeonholing of youth populations in order to control them through net widening and exposure to a series of predetermined interventions (see Goldson and Muncie 2006).

It is not, however, argued that early intervention in general is ineffective or unwarranted, nor that improving the quality of life for very young children is a bad thing. Indeed, there are numerous potential benefits to health, wellbeing, quality of life, access to opportunities etc of prosocial approaches that promote positive behaviour. However, what *is* asserted is that the link between *risk-focused* early intervention (at a very early age) and crime prevention is both far from proven and extremely difficult to confidently conclude from extant RFR, despite the definitiveness of governmental policy and practice in this area. The lack of supportive evidence for risk-focused early intervention has been brought into sharp focus by the public distancing by David Farrington and David Utting from previous definitive conclusions about the predictive utility of risk assessment focused on risk of offending onset:

> any notion that screening can enable policy makers to identify young children destined to join the 5 per cent of offenders responsible for 50–60 per cent of crime is fanciful. Even if there were no ethical objections to putting 'potential delinquent' labels round the necks of young children, there would continue to be statistical barriers . . . This demonstrates the dangers of assuming that antisocial five year olds are the criminals or drug abusers of tomorrow. (Sutton *et al.* 2004: 5)

Onset risk assessment replicates and animates the methodological problems of RFR at a number of levels; not only is the process based on another instrument (*Asset*) that demonstrates significant methodological (and theoretical) weaknesses, but this foundation instrument was itself based on original research that was critically flawed in a number of ways (e.g. due to over-simplification, imputation, determinism, psychosocial bias, scant evidence base). As such, *Onset* has updated, broadened and further engrained the mis-application of RFR within the youth justice process.

The new 'new youth justice': from risk assessment to the Scaled Approach

Such is the faith of the YJB in the results and conclusions of RFR and the *Asset* and *Onset* tools which have been based upon them, that it has sought to both broaden and deepen the extent to which risk assessment and risk focused interventions dominate youth justice policy and practice. This process began in 2002, when the YJB started to produce a series of Key Elements of Effective Practice to promote a consistent, 'evidence-based' approach to 'essential elements of practice with all young people at all stages of the Youth Justice System' (YJB 2003: 6). These key elements of effective practice consist of guidance manuals covering diverse aspects of youth justice practice and, to date, include: education, training and employment, mental health, substance use, young people who sexually abuse, offending behaviour programmes, parenting, restorative justice, mentoring, targeted neighbourhood prevention, final warning interventions, swift administration of justice, Intensive Surveillance and Supervision Programmes and custody and resettlement (http://www.yjb.gov.uk/ publications). Each guide has been produced by ECOTEC Research and Consulting Limited, largely in partnership with Nottingham Trent University. They all draw heavily on the 'what works' approach; a 'scientific', experimental basis for evaluating the robustness and 'effectiveness' of crime prevention interventions based on comparisons of intervention effects between control and recipient groups (see also Stephenson *et al.* 2007). It is important to recognise, however, that these guides form part of a system that links risk-focused assessment with risk-focused interventions and that this system is bound together by the central Key Element of Effective Practice (KEEP): *Assessment, Planning Interventions and Supervision*, which prescribes 'foundation activities which guide and shape all work with young people who offend' (YJB 2003: 6). *Assessment, Planning Interventions and Supervision* (APIS) was presented by the YJB as crucial to the successful execution of each of the other KEEPs. In order to fulfil the requirements of APIS to target effective services and interventions on assessed risk, the YJB prioritised 'dependable methods for analysing the risks that individuals will continue to commit crime, and for recognising the criminogenic needs that interventions should address' (YJB 2003: 5). These 'dependable methods' are now synonymous with the *Asset* and *Onset* risk assessment instruments.

APIS is far more than a manual for good practice and guide to risk assessment: it is an embedded system of practice management from which practitioners cannot (easily) deviate because it is the KEEP that underpins:

- practitioner training (both in-house YOT training and the foundation degree in youth justice run by the Open University and sponsored by the YJB);

- the Effective Practice Quality Assurance Framework with which 'practitioners audit their own performance within a framework of evidence-based practice' (Stephenson *et al.* 2007: 5); and, most importantly;

- the National Standards for Youth Justice Services, which set out 'the minimum expectations of staff and managers in the youth justice system' (YJB 2004: 19).

The managerialism, preventative ethos and risk-focus of APIS, the KEEPs and risk assessment in the YJS, embody a new 'new youth justice' (see

Goldson 2000) that has culminated in what is known as the scaled approach to youth justice: an approach which prescribes the level and type of intervention given to young people following risk assessment.

Youth Justice: the Scaled Approach

In their follow-up to *Misspent Youth*, entitled *Youth Justice 2004*, the Audit Commission concluded that 'YOTs should make better use of *Asset* to determine the amount as well as the nature of interventions with individuals using a scaled approach' (Audit Commission 2004: point 142). The report noted that such a risk-led approach had been hampered by practitioners lacking understanding in how to utilise *Asset* information. A subsequent inspection of YOTs consolidated this concern by stating that 'most YOTs had still to adopt a proportionate approach in working with the more vulnerable or challenging groups' (HMIP 2006: 25). The HMIP supported this criticism with the assertion that an insufficient number of YOT practitioners adequately link the results of risk assessments to the interventions that follow. As a response to these criticisms of youth justice practice, the YJB revised the National Standards for Youth Justice Services to incorporate the new *Scaled Approach* to intervention. The *Scaled Approach* involves 'tailoring the intensity of intervention to the assessment' (YJB 2007b: 4). It is intended to improve practice in relation to the completion of *Asset*, the writing of pre-sentence reports and intervention planning. Therefore, the *Scaled Approach* exemplifies the YJB's unflinching faith in *Asset* and risk-focused intervention as the most effective method of reducing reoffending; as a method of managing YOTs and their staff; and as the method for improving the quality of practice.

The *Scaled Approach* is to be a formal, explicit method of linking *Asset*-based assessed risk to: (1) the intensity of intervention deemed necessary and (2) the type of intervention to be provided. Details of how the *Scaled Approach* is intended to work in practice have been placed in the public domain by the YJB. In the *Scaled Approach*, practitioners use a total risk score (out of 64) comprised of scores (0–4) from the 12 *Asset* domains combined with the total scores from four static factors scored in the following way:

- *Offence type*: motoring offences/vehicle theft/unauthorised taking=4, burglary domestic and nondomestic=3, other offence=0.

- *Age at first Reprimand/Caution/Warning*: 10 to 12=4, 13 to 17=2, no previous reprimand/caution/warning=0.

- *Age at first conviction*: 10 to 13=4, 14 to 17=3, no previous convictions=0.

- *Number of previous convictions*: 4 or more = 4, 1 to 3 = 3, no previous convictions = 0.

(YJB 2009: 19)

The total risk score is then linked to a risk category/level: 'standard' (0–14), 'enhanced' (15–32) or 'intensive' (33–64). This risk category determines the level of 'risk of reoffending' exhibited by a young person and determines the type of intervention they receive in terms of:

- the *sentence* that the practitioner proposes to the court;

- the proposed *frequency of contact* between the practitioner in the first three months of the order (e.g. two contacts for low risk young people, four contacts for medium risk and 12 contacts for high-risk);

- the *content* of the intervention (i.e. the precise nature of the risk-focused interventions).

The *Scaled Approach* underpins a new sentencing framework for young offenders, headlined by the *Youth Rehabilitation Order*, a generic order to replace the plethora of community sentences currently available, which embodies 'a more targeted and tailored approach to interventions because there will no longer be a tiered set of orders through which a repeat offender would progress' (YJB 2007b: 4). The *Scaled Approach* is intended to improve the completion and utilisation of *Asset* with a view to enabling YOTs and YOT practitioners to more appropriately target their time and resources and to more effectively tailor interventions to individual risks (YJB 2009). For example, young people assessed as 'high risk' of reoffending will be subject to more intensive intervention and supervision than those measured at low risk (equivalent to refer 'standard' rating). The *Scaled Approach* reflects the youth justice principle of effective practice known as 'risk classification' – matching the level and intensity and type of interventions to the assessed seriousness of offending and the risk of reoffending (McGuire 1995).

The Scaled Approach: potential pitfalls

The *Scaled Approach* reflects and consolidates the extent to which the government in England and Wales has bought into developmental, deterministic readings of risk at the expense of theoretical explanations from other strands of RFR. The government is clearly of the view that psychosocial risk factors are the key (causal and predictive) influences on youth offending and should therefore form the focus of early and preventative interventions with young people in the YJS. However, very little robust evidence has been forthcoming from RFR to support the validity of risk-focused intervention and its applicability to all young people in the YJS (i.e. pre-offenders, offenders, re-offenders) in the present day. Such a lack of evidence effectively renders risk assessment and the *Scaled Approach* to be evidence-based practice without an actual evidence base. What makes the *Scaled Approach* different and an up-grading from previous approaches is the way in which APIS links risk assessment (however spurious) with predetermined risk-focused interventions and a specified intensity of intervention. Consequently, there are a number of methodological issues attendant to the introduction of the *Scaled Approach*, including:

- *Evidence-based practice?* – some may argue that the *Scaled Approach* offers nothing new to the context of existing practice within YOTs (i.e. practitioners are already doing it), except for even more prescriptive guidance around the risk-focused intervention that should follow from risk assessment; intervention that has a dubious validity in the evidence-base of extant RFR. Therefore, regardless of personal beliefs, professional knowledge, experience or conclusive evidence of a causal link between either risk factors and offending or risk-focused interventions and reductions in offending, the introduction of the *Scaled Approach* will further compel YOT practitioners to accept and work within this (risk factor prevention) paradigm as if it were evidence-based.

- *Disproportionate intervention* – young people may slip through the cracks of the approach or be criminalised by it. For example, serious offenders who measure as low risk following risk assessment may receive a minimal level of intervention, as intervention levels must be matched to demonstrable risk, yet this is unlikely to be in the interests of any party involved (e.g. offender, victim, practitioner, community, the YJB seeking reductions in youth offending). Conversely, a minor, one-off offender may receive intensive intervention if they are assessed to be high risk of reoffending, even though such intervention (possibly excessive in relation to the actual offence) may inadvertently stigmatise and criminalise that young person or, indeed, amplify their delinquency. The YJB has acknowledged this possibility in the *Scaled Approach* guidance by cautioning that 'practitioners should review the intervention level in the context of all other available information and consider whether there are any factors that indicate the intervention level may need to be increased or decreased' (YJB 2007b: 7) – a process known as 'having your cake and eating it'. In reality, however, the *Scaled Approach* heralds a more rigid matching of intervention to assessed risk level (compared to what has gone before) and tighter control of youth justice practice.

- *Exacerbating the identity crisis of risk assessment* – the main objective of the forthcoming approach has yet to be clarified with regards to whether it intends to reduce offending, reoffending or reconviction, whether it is to be more focused on reducing the *risk* of offending, reoffending or reconviction, whether there will be an equivalent or subsidiary focus on reducing the risk of serious harm and the risk of vulnerability, or whether the approach will be sufficiently broad to address all of these concerns.

The potential practicality and validity of the *Scaled Approach* in the YJS must be seriously evaluated, especially in view of the extent to which it could perpetuate and exacerbate the RFR-based methodological weaknesses of YJS risk assessment and its application within the RFPP (e.g. lack of evidence-base, developmental bias); themselves exacerbations of a methodologically-poor body of original RFR.

Misguided interventionism? Creating a non-evidence-based evidence base

there was no evidence that the [risk-focused] treatment program had deflected people from committing crimes. (McCord 1978: 286)

The *Scaled Approach* rests on the assumption that 'dynamic' risk factors are amenable to change by well-placed criminal justice policy and practice (Hannah-Moffat 2005). However, this central premise of the YJB's model of risk assessment, the *Scaled Approach* and the use of risk-focused youth justice interventions contradicts the conclusions offered by the pioneers of developmental RFR (Glueck and Glueck 1930) and developmental crime prevention (Cabot 1940; Bottoms and McClintock 1973; McCord 1978); all of whom found that young people grow out of crime and that there was no significant positive effect of early, risk-focused intervention on the risk of offending. Indeed, others have found that risk-focused youth justice interventions may even 'risk damaging the individuals they are designed to assist' (McCord 1978: 289; see also McAra and McVie 2007). The *Scaled Approach* offers an example, therefore, of an 'evidence-based', risk-focused approach that has been empirically-grounded in studies that refuted the need for, and efficacy of, risk-focused early intervention.

The *Scaled Approach* exemplifies the uncritical adoption of a particular reading of the findings and conclusions from developmental RFR. This lack of criticality and lack of understanding of RFR is the result of policy and strategy being politically-driven and set by government, yet handed over to others for implementation, such as civil servants from government departments or quasi-civil servants in agencies like the YJB for implementation. These 'half-experts' have pursued the *Scaled Approach* with an over-inflated and unjustified certainty about risk – having been fed a diet of simplified and partial, yet definitive, conclusions from flawed RFR which they have then turned into 'hard scientific fact'. Denied the right and opportunity for critical and reflective thought by their 'employer', they have driven the YJS and young people (as crash test dummy recipients of interventions) in the dark irrepressibly towards an unknown destination. Quantified risk factors have been readily translated into amenable targets for intervention to satisfy the managerialist demands of politicians and policy makers for practical, pragmatic, easily measurable and interpretable results (see also Muncie 2004). However, the lack of evidence and understanding from RFR of the risk–offending relationship has limited researchers, politicians, policy-makers and practitioners to extrapolating or hypothesising reasons for associations between certain factors and offending, therefore having to impute explanations of how risk-focused interventions may 'work' to prevent and reduce offending. If the extant 'evidence-base' cannot tell us how risk factors work, how these factors may precipitate youth offending or how the programmes they underpin actually reduce offending, subsequent research conclusions and 'evidence-based' policies and practices are built on sand (Case 2006).

Risk assessment: the methodological fallacy

The risk assessment of young people within the YJS has perpetrated and perpetuated a methodological fallacy. The purpose of this risk assessment has been to identify risk factors as suitable targets for interventions that can be 'tough on the causes of crime' and which can 'nip crime in the bud'. However, the risk factors identified through risk assessment have not been 'causes' or developmental 'predictors' and have lacked explanatory capability. Confident conclusions have made no concession to the degree of imputation required to draw explanatory conclusions regarding what are essentially correlates with offending, nor have they accounted for the definitional ambiguities of the measures of offending used, the inherent psychosocial bias of the risk measures or the inappropriate application of developmental RFR findings within risk assessment tools. The result has been a practice context in which the gloss of science and the standards of practice prescribed by the YJB (e.g. National Standards, KEEP) have beguiled and pressurised practitioners into imputing causality and making subjective, restricted and under-informed guesses about the influence of risk factors and the potential benefits of risk-focused interventions. Far from avoiding the pitfalls of actuarial and clinical processes, risk assessment in the YJS has embraced the limitations of both – the aggregated, deindividualised and prescriptive nature of actuarial justice and the subjective nature of clinical judgements. A limited understanding of risk has been perpetuated by risk assessment – one which has exploited a 'spurious scientificity' (Horsfield 2003) and which has privileged developmental explanations of offending, the influence of psychosocial risk factors and the utility of measuring risk factors as clinical variables, at the expense of a broader and more detailed exploration of risk constructions, mechanisms, processes and socio-structural factors that could incorporate explanations from other strands of RFR. The government agenda for practical and malleable targets for intervention has encouraged a rampant reductionism of the complexities of risk. The 'oversimplified technical fix' to a complex social reality (Stephenson *et al.* 2007) demanded by risk assessment and the *Scaled Approach* has stripped away the dynamism, life-force, nuance and immeasurable complexities of risk. Most importantly, the *Scaled Approach* to youth justice relies on an evidence-based that is at odds with the imputation that risk factors in the current lives of adolescents can be ameliorated through risk-focused interventions.

Risk assessment: from methodological fallacy to governmentality

(a) new industry of early intervention based on an ideology of 'risk' ... has become a tool of governmentality in the lives of young people. (Armstrong 2004: 102)

Some commentators have argued that risk assessment and risk-focused intervention have been exploited by the government to enable them (e.g. through making youth justice practitioners adhere to a prescribed evidence base) to measure, manage and control the lives of young people (see Goldson 2005). Risk-focused early intervention in particular has been criticised for widening the net of influence held by the state and the YJS (see O'Malley and Hutchinson 2007; Garland 2002). Risk assessment and the subsequent targeting of interventions may, for example, contravene the privacy, liberty and rights of the young people who receive them. Young people could become burdened by (actuarial) risk assessment because they live in circumstances that correlate highly with acts of offending (e.g. living in a 'high risk' neighbourhood) and are in a weak political position to resist classification (Silver and Miller 2002). This may lead to the marginalising, stigmatising and stereotyping of young people, who may already be disadvantaged and disaffected (economically, educationally, politically) – placing an unjustified 'scientific stamp' on the public's prejudice and fear (Silver and Miller 2002). However, in reality, a high-risk neighbourhood (e.g. a YIP area) is unlikely to contain only high-risk individuals, whilst high-risk young people (e.g. YISP participants) do not inevitably go on to offend. Therefore, there is an inherent danger that targeted interventions 'can exacerbate negative perceptions of particular areas or groups' (Percy-Smith 2000: 18), thus stigmatising and criminalising children and young people (and their families) by labelling them as 'potential offenders' and 'high risk' for the purpose of targeting interventions – the classic self-fulfilling prophecy. Risk-focused early interventions, inflicted on young people 'for their own good', have been viewed as widening the interventionist net and seeking to justify an

303

increasingly proactive, intensive and invasive approach with children and young people, families and communities (R. Smith 2003). A related criticism concerns how criminalisation processes (e.g. the individualisation of risk and the responsibilisation of young people by the government) and socio-structural risk factors (e.g. broken home, unemployment) have been inappropriately analysed and tackled without regard to policies which are class- and gender-biased nature of government policies (Cuneen and White 2006). Instead, the government has preferred to individualise risk, individualise interventions and thus absolve themselves of any responsibility for constructing and exacerbating youth offending and the risks that young people face in their daily lives.

Risks over rights

The YJS was once informed by the theoretical and ethical concerns of welfare, justice and (to a lesser extent) children's rights. This same YJS is now defined by risk. Policy and practice is underpinned by the assessment of risk and the planning of interventions to prevent and reduce this risk; an actuarial phenomena that has swept beyond YJS into the domains of social exclusion, health and access to employment (Sharland 2006). The use of risk assessment tools and the introduction of the *Scaled Approach* to risk-focused intervention has meant that:

> Children and their families are then constructed as repositories of risk factors, with predetermined risk trajectories ripe for intervention. (Kemshall 2008: 26)

For all methodological and political intents and purposes, children and young people in England and Wales who come into contact with the YJS have been defined and responded to in terms of the risk they present – the risk of offending (measured by *Onset*), reoffending, reconviction (measured by *Asset*), harming themselves and harming others. The identification of so-called 'predictive' factors has provided the evidence-base used to justify the YJB proselytising of risk-focused early, preventative interventions. The *Scaled Approach* formalises the explicit proportionality expected between risk assessment scores and the levels of intervention demanded from youth justice practitioners. This emphasis on risk serves the master of *prevention*; new Labour's 'third Way' approach to youth justice that has subsumed and supplanted more principled welfare and justice concerns in favour of 'nipping crime in the bud'. According to Kemshall:

> This approach has proved attractive because it appears to promise a more effective focus for policy, better targeting of programmes and

practitioner resources, and the emphasis on prevention is seen as both morally and economically desirable for dealing with youth crime. (Kemshall 2008: 24)

But what of the *rights* of children and young people to participate in and contribute to the processes by which they are defined and which inform the way they are treated? Moreover, what of their rights to full and equal participation in society and access to the opportunities that can foster positive outcomes? Risk-focused (early) intervention has been legitimated using evidence from RFR and applied in risk assessment instruments, but with scant regard for due process or the presence of an actual illegal behaviour, in contravention of several of the provisions of the UN Convention on the Rights of the Child (see Goldson 2003). This process, according to some, has criminalised child welfare and young people, ignored due process and subverted the legal tenet of innocent until proven guilty (see Goldson 2005). The use of risk as the normative touchstone for youth justice practice has, for some critical commentators (e.g. Goldson 2003), encouraged a deficit-focused, exclusionary, dehumanising, deindividualising and pessimistic view of young people as potential offenders/reoffenders – who must then be subjected to individualised, responsibilising risk-focused interventions 'for their own good'.

What civil servants have been acutely aware of, however, has been the managerialist governmental demand for accountable, measurable, quality assured and evidence-based methods of preventing youth offending that are efficient, effective and economical. APIS and the *Scaled Approach* enables government to control and manage YOT practice (in terms of what can and cannot be done to young people) in ways not previously possible or available (see also Haines and Drakeford 1998). The use of *Asset* and the results of evaluations of the instrument have shaped the debate about the causes and treatment of offending by young people. Goldson and Muncie (2006) have asserted that by uncritically accepting the statistical relationships between risk factors and measures of offending as uncomplicated, policy-makers conveniently avoid addressing the 'thematic complexities' of youth justice such as issues of welfare, justice, rights and punitiveness. It is as if 'instead, intervention is triggered by assessment, discretion and the spurious logic of prediction and actuarialism' (Goldson 2005: 264).

Risk assessment in the YJS has functioned as a self-fulfilling exercise to perpetuate a narrow, technical and deterministic understanding of psychosocial risk factors that are allegedly amenable to change through intervention, thus enabling the government to be seen to be addressing the youth crime 'problem'. However, because government understandings of youth offending have privileged quantitative, developmental risk, the 'myth' of the young person as crash test dummy hurtling towards pre-determined outcomes has become accepted uncritically by policy-

makers and has attained historical and cultural dominance as an explanation of youth offending in England and Wales (see Haw 2007).

The Government's use of evidence from research and practice to
underpin their risk-focused agenda for policy and practice (reflected in the
promotion and valorisation of risk assessment and the *Scaled Approach*)
has been lambasted as selective and uncritical, often employed to merely
confirm predetermined policy (D. Smith 2006; Muncie 2004; Wilcox 2003).
According to Bateman and Pitts (2005), findings from RFR and results
from risk assessments in the YJS have been selected primarily to fulfil
'psephologically-derived' policy goals, to both respond to and manipulate
politically driven objectives, rather than on the basis of the explanatory
power or practical efficacy of the RFR. There is a 'danger of regarding risk
assessment as a neutral, value-free, technical operation' (Haines and
Drakeford 1998: 217), whilst ignoring the moral overtones and punitive
political rhetoric. The Government's have been criticised for their un-
swerving support (demonstrated in policy formation, dissemination of
'effective' practice and funding for research) of a risk-focused, evidence-
based approach to youth offending centred on the technical, systematic
assessment of an established body of psychosocial risk factors (see D.
Smith 2006; Goldson and Muncie 2006; Pitts 2003a). Although such an
approach has undoubtedly proven to be readily comprehensible to
practitioners and the voting public, thus is practically-, financially- and
politically-convenient, it has also been selective about the evidence it has
created and unrealistic about the utility of this evidence. Some critics have
claimed that the Government has commissioned much (risk factor)
research in order to fulfil strategic, pre-existing policy objectives, what
France and Utting (2005) have defined as 'policy-based evidence', and that
the findings and conclusions of RFR have been subsequently interpreted,
disseminated and employed in a selective and self-fulfilling (rather than
evidence-based) manner by the government (Armstrong 2004).

Conclusion: risk assessment in the Youth Justice System – application without understanding

There is a basic commonsense logic to the research, policy and practice
implications of RFR The link is simple (if somewhat unsophisticated) –
once you have identified the factors that are statistically shown to be
causal or predictive of offending behaviour it then becomes a straightforward matter of changing those factors to change future or current
behaviour. This intuitive link between RFR and its policy and practice
correlates has been widely accepted and hugely influential in the YJS.
However, commonsense and intuition are extremely dangerous processes,
particularly when they are applied to highly complex and technical
research that has, in actuality, offered a limited, partial and imputed

'understanding' of risk (factors) and its relationship to offending. There-fore, a leap of faith has been required (although not acknowledged) to reach the conclusion that if risk factors are targeted and changed then the outcome (offending) can also be changed. The inherent ambiguities and incongruities of risk assessment in the YJS, combined with the method-ological weaknesses (e.g. factorisation, aggregation) that these processes have perpetrated and perpetuated, problematise the entire risk assessment exercise. The leap of faith required to execute such an uncritical, indefinitive and erroneous application of RFR findings to contemporary youth populations has been, consequently, more a leap of *blind* faith. Unfortunately, the over-zealous and ill-informed politicians and civil servants who have championed the use of risk assessment in the YJS have yet to realise that they are blind. It appears that politicians, policy makers, practitioners and risk factor researchers do not properly understand the risk assessment machine they have created. Risk assessment in the YJS of England and Wales has been partial in its choice and understanding of the RFR that forms its basis and partial in the understandings of the risk–offending relationship that it has been able to garner through its crude reductionist methods and analyses. The risk factors identified in national and international RFR and transported into policy and practice, particularly in England and Wales, have been depicted as if they have been identified 'objectively' through the appliance of science and that they are allegedly amenable to treatment in order to either prevent, reduce or cure delinquency. However, the positivistic and developmental empirical foundations of RFR and the privileging of artefact RFR have largely dictated what risk factors have been explored and how they have been understood. The 'objective' measurement, analysis and interpretation of ostensibly treatable risk factors that have underpinned the evidence-base for risk assessment and the *Scaled Approach* have been, in reality, prescribed by the YJB's selective, subjective and misinformed reading of RFR, that risk factors have a deterministic and/or predictive influence on offending or that this deterministic influence can actually be treated, and founded on scant empirical evidence that risk-focused early interventions actually 'work'. This has not only imbued risk assessment in the YJS with a degree of theoretical and methodological subjectivity but it has also led to the promotion (and widespread adoption) of a very restricted, yet poorly understood, model of delinquency causation and treatment. This is of particular concern because the developmentalists who have driven RFR (e.g. the Gluecks, Cabot, Farrington, Rutter, Thornberry, Hawkins) have seldom demonstrated that risk factors are actually either (1) really risk factors for offending at all and (2) that they are amenable to intervention with predictable and explicable results. Government claims that risk-focused policy and practice in the YJS have been 'evidence-based' have been founded and perpetuated on a narrow, partial, pseudoscientific misrepresentation and misapplication of the 'evidence' of risk and its relationship with offending (see Case 2007; Pitts 2003a). As a consequence, youth justice practitioners in England and Wales are required to conduct risk assessments, execute risk-focused interventions and impute definitive conclusions that exposure to risk factors leads to offending, despite a paucity of robust evidence that:

- risk factors are in any way precursors or causes of offending behaviour (as opposed to simple indicators or predictors of reporting offending in the future);

- prescribed interventions can change the level of risk experienced and presented by young people;

- risk-based interventions have any relationship at all to the prevention, reduction or treatment of youth offending.

Therefore, the situation has arisen whereby the espoused practical benefits of risk assessment and the *Scaled Approach* have been pursued in the YJS through an over-simplified and poorly-understood (mis)application of RFR findings at the expense of exploring a far more complex and abstract, but potentially more complete understanding of how risk may operate and may influence behaviour. The major concern with the mis-application of RFR is that these original findings were themselves partial and of dubious methodological robustness and validity, thus rendering the bedrock of youth justice practice little more than a set of methodologically-flawed, theoretically-biased and evidentially-sparse processes of questionable explanatory utility.

Chapter 7

Revisiting risk factor research, policy and practice

Risk factor research has achieved hegemony as a scientific, predictable and evidence-led foundation for policy, practice and research relating to the 'youth problem'. The much-vaunted advantages of RFR have centred on its use of positivistic, scientific, technical, clinical methodologies to produce universally-replicable and generalisable findings about how 'risk factors' *predict* offending, delinquency and antisocial behaviour by young people and the amenability of these factors to manipulation via practical, commonsense risk-focused interventions. The simplistic and readily understandable findings from RFR have become embedded in policy addressing youth problems, particularly youth offending and particularly in England and Wales (France and Homel 2006). By dint of its political appeal and claims to produce 'scientific fact' (France 2008), RFR has been effectively used to screen out other potential explanations of the aetiology of young people's social problems and other potential responses to it (see Bessant *et al.* 2003).

The hegemonic edifice of RFR, however, has masked an heterogeneity of approaches and methodological differences. RFR has been and continues to be diverse, both theoretically (although most theories have used developmentalism as their normative touchstone) and methodologically. However, these differences have been under-explained and under-explored in the literature and their consequences for explanations of youth offending and responses to it have remained hidden. This problem has been exacerbated by the (sometimes unjustified) claims of risk factor researchers and the uncritical, unequivocal adoption of over-simplified conclusions from RFR by politicians, policy makers and practitioners. Indeed, Laub (2006) has argued that RFR offers a prime example of how criminologists can ignore 'key facts' that run contrary to their own theoretical predilections and biases. Within RFR, different theories/

strands have struggled for explanatory supremacy and have attempted to achieve 'institutional hegemony by imposing their research agenda' (Laub 2006: 248). Yet this debate has been more private than public and the end result has been an unthinking and uncritical widespread adoption of narrow developmental risk factors first identified by the Gluecks and popularised by Farrington, without any proper understanding of this bias and the implications for both research and practice.

Armstrong (2004) has argued strongly that the unproblematic 'solutions' to the social problem of youth offending that have been provided by RFR have not only been theoretically-biased but also have been (in England and Wales) commissioned, interpreted and utilised selectively by the government to fulfil pre-ordained policy agendas (see also Goldson 2005), whilst the nature of 'risk' itself has been significantly under-theorised as a technical, psychosocial and apolitical concept. Consequently, RFR has become a somewhat self-fulfilling, methodologically-restricted exercise that has exemplified House's notion of 'status quo theory':

> Once research has been uncritically defined in a narrowly circum-scribed, quasi-positivistic way, then the almost inevitable result is . . . 'status quo' theory – that is, theory and research that tend to accept and reinforce prevailing ideological assumptions and 'regimes of truth', rather than being open to challenging and transcending them. (House 2007: 15)

Critical analysis has exposed the limitations, weaknesses, fallibilities and fallacies of RFR. This analysis has raised serious doubts about the legitimacy and validity of the methods, analysis, findings and conclusions of much RFR and its claims to be atheoretical, value free and scientific. The hegemony of developmentalism has precipitated and embedded a raft of methodological limitations, weaknesses and paradoxes within RFR, each of which have raised serious issues regarding the validity of the methodologies, analyses and conclusions that have driven the field and have engendered risk-based policy and practice within the Youth Justice System of England and Wales.

RFR methodologies: the paradox of simultaneous reductionism and over-generalisation

Methodologically, an insidious *reductionism* has pervaded RFR and has characterised the dominant artefact approach. However, the complexity of identified risk factors, at the same time, has been 'reduced' through the *over-generalisation* of their applicability to individual members of diverse, aggregated samples of young people, to young people in different countries, to young people in methodologically-different RFR studies, and to the explanation of different (homogenised) behaviours such as offending, reoffending, reconviction, delinquency and antisocial behaviour.

Central to the methodological reductionism within RFR has been the *simplistic over-simplification* of risk into quantifiable factors/variables that can be subject to statistical control and measured in terms of their statistical relationship with offending. This 'risk factorology' (France 2005) has been born of academic zeal and governmental pressure for positivist, 'scientific' methodologies that can produce generalisable, replicable and practical 'evidence' of risk. The simplistic over-simplification of risk has perpetuated a confidence and definitiveness regarding the developmental and deterministic influence of risk factors on offending and of protective factors on non-offending and desistance. Consequently, much store has been placed in identifying these factors through surveys and assessment tools and targeting them using practical risk-focused interventions – a paradigm that may be described as 'riskological pragmatism'. As Coles has asserted, RFR:

> employs a remarkably 'deductive', 'positivistic' and 'normative' approach to problem identification and problem solving. It suggests that social science is supremely confident that it knows the causes of problem behaviours and poor outcomes during youth transitions. This might be a very questionable assumption. (Coles 2000: 194)

Indeed, this positivistic and normative approach has been undermined by the rampant reductionism and 'dumbing down' within much RFR – the crude analysis of crude measures to produce crude conclusions and crude recommendations. The potentially complex, multi-faceted and dynamic processes of risk and protection and their potentially-complex relationships with offending, have been over-simplified, diluted and distorted to the point of no longer representing the circumstances, characteristics, traits, life events, mechanisms, processes and behaviour they purport to measure and have become devoid of any sensitivity or validity with respect to the real lives of individual young people. The production of artefactual evidence of risk has, therefore, engendered and necessitated levels of abstraction and generalisation that undermines any claim to have produced valid, real world knowledge. Indeed, without these levels of abstraction and generalisation, RFR could not have produced consistent and replicable findings. The *factorisation* of risk is now a standardised procedure within RFR. The reduction of risk to factors has rendered the unpredictable and incomprehensible to be predictable and comprehensible through standardisation, clinical, 'objective' measurement, and the inevitable replication of broadly-phrased risk measures using straightforward statistical analyses. Indeed, 'influential reviewers have concluded that the study of antisocial behaviour is stuck in the "risk-factor stage"' (Moffitt 2005: 533).

Reductionism through factorisation has simultaneously washed away the inherent qualitative complexity, nuance and depth of risk and protection in terms of, *inter alia*:

- how risk and protection may operate as mechanisms, processes and constructions (by young people);

- how risk and protection (as factors, mechanisms, processes and constructions) interrelate (e.g. the effects of risks on risks, the nature of the relationships between risk and protection);

- whether protection can function as a stand-alone, independent complex concept that should not be framed solely in relation to risk and should, therefore, be subjected to further independent scrutiny;

- how different manifestations of risk and protection relate to different forms of youth offending for specific individuals and different groups of young people at different times in different places.

The *homogenisation* of different categories of offending and groups of young people, often accompanied by the *aggregation* of both risk/ protection measures and the data produced by these groups of young people, has compounded the deleterious effects of reductionism on understandings of the relationships between risk, protection and offending. There has been a recurrent predilection for presenting 'offending' as an over-simplified, homogenised category (e.g. official, self-reported, general, serious, property) and then statistically analysing this generic category in relation to broad, composite measures of risk that have been aggregated across inappropriately and insensitive homogenised groups of young people (e.g. broad age ranges, different genders, ethnic backgrounds). Homogenisation and aggregation have facilitated statistical analyses of differences between the risk profiles of groups of young people within large samples. These differences have enabled understandable, generalised, even 'universal', factors and conclusions that have replicated previous RFR and have been used to inform and justify policy and practice. There has been a limited exploration, however, of specific measures of risk (e.g. the separate risk factors that form part of composite risk factors) for specific forms of offending (e.g. theft, vandalism, one-off offences) by specific young people or specific sub-groups (e.g. ethnic minorities, 11 year olds) at specific times in specific contexts, so identified risk factors may not be valid to or representative of the behaviour and circumstances of the young person to whom they have been attributed.

Paradoxically, the reductionist, standardised and homogenised methodologies of RFR have been undermined by an heterogeneity and ambiguity of foci – that has previously remained largely hidden and under-explored. There remains an inconsistency and lack of consensus regarding the precise working definitions of risk and protective factors and the nature of their proposed relationships with each other (e.g. interactive, cumulative, independent) and with offending (e.g. as linear causes, bidirectional causes, indirect causes through their impact on other causal risk factors, predictors, correlates, symptoms). There has been an equivalent lack of consensus over how to define and measure offending (e.g. due to different laws and differing social constructions of offending in different countries during different time periods) or, indeed, whether to take youth offending as the dependent variable at all or whether to assess the risk of reoffending, reconviction (e.g. in the case of *Asset* risk assessment), 'antisocial behaviour' or 'delinquency' (which can include measures of both antisocial behaviour and offending). Where antisocial behaviour and delinquency have been the adopted target measures (usually within RFR outside of England and Wales), there have been equivalent disparities between studies with regards to their definition and measurement (e.g. in the ISRD-1). The widespread ambiguities and disparities in the working definitions and understandings of central concepts within RFR raises serious problems regarding the replicability, universalism and particularly the validity of RFR findings due to the incomparability between the measures employed.

The risk measures reduced through factorisation, homogenisation and aggregation have been further reduced (in terms of scope) by the perpetuation of a *psychosocial bias* within RFR. Measures of risk and (the under-researched area of) protection have typically focused on the domains of family, school, neighbourhood/community and personal/ individual; the same domains privileged by the seminal criminological RFR of the Gluecks and the hugely-influential Cambridge Study in Delinquent Development. Consequently, direct influences on offending from other areas such as socio-structural factors (e.g. interactions with criminal justice agencies, local policy formations, poverty, unemployment), life events, turning points/life transitions and young people's constructions of risk have been relatively neglected. These alternative foci have not been ignored by RFR (see, for example, Sampson and Laub's life course model, the synthesised model of the Edinburgh Study and the Teesside studies), but RFR has typically explored their influence solely in terms of how they may create or exacerbate the psychosocial factors, which lead to offending. However, Cuneen and White (2006) have argued that the so-called 'social' risk factors identified in traditional artefact RFR (e.g. low socio-economic status, unemployment) should not be treated as specific causal (risk) factors, but rather as *consequences* of wider socio-structural features. Traditional reductionist and developmental RFR has, however, ignored the *generative* social processes that precipitate and exacerbate different risk factors and has eschewed investigation of life histories and young people's position in the wider social structure (Cuneen and White 2006; see also Hine 2006) that may offer more realistic understandings and explanations of youth behaviour. Therefore, the focus of much RFR has been on immediate, 'proximate', individual risk factors, with a restricted conception of socio-structural 'distal' risk factors as merely interacting with and exacerbating developmental anomalies (Pitts 2003a; Bessant *et al.* 2003).

RFR analyses: statistical replication and imputed temporal precedence

Analytically, the methodological reductionism of the dominant artefact form of RFR has engendered reductionist analysis based on *statistical comparisons* of aggregated risk levels between-groups (rather than within-groups or within-individuals). Analytical reductionism has been further demonstrated by the self-perpetuating statistical replication of broad, aggregated categories of risk in preference to the validation of these risk measures and the demonstration and explanation of their relationships with offending in the real world (outside of statistical manipulation). Therefore, a restricted set of crude, broadly-phrased, psychosocial 'inter-changeable indices' (see Lazarsfeld 1939) of risk, aggregated across homogenised groups of young people, have been statistically-linked to generalised measures of offending, contrary to the Gluecks' early caution that, when attempting to identify the risk factors for youth offending, 'statistical technique will not help us here' (Glueck and Glueck 1934: 243). This consistent, broad-brush methodological and analytical approach has inevitably fostered statistical reliability – the replication of different factors across groups, studies and countries. However, such superficial replication has neither established nor explained the existence or comparability of risk influences between and within groups, nor has it explored the validity of different factors as meaningful elements in the lives of the young people studied.

The most important contribution of statistical analysis to RFR has been in identifying risk and protective factors as alleged *predictors* and *causes* of future offending based on time-lagged analyses identifying the temporal ordering of factors and behaviour. For example, in the more common longitudinal form of RFR, regression techniques have been employed to measure the time-lagged relationship between risk factors assessed at time A (e.g. age 8–10 years in the Cambridge Study) and offending behaviour that has been officially-recorded and/or self-reported at time B (e.g. age 14–15 years), whilst simultaneously controlling (statistically) for the effects of other risk factors on offending. Most risk factor researchers have shied away from presenting the resultant statistical relationships as causal, which has been quite sensible because these researchers have been unable to fully *control* for all variables in the risk–offending equation (thus isolating the effects of particular risk factors in a clinical manner) or to adequately *explain* how factors actually lead to offending, or, for that matter, how risk-focused interventions may prevent/reduce offending. However, conclusions of predictive utility have been born of widespread and ill-advised *imputation* that, *inter alia*, temporal precedence in the measurement of risk over offending indicates temporal precedence in the onset of risk and that the temporal precedence of risk necessarily implies a substantive, explicable and linear influence over offending at that point or in the future. These conclusions have purportedly established the direction and deterministic nature of the relationship between specific risk factors and offending, thus justifying the label of 'risk' factor (as the factor supposedly increases the risk of a future offending outcome), with little consideration that these risk factors may be the products of other risks, may be the result of unreported or unrecorded offending at an earlier stage (or run concurrently to it) or that specific factors may sit far further back in the chain of influences that ultimately produce offending behaviour.

RFR conclusions: developmental determinism and the constructivist alternative

The definitiveness of the conclusions from RFR, especially artefact RFR (e.g. that risk factors are deterministic, predictive, universal, malleable and amenable to intervention) have, in reality, been a product of imputation from over-simplified, over-generalised, ambiguous and partial methodologies and analyses. The developmental determinism of these ostensibly 'evidence-based' conclusions has depicted children and young people as *crash test dummies* on an irrevocable course (trajectory, pathway) to offending unless they are in receipt of adult-prescribed, risk-focused intervention at an early stage in their lives or early in their offending 'career'.

Developmental risk factor researchers have begun to challenge their own deterministic biases by producing integrated, dynamic theories that have included consideration of the influence of life events, agency and situational factors. However, these theories have remained largely hypothetical (e.g. Farrington's Integrated Cognitive Antisocial Potential theory), imputed from cross-sectional research (e.g. Wikström's Developmental Ecological Action Theory) or, at their best, wedded (at least in part) to the developmental, reductionist and psychosocial biases that they have tried to avoid (e.g. Laub and Sampson's revised age graded theory of social control, the nascent explanatory model of the Edinburgh Study). Worse still, these methodological flaws and biases have been exacerbated by the uncritical and often inappropriate transportation of methods (notably the risk-based content of surveys), analyses and conclusions between studies conducted in different countries and with different populations of young people. The wholesale adoption of developmental factors and conclusions imported from longitudinal RFR into cross-sectional RFR has been particularly invalid. Developmental (childhood) risk factors have been uncritically applied to much older adolescent samples in cross-sectional RFR, the predictive influence of risk over time has been conflated with the current influence of risk in daily life and statistical correlations between risk and offending have often been taken to indicate predictive relationships. The potential utility of cross-sectional RFR in identifying risk and protective factors with currency that can inform temporary- and locally-relevant policy and practice has therefore been undermined and invalidated by poorly conceived and conducted research.

Critical scrutiny of RFR in England and Wales and research conducted internationally has indicated that the generalised, confident, definitive and deterministic conclusions from RFR have been founded on 'common-sense' imputations rather than a definitive, evidenced explanation/ understanding of the precise nature of the risk–offending relationship. Accordingly, there has been an inherent *black boxism* to the recommendations for risk-led interventions – a lack of definitive understanding about if, how or why 'what works' interventions impact on risk and offending behaviour for different groups of young people at different times in different locations. Notwithstanding this lack of understanding, the UK government (through the YJB) has promulgated a robust 'evidence base' of risk assessment and individualised interventions targeting psychosocial risk and protective factors, even though these interventions do not have an original, substantive evidential basis of their own. In the original RFR from which these ideas were drawn, risk-focused intervention was either downplayed (e.g. the Gluecks' emphasis on young people growing out of crime on their own), overlooked (e.g. in the Cambridge Study in Delinquent Development) or shown to have little effect (e.g. in the Cambridge-Somerville Youth Study and the Criminals Coming of Age study).

The methodological, analytical and interpretive limitations of artefactual and developmental RFR have been challenged (but not necessarily resolved at this point) by a constructivist pathways strand of RFR. Constructivist RFR has attempted to understand risk and offending as constructed and negotiated processes with inherent complexity and specific to individuals, demographic groups, locations, contexts, historical periods, life events and unpredictable critical moments. The constructivist pathways strand emerged in response to the artefact approach and has attempted to address the theoretical biases and the methodological weaknesses and limitations of the RFR that has shaped policy and practice responses to young people, for example, by utilising ethnographic approaches (e.g. biographies, histories) to elicit the voices of young people and to examine how they experience risk. Constructivists have asserted that young people are not crash test dummies who 'roll on deterministi-cally to foregone conclusions' (MacDonald 2007: 123) and thus their lives are not necessarily amenable to simplistic, unproblematic risk assessment and prediction. Constructivist RFR has evolved traditional understand-ings of risk factors by focusing on three 'Cs':

- *Currency* – how active risk factors in the daily lives of young people have influenced their offending behaviour, as opposed to this offending simply being the pre-determined result of exposure to risk factors in childhood.

- *Construction* – how risk can have different meanings to different people and can be differently constructed, experienced, negotiated and respon-ded to in an active manner, rather than simply experienced by passive 'crash test dummies'.

- *Context* – how the context in which risk is experienced (e.g. in neighbourhood/community contexts characterised by social depriva-tion, social dislocation, high unemployment and racial tension; as part of interactions in the YJS) can influence the individual's ability to actively negotiate their exposure to risk and protection.

These considerations have simultaneously broadened the foci of RFR and problematised existing understandings of the risk-factor–offending rela-tionship; such that constructivism may be viewed as having a potentially unconstructive, deleterious effect on a research movement that had been, until that point, easy to understand and readily accepted. The alternative explanation, unpalatable to adherents of artefact RFR, that the real world is just too complex, individualised and nuanced to be captured in predictive models has been rarely entertained. As Laub and Sampson have opined:

> The challenge is to find a middle ground between naïve reductionism and a wholism that does not allow for any precise explanation. (Laub and Sampson 2003: 277)

Yet, how realistic is this prospect? Whilst constructivist RFR did emerge in response to the reductionism of artefact approaches, the constructivist approach has been limited in acknowledging its debt to artefact RFR. The similarities between constructivist and artefact understandings of risk factors have been particularly evident in:

- *Developmentalism* – constructivist pathways RFR has been avowedly developmental (see Lawrence 2007), measuring young people's expo-sure to risk and their differing ability to negotiate and respond to this risk at different developmental stages in their lives. Developmentalism has ascribed a continued relevance (albeit a developmentally-contingent and constructed relevance) across the life course to the psychosocial, childhood-based risk factors of developmental RFR.

- *Determinism* – the constructivist approach *has* eschewed depicting young people as the passive crash test dummy of deterministic artefact models. However, the focus of constructivism has been limited to the young person's response to active risk factors within their current lives, all but ignoring the developmental potential of childhood risk factors to predict and influence future offending. Constructivist discourses *have* been imbued with a sense of determinism, but this has related to young people's ability to *self*-determine, recognise and negotiate risk and their own outcomes following exposure.

- *Lack of control* – constructivists have, as yet, made insufficient attempts to acknowledge and to account for the limitations in their own research designs and methodologies. There has been limited consideration of the influence of factors unmeasured in surveys that have not been reported for whatever reason, that have remained invisible to the researcher and the young person, or that simply cannot be adequately conceptualised for the purposes of analysis. Also overlooked thus far has been the potential of the young person's responses to be consciously or subconsciously biased in some way due to, *inter-alia*, demand characteristics (e.g. social desirability bias) or interview effects (e.g. leading questions, interview dynamics).

- *Psychosocial bias* – constructivist RFR, as much as it emerged in direct response to the weaknesses of the artefact approach, has adopted psychosocial risk factors as a normative touchstone, eagerly exploring and evaluating them in relation to how young people construct, negotiate and resist risk. There has been an assumption that the childhood psychosocial risk factors originally identified (by the Cambridge Study) as predictive of offending in adolescence should be a key component of any explanatory model of the active, current influence of risk factors on the offending of much older age groups of young people.

- *Predictive risk factors* – there has been an inherent contradiction between the robust critique of artefact approaches by constructivists and an implicit, uncritical acceptance of the key tenets of the developmental approach. It is as if the purported 'explanatory' models that have emerged from constructivist RFR have sought to explain offending by appropriating 'predictive' risk factors from developmental RFR and re-examining and re-validating their construction by young people in the present day in order to assert explanatory processes of risk factor influence. However, constructivist RFR has largely failed to acknowledge the methodological fallacies on which these re-badged predictive risk factors rest, nor has the model accounted sufficiently for the effects that a pervasive lack of control over sources of data and the respondent subjectivity has had on findings and subsequent conclusions.

- *Homogenisation and aggregation* – constructivism has not yet gone far enough in resisting the temptation to treat groups of young people as homogenous (notwithstanding the fact that these groups have been the inherently disparate and idiosyncratic 'hard to reach' groups traditionally neglected by artefact RFR), in order to generalise findings that can feed into an explanatory model. This may, however, indicate a more general limitation of theory development within the social sciences (as yet to be addressed by RFR), in that it relies on applicability, generalisability and replicability to enable validation.

The authors' journey to a better understanding of risk and offending – some personal reflections

When we originally took the decision to produce this book, we had been conducting RFR for several years. Throughout this time, however, we had been struck by the insensitive (e.g. homogenised, aggregated) nature of RFR methodologies and analyses and this had led us to prioritise the identification of risk factors for different forms of offending carried out by different genders at specific ages (see, for example, Haines and Case 2005). Nevertheless, our methodologies, analyses and conclusions had been underpinned by an artefactualism, which became increasingly difficult to reconcile with our inclusionary, 'children first' perspective of young people that prioritised prosocial outcomes and access to rights and entitlements. Consequently, we began to engage with some of the more progressive RFR perspectives (notably the constructivist pathways model) and to examine the hegemonic conceptions of the risk–offending relationship with a more critical eye (see, for example, Haines and Case 2008; Case 2006, 2007; Case *et al.* 2005). It soon became clear that there was a continuum of debate within the RFR field, characterised by two distinct, equally dogmatic and intensely committed sides – ranging from the almost proselytising, religious fervour amongst developmental RFR devotees to the hyper-critical (yet often cursory), ethically-driven and fatalistic view of certain critical criminologists and social commentators. It became even clearer that the expanding corpus of RFR urgently needed to be exposed to a detailed academic critique, particularly in relation to RFR methodologies, which had never been subject to extensive evaluation. We embarked on this journey resolved to offer a balanced critique, rather than aligning ourselves with either artefact or constructivist researchers, or with the avowed critics. The intention was, therefore, to occupy the middle ground and to balance the rhetoric and reality of RFR. What we have found on our journey has been eye-opening, enlightening, encouraging and frequently shocking. We have felt simultaneously validated and disappointed by the extent to which our project has been necessary and fills a huge gap in the literature.

It became evident from a very early stage that the vast majority of the RFR literature had a developmental basis and that critics of RFR were overwhelmingly critics of this developmental form of RFR. It soon became clearer still that there had been an alarming level of imputation and generalisation by both advocates and critics of RFR based on uncritical and superficial readings of the original research, or even the uncritical acceptance of partial conclusions from secondary sources. Perhaps our most shocking discoveries were the *lack of consensus* within RFR about its central concepts (e.g. how to define risk factors) and tenets (e.g. the hypothesised nature of the risk-factor–offending relationship), the *poor quality methodologies* employed in RFR (e.g. the widespread use of crude factorisation processes) and the *simplistic analyses of aggregated data* which led to, what often seemed to us to be, spurious conclusions.

Furthermore, a closer inspection of the earliest RFR brought to light the degree to which subsequent RFR has been founded on a misreading or even non-reading of the original research studies. For example, a detailed reading of the early research of Sheldon and Eleanor Glueck highlighted their conclusion that *maturation through ageing* was considered to be the major influence on desistence from offending. Whilst this conclusion does not necessarily undermine or invalidate developmental understandings of how risk influences offending, we were struck by the implication of this conclusion for the efficacy (even necessity) of risk-focused intervention in adolescence and how its implications have been sidelined and overlooked in subsequent RFR. This selective (mis)representation of previous work was to be an ongoing trait of RFR in our view. There was an equivalent lack of evidence base in the early RFR literature that risk-focused interventions could work (e.g. the Cambridge Study in Delinquent Development did not contain an intervention element) or that these interventions did work when implemented (e.g. as demonstrated by the counter-intuitive results of the *Criminals Coming of Age* study).

It has been evident within our arguments that we have been alarmed by the sometimes outrageous and frequently unsubstantiated conclusions from RFR. These conclusions, on closer inspection, have been based on partial or inaccurate readings of the original research, have 'imputed with impunity' from limited data and have been intent on replicating findings from a starting point that the original risk factors were valid to all young people at all times in all places, so required no further exploration. The self-perpetuating nature of artefact RFR appears to us to have been the product of a theoretical, ethical and practical commitment amongst researchers to better understand the aetiology of youth offending and to provide solutions to policy makers and practitioners operating in the real world. Unfortunately, in their haste to validate risk-based understandings of youth offending and to produce practical conclusions, risk factor researchers seem to have frequently (perhaps inadvertently) gone beyond the scope of their data, conveniently ignoring or marginalising problematic findings (e.g. the influence of maturation, the lack of evidence base for risk-focused interventions) and taking for granted the selective readings of original sources (e.g. in reviews of international RFR by 'experts' in the field). We found this pervasive trait of oversimplifying the 'headlines' from RFR to be particularly problematic. On reflection, the oversimplification of methodologies, analyses, findings and conclusions have been driven by several factors:

- the need for academics to provide comprehensible and practical summaries and recommendations to laypeople such as politicians, policy makers, practitioners, young people and the general public;

- the production of summaries and recommendations by civil servants oblivious to the political drivers, theoretical biases and methodological weaknesses that have distorted their understandings;

- the uncritical acceptance and importation of key elements of previous RFR presented selectively in secondary sources or following selective interpretation of the original research;

- the replication of previous RFR (or elements of it) on the mistaken assumption that this original research had been methodologically-robust and thus constituted a validated evidence base for RFR.

When sourcing the RFR literature, it became clear that the partial (in the dual sense of limited and biased) reading, interpretation and application of RFR had emerged from a progressive watering down process, whereby key messages were extricated from the original RFR and selectively interpreted and presented in secondary sources, which were then reviewed in further RFR and were subject to further watering down and oversimplification, and so it went on. Aside from the practical need to (over) simplify RFR, the partial presentation of RFR methods, findings and conclusions could have been a result of the inaccessibility of original research publications. For example, many of the original studies of the Gluecks (apart from *Unraveling Juvenile Delinquency*) were difficult to obtain, as were the seldom-cited original publication relating to the Cambridge Study in Delinquent Development (West 1969), the original Cambridge-Somerville Youth Study publications of Cabot and the Criminals Coming of Age study (Bottoms and McClintock 1973). Furthermore, several of the more important RFR studies and reviews have failed to provide comprehensive, detailed methodological information (e.g. links to theoretical background, questionnaire content, processes of factorisation, statistical analysis used) in an accessible form. Instead, readers have been presented with selective, superficial results in cursory summaries (e.g. Farrington's Understanding and Preventing Youth Crime review, the SCoPIC partnership studies), some with limited theoretical background and critical evaluation (e.g. the Home Office Youth Lifestyles Survey, the Communities that Care Youth at Risk study, the Offending Crime and Justice Survey), some in edited texts (e.g. the Causes and Correlates Studies, the Social Development Model, the Seattle Social Development Project, the Montréal Longitudinal and Experimental Study, the ICAP theory, the DEAT). Other sources of RFR have provided far more comprehensive and accessible information regarding their theoretical background, methodologies and analytical procedures and these sources have usually been far more willing and able to provide critical evaluation of their central tenets, procedures and conclusions. Such comprehensiveness, accessibility and critical reflection has been particularly evident in the work of Gluecks, Sampson and Laub, the Pathways Into and Out of Crime partnership studies and the Antisocial Behaviour by Young People review. Detailed theoretical and methodological reviews of the Edinburgh Study of Youth Transitions and Crime and the Social Contexts of Pathways Into Crime partnership studies are forthcoming, but have been notable by their absence to date. Whilst publications relating to the Cambridge Study have been both accessible and ostensibly comprehensive in methodological detail (certainly relative to most other RFR studies), their degree of critical reflection (beyond superficial and easily-rectified methodological targets) has been at once selective and disappointing.

Our overriding disappointment throughout our journey of critical reflection on RFR has been that this purportedly scientific and evidence-based field, one that has produced findings so influential within the Youth Justice System, has lacked transparency, rigour, consistency and reflexivity in its investigations of risk, protection and youth offending. Consequently, whilst we have attempted, where possible, to offer a balanced critique of RFR, it has become increasingly clear to us that realistic, holistic, sensitive and dynamic understandings of risk are notable by their absence in the objectives and outcomes of RFR. Instead, RFR has been undermined by an insidious, yet alarmingly unreflective, reliance on developmentalism as its frame of reference and a desire to inform policy through user-friendly, simplified (dumbed down) conclusions. It is ironic that it has been risk factor researchers themselves who have been the crash test dummies, often hurtling towards predetermined research outcomes that have neglected (yet imputed) two crucial issues: the *validity* of risk to the real lives of young people and *explanation* of the relationships between risk and youth offending. Despite over half a century of research, we still lack a clear understanding of risk and its relationship to the behaviour of young people. Furthermore, the evidence that certain risks cause offending and that these risks can be targeted to reduce offending has simply not been provided.

Bibliography

Achenbach, T.M. and Edelbrock, C. (1983) *Manual for the Child Behavior Checklist and Revised Child Behavior Profile.* Burlington, VT: Queen City Printers.

Agnew, R. (2005) *Why Do Criminals Offend? A General Theory of Crime and Delinquency.* Los Angeles, CA: Roxbury Publishing Company.

Akers, R. (1985) *Deviant Behavior: A Social Learning Approach.* Belmont, CA: Wadsworth.

Anderson, B., Beinart, S., Farrington, D.P., Longman, J., Sturgis, P. and Utting, D. (2001) *Risk and Protective Factors Associated with Youth Crime and Effective Interventions to Prevent It.* Youth Justice Board Research Note No. 5. London: Youth Justice Board.

Annison, J. (2005) 'Risk and protection', in T. Bateman and J. Pitts (eds) *The RHP Companion to Youth Justice.* Lyme Regis: Russell House.

ARCS Ltd (2008) *Reviewing the Effectiveness of Community Safety Policy and Practice – An Overview of Current Debates and their Background.* Montréal, QB: International Centre for the Prevention of Crime.

Armstrong, D. (2004) 'A risky business? Research, policy, governmentality and youth offending', *Youth Justice*, 4(2): 100–16.

Armstrong, D., Hine, J., Hacking, S., Armaos, R., Jones, R., Klessinger, N. and France, A. (2005) *Children, Risk and Crime: The On Track Youth Lifestyles Surveys.* Home Office Research Study 278. London: Home Office.

Ashcroft, J., Daniels, D. and Hart, S. (2004) *Evaluating GREAT: A School-Based Gang Prevention Program.* Washington, DC: National Institute of Justice, US Department of Justice.

Ashford, B. (2007) *Towards a Crime Prevention Strategy.* London: Youth Justice Board.

Audit Commission (1996) *Misspent Youth: Young People and Crime.* London: Audit Commission.

Audit Commission (1998) *Misspent Youth: The Challenge for Youth Justice.* London: Audit Commission.

Audit Commission (2004) *Youth Justice 2004.* London: Audit Commission.

Ayers, C.D., Williams, J.H.W., Hawkins, J.D., Peterson, P.L., Catalano, R.F. and Abbott, R.D. (1999). 'Assessing correlates of onset, escalation, deescalation, and desistance of delinquent behavior', *Journal of Quantitative Criminology*, 15: 277–306.

Baker, K. (2005) 'Assessment in youth justice: Professional discretion and the use of Asset', *Youth Justice*, 5: 106–22.

Baker, K., Jones, S., Roberts, C. and Merrington, S. (2002) *Validity and Reliability of Asset*. London: Youth Justice Board.

Baker, K., Jones, S., Roberts, C. and Merrington, S. (2005) *Further Development of Asset*. London: Youth Justice Board.

Bateman, T. and Pitts, J. (2005) *The RHP Companion to Youth Justice*. Lyme Regis: Russell House.

Beck, U. (1992) *Risk Society: Towards a New Modernity*. London: Sage.

Beinert, S., Anderson, B., Lee, S. and Utting, D. (2002) *Youth at Risk? A National Survey of Risk Factors, Protective Factors and Problem Behaviour Among Young People in England, Scotland and Wales*. London: Communities that Care.

Berger, P.L. and Luckmann, T. (1966) *The Social Construction of Reality: A Treatise its the Sociology of Knowledge*. Garden City, NY: Anchor Books.

Bessant, J., Hil, R. and Watts, R. (2003) *Discovering Risk: Social Research and Policy Making*. New York: Peter Lang.

Bhabra, S., Dinos, S. and Ghate, D. (2006a) *Young People, Risk, and Protection: A Major Survey of Primary Schools in On Track Areas*. London: Department for Education and Skills.

Bhabra, S., Dinos, S. and Ghate, D. (2006b) *Young People, Risk, and Protection: A Major Survey of Secondary Schools in On Track Areas*. London: Department for Education and Skills.

Blyth, M., Solomon, E. and Baker, K. (2007) *Young People and Risk*. Bristol: Policy Press.

Boeck, T., Fleming, J. and Kemshall, H. (2006) 'The context of risk decisions: Does social capital make a difference?' [Online]. Available at: http://www.qualitative-research.net/index.php/fqs/article/view/55 [accessed 17 March 2009].

Bonta, J. (1996) 'Risk-needs assessment and treatment', in A.T. Harland (ed.) *Choosing Correctional Options that Work*. Thousand Oaks, CA: Sage.

Bottoms, A.E. and McClintock, F.H. (1973) *Criminals Coming of Age. A Study of Institutional Adaptation in the Treatment of Adolescent Offenders*. London: Heinemann.

Bottoms, A.E., Shapland, J. and Muir, G. (2006) 'Offending and steps towards desistance within the social contexts of early adulthood', *Assessing the Role of Individual Differences and the Environment in Crime Causation. Third Annual SCoPiC Conference*, Cambridge, December 2006.

Bottoms A.E., Shapland, J., Costello, A., Holmes, D. and Muir, G. (2004) 'Towards desistance: Theoretical underpinnings for an empirical study', *Howard Journal*, 43(4): 368–89.

Bourdieu, P. (1977) *Outline of a Theory of Practice*. Cambridge: Cambridge University Press.

Bradshaw, P. and Smith, D.J. (2005) *Gang Membership and Teenage Offending*, Edinburgh Study of Youth Transitions and Crime Research Digest No. 8. Edinburgh: The University of Edinburgh.

Bronfenbrenner, U. and Morris, P.A. (1998) 'The ecology of developmental processes', in W. Damon and R.M. Lerner (eds) *Handbook of Child Psychology: Vol. 1: Theoretical Models of Human Development*. New York: Wiley.

Brown, S. (2005) *Understanding Youth and Crime. Listening to Youth?* Maidenhead: Open University Press.

Browning, K., Huizinga, D., Loeber, R. and Thornberry, T. (1999) *Causes and Correlates of Delinquency Program. OJJDP Fact Sheet*. Washington, DC: Office of Juvenile Justice and Delinquency Prevention.

Budd, T., Sharp, C. and Mayhew, P. (2005a) *Offending in England and Wales: First results from the 2003 Crime and Justice Survey*. London: Home Office.

Budd, T., Sharp, C., Weir, G., Wilson, D. and Owen, N. (2005b) *Young People and Crime: Findings from the 2004 Offending, Crime and Justice Survey*. London: Home Office.

Bunge, M. (2006) *Chasing Reality: Strife over Realism*. Toronto, ON: University of Toronto Press.

Burnett, R. (2007) 'Never too early? Reflections on research and interventions for early developmental prevention of serious harm', in M. Blyth, E. Solomon and K. Baker (eds) *Young People and Risk*. Bristol: Policy Press.

Cabot, R. (1930) 'Foreword', in S. Glueck and E. Glueck (authors) *500 Criminal Careers*. New York: Alfred Knopf.

Cabot, R. (1940) 'A long-term study of children: The Cambridge-Somerville Youth Study', *Child Development*, 11(2): 143–51.

Case, S.P. (2004) *Promoting Prevention: Evaluating a Multi-Agency Initiative to Prevent Youth Offending in Swansea. Unpublished PhD Thesis*. Swansea: Swansea University.

Case, S.P. (2006) 'Young people "at risk" of what? Challenging risk-focused early intervention as crime prevention', *Youth Justice*, 6(3): 171–9.

Case, S.P. (2007) 'Questioning the "evidence" of risk that underpins evidence-led youth justice interventions', *Youth Justice*, 7(2): 91–106.

Case, S.P., Clutton, S. and Haines, K.R. (2005) 'Extending entitlement: A Welsh policy for children', *Wales Journal of Law and Policy*, 4(2): 187–202.

Case, S.P. and Haines, K.R. (2004) 'Promoting prevention: Evaluating a multi-agency initiative of youth consultation and crime prevention in Swansea', *Children and Society*, 18(5): 355–70.

Case, S.P. and Haines, K.R. (2007) 'Offending by young people: A further risk factor analysis', *Security Journal*, 20(2): 96–110.

Case, S.P. and Haines, K.R. (2008) 'Factors shaping substance use by young people', *Journal of Substance Use*, 13(1): 1–15.

Cashmore, J. (2001) 'Early experience and brain development', *National Child Protection Clearinghouse Newsletter*, 6–9.

Catalano, R.F. and Hawkins, J.D. (1996) 'The Social Development Model: A theory of anti-social behaviour', in J. Hawkins (ed.) *Delinquency and Crime: Current Theories*. Cambridge: Cambridge University Press.

Catalano, R.F., Berglund, M., Ryan, J., Lonczak, H. and Hawkins, D. (2004) 'Positive youth development in the United States: Research findings on evaluations of positive youth development programs', *Annals of the American Academy of Political and Social Sciences*, 59: 98–124.

Catalano, R.F., Park, J., Harachi, T.W., Haggerty, K.P., Abbott, R.D. and Hawkins J.D. (2005) 'Mediating the effects of poverty, gender, individual characteristics and external constraints on antisocial behaviour: A test of the Social Development Model and implications for developmental life-course theory', in D.P. Farrington (ed.) *Integrated Developmental and Life-Course Theories of Offending*. New Brunswick, NJ: Transaction.

Chief Secretary to the Treasury (2003) *Every Child Matters, Cm 5860*. London: The Stationary Office.

Chung, I-J., Hill, K.G., Hawkins, J.D., Gilchrist, L.D. and Nagin, D. (2002) 'Childhood predictors of offence trajectories', *Journal of Research in Crime and Delinquency*, 39: 60–90.

City and County of Swansea (2001) *Safer Swansea: A Crime and Disorder Crime and Disorder Reduction Strategy*. Swansea: Community Safety Department, City and County of Swansea.

Coles, B. (2000) *Joined Up Youth Research, Policy and Practice*. Leicester: Youth Work Press.

Cook, T.D. and Campbell, D.T. (1979) *Quasi-experimentation: Design and Analysis for Field Settings*. Chicago, IL: Rand McNally.

Crawford, A. and Newburn, T. (2003) *Youth Offending and Restorative Justice: Implementing Reform in Youth Justice*. Cullompton: Willan Publishing.

Cuneen, C. and White, R. (2006) 'Australia: Control, containment or empowerment?' in J. Muncie and B. Goldson (eds) *Comparative Youth Justice*. London: Sage.

Durlak, J.A. (1998) 'Common risk and protective factors in successful prevention programs: Prevention science research with children, adolescents and families', *American Journal of Orthopsychiatry*, 68(4): 512–20.

Eadie T. and Canton R. (2002) 'Practising in a context of ambivalence: The challenge for youth justice workers', *Youth Justice*, 2(1): 14–26.

Edwards, L. and Hatch, B. (2003) *Passing Time. A Report about Young People and Communities*. London: Institute for Public Policy Research.

Elder, G.H., Kirkpatrick Johnson, M. and Crosnoe, R. (2004) 'The emergence and development of life course theory', in J.T. Mortimer and M.J. Shanahan (eds) *Handbook of the Life Course*. New York: Springer.

Elliott, D.S., Huizinga, D. and Ageton, S.S. (1985) *Explaining Delinquency and Drug Use*. Beverly Hills, CA: Sage.

Elliott, D.S., Ageton, S.S., Huizinga, D., Knowles, B.A. and Canter, R.J. (1983) *The Prevalence and Incidence of Delinquent Behaviour. The National Youth Survey Report No. 26*. Boulder, CO: Behavioral Research Institute.

Evans, T. and Harris, J. (2004) 'Street-level bureaucracy, social work and the (exaggerated) death of discretion', *British Journal of Social Work*, 34: 871–96.

Farrington, D.P. (1988) 'Studying changes within individuals: The causes of offending', in M. Rutter (ed.) *Studies of Psychosocial Risk: The Power of Longitudinal Data, 158–183*. Cambridge: Cambridge University Press.

Farrington, D.P. (1990) 'Implications of criminal career research for the prevention of offending', *Journal of Adolescence*, 13(2): 93–113.

Farrington, D.P. (1996) *Understanding and Preventing Youth Crime*. York: Joseph Rowntree Foundation.

Farrington, D.P. (1997) 'Human development and criminal careers', in M. Maguire, R. Morgan and R. Reiner (eds) *The Oxford Handbook of Criminology*, 2nd edn. Oxford: Oxford University Press.

Farrington, D.P. (1999) 'A criminological research agenda for the next millennium', *Journal of Offender Therapy and Comparative Criminology*, 43: 154–67.

Farrington, D.P. (2000) 'Explaining and preventing crime: The globalization of knowledge', *Criminology*, 38(1): 1–24.

Farrington, D.P. (2002) 'Developmental criminology and risk-focused prevention', in M. Maguire, R. Morgan and R. Reiner (eds) *The Oxford Handbook of Criminology*, 3rd edn. Oxford: Oxford University Press.

Farrington, D.P. (2003) 'Key results from the first forty years of the Cambridge Study in Delinquent Development', in T.P Thornberry and M.D. Krohn (eds) *Taking Stock of Delinquency: An Overview of Findings from Contemporary Longitudinal Studies*. New York: Kluwer.

Farrington, D.P. (2005) 'The Integrated Cognitive Antisocial Development (ICAP) theory', in D.P. Farrington (ed.) *Integrated Developmental and Life-Course Theories of Offending*. New Brunswick, NJ: Transaction.

Farrington, D.P. (2007) 'Childhood risk factors and risk-focused prevention', in M. Maguire, R. Morgan and R. Reiner (eds) *The Oxford Handbook of Criminology*, 4th edn. Oxford: Oxford University Press.

Farrington, D.P., Coid, J., Harnett, L., Jolliffe, D., Soteriou, N., Turner, R. and West, D. (2006) *Criminal Careers and Life Success: New Findings from the Cambridge Study in Delinquent Development*, Research Findings 281. London: Home Office.

Farrington, D.P., Gallagher, B., Morley, L., St. Ledger, R.J. and West, D.J. (1986) 'Unemployment, school leaving and crime', *British Journal of Criminology*, 26(4), 335–56.

Farrington, D.P. and Hawkins, J.D. (1991) 'Predicting participation, early onset, and later persistence in officially recorded offending,' *Criminal Behaviour and Mental Health*, 1: 1–33.

Farrington, D.P., Langan, P.A. and Wikström, P-O. (1994) 'Changes in crime and punishment in America, England and Sweden between the 1980s and the 1990s', *Studies in Crime and Crime Prevention*, 3: 104–31.

Farrington, D.P. and Loeber, R. (1999) 'Transatlantic replicability of risk factors in the development of delinquency', in P. Cohen, C. Slomkowski and L. Robins (eds) *Historical and Geographical Influences on Psychopathology*. Mahwah, NY: Lawrence Erlbaum.

Farrington, D.P. and Painter, K.A. (2004) *Gender Differences in Offending: Implications for Risk-focused Prevention*. Home Office Findings 196. London: Home Office.

Feeley, M.M. and Simon, J. (1992) 'The new penology: notes on the emerging strategy of corrections and its implications', *Criminology*, 30: 449–74.

Feeley, M.M. and Simon, J. (1994) 'Actuarial justice: the emerging new criminal law', in D. Nelken (ed.) *The Futures of Criminology*. London: Sage.

Field, A. (2005) *Discovering Statistics Using SPSS*. London: Sage.

Flood-Page, C., Campbell, S., Harrington, V., and Miller, J. (2000) *Youth Crime: Findings from the 1998/99 Youth Lifestyles Survey*. Home Office Research Study 209. London: Home Office.

France, A. (2005) 'Risk factorology and the youth question', *British Sociological Association Conference*, York University, March 2005.

France, A. (2008) 'Risk factor analysis and the youth question', *Journal of Youth Studies*, 11(1): 1–15.

France, A. and Crow, I. (2005) 'Using the "risk factor paradigm" in prevention: lessons from the evaluation of Communities that Care', *Children and Society*, 19(2): 172–84.

France, A. and Homel, R. (2006) 'Societal access routes and developmental pathways: Putting social structure and young people's voices into the analysis of pathways into and out of crime', *Australian New Zealand Journal of Criminology*, 39(3): 295–309.

France, A. and Homel, R. (2007) *Pathways and Crime Prevention: Theory, Policy and Practice*. Cullompton: Willan Publishing.

Furlong, A. and Cartmel, F. (2006) *Young People and Social Change: New Perspectives*. Buckingham: Open University Press.

Garland, D. (2002) *The Culture of Control*. Oxford: Oxford University Press.

Gibbens, T.C.N. (1963) *Psychiatric Studies of Borstal Lads*. Oxford: Oxford University Press.

Glueck, S. and Glueck, E. (1930) *500 Criminal Careers*. New York: Alfred Knopf.

Glueck, S. and Glueck, E. (1934) *One Thousand Juvenile Delinquents*. Cambridge: Cambridge University Press.

Glueck, S. and Glueck, E. (1937) *Later Criminal Careers*. New York: Commonwealth Fund.

Glueck, S. and Glueck, E. (1950) *Unraveling Juvenile Delinquency*. New York: Commonwealth Fund.

Goldblatt, P. and Lewis, C. (1998) *Reducing Offending: An Assessment of Research Evidence on Ways of Dealing with Offending Behaviour*. Home Office Research Study 187. London: Home Office.

Goldson, B. (2000) *The New Youth Justice*. Lyme Regis: Russell House.

Goldson, B. (2003) 'Tough on children: Tough on justice', paper presented at the Centre for Studies in Crime and Social Justice (Edge Hill) in collaboration with the European Group for the Study of Deviance and Social Control. Chester, UK.

Goldson, B. (2005) 'Taking liberties: Policy and the punitive turn', in H. Hendrick (ed.) *Child Welfare and Social Policy*. Bristol: Policy Press.

Goldson, B. and Muncie, J. (2006) *Youth Crime and Justice*. London: Sage.

Goodman, R. (1997) 'The strengths and difficulties questionnaire: A research note', *Journal of Child Psychology and Psychiatry*, 38: 581–6.

Graham, J. and Bowling, B. (1995) *Young People and Crime*. Home Office Research Study 145. London: Home Office.

Gray, P. (2005) 'The politics of risk and young offenders' experiences of social exclusion and restorative justice', *British Journal of Criminology*, 45: 938–57.

Grove, W.M. and Meehl, P.E. (1996) 'Comparative efficiency of informal (subjective, impressionistic) and formal (mechanical, algorithmic) prediction', *Psychology, Public Policy and Law*, 2: 293–323.

Hackett, S. (2005) 'Risk and resilience: Two sides of the same coin', *Assessment and Child Protection Conference*, Bonnington Hotel, March 2005.

Hagell, A. and Newburn, T. (1994) *Persistent Young Offenders*. London: Policy Studies Institute.

Haines, K.R. (1999) 'Crime as a social problem', *European Journal on Criminal Policy and Research*, 17(2): 263–75.

Haines, K.R. and Case, S.P. (2005) 'Promoting prevention: Targeting family-based risk and protective factors for drug use and youth offending in Swansea', *British Journal of Social Work*, 35(2): 1–18.

Haines, K.R. and Case, S.P. (2008) 'The rhetoric and reality of the Risk Factor Prevention Paradigm approach to preventing and reducing youth offending', *Youth Justice*, 8(1): 5–20.

Haines, K.R. and Drakeford, M. (1998) *Young People and Youth Justice*. Basingstoke: Macmillan.

Hammersley, R., Marsland, L. and Reid, M. (2003) *Substance Use by Young Offenders: The Impact of the Normalisation of Drug Use in the Early Years of the 21st Century*. Home Office Research Study 261. London: Home Office.

Hannah-Moffat, K. (2005) 'Criminogenic needs and the transformative risk subject' *Punishment and Society*, 7(1): 29–51.

Hansen, K. and Plewis, I. (2004) *Children at Risk: How Evidence from British Cohort Data can Inform the Debate on Prevention*. London: University of London.

Harcourt, B. (2007) *Against Prediction*. Chicago, IL: University of Chicago Press.

Hargreaves, D. (2007) 'Teaching as a research-based profession: Possibilities and prospects', in M. Hammersley (ed.) *Educational Research and Evidence-based Practice*. London: Sage.

Haw, K. (2007) 'Risk factors and pathways into and out of crime: Misleading, misinterpreted or mythic? From generative metaphor to professional myth', in J.D Hawkins and R.F. Catalano (1992) *Communities that Care*. San Francisco: Jossey-Bass.

Hawkins, J.D. and Weis, J.G. (1985) 'The social development model: An integrated approach to delinquency prevention', *Journal of Primary Prevention*, 6: 73–97.

Hawkins, J.D., Catalano, R.F., Kosterman, R., Abbott, R. and Hill, K.G. (1999) 'Preventing adolescent health-risk behaviours by strengthening protection during childhood', *Archive of Paediatrics and Adolescent Medicine'*, 153: 226–34.

Hawkins, J.D., Smith, B.H., Hill, K.G., Kosterman, R., Catalano, R.F. and Abbott. R.D. (2003) 'Understanding and preventing crime and violence. Findings from the Seattle Social Development Project', in T.P. Thornberry and M.D. Krohn (eds) *Taking Stock of Delinquency: An Overview of Findings from Contemporary Longitudinal Studies*. New York: Kluwer.

Hawkins, J.D., Von Kleve, E. and Catalano, R.F. (1991) 'Reducing early childhood aggression: Results of a primary prevention program', *Journal of the American Academy of Childhood and Adolescent Psychiatry*, 30: 208–17.

Herrenkohl, T.I., Maguin, E., Hill, K.G., Hawkins, J.D., Abbott, R.D. and Catalano, R.F. (2000) 'Developmental risk factors for youth violence', *Journal of Adolescent Health*, 26: 176–86.

Hill, K.G., Collins, L.M. and Hawkins, J.D. (2002). 'Examining the progression of offenses in the behavioral repertoire: A Latent Transition Analysis of the development of delinquency and substance use'. Unpublished.

Hill, M., Davis, J., Prout, A. and Tisdall, K. (2004) 'Moving the participation agenda forward', *Children & Society*, 18(2): 77–96.

Hine, J. (2005) 'Early intervention: the view from On Track', *Children and Society*, 19(2): 117–30.

Hine, J. (2006) 'Young people, pathways and crime: context and complexity', *Pathways into and out of Crime: Taking Stock and Moving Forward: International Symposium*. Leicester, April 2006.

Hine, J. (2008) Personal communication [Email]. August 2008.

Hine, J., France, A., Dunkerton, L. and Armstrong, D. (2007) 'Risk and resilience in children who are offending, excluded from school or who have behaviour problems' [Online]. Available at: http://www.pcrrd.group.shef.ac.uk/reports/project_1.pdf [accessed 17 March 2009].

Hirschi, T. (1969) *Causes of Delinquency*. Berkeley, CA: University of California Press.

Hirschi, T. and Selvin, H.C. (1967) *Delinquency Research: An Appraisal of Analytic Methods*. New York: Free Press.

HMIP (2006) *Joint Inspection of Youth Offending Teams of England and Wales*. London: HMIP.

Home Office (1998) *The Crime and Disorder Act*. London: Home Office.

Horlick-Jones, T. (1998) 'Meaning and contextualisation in risk assessment', *Reliability Engineering and System Safety*, 5: 79–89.

Homel, R. (2005) 'Developmental crime prevention', in N. Tilley (ed.) *Handbook of Crime Prevention and Community Safety*. Cullompton: Willan Publishing.

Horsfield, A. (2003) 'Risk assessment: Who needs it?' *Probation Journal*, 50(4): 374–9.

House, R. (2007) 'Research must fight status quo', *Times Higher Education*, 19 November.

House of Commons Home Affairs Committee (1993) *Juvenile Offenders. Sixth Report*. London: House of Commons.

Hughes, G., Muncie, J. and McLaughlin, E. (2002) *Crime Prevention and Community Safety: New Directions*. London: Sage.

Huizinga, D. (1997) Risk and protective factors for successful adolescence. Paper presented at the National Institute of Justice Conference on Evaluation and Research. Washington, DC, USA.

Huizinga, D. and Espiritu, R. (1999) *Delinquent Behavior of Youth in the Juvenile Justice System*. Pittsburgh, PA: National Center for Juvenile Justice.

Huizinga, D., Esbensen, F. and Weiher, A. (1991) 'Are there multiple paths to delinquency?' *Journal of Criminal Law and Criminology*, 82: 83–118.

Huizinga, D., Weiher, A.W., Espiritu, R. and Esbensen, F. (2003) 'Delinquency and crime. Some highlights from the Denver Youth Survey', in T.P. Thornberry and M.D. Krohn (eds) *Taking Stock of Delinquency: An Overview of Findings from Contemporary Longitudinal Studies*. New York: Kluwer.

Johnston, J., MacDonald, R., Mason, P., Ridley, L. and Webster, C. (2000) *Snakes & Ladders: Young People, Transitions and Social Exclusion*. Bristol: Policy Press.

Junger-Tas, J., Marshall, I.H. and Ribeaud, D. (2003) *Delinquency in an International Perspective: The International Self-Reported Delinquency Study*. The Hague: Kugler.

Junger-Tas, J., Terlouw. G.J. and Klein, M.W. (1994) *Delinquent Behavior among Young People in the Western World*. Amsterdam: Kugler.

Katz, J. (1988) *Seductions of Crime*. New York: Basic Book.

Kazdin, A.E., Kraemer, H.C., Kessler, R.C., Kupfer, D.J. and Offord, D.R. (1997) 'Contributions of risk factor research to developmental psychopathology', *Clinical Psychology Review*, 17: 375–406.

Kemshall, H. (2003) *Understanding Risk in Criminal Justice*. Maidenhead: Open University Press.

Kemshall, H. (2007) 'Risk assessment and risk management: The right approach?' in M. Blyth, E. Solomon and K. Baker (eds) *Young People and Risk*. Bristol: Policy Press.

Kemshall, H. (2008) 'Risk, rights and justice: Understanding and responding to youth risk', *Youth Justice*, 8(1): 21–38.

Kemshall, H., Boeck, T. and Fleming, J. (2008) 'Social capital and its impact on risk, protection and resilience in young people' [Online]. Available at: http://www.pcrrd.group.shef.ac.uk/reports/project_4.pdf [accessed 17 March 2009].

Kemshall, H., Marsland, L., Boeck, T. and Dunkerton, L. (2006) 'Young people, pathways and crime: Beyond risk factors', *Australian and New Zealand Journal of Criminology*, 39(3): 354–70.

Kemshall, H., Marsland, L., Boeck, T. and Dunkerton, L. (2007) 'Young people, pathways and crime: Beyond risk factors', in A. France and R. Homel (eds) *Pathways and Crime Prevention. Theory, Policy and Practice*. Cullompton: Willan Publishing.

Kosterman, R., Hawkins, J.D., Guo, J., Catalano, R.F. and Abbott, R.D. (2000) 'The dynamics of alcohol and marijuana initiation: patterns and predictors of first use in adolescence', *American Journal of Public Health*, 90: 360–6.

Kraemer, H., Stice, E., Kazdin, A., Offord, D. and Kupfer, D. (2001) 'How do risk factors work together? Mediators, moderators, and independent, overlapping, and proxy risk factors', *American Journal of Psychiatry*, 158: 848–56.

Kraemer, H.C., Lowe, K.K., and Kupfer, D.J. (2005) *To Your Health: How to Understand What Research Tells Us About Risk*. New York: Oxford University Press.

Krohn, M.D. (1986) 'The web of conformity: A network approach to the explanation of delinquent behavior', *Social Problems*, 33: 581–93.

Laub, J. (2006) 'Edwin H. Sutherland and the Michael-Adler Report: Searching for the soul of Criminology 70 Years Later. The 2005 Sutherland Award Address', *Criminology*, 44(2): 235–58.

Laub, J. and Sampson, R. (2003) *Shared Beginnings, Delinquent Lives. Delinquent Boys to Age 70*. London: Harvard University Press.

Lawrence, J. (2007) Taking the developmental pathways approach to understanding and preventing antisocial behaviour. In A. France and R. Homel (eds) *Pathways and crime prevention. Theory, policy and practice*. Cullompton: Willan.

Lawy, R. (2002) 'Risk stories: Youth identities, learning and everyday risk', *Journal of Youth Studies*, 5(4): 407–23.

Layder, D. (1998) *Sociological Practice: Linking Theory and Social Research*. London: Sage.

Lazarsfeld, P.F. (1939) 'Interchangeability of indices in the measurement of economic influences', *Journal of Applied Psychology*, 23(1): 33–45.

Leacock, V. and Sparks, R. (2002) 'Riskiness and at-risk-ness: some ambiguous features of the current penal landscape', in N. Gray, J. Laing and L. Noaks (eds) *Criminal Justice, Mental Health and the Politics of Risk*. London: Cavendish.

LeBel, T.P., Burnett, R., Maruna, S. and Bushway, S. (2008) 'The "chicken and egg" of subjective and social factors in desistance from crime', *European Journal of Criminology*, 5(2): 131–59.

Lindström, P. (1996) 'Family interaction, neighbourhood context and deviant behavior: A research note', *Studies on Crime and Crime Prevention*, 5: 113–19.

Loeber, R. and Farrington, D.P. (2000) *Child Delinquents: Development, Intervention and Service Needs*. Thousand Oaks, CA: Sage.

Loeber, R. and Hay, D.F. (1997) 'Key issues in the development of aggression and violence from childhood to early adulthood', *Annual Review of Psychology*, 48: 371–410.

Loeber, R., Farrington, D.P., Stouthamer-Loeber, M., Moffitt, T.E., Caspi, A., White, H. Wei, E. and Beyers. J.M. (2003) 'The development of male offending. Key findings from fourteen years of the Pittsburgh Youth Study', in T.P. Thornberry and M.D. Krohn (eds) *Taking Stock of Delinquency: An Overview of Findings from Contemporary Longitudinal Studies*. New York: Kluwer.

Loeber, R., Farrington, D.P., Stouthamer-Loeber, M. and Van Kammen, W.B. (1998) 'Multiple risk factors for multi-problem boys: Co-occurrence of delinquency, substance use, attention deficit, conduct problems, physical aggression, covert behaviour, depressed mood, and shy/withdrawn behavior', in R. Jessor (ed.) *New Perspectives on Adolescent Risk Behavior*. Cambridge: Cambridge University Press.

Loeber, R., Stouthamer-Loeber, M., Van Kammen, W.B. and Farrington, D.P. (1989) 'Development of a new measure of self-reported antisocial behavior for young children: Prevalence and reliability', in M. Klein (ed.) *Cross-National Research in Self-Reported Crime and Delinquency*. Boston, MA: Kluwer-Nijhoff.

Lupton, D. (1999) *Risk*. New York: Routledge.

Lynam, D., Moffitt, T, and Stouthamer-Loeber, M. (1993) 'Explaining the relation between IQ and delinquency: Class, race, test motivation, school failure, or self-control?', *Journal of Abnormal Psychology*, 102: 187–96.

MacDonald, R. (2007) 'Social exclusion, youth transitions and criminal careers: Five critical reflections on "risk"', in A. France and R. Homel (2007) *Pathways and Crime Prevention. Theory, Policy and Practice*. Cullompton: Willan Publishing.

MacDonald, R. and Marsh, J. (2005) *Disconnected Youth? Growing Up in Britain's Poor Neighbourhoods*. Basingstoke: Palgrave.

Maruna, S. (2001) *Making Good: How Ex-Convicts Reform and Rebuild Their Lives*. Washington, DC: American Psychological Association.

Mason, P. and Prior, D. (2008) 'The Children's Fund and the prevention of crime and anti-social behaviour', *Criminology and Criminal Justice*, 8(3): 279–96.

McAra, L. and McVie, S. (2005) 'The usual suspects? Street-life, young offenders and the police', *Criminal Justice*, 5(1): 5–36.

McAra, L. and McVie, S. (2007) 'Youth Justice? The impact of system contact on patterns of desistance from offending', *European Journal of Criminology*, 4(3): 315–45.

McCarthy, P., Laing, K. and Walker, J. (2004) *Offenders of the Future: Assessing the Risk of Children and Young People Becoming Involved in Criminal or Antisocial Behaviour*. London: Department for Education and Skills.

McCord, J. (1978) 'A thirty year follow-up of treatment effects', *American Psychologist*, March, 284–9.

McCord, J. (1979) 'Some child-rearing antecedents of criminal behaviour in adult men', *Journal of Personality and Social Psychology*, 37: 1477–86.

McCord, J. and McCord, W. (1959) 'A follow-up report on the Cambridge-Somerville Youth Study', *The ANNALS of the American Academy of Political and Social Science*, 322(1): 89–96.

McGuire, J. (1995) *What Works: Reducing Re-offending: Guidelines from Research and Practice*. Chichester: Wiley.

McKinlay, J.B. and Marceau, L.D. (2000) 'To boldly go . . .', *American Journal of Public Health*, 90(1): 25–33.

McVie, S. (2003) *Edinburgh Study Technical Report: Sweeps 3 and 4* [Online]. Available at: http://www.law.ed.ac.uk/cls/esytc/findings/technicalrepor t3and4.pdf [accessed 17 March 2009].

Mead, G.H. (1934) *Mind, Self, and Society*. Chicago, IL: University of Chicago Press.

Moffitt, T.E. (1991) '"Life-course-persistent" and "adolescence-limited" antisocial behavior: A developmental taxonomy', *Psychological Review*, 100: 674–701.

Moffitt, T.E. (2005) 'The new look of behavioral genetics in developmental psychopathology: gene-environment interplay in antisocial behaviors', *Psychological Bulletin*, 131(4): 533–54.

Moffitt, T.E. (2006) 'Life-course persistent versus adolescence-limited antisocial behavior', in D. Cicchetti and D. Cohen (eds) *Developmental Psychopathology*, 2nd edn. New York: Wiley.

Moffitt, T.E. (no date) *The Environmental Risk Longitudinal Twin Study (E-Risk)* [Online]. Available at: http://www.scopic.ac.uk/StudiesERisk.html [accessed 18 March 2009].

Moffitt, T.E., Caspi, A., Rutter, M. and Silva, P.A. (2001) Sex *Differences in Antisocial Behaviour*. Cambridge: Cambridge University Press.

Moffitt, T.E. and the E-Risk Team (2002) 'Teen-aged mothers in contemporary Britain', *Journal of Child Psychology and Psychiatry*, 43: 727–42.

Moffitt, T.E. and Odgers, C. (2007) 'Does neighbourhood social context influence children's pathways into conduct problems from age 5 to 10 years?' *Assessing the Role of Individual Differences and the Environment in Crime Causation. Third Annual SCoPiC Conference*, Cambridge, December 2006.

Moffitt, T.E. and Silva, P.A. (1988) 'IQ and delinquency: A direct test of differential detection hypothesis', *Journal of Abnormal Psychology*, 97: 330–3.

Morgan Harris Burrows (2003) *Evaluation of the Youth Inclusion Programme*. London: MHB.

Muncie, J. (2004) *Youth and Crime*. London: Sage.

Murray, J., Farrington, D.P. and Eisner, M.P. (in press) 'Drawing conclusions about causes from systematic reviews of risk factors: The Cambridge Quality Checklists', *Journal of Experimental Criminology*, 5(1).

Nagin, D.S. and Tremblay, R.E. (2001) 'Parental and early childhood predictors of persistent physical aggression in boys from kindergarten to high school', *Archives of General Psychiatry*, 58: 389–94.

Nagin, D.S. and Tremblay, R.E. (2005) 'Developmental trajectory groups: Fact or a useful statistical fiction?', *Criminology*, 43(4): 873–904.

National Assembly for Wales (2000) *Better Wales*. Cardiff: National Assembly for Wales.

National Assembly Policy Unit (2002) *Extending Entitlement: Support for 11 to 25 year olds in Wales. Direction and Guidance*. Cardiff: National Assembly for Wales.

O'Donnell, J., Hawkins, J.D. and Abbott, R.D. (1995) 'Predicting serious delinquency and substance use among aggressive boys', *Journal of Consulting and Clinical Psychology*, 63: 529–37.

O'Mahony, D. (2008) 'The risk factors prevention paradigm and the causes of crime: A deceptively useful blueprint', *Youth Justice 2008: Measuring Compliance with International Standards Conference*, Cork University, Republic of Ireland, April 2008.

O'Malley, P. and Hutchinson, S. (2007) 'Reinventing prevention: Why did 'crime prevention' develop so late?' *British Journal of Criminology*, 47: 373–89.

Pawson, R. and Tilley, N. (1998) *Realistic Evaluation*. London: Sage.

Payne, M., Williams, M. and Chamberland, S. (2004) 'Methodological pluralism in British sociology', *Sociology*, 38: 153–64.

Pearce, N. (1996) 'Traditional epidemiology, modern epidemiology, and public health', *American Journal of Public Health*, 86: 678–83.

Pearson, G. (1983) *Hooligan: A History of Respectable Fears*. Basingstoke: Macmillan.

Percy-Smith, J. (2000) *Policy Responses to Social Exclusion*. Buckingham: Open University Press.

Piquero, A.R., Farrington, D.P. and Blumstein, A. (2007) *Key Issues in Criminal Careers Research: New Analyses from the Cambridge Study in Delinquent Development*. Cambridge: Cambridge University Press.

Pitts, J. (2001) 'Korrectional Karaoke: New Labour and the zombification of youth justice', *Youth Justice*,1: 3–16.

Pitts, J. (2003a) *The New Politics of Youth Crime: Discipline or Solidarity?* Lyme Regis: Russell House.

Pitts, J. (2003b) 'Changing youth justice', *Youth Justice*, 3: 5–20.

Pitts, J. (2005) 'No boundaries – The anti-social behaviour industry and young people', *Community Safety Journal*, 5(1).

Pollard, J.A., Hawkins, J.D. and Arthur, M.W. (1999) 'Risk and protection: Are both necessary to understand diverse behavioral outcomes in adolescence?' *Social Work Research*, 23(3): 145–58.

Porteous, D. (2007) 'The prevention of youth crime: A risky business?', in B. Thom, R. Sales and J. Pearce (eds) *Growing Up With Risk*. Bristol: Policy Press.

Powers, E., Witmer, H. and Allport, G.W. (1951) *An Experiment in the Prevention of Delinquency*. New York: Columbia University Press.

Prelow, H., Loukas, A. and Jordan-Green, L. (2007) 'Socioenvironmental risk and adjustment in Latino youth: The mediating effects of family processes and social competence', *Journal of Youth and Adolescence*, 36(4): 465–76.

Prior, D. and Paris, A. (2005) *Preventing Children's Involvement in Crime and Anti-social Behaviour: A Literature Review*. Birmingham: Department for Education and Skills.

Pulkkinen, L. (1988) 'Delinquent development: Theoretical and empirical considerations', in M. Rutter (ed.) *Studies of Psychosocial Risk*. Cambridge: Cambridge University Press.

Pulkkinen, L. and Tremblay, R.E. (1992) 'Patterns of boys' social adjustment in two cultures and at different ages: A longitudinal perspective', *International Journal of Behavioural Development*, 15(4): 527–53.

Radzinowicz, L. (1973) 'Foreword', in D.J. West and D.P Farrington (authors) *Who Becomes Delinquent?* London: Heinemann.

Reiss, A. (1951) 'Unraveling juvenile delinquency: An appraisal of the research methods', *American Journal of Sociology*, 57: 115–120.

Roberts, C., Burnett, R., Kirby, A. and Hamill, H. (1996) *A System for Evaluating Probation Practice: Report of a Method Devised and Piloted by the Oxford Probation Studies Unit and Warwickshire Probation Service*. Oxford: University of Oxford Centre for Criminological Research.

Robinson, G. (2003) 'Risk and risk assessment', in W.-H. Chui and M. Nellis (eds) *Probation: Theories, Practice and Research*. Harlow: Pearson Education.

Robson, C. (2002) *Real World Research: A Resource for Social Scientists and Practitioner-researchers*. Oxford: Blackwell.

Rose, A.G. (1954) *Five Hundred Borstal Boys*. London: Blackwell.

Rutter, M. (1987) 'Psychosocial resilience and protective mechanisms', *American Journal of Orthopsychiatry*, 57(3): 316–331.

Rutter, M. and Giller, H. (1983) *Juvenile Delinquency: Trends and Perspective*. Harmondsworth: Penguin.

Rutter, M., Quinton, D. and Hill, J. (1990) 'Adult outcomes of institution reared children: Males and females compared', in L.N. Robins and M. Rutter (eds) *Straight and Devious Pathways from Childhood to Adulthood*. Cambridge: Cambridge University Press.

Rutter, M.J., Giller, H. and Hagell, A. (1998) *Antisocial Behaviour by Young People*. Cambridge: Cambridge University Press.

Sampson, R.J. and Laub, J.H. (1993) *Crime in the Making: Pathways and Turning Points through Life*. Harvard: Harvard University Press.

Sampson, R.J. and Laub, J.H. (2005) 'A general age-graded theory of crime: Lessons learned and the future of life-course criminology', in D.P. Farrington (ed.) *Integrated Developmental and Life-Course Theories of Offending*. New Brunswick, NJ: Transaction.

Sampson, R.J., Raudenbush, S.W. and Earls, F. (1997) 'Neighborhoods and Violent Crime: A Multilevel Study of Collective Efficacy', *Science*, 15: 918–24.

Schoon, I. (2006) *Risk and Resilience: Adaptations in Changing Times*. Cambridge: Cambridge University Press.

Sharland, E. (2006) 'Young people, risk taking and risk making', *British Journal of Social Work*, 36(2): 247–65.

Sherman, L., Gottfredson D., MacKenzie, D., Eck, J., Reuter, P. and Bushway, S. (1998) *Preventing Crime: What Works, What Doesn't, What's Promising*. Baltimore, MD: Department of Criminology and Criminal Justice, University of Maryland.

Silver, E. (2001) 'Extending social disorganization theory: A multi-level approach to the study of violence among persons with mental illness', *Criminology*, 38: 1043–74.

Silver, E. and Miller, L.L. (2002) 'A cautionary note on the use of actuarial risk assessment tools for social control', *Crime and Delinquency*, 48(1): 138–61.

Smith, D. (2006) 'Youth crime and justice: Research, evaluation and evidence', in B. Goldson and J. Muncie (eds) *Youth Crime and Justice*. London: Sage.

Smith, D. (2007) 'Crime and the life course', in M. Maguire, R. Morgan and R. Reiner (eds) *The Oxford Handbook of Criminology*. Oxford: Oxford University Press.

Smith, D.J. (2006), *Social Inclusion and Early Desistance from Crime*. Edinburgh Study of Youth Transitions and Crime Research Digest No.12. Edinburgh: The University of Edinburgh.

Smith, D.J. and McAra, L. (2004) *Gender and Youth Offending*, Edinburgh Study of Youth Transitions and Crime Research Digest No. 2. Edinburgh: The University of Edinburgh.

Smith, D.J. and McVie, S. (2003) 'Theory and Method in the Edinburgh Study of Youth Transitions and Crime', *British Journal of Criminology*, 43(1):169–95.

Smith, D.J., McVie, S., Woodward, R., Shute, J. and McAra, L. (2001) *The Edinburgh Study of Youth Transitions and Crime: Key Findings at Ages 12 and 13*. Edinburgh Study of Youth Transitions and Crime Research Digest No. 1 [Online]. Available at: http://www.law.ed.ac.uk/cls/esytc/findings/digest1.htm [accessed 17 March 2009].

Smith, R. (2006) *Youth Justice: Ideas, Policy and Practice*. Cullompton: Willan Publishing.

Solomon, E. and Garside, R. (2008*) Ten Years of Labour's Youth Justice Reforms: An Independent Audit*. London: Centre for Crime and Justice Studies, Kings College London.

Souhami, A. (2007) *Transforming Youth Justice: Occupational Identity and Cultural Change*. Cullompton: Willan Publishing.

Stephenson, M., Giller, H. and Brown, S. (2007) *Effective Practice in Youth Justice*. Cullompton: Willan Publishing.

Stouthamer-Loeber, M., Loeber, R., Wei, E., Farrington, D.P. and Wikström, P-O. (2002) 'Risk and promotive effects in the explanation of persistent serious delinquency in boys', *Journal of Clinical and Consulting Psychology*, 70: 111–23.

Susser, M. (1998) 'Does risk factor epidemiology put epidemiology at risk? Peering into the future', *Journal of Epidemiology and Community Health*, 52(10): 608–11.

Sutherland, E.H. (1934) *Principles of Criminology*. Philadelphia, PA: J.B. Lippincott.

Sutherland, E.H. and Cressey D.R. (1974) *Criminology*, 9th edn. Philadelphia, PA: J.B. Lippincott.

Sutton, C., Utting, D. and Farrington, D.P. (2004) *Support from the Start: Working with Young Children and their Families to Reduce the Risks of Crime and Antisocial Behaviour*. London: Department for Education and Skills.

Thornberry, T.P. (1987) 'Toward an interactional theory of delinquency', *Criminology*, 25(4): 863–92.

Thornberry, T.P. (1994) *Violent Families and Youth Violence. OJJDP Fact Sheet 21*. Washington: Office of Juvenile Justice and Delinquency Prevention.

Thornberry, T.P., Huizinga, D. and Loeber, R. (2004) 'The Causes and Correlates studies: Findings and policy implications', *Juvenile Justice*, 10(1): 3–19.

Thornberry, T.P. and Krohn, M.D. (2003) *Taking Stock of Delinquency: An Overview of Findings from Contemporary Longitudinal Studies*. New York: Kluwer.

Thornberry, T.P., Lizotte, A.J., Krohn, M.D., Farnworth, M. and Jang, S.J. (1991) 'Testing interactional theory: An examination of reciprocal causal relationship among family, school, and delinquency', *Journal of Criminal Law and Criminology*, 82(1): 3–35.

Thornberry, T.P., Lizotte, A.J., Krohn, M.D., Smith, C.A. and Porter, P.K. (2003) 'Causes and consequences of delinquency. Findings from the Rochester Youth Development Study', in T.P. Thornberry and M.D. Krohn (eds) *Taking Stock of Delinquency: An Overview of Findings from Contemporary Longitudinal Studies*. New York: Kluwer.

Thornberry, T.P. and Krohn, M.D. (2003) *Taking Stock of Delinquency: An Overview of Findings from Contemporary Longitudinal Studies*. New York: Kluwer.

Tonry, M. and Farrington, D.P. (1995) *Building a Safer Society: Strategic Approaches to Crime Prevention*. Chicago, IL: University of Chicago Press.

Tremblay, R.E., Desmarais-Gervais, L., Gagnon, C. and Charlebois, P. (1987) 'The Preschool Behaviour Questionnaire: Stability of its factor structure between cultures, sexes, ages and socioeconomic classes', *International Journal of Behavioral Development*, 10(4): 467–84.

Tremblay, R.E., Phil, R.O., Vitaro, F. and Dobkin, P.L. (1994) 'Predicting early onset of male antisocial behavior from preschool behavior', *Archives of General Psychiatry*, 51: 732–39.

Tremblay, R.E., Vitaro, F., Nagin, F., Pagani, L. and Seguin, J. (2003) 'The Montréal Longitudinal Experimental Study. Rediscovering the power of descriptions', in Thornberry, T.P. and Krohn, M.D. (2003) *Taking Stock of Delinquency: An Overview of Findings from Contemporary Longitudinal Studies*. New York: Kluwer.

Ungar, M. (2004) 'A constructionist discourse on resilience: Multiple contexts, multiple realities among at-risk children and youth', *Youth and Society*, 35: 341–65.

UNICEF (1989) *United Nations Convention on the Rights of the Child*. London: UNICEF.

Walker, J. and McCarthy, P. (2005) 'Parents in prison: The impact on children', in G. Preston (ed.) *At Greatest Risk: The Children Most Likely to be Poor*. London: Child Poverty Action Group.

Walker, J., Thompson, C., Laing, K., Raybould, S., Coombes, S., Proctor, S. and Wren, C. (2007) *Youth Inclusion and Support Panels: Preventing Crime and Antisocial Behaviour?* London: Department of Education and Skills.

Webster, C. (2007) 'Criminal careers in theoretical context: Biography, history and risk', *European Society of Criminology Conference*, Bologna, Italy, September 2007.

Webster, C., Simpson, D., MacDonald, R., Abbas, A., Cieslik, M., Shildrick, T. and Simpson, M. (2004) *Poor Transitions: Social Exclusion and Young Adults*. Bristol: Policy Press.

Webster, C., MacDonald, R. and Simpson, M. (2006) 'Predicting criminality: Risk/protective factors, neighbourhood influence and desistance', *Youth Justice* 6(1): 7–22.

West, D.J. (1969) *Present Conduct and Future Delinquency*. London: Heinemann.

West, D.J. (1982) *Delinquency: Its Roots, Careers and Prospects*. London: Heinemann.

West, D.J. and Farrington, D.P. (1973) *Who Becomes Delinquent?* London: Heinemann.

West, D.J. and Farrington, D.P. (1977) *The Delinquent Way of Life*. London: Heinemann.

White, R. (2008) 'Disputed definitions and fluid identities: The limitations of social profiling in relation to ethnic youth gangs', *Youth Justice*, 8: 149–61.

Whyte, B. (2004) 'Effectiveness, research and youth justice', *Youth Justice*, 4: 3–21.

Wilkins, L. (1969) 'Data and delinquency', *Yale Law Journal*, 78: 731–37.

Wikström, P-O. (2005) 'The social origins of pathways in crime: Towards a Developmental Ecological Action Theory of Crime Involvement and its changes', in D.P. Farrington (ed.) *Integrated Developmental and Life-Course Theories of Offending*. New Brunswick, NJ: Transaction.

Wikström, P-O. (2006a) 'Does neighbourhood disadvantage influence pathways into crime?', *Assessing the Role of Individual Differences and the Environment in Crime Causation. Third Annual SCoPiC Conference*, Cambridge, December 2006.

Wikström, P-O. (2006b) 'Individuals, settings and acts of crime: Situational mechanisms and the explanation of crime', in P-O Wikström and R. Sampson (eds) *The Explanation of Crime: Context, Mechanisms and Development*. Cambridge: Cambridge University Press.

Wikström, P-O. (2008) 'In search of causes and explanations of crime', in R. King and E. Wincup (eds) *Doing Research on Crime and Justice*. Oxford: Oxford University Press.

Wikström, P-O. (no date) [Online]. Available at: http://www.scopic.ac.uk/index.html [accessed 18 March 2009].

Wikström, P-O. and Butterworth, D. (2006) *Adolescent Crime: Individual Differences and Lifestyles*. Cullompton: Willan Publishing.

Wikström, T. and Loeber, R. (1998) 'Individual risk factors, Neighbourhood SES and juvenile offending', in M. Tonry (ed.) *The Handbook of Crime and Punishment*. New York: OUP.

Wikström, P-O. and Loeber, R. (2000) 'Do disadvantaged neighborhoods cause well-adjusted children to become adolescent delinquents? A study of male juvenile serious offending, risk and protective factors and neighborhood context', *Criminology*, 38(4): 1109–42.

Wikström, P-O. and Sampson, R. (2003) 'Social mechanisms of community influences on crime and pathways in criminality', in B. Lahey, T.E. Moffitt, and A. Caspi (eds) *Causes of Conduct Disorder and Serious Juvenile Delinquency*. New York: Guilford Press.

Wilcox, A. (2003) 'Evidence-based youth justice? Some valuable lessons from an evaluation for the Youth Justice Board', *Youth Justice*, 3: 21–35.

Wilson, D., Sharp, C. and Patterson, A. (2006) *Young People and Crime: Findings from the 2005 Offending, Crime and Justice Survey*. London: Home Office.

Youth Justice Board (2000) *ASSET: Explanatory Notes*. London: Youth Justice Board.

Youth Justice Board (2003) *Assessment, Planning Interventions and Supervision*. London: Youth Justice Board.

Youth Justice Board (2004) *National Standards for Youth Justice Services*. London: Youth Justice Board.

Youth Justice Board (2005a) *Risk and Protective Factors*. London: Youth Justice Board.

Youth Justice Board (2005b) *Role of Risk and Protective Factors*. London: Youth Justice Board.

Youth Justice Board (2006a) *Onset Referral and Screening – Guidance*. London: Youth Justice Board.

Youth Justice Board (2006b) *Onset Referral and Screening Form*. London: Youth Justice Board.

Youth Justice Board (2006c) *Onset Assessment Form*. London: Youth Justice Board.

Youth Justice Board (2006d) *Onset Over to YOU! Questionnaire for Young People*. London: Youth Justice Board.

Youth Justice Board (2006e) *YIP Management Guidance*. London: Youth Justice Board.

Youth Justice Board (2007a) *ASSET Young Offender Assessment Profile* [Online]. Available at: http://www.yjb.gov.uk/en-gb/practitioners/Assessment/Asset.htm [accessed 17 March 2009].

Youth Justice Board (2007b) *Youth Justice: The Scaled Approach*. London: Youth Justice Board.

Youth Justice Board (2008) *Assessment, Planning Interventions and Supervision*. London: Youth Justice Board.

Youth Justice Board (2009) *Youth Justice: The Scaled Approach. A Framework for Assessment and Interventions. Post-Consultation Version Two*. London: Youth Justice Board.

Index

Added to a page number 't' denotes a table.